WORD of LIFE™

Grade 6
The Word of God:
Jesus Christ and Sacred Scripture

Student Text

Augustine Institute   Ignatius Press

Nihil obstat:	Tomas Fuerte, S.T.L. *Censor Librorum*
Imprimatur:	+Most Reverend Samuel J. Aquila, S.T.L. Archbishop of Denver Denver, Colorado, USA June 28, 2023

Middle School Series Editor: Benjamin Akers, S.T.D.

Writing and Editorial Team: Kevin A. Clemens, M.A.; Anthony S. Fortunato, D.Min.; Erik L. Hesla, M.T.S.; Roberto M. Chavez, M.Div., M.Ed.; Constance M. Schmidt, M.Ed., M.A.; Katharine L. Albright, M.T.S., M.A.; Kimberly S. Barber, M.A.; Meghan M. Martinez, M.A.; Ashley E. Crane, M.A.; Joan Watson, M.A.; Jacob P. Pride, Ph.D.; David J. Dashiell, M.A.; Tomas Sandoval; Cecilia B. Wood; Lydia J. Whitten, M.A.; Ann Diaz, M.A.

Creative Director: Ben Dybas

Graphic Designers: Kirk Flory; Mike Fontecchio; Tina Sheppard

Illustrations: Alessandro Valdrighi

The Gospel of Matthew CSV™, copyright © 2022 by Augustine Institute. All rights reserved.

With the exception of quotations from the Gospel of Matthew, Scripture quotations have been taken from the Revised Standard Version of the Holy Bible, Second Catholic Edition, © 2006. The Revised Standard Version of the Holy Bible: the Old Testament, © 1952, 2006; the Apocrypha, © 1957, 2006; the New Testament, © 1946, 2006; the Catholic Edition of the Old Testament, incorporating the Apocrypha, © 1966, 2006, the Catholic Edition of the New Testament, © 1965, 2006 by the Division of Christian Education of the National Council of the Churches of Christ in the United States of America. All rights reserved.

Excerpts from the English translation of The Roman Missal © 2010, International Commission on English in the Liturgy Corporation. All rights reserved.

Excerpts from the English translation of the *Catechism of the Catholic Church*, Second Edition, © 1994, 1997, 2000 by Libreria Editrice Vaticana—United States Catholic Conference, Washington, D.C. All rights reserved.

Cover design by John Herreid and Ben Dybas
Pantocrator by Chris Pelicano
Cover photography by Ryan Bradshaw
© 2024 Augustine Institute and Ignatius Press
All rights reserved
ISBN: 978-1-955305-82-2
Printed by Friesens Corporation in Altona, MB, Canada, April 2024
Job Number 302804
In compliance with the Consumer Protection Safety Act, 2008

Contents

The Gospel according to Matthew 1

Unit One — The Good News

Saint Jerome 31

Chapter One — Jesus, Who Is Called the Christ 35
Chapter Two — The Gospel of the Kingdom 43
Chapter Three — The Crucified Lord of Glory 51
Chapter Four — Sacred Scripture, the Inspired Word 59
Chapter Five — Jesus Christ, the Incarnate Word 69

Unit Two — In the Beginning

Saint Teresa Benedicta of the Cross (Edith Stein) 81

Chapter Six — Creator of Heaven and Earth 85
Chapter Seven — "Through the Devil's Envy" 95
Chapter Eight — The God of Abraham, Isaac, and Jacob 105
Chapter Nine — Jesus, the Son of Abraham 115

Unit Three — You Shall Be My People

Saint Josephine Bakhita 127

Chapter Ten — Out of Egypt 131
Chapter Eleven — A Land Flowing with Milk and Honey 141
Chapter Twelve — Jesus, the New Moses 151

Unit Four — The Kingdom of the Lord

Saint Gregory the Great 163

Chapter Thirteen — The Lord Raised Up Judges 167
Chapter Fourteen — David the King 177
Chapter Fifteen — The House of David 187
Chapter Sixteen — The Mission of the Prophets 197
Chapter Seventeen — Into Exile 207
Chapter Eighteen — Jesus, the Son of David 217

Unit Five — The Coming of the Anointed One

Blessed Franz Jägerstätter 229

Chapter Nineteen — An Everlasting Kingdom 233
Chapter Twenty — I Will Bring Them Back 243

Chapter Twenty-One	Zeal for the Law	253
Chapter Twenty-Two	Jesus, the Son of Man	263

Unit Six — God with Us

	Saint Teresa of Avila	275
Chapter Twenty-Three	The Fullness of Time	279
Chapter Twenty-Four	Jesus, Emmanuel	289

Liturgical Year Unit

Advent	299
Epiphany	307
Lent	315
Easter	323

Appendixes

The Canon of Sacred Scripture	331
Looking Up Bible Passages	332
Salvation History Overview	334
Catholic Prayers	335
Some Prayers of the Mass	337
The Rosary	338
Our Catholic Faith	339
The Seven Sacraments	340
Resources to Prepare for the Sacrament of Reconciliation	342
The Liturgical Year	344
Growing in Virtue	345
Tour of a Catholic Church	346
Words to Know	348
Endnotes	352
Art Credits	356

THE GOSPEL ACCORDING TO
MATTHEW

The Genealogy of Jesus Christ

1 ¹The book of the genealogy of Jesus Christ, the son of David, the son of Abraham.

²Abraham begot Isaac, Isaac begot Jacob, Jacob begot Judah and his brothers, ³Judah begot Perez and Zerah by Tamar, Perez begot Hezron, Hezron begot Aram, ⁴Aram begot Aminadab, Aminadab begot Nahshon, Nahshon begot Salmon, ⁵Salmon begot Boaz by Rahab, Boaz begot Obed by Ruth, Obed begot Jesse, ⁶and Jesse begot David the king.

David begot Solomon by the wife of Uriah, ⁷Solomon begot Rehoboam, Rehoboam begot Abijah, Abijah begot Asa, ⁸Asa begot Jehoshaphat, Jehoshaphat begot Joram, Joram begot Uzziah, ⁹Uzziah begot Jotham, Jotham begot Ahaz, Ahaz begot Hezekiah, ¹⁰Hezekiah begot Manasseh, Manasseh begot Amon, Amon begot Josiah, ¹¹and Josiah begot Jechoniah and his brothers, at the time of the Babylonian exile.

¹²After the Babylonian exile, Jechoniah begot Shealtiel, Shealtiel begot Zerubbabel, ¹³Zerubbabel begot Abiud, Abiud begot Eliakim, Eliakim begot Azor, ¹⁴Azor begot Zadok, Zadok begot Achim, Achim begot Eliud, ¹⁵Eliud begot Eleazar, Eleazar begot Matthan, Matthan begot Jacob, ¹⁶and Jacob begot Joseph the husband of Mary, of whom Jesus was born, who is called the Christ.

¹⁷So all the generations from Abraham to David were fourteen generations; and from David to the Babylonian exile, fourteen generations; and from the Babylonian exile to the Christ, fourteen generations.

The Birth of Jesus Christ

¹⁸Now the birth of Jesus Christ took place in this way. When his mother Mary had been betrothed to Joseph, before they came together, she was found to be with child of the Holy Spirit. ¹⁹And Joseph her husband, being a righteous man and unwilling to expose her to shame, decided to divorce her secretly. ²⁰But while he was considering these things, behold, an angel of the Lord appeared to him in a dream, saying, "Joseph, son of David, do not fear to take Mary your wife, for the child conceived in her is of the Holy Spirit. ²¹She will bear a son, and you shall call his name Jesus, for he will save his people from their sins." ²²Now all this took place so that what was spoken by the Lord through the prophet might be fulfilled,

²³"Behold, the virgin shall be with
child and bear a son, and they shall
call his name Emmanuel,"

which means, "God with us." ²⁴When Joseph rose from sleep, he did as the angel of the Lord commanded him and took his wife. ²⁵And he did not know her until she bore a son, and he called his name Jesus.

The Magi from the East

2 ¹Now after Jesus was born in Bethlehem of Judea in the days of Herod the king, behold, magi from the east came to Jerusalem, ²saying, "Where is he who was born king of the Jews? For we have seen his star at its rising and have come to worship him." ³But when Herod the king heard this, he was troubled, and all Jerusalem with him. ⁴And assembling all the chief priests and scribes of the people, he inquired of them where the Christ would be born. ⁵They said to him, "In Bethlehem of Judea, for so it is written through the prophet,

⁶'And you Bethlehem, land of Judah, are
by no means least among the rulers of
Judah, for from you shall come a ruler,
who will shepherd my people Israel.'"

⁷Then Herod secretly called the magi and determined from them the time when the star appeared. ⁸And he sent them to Bethlehem and said, "Go and search diligently for the child. And when you have found him, report back to me, so that I too may come and worship him."

⁹When they had heard the king, they departed. And behold, the star which they had seen at its rising went before them, until it came to rest over where the child was. ¹⁰When they saw the star, they rejoiced with exceedingly great joy. ¹¹And coming into the house, they saw the child with Mary his mother, and they fell down and worshiped him. And opening their treasures, they presented him with gifts of gold, frankincense, and myrrh. ¹²And having been warned in a dream not to return to Herod, they departed to their own country by another way.

The Flight to Egypt

¹³When they had departed, behold, an angel of the Lord appeared to Joseph in a dream, saying, "Rise, take the child and his mother and flee into Egypt, and stay there until I tell you, for Herod is about to search for the child, to destroy him." ¹⁴So he rose and took the child and his mother by night and went away into Egypt. ¹⁵And he stayed there until the death of Herod, so that what was spoken by the Lord through the prophet might be fulfilled, "Out of Egypt I have called my son."

The Massacre of the Infants

¹⁶Then, when Herod saw that he had been tricked by the magi, he was very angry. And he sent and killed all the children in Bethlehem and in all its surrounding regions, from two years old and under, according to the time he had ascertained from the magi. ¹⁷Then was fulfilled what was spoken through Jeremiah the prophet,

¹⁸"A voice was heard in Ramah,
wailing and great lamentation,
Rachel weeping for her children,
and she would not be comforted,
because they are no more."

The Return from Egypt

¹⁹When Herod died, behold, an angel of the Lord appeared in a dream to Joseph in Egypt, ²⁰saying, "Rise, take the child and his mother and go to the land of Israel, for those who sought the life of the child are dead." ²¹And he rose and took the child and his mother and came into the land of Israel. ²²But when he heard that Archelaus reigned over Judea in place of his father Herod, he was afraid to go there. And being warned in a dream, he went away to the territory of Galilee. ²³And he came and dwelt in a city called Nazareth, so that what was spoken through the prophets might be fulfilled, "He shall be called a Nazarene."

The Preaching of John the Baptist

3 ¹In those days John the Baptist came preaching in the wilderness of Judea, ²saying, "Repent, for the kingdom of heaven is at hand!" ³For this is he who was spoken of through Isaiah the prophet,

"A voice of one crying out
in the wilderness:
'Prepare the way of the Lord,
make his paths straight!'"

⁴Now John himself wore a garment of camel's hair and a leather belt around his waist, and his food was locusts and wild honey. ⁵Then Jerusalem and all Judea and all the region surrounding the Jordan went out to him, ⁶and they were baptized by him in the Jordan river, confessing their sins.

⁷But when he saw many of the Pharisees and Sadducees coming for his baptism, he said to them, "You brood of vipers! Who warned you to flee from the coming wrath? ⁸Bear fruit that is worthy of repentance. ⁹Do not think to say to yourselves, 'We have Abraham as our father.' For I say to you, God is able to raise up children for Abraham from these stones! ¹⁰Even now the axe is laid to the root of the trees. Therefore, every tree that does not bear good fruit is cut down and thrown into the fire. ¹¹I baptize you in water for repentance, but the one who is coming after me is mightier than I, whose sandals I am not worthy to carry. He will baptize you in the Holy Spirit and in fire. ¹²His winnowing fork is in his hand, and he will cleanse his threshing floor and gather his wheat into the granary. But the chaff he will burn with unquenchable fire."

The Baptism of Jesus

¹³Then Jesus came from Galilee to John at the Jordan, to be baptized by him. ¹⁴But John would have prevented him, saying, "I need to be baptized by you; yet you come to me?" ¹⁵But Jesus answered and said to him, "Let it be so now, for in this way it is fitting for us to fulfill all righteousness." Then he consented. ¹⁶And when Jesus was baptized, he immediately came up from the water, and behold, the heavens were opened to him, and he saw the Spirit of God descending like a dove and coming upon him. ¹⁷And behold, a voice from the heavens said, "This is my beloved Son, in whom I am well pleased."

The Temptations of Jesus

4 ¹Then Jesus was led by the Spirit into the wilderness to be tempted by the devil. ²And after fasting forty days and forty nights, he was hungry. ³And the tempter came and said to him, "If you are the Son of God, command these stones to become loaves of bread." ⁴But he answered and said, "It is written,

'Man shall not live by bread alone,
but by every word that comes
forth from the mouth of God.'"

⁵Then the devil took him to the holy city and placed him on the ledge of the temple. ⁶And he said to him, "If you are the Son of God, throw yourself down, for it is written,

'He will command his angels concerning you,
and on their hands they will bear you up,
lest you strike your foot against a stone.'"
⁷Jesus said to him, "Again, it is written,
'You shall not put the Lord your God to the test.'"
⁸Again, the devil took him to a very high mountain and showed him all the kingdoms of the world and their glory. ⁹And he said to him, "All these things I will give to you, if you will fall down and worship me." ¹⁰Then Jesus said to him, "Be gone, Satan! For it is written,
'You shall worship the Lord your God,
and him only shall you serve.'"
¹¹Then the devil left him. And behold, angels came and ministered to him.

Jesus Begins to Preach in Galilee

¹²Now when he heard that John had been handed over to the authorities, he went away into Galilee. ¹³And leaving Nazareth, he came and dwelt in Capernaum by the sea, in the regions of Zebulun and Naphtali, ¹⁴so that what was spoken through Isaiah the prophet might be fulfilled,
¹⁵"Land of Zebulun and land of Naphtali,
the way of the sea, beyond the Jordan,
Galilee of the Gentiles.
¹⁶The people who sit in darkness
have seen a great light,
and on those who sit in the
region and shadow of death,
light has dawned."
¹⁷From then on, Jesus began to preach and to say, "Repent, for the kingdom of heaven is at hand!" ¹⁸Now as he was walking beside the sea of Galilee, he saw two brothers: Simon, who is called Peter, and Andrew his brother. They were casting a net into the sea, for they were fishermen. ¹⁹And he said to them, "Follow me, and I will make you fishers of men." ²⁰Immediately they left their nets and followed him.
²¹And going on from there, he saw two other brothers: James the son of Zebedee and John his brother. They were in the boat with Zebedee their father, mending their nets. And he called them. ²²Immediately they left the boat and their father and followed him.
²³And he went throughout all Galilee, teaching in their synagogues, preaching the gospel of the kingdom, and healing every disease and every sickness among the people. ²⁴So his fame spread throughout all Syria. And they brought to him all the sick who had various illnesses and were afflicted with torments, those possessed by demons, those who suffered from seizures, and paralytics, and he healed them. ²⁵And many crowds followed him from Galilee, the Decapolis, Jerusalem, Judea, and from beyond the Jordan.

The Beatitudes

5 ¹When he saw the crowds, he went up the mountain. And when he sat down, his disciples came to him. ²And he opened his mouth and taught them, saying:
³"Blessed are the poor in spirit, for theirs is the kingdom of heaven.
⁴"Blessed are those who mourn, for they shall be comforted.
⁵"Blessed are the meek, for they shall inherit the earth.
⁶"Blessed are those who hunger and thirst for righteousness, for they shall be filled.
⁷"Blessed are the merciful, for they shall receive mercy.
⁸"Blessed are the pure in heart, for they shall see God.
⁹"Blessed are the peacemakers, for they shall be called sons of God.
¹⁰"Blessed are those who are persecuted for the sake of righteousness, for theirs is the kingdom of heaven.
¹¹"Blessed are you whenever they insult you and persecute you and say all kinds of evil things against you falsely because of me. ¹²Rejoice and be glad, for your reward is great in heaven. For in the same way they persecuted the prophets who came before you.

Salt of the Earth, Light of the World

¹³"You are the salt of the earth. But if salt has lost its flavor, how will it be made salty again? It is no longer good for anything except to be thrown out and trampled underfoot.
¹⁴"You are the light of the world. A city set on a hill cannot be hidden. ¹⁵Nor does anyone light a lamp and put it under a bushel basket, but on a lampstand, and it gives light to all in the house. ¹⁶In the same way, let your light shine before others, so that they may see your good works and glorify your Father in heaven.

To Fulfill the Law and the Prophets

¹⁷"Do not think that I have come to abolish the law or the prophets. I have not come to abolish, but to fulfill. ¹⁸For amen, I say to you, until heaven and earth pass away, not one letter or part of a letter shall pass away from the law until all is accomplished. ¹⁹Whoever therefore loosens one of the least of these

commandments and teaches others to do so will be called least in the kingdom of heaven. But whoever does them and teaches them will be called great in the kingdom of heaven. [20]For I say to you, unless your righteousness surpasses that of the scribes and Pharisees, you will never enter the kingdom of heaven.

Murder and Anger

[21]"You have heard that it was said to those of old, 'You shall not murder,' and 'Whoever murders will be liable to judgment.' [22]But I say to you, everyone who is angry with his brother will be liable to judgment. And whoever says '*Raka*!' to his brother will be liable to the Sanhedrin. And whoever says 'You fool!' will be liable to the Gehenna of fire. [23]So if you bring your gift to the altar and there remember that your brother has anything against you, [24]leave your gift there before the altar and go. First be reconciled with your brother, and then come and offer your gift. [25]Make friends with your adversary quickly while you are with him on the way, lest your adversary hand you over to the judge, and the judge to the guard, and you be thrown into prison. [26]Amen, I say to you, you will never get out until you have paid the last penny.

Adultery and Covetous Looks

[27]"You have heard that it was said, 'You shall not commit adultery.' [28]But I say to you, everyone who looks at a woman in order to covet her has already committed adultery with her in his heart. [29]If your right eye leads you to sin, pluck it out and throw it away. It is better for you that one of your members perish than that your whole body be cast into Gehenna. [30]And if your right hand leads you to sin, cut it off and throw it away. It is better for you that one of your members perish than that your whole body go into Gehenna.

Divorce and Remarriage

[31]"It was said, 'Whoever divorces his wife must give her a bill of divorce.' [32]But I say to you, whoever divorces his wife, except for a case of sexual immorality, makes her commit adultery. And whoever marries a divorced woman commits adultery.

Oaths and Swearing

[33]"Again, you have heard that it was said to those of old, 'You shall not swear falsely, but you shall keep your oaths to the Lord.' [34]But I say to you, do not swear at all, either by heaven, because it is God's throne, [35]or by the earth, because it is his footstool, or by Jerusalem, because it is the city of the great King. [36]Nor shall you swear by your head, because you cannot make one hair white or black. [37]Let your 'Yes' be 'Yes' and your 'No' be 'No.' Anything more than this is from the evil one.

Turn the Other Cheek

[38]"You have heard that it was said, 'An eye for an eye and a tooth for a tooth.' [39]But I say to you, do not resist one who is evil. But if anyone strikes you on your right cheek, turn the other to him also. [40]And if anyone wants to sue you and take your tunic, give him your cloak as well. [41]And if anyone forces you to go one mile, go with him two miles. [42]Give to the one who begs you, and do not turn away from the one who would borrow from you.

Hatred and Love of Enemies

[43]"You have heard that it was said, 'You shall love your neighbor and hate your enemy.' [44]But I say to you, love your enemies and pray for those who persecute you, [45]so that you may be sons of your Father who is in heaven. For he makes his sun rise on the evil and the good, and he sends rain on the righteous and the unrighteous. [46]For if you love those who love you, what reward do you have? Do not even the tax collectors do the same? [47]And if you greet only your brothers, what more are you doing than others? Do not even the Gentiles do the same? [48]Be perfect, therefore, as your heavenly Father is perfect.

Almsgiving in Secret

6 [1]"Beware of practicing your righteousness before others in order to be seen by them. Otherwise, you have no reward with your Father in heaven. [2]Therefore, when you give alms, do not blow a trumpet before you as the hypocrites do in the synagogues and in the streets, so that they may be praised by others. Amen, I say to you, they have their reward. [3]But when you give alms, do not let your left hand know what your right hand is doing, [4]so that your alms may be in secret. And your Father, who sees in secret, will repay you.

Prayer in Secret

[5]"When you pray, do not be like the hypocrites, for they love to stand and pray in the synagogues and on the street corners, so that they may be seen by others. Amen, I say to you, they have received their reward. [6]But you, when you pray, go into your inner room, and close your door and pray to your Father who is in secret. And your Father, who sees in secret, will repay you. [7]And when you pray, do not babble

like the Gentiles, for they think they will be heard because of their many words. ⁸Do not be like them, for your Father knows what you need before you ask him.

The Our Father

⁹"Pray, therefore, in this way:
'Our Father in heaven,
your name be hallowed,
¹⁰your kingdom come,
your will be done,
on earth as it is in heaven.
¹¹Give us this day our daily bread.
¹²And forgive us our debts,
as we forgive our debtors.
¹³And lead us not into temptation,
but deliver us from the evil one.'

¹⁴For if you forgive others their trespasses, your heavenly Father will also forgive you. ¹⁵But if you do not forgive them, neither will your Father forgive your trespasses.

Fasting in Secret

¹⁶"When you fast, do not look sad, like the hypocrites. For they change their appearance so that their fasting may be seen by others. Amen, I say to you, they have their reward. ¹⁷But when you fast, anoint your head and wash your face, ¹⁸so that your fasting may not be seen by others, but by your Father who is in secret. And your Father, who sees in secret, will repay you.

Treasure in Heaven

¹⁹"Do not store up for yourselves treasures on earth, where moth and rust consume, and where thieves break in and steal. ²⁰But store up for yourselves treasures in heaven, where moth and rust do not consume, and where thieves do not break in and steal. ²¹For where your treasure is, there will your heart be also.

²²"The lamp of the body is the eye. If, therefore, your eye is generous, your whole body will be full of light. ²³But if your eye is evil, your whole body will be full of darkness. If, therefore, the light in you is darkness, how great is that darkness!

²⁴"No one can serve two masters. For either he will hate the one and love the other, or he will be devoted to the one and despise the other. You cannot serve God and mammon.

Do Not Be Anxious

²⁵"Therefore, I say to you, do not be anxious about your life, what you will eat, or about your body, what you will wear. Is not life more than food and the body more than clothing? ²⁶Look at the birds of heaven. They neither sow, nor reap, nor gather into barns, and yet your heavenly Father feeds them. Are you not worth more than they? ²⁷Who among you by being anxious can add one cubit to his span of life? ²⁸And why are you anxious about clothing? Consider the lilies of the field, how they grow. They neither toil nor spin. ²⁹yet I say to you, not even Solomon in all his glory was dressed like one of these. ³⁰But if God so clothes the grass of the field, which today is here and tomorrow is cast into the oven, will he not much more clothe you, O you of little faith? ³¹Therefore, do not be anxious, saying, 'What will we eat?' or 'What will we drink?' or 'What will we wear?' ³²For the Gentiles seek after all these things, and your heavenly Father knows that you need them all. ³³But seek first the kingdom of God and his righteousness, and all these things will be added to you. ³⁴Therefore, do not be anxious about tomorrow, for tomorrow will be anxious for itself. Today's trouble is enough for today.

Do Not Judge

7 ¹"Judge not, so that you may not be judged. ²For with the judgment you make you will be judged, and the measure you give will be the measure you receive ³Why do you see the splinter in your brother's eye, but do not notice the wooden beam in your own eye? ⁴Or how will you say to your brother, 'Let me remove the splinter from your eye,' when behold, there is a wooden beam in your own eye? ⁵You hypocrite! First remove the wooden beam from your own eye, and then you will see clearly to remove the splinter from your brother's eye.

Dogs and Swine

⁶"Do not give what is holy to dogs, or cast your pearls before swine, lest they trample them underfoot and turn and tear you in pieces.

Ask, Seek, Knock

⁷"Ask, and it shall be given to you; seek, and you shall find; knock, and it shall be opened to you. ⁸For everyone who asks receives, and the one who seeks finds, and to the one who knocks, it shall be opened. ⁹Who among you, if his son asks him for bread, will give him a stone? ¹⁰Or if he asks for a fish, will give him a snake? ¹¹So if you, who are evil, know how to give good gifts to your children, how much more will your Father in heaven give good things to those who ask him!

The Golden Rule

¹²"Therefore, do to others whatever you would have them do to you. For this is the law and the prophets.

The Two Ways

¹³"Enter through the narrow gate, for the gate is wide and the way is easy that leads to destruction, and those who enter through it are many. ¹⁴But the gate is narrow and the way is hard that leads to life, and those who find it are few.

By Their Fruits You Shall Know Them

¹⁵"Beware of false prophets, who come to you in sheep's clothing but inwardly are ravenous wolves. ¹⁶By their fruits you shall know them. Are grapes gathered from thorns, or figs from thistles? ¹⁷In the same way, every good tree bears good fruit, but a bad tree bears evil fruit. ¹⁸A good tree cannot bear evil fruit, nor can a bad tree bear good fruit. ¹⁹Every tree not bearing good fruit is cut down and cast into the fire. ²⁰So by their fruits you shall know them.

²¹"Not everyone who says to me, 'Lord, Lord,' will enter the kingdom of heaven, but rather the one who does the will of my Father in heaven. ²²Many will say to me on that day, 'Lord, Lord, did we not prophesy in your name, and cast out demons in your name, and do many deeds of power in your name?' ²³Then I will declare to them, 'I never knew you. Depart from me, you evildoers.'"

The Wise Man and the Foolish Man

²⁴"Everyone therefore who hears these words of mine and does them will be like a wise man who built his house on the rock. ²⁵The rain fell, the floods came, and the winds blew and beat on that house. But it did not fall, for it was founded on the rock. ²⁶And everyone who hears these words of mine and does not do them will be like a foolish man who built his house upon the sand. ²⁷The rain fell, the floods came, and the winds blew and beat upon that house. And it fell, and great was its fall."

²⁸Now when Jesus had finished these words, the crowds were astonished at his teaching. ²⁹For he taught them as one having authority, and not as their scribes.

Jesus Heals a Leper

8 ¹When he came down from the mountain, many crowds followed him. ²And behold, a leper came and worshiped him, saying, "Lord, if you will it, you can make me clean." ³And he stretched out his hand and touched him, saying, "I will it; be made clean." And immediately his leprosy was cleansed. ⁴And Jesus said to him, "See that you tell no one. But go, show yourself to the priest and offer the gift that Moses commanded, for a testimony to them."

The Faith of the Centurion

⁵And when he entered Capernaum, a centurion came to him and begged him, ⁶saying, "Lord, my servant lies at home paralyzed, suffering terribly." ⁷And he said to him, "I will come and heal him." ⁸The centurion answered and said, "Lord, I am not worthy that you should enter under my roof, but only say the word, and my servant shall be healed. ⁹For I too am a man under authority, with soldiers under me. And I say to this one, 'Go,' and he goes; and to another, 'Come,' and he comes; and to my servant, 'Do this,' and he does it."

¹⁰When Jesus heard this, he marveled and said to those who followed him, "Amen, I say to you, with no one in Israel have I found such faith! ¹¹And I say to you, many shall come from east and west and recline at table with Abraham, Isaac, and Jacob, in the kingdom of heaven. ¹²But the sons of the kingdom shall be cast out into the outer darkness, where there shall be weeping and gnashing of teeth." ¹³And Jesus said to the centurion, "Go. As you have believed, so let it be done for you." And his servant was healed in that hour.

Jesus Heals the Sick

¹⁴When Jesus entered Peter's house, he saw his mother-in-law lying down and burning with fever. ¹⁵So he touched her hand, and the fever left her. And she rose up and ministered to him.

¹⁶When it was evening, they brought to him many who were demon-possessed. And he cast out the spirits with a word and healed all who were sick, ¹⁷so that what was spoken through Isaiah the prophet might be fulfilled,

"He took our infirmities,
and bore our diseases."

Following Jesus

¹⁸Now when Jesus saw a crowd around him, he gave orders to depart to the other side. ¹⁹And a scribe came and said to him, "Teacher, I will follow you wherever you go." ²⁰And Jesus said to him, "Foxes have holes, and the birds of heaven have nests, but the Son of Man has nowhere to lay his head." ²¹And another of his disciples said to him, "Lord, allow me

first to go and bury my father." ²²But Jesus said to him, "Follow me, and let the dead bury their dead."

Jesus Stills a Storm

²³And when he got into the boat, his disciples followed him. ²⁴And behold, a great storm arose on the sea, so that the boat was being swamped by the waves. But he was asleep. ²⁵And they came and woke him, saying, "Lord, save us, we are perishing!" ²⁶And he said to them, "Why are you fearful, O you of little faith?" Then he rose and rebuked the winds and the sea. And there was a great calm. ²⁷But the men marveled and said, "What kind of man is this, that even the winds and the sea obey him?"

Jesus Heals Two Demon-Possessed Men

²⁸When he came to the other side, to the region of the Gadarenes, two demon-possessed men met him, coming out of the tombs. They were so violent that no one was ever able to travel that way. ²⁹And behold, they cried out, saying, "What have you to do with us, Son of God? Have you come here to torment us before the time?" ³⁰Now a herd of many swine was feeding far from them. ³¹So the demons begged him, saying, "If you cast us out, send us into the herd of swine." ³²And he said to them, "Go." When they came out, they went into the swine. And behold, the whole herd rushed down the bank into the sea and died in the waters. ³³And the herders fled, and they went away into the city and told everything, including what had happened to the demon-possessed men. ³⁴And behold, the whole city came out to meet Jesus. And when they saw him, they begged him to leave their region.

Jesus Heals a Paralytic

9 ¹After getting into a boat, he crossed over to the other side and came into his own city. ²And behold, they brought to him a paralytic lying on a mat. And when Jesus saw their faith, he said to the paralytic, "Take heart, son; your sins are forgiven." ³And behold, some of the scribes said to themselves, "This man is blaspheming!" ⁴But when Jesus saw their thoughts, he said, "Why do you think evil in your hearts? ⁵For which is easier? To say, 'Your sins are forgiven,' or to say, 'Rise and walk?' ⁶But so that you may know that the Son of Man has authority on earth to forgive sins"—then he said to the paralytic, "Rise, take up your mat, and go to your house." ⁷And he rose and departed to his house. ⁸When the crowds saw it, they were afraid, and they glorified God, who had given such authority to men.

Jesus Calls Matthew the Tax Collector

⁹As Jesus was passing along from there, he saw a man named Matthew sitting at the tax booth, and he said to him, "Follow me." And he rose and followed him.

¹⁰And as he was reclining at table in the house, behold, many tax collectors and sinners came and were reclining with Jesus and his disciples. ¹¹And when the Pharisees saw it, they said to his disciples, "Why does your teacher eat with tax collectors and sinners?" ¹²But when he heard it, he said "Those who are healthy have no need for a physician, but those who are sick. ¹³But go and learn what this means, 'I desire mercy, and not sacrifice.' For I have come not to call the righteous, but sinners."

A Question about Fasting

¹⁴Then the disciples of John came to him and said, "Why do we and the Pharisees fast frequently, but your disciples do not fast?" ¹⁵And Jesus said to them, "Can the groomsmen mourn as long as the bridegroom is with them? But the days will come when the bridegroom will be taken away from them, and then they shall fast. ¹⁶No one puts a piece of unshrunken cloth on an old garment, for the patch pulls away from the garment, and a worse tear is made. ¹⁷Nor do they put new wine into old wineskins. Otherwise the skins burst, the wine spills out, and the skins are destroyed. But they put new wine into new wineskins, and both are preserved."

A Ruler's Daughter and the Woman with a Hemorrhage

¹⁸While he was saying these things to them, behold, a ruler came and worshiped him, saying, "My daughter has just died. But come, lay your hand upon her, and she will live." ¹⁹And Jesus rose up and followed him, along with his disciples.

²⁰And behold, a woman who had been suffering with a hemorrhage for twelve years came up behind him and touched the fringe of his garment. ²¹For she said to herself, "If only I touch his garment, I will be saved." ²²But when Jesus turned around and saw her, he said, "Take heart, daughter; your faith has saved you." And the woman was healed from that hour.

²³And when Jesus came into the ruler's house and saw the flute-players and the crowd making a commotion, ²⁴he said, "Go away! For the girl is not dead, but sleeping." And they laughed at him. ²⁵But when the crowd was sent out, he went inside and took her hand, and the girl arose. ²⁶And the news of this went out into all that land.

Jesus Heals Two Blind Men

²⁷When Jesus passed on from there, two blind men followed him, crying out and saying, "Have mercy on us, Son of David!" ²⁸And when he came into the house, the blind men came to him. And Jesus said to them, "Do you believe that I am able to do this?" They said to him, "Yes, Lord." ²⁹Then he touched their eyes, saying, "As you have believed, so let it be done to you." ³⁰And their eyes were opened. And Jesus sternly warned them, saying, "See that no one knows of it." ³¹But they went out and spread word of him in all that land.

Jesus Heals a Mute Demon-Possessed Man

³²As they were going out, behold, a demon-possessed man who was mute was brought to him. ³³And when the demon had been cast out, the mute man spoke, and the crowds marveled, saying, "Never has anything like this appeared in Israel!" ³⁴But the Pharisees said, "By the prince of demons he casts out demons."

The Harvest and the Laborers

³⁵And Jesus went around all the cities and villages, teaching in their synagogues, preaching the gospel of the kingdom, and healing every disease and every sickness. ³⁶But when he saw the crowds, he had compassion on them, because they were weary and scattered like sheep without a shepherd. ³⁷Then he said to his disciples, "The harvest is plentiful, but the laborers are few. ³⁸Therefore, ask the Lord of the harvest to send out laborers into his harvest."

Jesus Calls the Twelve Disciples

10 ¹After calling his twelve disciples to himself, he gave them authority over unclean spirits, to cast them out, and to heal every disease and every sickness. ²Now these are the names of the twelve apostles: first, Simon, who is called Peter, and Andrew his brother; then James the son of Zebedee and John his brother; ³Philip and Bartholomew; Thomas and Matthew the tax collector; James the son of Alphaeus and Thaddaeus; ⁴Simon the Cananean and Judas Iscariot, who betrayed him.

Jesus Sends the Twelve

⁵Jesus sent out these twelve and commanded them, saying, "Do not go along a road of the Gentiles, and do not enter any city of the Samaritans. ⁶Go rather to the lost sheep of the house of Israel. ⁷And preach as you go, saying, 'The kingdom of heaven is at hand.' ⁸Heal the sick, raise the dead, cleanse lepers, cast out demons. Freely you have received; freely give. ⁹Acquire no gold, or silver, or copper to put in your belts; ¹⁰and take no bag for the journey, or two cloaks, or sandals, or a staff. For the laborer deserves his food.

¹¹"And whatever city or village you enter, search for who is worthy in it, and remain there until you go away. ¹²When you enter a house, greet it. ¹³And if the house is worthy, let your peace come upon it; but if it is not worthy, let your peace return to you. ¹⁴And whoever will not receive you or hear your words, when you go out of that house or city, shake off the dust from your feet. ¹⁵Amen, I say to you, it shall be more tolerable for the land of Sodom and Gomorrah on the day of judgment than for that city.

You Will Be Hated by All

¹⁶"Behold, I send you out as sheep in the midst of wolves. Therefore, be wise as serpents and innocent as doves. ¹⁷But beware of men, for they will hand you over to sanhedrins and flog you in their synagogues. ¹⁸And you will be brought before governors and kings for my sake, for testimony to them and the Gentiles. ¹⁹But when they hand you over, do not be anxious about how you are to speak or what you are to say, for what you are to say will be given to you in that hour. ²⁰For it is not you who speak, but the Spirit of your Father who speaks in you.

²¹"Brother will hand over brother to death, and a father his child, and children will rise up against parents and put them to death. ²²And you will be hated by all because of my name. But the one who endures to the end shall be saved. ²³Whenever they persecute you in one city, flee to another. For amen, I say to you, you will not finish going through the cities of Israel before the Son of Man comes.

²⁴"A disciple is not above his teacher, nor a servant above his master. ²⁵It is enough for the disciple to be like his teacher, and the servant like his master. If they have called the master of the house Beelzebul, how much more the members of his house!

Do Not Fear Them

²⁶"So do not fear them. For nothing is hidden that will not be revealed, and nothing secret that will not be known. ²⁷What I say to you in the dark, say in the light, and what you hear whispered in your ear, preach upon the housetops. ²⁸And do not fear those who kill the body but are not able to kill the soul. Rather, fear him who is able to destroy both soul and body in Gehenna. ²⁹Are not two sparrows sold for a copper coin? Yet not one of them will fall to the

ground apart from your Father. ³⁰Even the hairs of your head are all counted. ³¹So do not fear. You are worth more than many sparrows.

³²"Everyone therefore who confesses me before men, I also will confess before my Father who is in heaven. ³³But whoever denies me before men, I also will deny before my Father who is in heaven.

Not Peace, But a Sword

³⁴"Do not think that I have come to cast peace upon the earth. I have not come to cast peace, but a sword. ³⁵For I have come to turn

'a man against his father,
and a daughter against her mother,
and a daughter-in-law against
her mother-in-law.
³⁶And a man's enemies will be
from his own household.'

³⁷"Whoever loves father or mother more than me is not worthy of me, and whoever loves son or daughter more than me is not worthy of me. ³⁸And whoever does not take up his cross and follow me is not worthy of me. ³⁹Whoever finds his life will lose it, and whoever loses his life for my sake will find it.

The Reward for Receiving Disciples

⁴⁰"Whoever receives you receives me, and whoever receives me receives him who sent me. ⁴¹Whoever receives a prophet in the name of a prophet will receive a prophet's reward, and whoever receives a righteous person in the name of a righteous person will receive the reward of the righteous. ⁴²And whoever gives even a cup of cold water to drink to one of these little ones in the name of a disciple—amen, I say to you, he shall by no means lose his reward."

11 ¹Now when Jesus had finished instructing his twelve disciples, he left there to teach and to preach in their cities.

Jesus and John the Baptist

²Now when John heard in prison about the works of the Christ, he sent word through his disciples ³and said to him, "Are you the one who is to come, or shall we wait for another?" ⁴And Jesus answered and said to them, "Go tell John what you hear and see: ⁵the blind receive their sight, the lame walk, the lepers are cleansed, the deaf hear, the dead are raised, and the poor have good news proclaimed to them. ⁶And blessed is he who is not scandalized by me." ⁷As they were going, Jesus began to say to the crowds regarding John, "What did you go out into the wilderness to see? A reed shaken by the wind? ⁸What then did you go out to see? A man clothed in soft garments? Behold, those who wear soft garments are in the houses of kings. ⁹What then did you go out to see? A prophet? Yes, I say to you, and more than a prophet. ¹⁰This is he of whom it is written,

'Behold, I am sending my
messenger before your face,
who will prepare your way before you.'

¹¹Amen, I say to you, among those born of women there has arisen no one greater than John the Baptist. Yet the one who is least in the kingdom of heaven is greater than he. ¹²And from the days of John the Baptist until now, the kingdom of heaven has suffered violence, and the violent seize it by force. ¹³For all the prophets and the law prophesied until John, ¹⁴and if you are willing to accept it, he is Elijah who is to come. ¹⁵Whoever has ears, let him hear!

¹⁶"But to what shall I compare this generation? It is like children sitting in the marketplaces, who call out to others, ¹⁷saying,

'We played the flute for you, but you did not dance,
we sang a lament, but you did not mourn.'

¹⁸For John came neither eating nor drinking, and they say, 'He has a demon!' ¹⁹The Son of Man came eating and drinking, and they say, 'Behold a glutton and a drunkard, a friend of tax-collectors and sinners!' But wisdom is justified by her works."

Jesus Reprimands Those Who Do Not Repent

²⁰Then he began to reprimand the cities in which most of his deeds of power were done, because they did not repent. ²¹"Woe to you, Chorazin! Woe to you, Bethsaida! For if the deeds of power done in you had been done in Tyre and Sidon, they would have repented long ago in sackcloth and ashes. ²²But I say to you, it shall be more tolerable for Tyre and Sidon on the day of judgment than for you. ²³And you, Capernaum, will you be exalted to heaven? You shall be brought down to hell. For if the deeds of power done in you had been done in Sodom, it would have remained until this day. ²⁴But I say to you, it shall be more tolerable for the land of Sodom on the day of judgment than for you."

The Father and the Son

²⁵At that time Jesus said, "I praise you, Father, Lord of heaven and earth, because you have hidden these things from the wise and understanding and have revealed them to little ones. ²⁶Yes, Father, for so

it has seemed good in your sight. ²⁷All things have been handed over to me by my Father. No one knows the Son except the Father, and no one knows the Father except the Son and anyone to whom the Son chooses to reveal him."

²⁸"Come to me, all you who are weary and burdened, and I will give you rest. ²⁹Take my yoke upon you, and learn from me, for I am meek and humble in heart, and you will find rest for your souls. ³⁰For my yoke is sweet, and my burden is light."

The Lord of the Sabbath

12 ¹At that time, Jesus went through the grain fields on the Sabbath. Now his disciples were hungry, and they began to pick the heads of grain and eat them. ²But when the Pharisees saw it, they said to him, "Behold, your disciples are doing what is not lawful on the Sabbath." ³But he said to them, "Have you not read what David did, when he was hungry, and those with him? ⁴How he went into the house of God and ate the bread of the Presence, which was not lawful for him to eat, nor for those with him, but only for the priests? ⁵Or have you not read in the law that on the Sabbath the priests in the temple profane the Sabbath, yet are innocent? ⁶But I say to you, something greater than the temple is here. ⁷And if you had known what this means, 'I desire mercy, and not sacrifice,' you would not have condemned the innocent. ⁸For the Son of Man is Lord of the Sabbath."

The Man with the Withered Hand

⁹When he left there, he entered their synagogue. ¹⁰And behold, there was a man with a withered hand. And they asked him, saying, "Is it lawful to heal on the Sabbath?"—so that they might accuse him. ¹¹And he said to them, "Which one of you who has one sheep, if it falls into a pit on the Sabbath, will not take hold of it and lift it out? ¹²How much more valuable is a person than a sheep! Therefore, it is lawful to do good on the Sabbath." ¹³Then he said to the man, "Stretch out your hand." And he stretched it out, and it was restored to health like his other hand. ¹⁴Then the Pharisees went out and took counsel against him, in order to destroy him.

The Chosen Servant

¹⁵But Jesus, knowing this, withdrew from there. And many crowds followed him, and he healed them all. ¹⁶And he warned them not to make him known, ¹⁷so that what was spoken through Isaiah the prophet might be fulfilled,

¹⁸"Behold my servant, whom I have chosen,
my beloved, in whom my soul is well pleased;
I will put my Spirit upon him,
and he will proclaim judgment to the Gentiles.
¹⁹He will not quarrel or shout,
nor will anyone hear his voice in the streets.
²⁰A bruised reed he will not break,
and a smoldering wick he will not quench,
until he brings judgment to victory.
²¹And in his name the Gentiles will hope."

Jesus and Beelzebul

²²Then a demon-possessed man who was blind and mute was brought to him. And he healed him, so that the mute man was able to speak and to see. ²³And all the crowds were amazed and said, "Can this be the son of David?" ²⁴But when the Pharisees heard it, they said, "It is only by Beelzebul, the prince of demons, that this man casts out demons." ²⁵But knowing their thoughts, he said to them, "Every kingdom divided against itself is made desolate, and every city or house divided against itself will not stand. ²⁶And if Satan casts out Satan, he is divided against himself. How then will his kingdom stand? ²⁷If I cast out demons by Beelzebul, by whom do your sons cast them out? Therefore they will be your judges. ²⁸But if by the Spirit of God I cast out demons, then the kingdom of God has come upon you. ²⁹Or how can someone break into the house of a strong man and steal his things, unless he first binds the strong man? Then he will plunder his house. ³⁰Whoever is not with me is against me, and whoever does not gather with me scatters.

Blasphemy Against the Holy Spirit

³¹"Therefore I say to you, people will be forgiven for every sin and blasphemy, but blasphemy against the Spirit will not be forgiven. ³²Whoever speaks a word against the Son of Man will be forgiven, but whoever speaks against the Holy Spirit will not be forgiven, either in this age or in the age to come.

The Good Tree and the Bad Tree

³³"Either make the tree good and its fruit good, or else make the tree bad and its fruit bad. For the tree is known by its fruit. ³⁴You brood of vipers! How can you speak good things when you are evil? For out of the abundance of the heart the mouth speaks. ³⁵The good person out of his good treasure brings forth good, and the evil person out of his evil treasure brings forth evil. ³⁶I say to you, on the day of judgment, you will

give an account for every careless word you speak. ³⁷For by your words you will be justified, and by your words you will be condemned."

The Sign of Jonah

³⁸Then some of the scribes and Pharisees answered him, saying, "Teacher, we wish to see a sign from you." ³⁹But he answered and said to them, "An evil and adulterous generation seeks after a sign, but no sign will be given to it except the sign of Jonah the prophet. ⁴⁰For just as Jonah was in the belly of the fish three days and three nights, so will the Son of Man be in the heart of the earth three days and three nights. ⁴¹The men of Nineveh will arise at the judgment with this generation and condemn it, for they repented at the preaching of Jonah. And behold, something greater than Jonah is here! ⁴²The queen of the south will be raised up at the judgment with this generation and condemn it, for she came from the ends of the earth to hear the wisdom of Solomon. And behold, something greater than Solomon is here!

The Unclean Spirit

⁴³"Whenever an unclean spirit has gone out of a person, it goes about through waterless places seeking rest, but it finds none. ⁴⁴Then it says, 'I will return to my house from which I came.' And when it comes, it finds it empty, swept, and put in order. ⁴⁵Then it goes and takes with it seven other spirits more evil than itself, and they enter and dwell there. And the last state of that person is worse than the first. So will it be with this evil generation."

The Mother and Brothers of Jesus

⁴⁶While he was still speaking to the crowds, behold, his mother and his brothers stood outside, seeking to speak with him. ⁴⁷Then someone said to him, "Behold, your mother and your brothers are standing outside, seeking to speak with you." ⁴⁸But he answered and said to the one speaking to him, "Who is my mother, and who are my brothers?" ⁴⁹And he stretched out his hand over his disciples, and said, "Behold, my mother and my brothers. ⁵⁰For whoever does the will of my Father who is in heaven is my brother, and sister, and mother."

Jesus Teaches the Crowd on the Shore

13 ¹On that day, Jesus went out of the house and sat beside the sea. ²And many crowds were gathered to him, so that he got into a boat and sat down. And all the crowd stood on the shore.

The Parable of the Sower

³And he spoke many things to them in parables, saying, "Behold, the sower went out to sow. ⁴And while he sowed, some seeds fell beside the path, and the birds came and ate them up. ⁵Others fell upon rocky ground where they did not have much soil, and immediately they sprang up, because they had no depth of soil. ⁶But when the sun came up they were scorched, and because they had no root, they withered. ⁷Others fell among thorns, and the thorns grew up and choked them. ⁸But others fell on good soil, and produced fruit: some a hundredfold, some sixty, some thirty. ⁹Whoever has ears, let him hear!"

Why Jesus Speaks in Parables

¹⁰And the disciples came and said to him, "Why do you speak to them in parables?" ¹¹He answered and said to them, "To you it has been given to know the mysteries of the kingdom of heaven, but to them it has not been given. ¹²For whoever has, more will be given to him, and he will have in abundance. But whoever does not have, even what he has will be taken away from him. ¹³For this reason I speak to them in parables: because seeing, they do not see, and hearing, they do not hear, nor do they understand. ¹⁴In them is fulfilled the prophecy of Isaiah, which says,

'Hearing, you will hear, but not understand,
and seeing, you will see, but not perceive.
¹⁵For the heart of this people has grown fat,
and their ears have grown hard of hearing,
and they have closed their eyes,
lest they see with their eyes,
and hear with their ears,
and understand with their heart,
and they turn, and I heal them.'

¹⁶But blessed are your eyes, for they see, and your ears, for they hear. ¹⁷Amen, I say to you, many prophets and righteous people longed to see what you see, and did not see it, and to hear what you hear, and did not hear it!

The Parable of the Sower Explained

¹⁸"Hear then the parable of the sower: ¹⁹when anyone hears the word of the kingdom and does not understand, the evil one comes and takes away what was sown in his heart—this is what was sown beside the path. ²⁰As for what was sown upon the rocky ground—this is the one who hears the word, and immediately receives it with joy. ²¹Yet he has no root in himself, but lasts only for a little while. And when

tribulation or persecution happens because of the word, immediately he falls away. ²²As for what was sown among the thorns—this is the one who hears the word, but the cares of this age and the deception of riches choke the word, and it becomes fruitless. ²³As for what was sown upon good soil—this is the one who hears the word and understands it. He indeed bears fruit and produces: in one case a hundredfold, in another sixty, and in another thirty."

The Weeds and the Wheat

²⁴He put another parable before them, saying, "The kingdom of heaven may be compared to a man who sowed good seed in his field. ²⁵But while everyone slept, his enemy came and sowed weeds in the midst of the wheat, and went away. ²⁶When the plants sprouted and bore grain, the weeds also appeared. ²⁷Then the servants of the master of the house came and said to him, 'Master, did you not sow good seed in your field? Where then did the weeds come from?' ²⁸He said to them, 'An enemy has done this.' The servants said to him, 'Then do you want us to go and gather them up?' ²⁹But he said, 'No, lest in gathering up the weeds, you uproot the wheat along with them. ³⁰Let both grow together until the harvest. And at the time of the harvest, I will say to the reapers, First gather the weeds and bind them in bundles to burn them, but gather the wheat into my granary.'"

The Mustard Seed

³¹He put another parable before them, saying, "The kingdom of heaven is like a mustard seed, which a man took and sowed in his field. ³²It is the smallest of all seeds, but when it is grown, it is the greatest of herbs and becomes a tree, so that the birds of heaven come and nest in its branches."

The Leaven

³³He spoke to them another parable: "The kingdom of heaven is like leaven, which a woman took and hid in three measures of flour until it was all leavened."

The Parables and the Prophet

³⁴All these things Jesus spoke in parables to the crowds. He spoke nothing to them without a parable, ³⁵so that what was spoken through the prophet might be fulfilled,

"I will open my mouth in parables;
I will proclaim things hidden since
the foundation of the world."

The Parable of the Weeds Explained

³⁶Then he dismissed the crowds and went into the house. And his disciples came to him, saying, "Explain to us the parable of the weeds of the field." ³⁷He answered and said, "The one who sows the good seed is the Son of Man; ³⁸the field is the world, and the good seed are the sons of the kingdom. But the weeds are the sons of the evil one; ³⁹the enemy who sowed them is the devil; the harvest is the end of the age, and the reapers are the angels. ⁴⁰Just as the weeds are gathered and burned with fire, so will it be at the end of the age. ⁴¹The Son of Man will send forth his angels, and they will gather out of his kingdom all who lead others to sin and those who commit lawlessness. ⁴²And they will cast them into the furnace of fire, where there shall be weeping and gnashing of teeth. ⁴³Then the righteous will shine like the sun in the kingdom of their Father. Whoever has ears, let him hear!

The Hidden Treasure

⁴⁴"The kingdom of heaven is like a treasure hidden in a field, which a man found and hid. Then, in his joy, he went and sold all that he had and bought that field.

The Pearl of Great Price

⁴⁵"Again, the kingdom of heaven is like a merchant seeking fine pearls. ⁴⁶When he found one pearl of great price, he went and sold all that he had and bought it.

The Dragnet

⁴⁷"Again, the kingdom of heaven is like a dragnet that was cast into the sea and gathered fish of every kind. ⁴⁸When it was full, they pulled it up on the shore and sat down and gathered the good into vessels, but the bad they cast out. ⁴⁹So will it be at the end of the age. The angels will come forth and separate the evil from the midst of the righteous, ⁵⁰and they will cast them into the furnace of fire, where there shall be weeping and gnashing of teeth.

The Scribe in the Kingdom of Heaven

⁵¹"Have you understood all these things?" They said to him, "Yes." ⁵²He said to them, "For this reason, every scribe who has become a disciple of the kingdom of heaven is like the master of a house, who brings out of his treasure both the new and the old."

A Prophet in His Hometown

⁵³Now when Jesus had finished these parables, he went away from there. ⁵⁴And when he came into his hometown, he taught them in their synagogue, so that they were astonished and said, "Where did this man get this wisdom and these powers? ⁵⁵Is this not the carpenter's son? Is not his mother called Mary, and are not his brothers James and Joseph and Simon and Jude? ⁵⁶And his sisters, are they not all with us? So where did this man get all this?" ⁵⁷And they were scandalized by him. But Jesus said to them, "No prophet is without honor except in his hometown and in his own house." ⁵⁸And he did not do many deeds of power there, because of their unbelief.

The Beheading of John the Baptist

14 ¹At that time Herod the tetrarch heard of the fame of Jesus, ²and he said to his servants, "This is John the Baptist! He has been raised from the dead, and this is why these powers are at work in him." ³For Herod had arrested John, bound him, and put him in prison because of Herodias, the wife of Philip his brother. ⁴For John had said to him, "It is not lawful for you to have her." ⁵And though he wanted to put him to death, he was afraid of the crowd, because they held him to be a prophet.

⁶But when Herod's birthday came, the daughter of Herodias danced in their midst and pleased Herod. ⁷So he promised with an oath to give her whatever she asked. ⁸And prompted by her mother, she said, "Give me here on a platter the head of John the Baptist." ⁹Although the king was grieved, for the sake of the oath and those who sat at table with him, he ordered it to be given. ¹⁰And he sent and beheaded John in prison. ¹¹And his head was brought in on a platter and given to the girl, and she brought it to her mother. ¹²Then his disciples came and took the body and buried it. And they went and told Jesus.

The Feeding of the Five Thousand

¹³Now when Jesus heard of this, he withdrew from there in a boat to a deserted place by himself. But when the crowds heard, they followed him on foot from the cities. ¹⁴When he came ashore, he saw the great crowd, and he had compassion on them and healed their sick. ¹⁵And when it was evening, the disciples came to him and said, "This is a deserted place, and the hour is now past. Send the crowd away, so that they may go into the villages and buy food for themselves." ¹⁶But Jesus said to them, "They need not go away. You give them something to eat." ¹⁷They said to him, "We have nothing here except five loaves of bread and two fish." ¹⁸So he said, "Bring them here to me." ¹⁹And he ordered the crowd to recline on the grass. Taking the five loaves and the two fish and looking up to heaven, he said the blessing, broke the loaves, and gave them to his disciples. And his disciples gave them to the crowd. ²⁰Then they all ate and were filled. And they took up what remained of the broken pieces, twelve baskets full. ²¹Those who had eaten were about five thousand men, besides women and children.

Jesus Walks on the Sea

²²And immediately he made his disciples get into the boat and go before him to the other side, while he sent away the crowds. ²³And when he had sent the crowds away, he went up the mountain by himself to pray. And when it was evening, he was there alone. ²⁴Now the boat was already miles away from the land, being battered by the waves, for the wind was against it. ²⁵And in the fourth watch of the night, he came to them, walking on the sea. ²⁶And when the disciples saw him walking on the sea, they were frightened, saying, "It is a ghost!" And they cried out in fear. ²⁷But immediately Jesus spoke to them, saying, "Take heart! I am; do not fear." ²⁸And Peter answered him and said, "Lord, if it is you, command me to come to you on the waters." ²⁹And he said, "Come!" And when Peter stepped out of the boat, he walked on the waters and came to Jesus. ³⁰But when he saw the strong wind, he was afraid. And beginning to sink, he cried out, saying, "Lord, save me!" ³¹And immediately Jesus stretched out his hand, took hold of him, and said to him, "O you of little faith, why did you doubt?" ³²And when they climbed into the boat, the wind ceased. ³³Then those who were in the boat worshiped him, saying, "Truly you are the Son of God!"

Jesus in the Land of Gennesaret

³⁴And when they had crossed over, they came ashore to Gennesaret. ³⁵And when the people of that place recognized him, they sent word into all that surrounding region and brought to him all the sick. ³⁶And they were begging him that they might touch only the fringe of his garment. And all who touched it were healed.

The Pharisees and Their Tradition

15 ¹Then Pharisees and scribes came to Jesus from Jerusalem, saying, ²"Why do your disciples transgress the tradition of the elders?

For they do not wash their hands when they eat." ³But he answered and said to them, "Why do you transgress the commandment of God for the sake of your tradition? ⁴For God said, 'Honor your father and mother,' and, 'Whoever curses his father or mother must die.' ⁵But you say, 'Whoever says to his father or mother, "Whatever you are owed from me is a gift to God," ⁶he need not honor his father.' You have made void the word of God for the sake of your tradition. ⁷You hypocrites! Well did Isaiah prophesy about you, saying,

> ⁸"This people honors me with their lips,
> but their heart is far away from me.
> ⁹In vain do they worship me,
> teaching as doctrines the
> commandments of men.'"

What Defiles a Person

¹⁰And he called the crowd to himself and said to them, "Hear and understand: ¹¹it is not what goes into the mouth that defiles a person, but what comes out of the mouth; this defiles a person." ¹²Then his disciples came and said to him, "Do you know that the Pharisees were scandalized when they heard this saying?" ¹³But he answered and said, "Every plant that my heavenly Father has not planted will be uprooted. ¹⁴Leave them alone. They are blind guides of the blind. If one blind person leads another, both will fall into a pit." ¹⁵Then Peter answered and said to him, "Explain to us this parable." ¹⁶And Jesus said, "Are you also still without understanding? ¹⁷Do you not perceive that everything that goes into the mouth enters the stomach and is expelled into the sewer? ¹⁸But those things which proceed from the mouth come out of the heart, and they defile a person. ¹⁹For out of the heart come evil thoughts, murders, adulteries, sexual sins, thefts, false testimonies, blasphemies. ²⁰These are the things that defile a person, but to eat with unwashed hands does not defile a person."

The Canaanite Woman

²¹Then Jesus went away from there and departed into the district of Tyre and Sidon. ²²And behold, a Canaanite woman from that region came and cried out, saying, "Have mercy on me, Lord, Son of David! My daughter is cruelly tormented by a demon." ²³But he did not answer her a word. And his disciples came and begged him, saying, "Send her away, for she is crying out after us." ²⁴But he answered and said, "I was sent only to the lost sheep of the house of Israel." ²⁵Then she came and worshiped him, saying, "Lord, help me!" ²⁶But he answered and said, "It is not good to take the bread of the children and throw it to the dogs." ²⁷But she said, "Yes, Lord, but even the dogs eat the crumbs that fall from their masters' table." ²⁸Then Jesus answered and said to her, "O woman, great is your faith! Let it be done for you as you wish." And her daughter was healed from that hour.

Jesus Heals the Crowds on the Mountain

²⁹And Jesus left there and walked along beside the sea of Galilee. And he went up the mountain, where he sat down. ³⁰Many crowds came to him, bringing with them those who were lame, blind, maimed, mute, and many others, and they laid them down at his feet. And he healed them, ³¹so that the crowd marveled when they saw the mute speaking, the maimed made whole, the lame walking, and the blind seeing. And they glorified the God of Israel.

The Feeding of the Four Thousand

³²Then Jesus called his disciples to himself and said, "I have compassion for the crowd, since they have remained with me for three days now and have nothing to eat. And I am not willing to send them away fasting, lest they faint on the road." ³³His disciples said to him, "Where can we get enough bread in this desolate place to satisfy such a crowd?" ³⁴And Jesus said to them, "How many loaves do you have?" And they said, "Seven, and a few small fish." ³⁵Then he ordered the crowd to sit on the ground. ³⁶And he took the seven loaves and the fish, and having given thanks, he broke them and gave them to his disciples, and the disciples gave them to the crowds. ³⁷Then they all ate and were filled. And they took up what remained of the broken pieces, seven baskets full. ³⁸Those who had eaten were four thousand men, besides women and children. ³⁹And after he sent away the crowds, he got into the boat and came into the region of Magadan.

The Signs of the Times

16 ¹Now the Pharisees and Sadducees came to test him, and they asked him to show them a sign from heaven. ²He answered and said to them, "When it is evening, you say, 'It will be good weather, for the sky is red.' ³And in the morning, 'It will be bad weather today, for the sky is red and threatening.' You know how to judge the face of the sky, but not the signs of the times. ⁴An evil and adulterous generation seeks a sign, but no sign will be given to it except the sign of Jonah." And he left them and went away.

The Leaven of the Pharisees and the Sadducees

⁵And when his disciples came to the other side, they had forgotten to bring bread. ⁶Then Jesus said to them, "Watch, and beware of the leaven of the Pharisees and the Sadducees." ⁷And they were discussing it among themselves, saying, "We did not bring bread!" ⁸But knowing this, Jesus said, "O you of little faith, why are you discussing among yourselves that you have no bread? ⁹Do you not yet understand? Or do you not remember the five loaves for the five thousand, and how many baskets you took up? ¹⁰Or the seven loaves for the four thousand, and how many baskets you took up? ¹¹How do you not understand that I did not speak to you about bread? Beware of the leaven of the Pharisees and the Sadducees." ¹²Then they realized that he had not told them to beware of the leaven of bread, but of the teaching of the Pharisees and the Sadducees.

Jesus, Peter, and the Keys of the Kingdom

¹³When Jesus came into the district of Caesarea Philippi, he asked his disciples, "Who do people say that the Son of Man is?" ¹⁴And they said, "Some say John the Baptist, others Elijah, still others say Jeremiah or one of the prophets." ¹⁵He said to them, "But you, who do you say that I am?" ¹⁶Simon Peter answered and said, "You are the Christ, the Son of the living God." ¹⁷And Jesus answered and said to him, "Blessed are you, Simon Bar-Jonah, for flesh and blood has not revealed this to you, but my Father who is in heaven. ¹⁸And I say to you, you are Peter, and upon this rock I will build my Church, and the gates of hell shall not prevail against it. ¹⁹I will give you the keys of the kingdom of heaven. Whatever you bind on earth shall be bound in heaven, and whatever you loose on earth shall be loosed in heaven." ²⁰Then he commanded his disciples to tell no one that he was the Christ.

Peter Rebukes Jesus

²¹From then on Jesus began to show his disciples that he must go to Jerusalem and suffer many things from the elders and chief priests and scribes, and be killed, and on the third day be raised. ²²Then Peter took him aside and began to rebuke him, saying, "Far be it from you, Lord! Surely this shall never happen to you." ²³But he turned and said to Peter, "Get behind me, Satan! You are a stumbling block to me, for you are not thinking the things of God, but the things of men."

Whoever Loses His Life Will Find It

²⁴Then Jesus said to his disciples, "If anyone wants to come after me, let him deny himself and take up his cross and follow me. ²⁵For whoever would save his life will lose it, but whoever loses his life for my sake will find it. ²⁶For what shall it profit someone if he gains the whole world, but suffers the loss of his soul? Or what will someone give in exchange for his soul? ²⁷For the Son of Man is about to come in the glory of his Father with his angels, and then he will repay each person according to his works. ²⁸Amen, I say to you, there are some standing here who shall not taste death until they see the Son of Man coming in his kingdom."

The Transfiguration

17 ¹After six days, Jesus took with him Peter and James and John his brother and led them up a high mountain by themselves. ²And he was transfigured before them, and his face shone like the sun, and his garments became white as light. ³And behold, Moses and Elijah appeared to them and were talking with him. ⁴Then Peter answered and said to Jesus, "Lord, it is good for us to be here. If you wish, I will make three tabernacles here, one for you, one for Moses, and one for Elijah." ⁵While he was still speaking, behold, a luminous cloud overshadowed them. And behold, a voice from the cloud said, "This is my beloved Son, in whom I am well pleased. Listen to him!" ⁶And when the disciples heard this, they fell on their faces and were filled with fear. ⁷But Jesus came and touched them and said, "Rise, and do not fear." ⁸And when they lifted up their eyes, they saw no one but Jesus alone. ⁹And as they were coming down from the mountain, Jesus commanded them saying, "Tell no one about the vision until the Son of Man is raised from the dead."

Elijah Has Already Come

¹⁰And his disciples asked him, "Why then do the scribes say that Elijah must come first?" ¹¹He answered and said, "Elijah does come, and he will restore all things. ¹²But I say to you that Elijah has already come, and they did not recognize him, but they did to him whatever they wanted. So too the Son of Man is about to suffer at their hands." ¹³Then the disciples understood that he had spoken to them of John the Baptist.

Jesus Casts Out a Demon from a Man's Son

¹⁴And when they came to the crowd, a man came and knelt before him, ¹⁵saying, "Lord, have mercy on

my son, for he has seizures and suffers terribly. For he often falls into the fire, and often into the water. **16**So I brought him to your disciples, but they were not able to heal him." **17**Then Jesus answered and said, "O faithless and perverse generation, how long will I be with you? How long will I endure you? Bring him here to me." **18**And Jesus rebuked the demon, and it came out of him, and the child was healed from that hour. **19**Then the disciples came to Jesus privately and said, "Why were we not able to cast it out?" **20**And he said to them, "Because of your little faith. For amen, I say to you, if you have faith like a mustard seed, you will say to this mountain, 'Move from here to there,' and it will move. And nothing will be impossible for you."

Jesus Predicts His Death and Resurrection

22And while they were gathering in Galilee, Jesus said to them, "The Son of Man is about to be betrayed into the hands of men. **23**They will kill him, and on the third day he will be raised." And they were very sorrowful.

Jesus, Peter, and the Temple Tax

24When they came into Capernaum, the collectors of the temple tax came to Peter and said: "Does your teacher not pay the temple tax?" **25**He said, "Yes." And when he came into the house, Jesus spoke to him first, asking, "What do you think, Simon? From whom do the kings of the earth collect toll or tax? From their sons, or from others?" **26**Peter said to him, "From others." Jesus said to him, "Then the sons are free. **27**Yet, lest we scandalize them, go to the sea, cast a fishhook, and take the first fish that comes up. And when you open its mouth, you will find a silver coin worth four drachmas. Take that, and give it to them for me and for you."

The Greatest in the Kingdom

18

1At that hour, the disciples came to Jesus, saying, "Who then is greatest in the kingdom of heaven?" **2**And calling a little child to himself, he stood him in their midst **3**and said, "Amen, I say to you, unless you turn and become like little children, you will never enter the kingdom of heaven. **4**Therefore, whoever humbles himself like this little child is the greatest in the kingdom of heaven. **5**And whoever receives one such little child in my name, receives me.

Scandals

6"But whoever leads one of these little ones who believes in me into sin, it would be better for him to have a great millstone hung around his neck and be drowned in the depths of the sea. **7**Woe to the world because of scandals! For scandals must come, but woe to the one through whom the scandal comes!

8"So if your hand or your foot leads you to sin, cut it off and throw it away. It is better for you to enter life maimed or lame than to have two hands or two feet and be cast into the eternal fire. **9**And if your eye leads you to sin, pluck it out and throw it away. It is better for you to enter life with one eye than to have two eyes and be cast into the Gehenna of fire.

Angels in Heaven

10"See that you do not despise one of these little ones. For I say to you, in heaven their angels continually see the face of my Father who is in heaven.

The Lost Sheep

12"What do you think? If a man has a hundred sheep, and one of them goes astray, will he not leave the ninety-nine on the mountains and go in search of the one gone astray? **13**Amen, I say to you, if he finds it, he rejoices over it more than over the ninety-nine that did not go astray. **14**In the same way, it is not the will of your Father who is in heaven that one of these little ones should perish.

If Your Brother Sins Against You

15"If your brother sins against you, go, tell him his fault between you and him alone. If he listens to you, you have gained your brother. **16**But if he does not listen, take with you one or two others, so that 'every word may be established from the mouth of two or three witnesses.' **17**And if he refuses to listen to them, tell the church. But if he refuses to listen even to the church, let him be to you like a Gentile or a tax collector. **18**Amen, I say to you, whatever you bind on earth shall be bound in heaven, and whatever you loose on earth shall be loosed in heaven. **19**Again, amen I say to you, if two of you agree on earth about anything they ask, it shall be done for them by my Father who is in heaven. **20**For where two or three are gathered in my name, there I am in the midst of them."

The Unforgiving Servant

21Then Peter came and said to him, "Lord, how many times will my brother sin against me and I forgive him? Up to seven times?" **22**Jesus said to him, "I say to you, not up to seven times, but up to seventy-seven times.

23"For this reason, the kingdom of heaven may be

compared to a king who wished to settle accounts with his servants. ²⁴When he began to settle accounts, one was brought to him who owed ten thousand talents. ²⁵But because he did not have the money to pay, his master ordered him to be sold, along with his wife and children and all that he had, and payment to be made. ²⁶So the servant fell down and worshiped him, saying, 'Have patience with me, and I will pay you everything.' ²⁷Then the lord of that servant, moved with compassion, released him and forgave him the debt. ²⁸But when the same servant went out, he found one of his fellow servants who owed him one hundred denarii. And he seized him and began choking him, saying, 'Pay what you owe!' ²⁹So his fellow servant fell down and begged him, saying, 'Have patience with me, and I will pay you.' ³⁰But he would not. Instead he went and cast him into prison, until he should pay what was owed.

³¹For this reason, when his fellow servants saw what had taken place, they were extremely sorrowful. So they went and told their lord all that had taken place. ³²Then his lord called him and said to him, "You evil servant! I forgave you all that debt because you begged me. ³³Should you not have had mercy on your fellow servant, just as I had mercy on you?' ³⁴And the lord was angry, and he handed him over to the torturers until he should pay all the debt. ³⁵So my heavenly Father will also do to each one of you, if you do not forgive your brother from your heart."

Jesus Comes into Judea

19 ¹Now when Jesus had finished these words, he departed from Galilee and came into the regions of Judea beyond the Jordan. ²And many crowds followed him, and he healed them there.

Divorce and Remarriage

³And Pharisees came to him in order to test him, saying, "Is it lawful for a man to divorce his wife for any reason?" ⁴And he answered and said, "Have you not read that from the beginning, the Creator 'made them male and female' ⁵and said, 'For this reason a man shall leave his father and mother and be joined to his wife, and the two shall become one flesh'? ⁶So they are no longer two, but one flesh. Therefore, what God has yoked together, let no one separate." ⁷They said to him, "Why then did Moses command us to give her a bill of divorce and send her away?" ⁸He said to them, "Moses permitted you to divorce your wives because of your hardness of heart, but from the beginning it was not so. ⁹But I say to you, whoever divorces his wife, except for sexual immorality, and marries another, commits adultery."

Eunuchs for the Sake of the Kingdom

¹⁰The disciples said to him, "If this is the case of a man with his wife, it is better not to marry!" ¹¹But he said to them, "Not everyone receives this word, but only those to whom it is given. ¹²For there are some eunuchs who were born eunuchs from their mother's womb, and there are some who were made eunuchs by men, and there are some who have made themselves eunuchs for the sake of the kingdom of heaven. Whoever is able to receive this, let him receive it."

Let the Little Children Come to Me

¹³Then little children were brought to him so that he might lay hands on them and pray. And the disciples rebuked them. ¹⁴But Jesus said, "Let the little children come to me, and do not prevent them, for the kingdom of heaven belongs to such as these." ¹⁵And he laid his hands on them and went away from there.

The Rich Young Man

¹⁶And behold, someone came to him and said, "Teacher, what good must I do to have eternal life?" ¹⁷But he said to him, "Why do you ask me about the good? There is one who is good. If you wish to enter into life, keep the commandments."

¹⁸He said to him, "Which ones?" Jesus said, "'You shall not murder, You shall not commit adultery, You shall not steal, You shall not bear false witness, ¹⁹Honor your father and mother, and You shall love your neighbor as yourself.'" ²⁰The young man said to him, "All these I have kept. What do I still lack?" ²¹Jesus said to him, "If you wish to be perfect, go, sell what you have and give to the poor, and you will have treasure in heaven. And come, follow me." ²²But when the young man heard this word, he went away grieving, for he had many possessions.

The Rich and the Kingdom of Heaven

²³Then Jesus said to his disciples, "Amen, I say to you, it will be difficult for one who is rich to enter the kingdom of heaven. ²⁴Again I say to you, it is easier for a camel to go through the eye of a needle than for a rich man to enter the kingdom of God." ²⁵When the disciples heard it, they were utterly astonished and said, "Who then can be saved?" ²⁶But Jesus looked at them and said, "With man, this is impossible, but with God, all things are possible."

The Twelve Thrones and the Twelve Tribes

²⁷Then Peter answered and said to him, "See, we have left everything and followed you. What then will we have?" ²⁸And Jesus said to him, "Amen, I say to you, in the new creation, when the Son of Man sits upon his throne of glory, you who have followed me will also sit upon twelve thrones, judging the twelve tribes of Israel. ²⁹And everyone who has left houses, or brothers, or sisters, or father, or mother, or children, or fields for the sake of my name, will receive a hundredfold and inherit eternal life. ³⁰But many who are first shall be last, and the last first.

The Workers in the Vineyard

20 ¹"For the kingdom of heaven is like the master of a house who went out early in the morning to hire workers for his vineyard. ²When he had agreed to give the workers a denarius for the day, he sent them into his vineyard. ³And going out at about the third hour, he saw others standing idle in the marketplace. ⁴And he said to them, 'You also go into the vineyard, and whatever is just, I will give you.' ⁵So they went. And going out again around the sixth hour and the ninth hour, he did likewise. ⁶Around the eleventh hour, he went out and found others standing and said to them, 'Why do you stand here idle the whole day?' ⁷They said to him, 'Because no one hired us.' He said to them, 'You also go into the vineyard.'

⁸"When it was evening, the master of the vineyard said to his foreman, 'Call the workers and pay them their wage, beginning with the last and proceeding to the first.' ⁹And those who came around the eleventh hour each received one denarius. ¹⁰And when the first came, they thought they would receive more, but they also received one denarius. ¹¹And when they received it, they murmured against the master of the house, ¹²saying, 'These last worked one hour, and you have made them equal to us, who endured the burden of the day and the burning heat!' ¹³But he answered one of them and said, 'Friend, I did you no injustice. Did you not agree with me for a denarius? ¹⁴Take what is yours and go, for I wish to give this last one exactly what I gave you. ¹⁵Or am I not allowed to do what I will with what is mine? Or is your eye evil because I am good?' ¹⁶In this way, the last shall be first and the first shall be last."

Jesus Predicts His Death and Resurrection a Third Time

¹⁷As Jesus was going up to Jerusalem, he took the twelve disciples aside by themselves, and he said to them on the way, ¹⁸"Behold, we are going up to Jerusalem, and the Son of Man will be handed over to the chief priests and scribes, and they will condemn him to death. ¹⁹And they will hand him over to the Gentiles to be mocked and scourged and crucified, and on the third day he will be raised."

The Request of the Mother of James and John

²⁰Then the mother of the sons of Zebedee came to him with her sons. And worshiping him, she asked him for something. ²¹But he said to her, "What do you wish?" She said to him, "Declare that these two sons of mine may sit, one at your right hand and one at your left, in your kingdom." ²²But Jesus answered and said, "You do not know what you are asking. Are you able to drink the cup that I am about to drink?" They said to him, "We are able." ²³He said to them, "You will drink my cup, but to sit at my right hand and at my left is not mine to give, but is for those for whom it is prepared by my Father."

²⁴And when the ten heard it, they were indignant at the two brothers. ²⁵But Jesus called them to himself and said, "You know that the rulers of the Gentiles lord it over them, and their great ones exercise authority over them. ²⁶It shall not be so among you. But whoever wishes to become great among you must be your minister, ²⁷and whoever wishes to be first among you must be your servant, ²⁸just as the Son of Man did not come to be served but to serve, and to give his life as a ransom for many."

Jesus Heals Two Blind Men

²⁹As they were going out from Jericho, a great crowd followed him. ³⁰And behold, two blind men were sitting beside the road. When they heard that Jesus was passing by, they cried out, saying, "Have mercy on us, Lord, son of David!" ³¹And the crowd rebuked them in order to silence them. But they cried out louder and said, "Have mercy on us, Lord, son of David!" ³²And Jesus stood still, and he called them and said, "What do you want me to do for you?" ³³They said to him, "Lord, let our eyes be opened." ³⁴So Jesus had compassion on them and touched their eyes, and immediately they were able to see, and they followed him.

Jesus Enters into Jerusalem

21 ¹When they drew near to Jerusalem and came to Bethphage on the Mount of Olives, Jesus then sent two disciples, ²saying to them, "Go into the village opposite you, and immediately you will find a donkey tied and a colt with her. Untie them and bring them to me. ³And if anyone says anything to you, say, 'The Lord has need of them,' and he will send them immediately." ⁴Now this took place, so that what was spoken through the prophet might be fulfilled,

⁵"Tell the daughter of Zion,
'Behold, your King comes to you,
meek and riding on a donkey,
and on a colt, the foal of a beast of burden.'"

⁶And the disciples went and did as Jesus commanded them. ⁷They brought the donkey and the colt and placed their garments on them, and he sat on them. ⁸And a very large crowd spread their garments on the road. Others cut branches from the trees and spread them on the road. ⁹And the crowds that went before him and those that followed cried out, saying,

"Hosanna to the Son of David!
'Blessed is he who comes in
the name of the Lord!'
Hosanna in the highest!"

¹⁰And when he entered Jerusalem, the whole city shook, saying, "Who is this?" ¹¹The crowds were saying, "This is the prophet Jesus from Nazareth of Galilee." ¹²And Jesus went into the temple and cast out all those who sold and bought in the temple. And he overturned the tables of the moneychangers and the seats of those who sold doves. ¹³And he said to them, "It is written,

'My house shall be called a house of prayer,'
but you are making it 'a den of thieves.'"

¹⁴And the blind and the lame came to him in the temple, and he healed them. ¹⁵When the chief priests and the scribes saw the wonders he had done and the children crying out in the temple, saying, "Hosanna to the Son of David!" they were indignant. ¹⁶And they said to him, "Do you hear what these people are saying?" Jesus said to them, "Yes. Have you never read:

'Out of the mouths of babes and nurslings,
you have perfected praise'?"

¹⁷And leaving them, he went out of the city to Bethany and spent the night there.

Jesus and the Fig Tree

¹⁸Now, in the morning, as he was returning to the city, he was hungry. ¹⁹Seeing a fig tree on the way, he went to it but found nothing on it except leaves. And he said to it, "May no fruit ever come from you again!" And the fig tree withered at once. ²⁰When the disciples saw it, they marveled and said, "How did the fig tree wither at once?" ²¹Jesus answered and said to them, "Amen, I say to you, if you have faith and do not doubt, not only will you do what was done to the fig tree, but even if you say to this mountain, 'Be lifted up and cast into the sea,' it will be done. ²²And whatever you ask in prayer, you will receive, if you have faith."

The Authority of Jesus and John the Baptist

²³When he had come into the temple, the chief priests and the elders of the people came to him as he was teaching and said, "By what authority do you do these things? And who gave you this authority?" ²⁴And Jesus answered and said to them, "I too will ask you one question, and if you answer me, then I will also tell you by what authority I do these things. ²⁵The baptism of John: where was it from? From heaven, or from men?" And they discussed it among themselves saying, "If we say, 'From heaven,' he will say to us, 'Why then did you not believe him?' ²⁶But if we say, 'From men,' we fear the crowd, for they all hold John to be a prophet." ²⁷So they answered Jesus and said, "We do not know." And he said to them, "Neither will I tell you by what authority I do these things."

The Two Children

²⁸"What do you think? A man had two children. And he came to the first and said, 'Child, go and work in the vineyard today.' ²⁹He answered and said, 'I will not.' But later he changed his mind and went. ³⁰And he came to the other and said likewise. And he answered and said, 'I will, sir.' But he did not go. ³¹Which of the two did the will of the father?" They said, "The first." Jesus said to them, "Amen, I say to you, tax collectors and prostitutes are entering the kingdom of God ahead of you, ³²for John came to you in the way of righteousness, and you did not believe him. But tax collectors and prostitutes believed him. Yet when you saw it, even then you did not change your mind and believe him.

The Wicked Tenants

³³"Hear another parable: there was a master of a house who planted a vineyard, put a fence around it, dug a winepress in it, and built a tower. Then he rented it out to tenant farmers and went on a journey. ³⁴And when the season for fruit drew near, he sent his servants to the tenants to collect its fruits. ³⁵And the tenants took his servants, beat one, killed another, and stoned another. ³⁶Again, he sent other servants, more than the first, and they did the same to them. ³⁷Afterward he sent his son to them, saying, 'They will respect my son.' ³⁸But when the tenants saw the son, they said to themselves, 'This is the heir. Come, let us kill him and take his inheritance.' ³⁹And they

took him and cast him out of the vineyard and killed him. ⁴⁰So when the master of the vineyard comes, what will he do to those tenants?" ⁴¹They said to him, "He will bring those evil men to an evil end and lease the vineyard to other tenants, who will give him the fruits in their seasons." ⁴²Jesus said to them, "Have you never read in the scriptures,

'The stone which the builders rejected,
has become the cornerstone.
This was the Lord's doing,
and it is marvelous in our eyes'?

⁴³For this reason I say to you that the kingdom of God will be taken from you and given to a people producing its fruits. ⁴⁴The one who falls on this stone will be broken in pieces, and on whomever it falls, it will crush him."

⁴⁵And when the chief priests and the Pharisees heard his parables, they knew that he was speaking about them. ⁴⁶And although they sought to arrest him, they feared the crowds, because they held him to be a prophet.

The Royal Wedding Feast

22 ¹Once again Jesus spoke to them in parables, saying, ²"The kingdom of heaven may be compared to a king who held a wedding feast for his son. ³He sent his servants to call those who had been invited to the wedding feast, but they did not want to come. ⁴Again, he sent other servants and said, 'Say to those who were called: behold, I have prepared my feast, my bulls and fatted calves have been slaughtered, and all is ready. Come to the wedding feast.' ⁵But they ignored it and went away, one to his field, another to his business. ⁶And the rest seized his servants and mistreated them and killed them.

⁷"Now the king was angry, so he sent his armies and destroyed those murderers and burned their city. ⁸Then he said to his servants, 'The wedding feast is ready, but those who were called were not worthy. ⁹Go therefore to the roads leading out of the city and call as many as you can find to the wedding feast.' ¹⁰And those servants went out to the roads, and gathered together everyone they found, both the evil and the good. And the wedding feast was filled with guests. ¹¹But when the king came in to see the guests at table, he saw there a man who was not wearing a wedding garment. ¹²And he said to him, 'Friend, how did you come in here without a wedding garment?' But he was silent. ¹³Then the king said to the ministers, 'Bind his feet and hands and cast him into the outer darkness, where there shall be weeping and gnashing of teeth.' ¹⁴For many are called, but few are chosen."

The Question about Paying Taxes to Caesar

¹⁵Then the Pharisees went and took counsel about how to trap him in his words. ¹⁶And they sent their disciples to him with the Herodians, saying, "Teacher, we know that you are truthful, and that you teach the way of God in truth and are not concerned with anyone's opinion. For you do not regard a person's status. ¹⁷Tell us then, what do you think? Is it lawful to pay the census tax to Caesar or not?" ¹⁸But Jesus knew their evil and said, "Why do you test me, you hypocrites? ¹⁹Show me the coin for the tax." So they brought him a denarius. ²⁰And he said to them, "Whose image and inscription is this?" ²¹They said to him, "Caesar's." Then he said to them, "Therefore render to Caesar the things that are Caesar's, and to God the things that are God's." ²²When they heard it, they marveled, and they left him and went away.

The Question about the Resurrection

²³On that day, the Sadducees, who say there is no resurrection, came to him and asked him, saying, ²⁴"Teacher, Moses said, 'If someone dies without having children, his brother shall marry his wife and raise up offspring for his brother.' ²⁵Now there were seven brothers among us. After the first was married, he died. But having no offspring, he left his wife to his brother. ²⁶Likewise, the second also died, and the third, all the way to the seventh. ²⁷After them all, the wife died. ²⁸Therefore, in the resurrection, of the seven brothers, whose wife will she be? For they all had her." ²⁹Jesus answered and said to them, "You are wrong, because you do not know the Scriptures or the power of God. ³⁰For in the resurrection they neither marry nor are given in marriage, but are like angels in heaven. ³¹Regarding the resurrection of the dead, have you not read what was spoken to you by God, ³²'I am the God of Abraham, the God of Isaac, and the God of Jacob'? He is not the God of the dead, but of the living." ³³And when the crowds heard it, they were astonished at his teaching.

The Question about the Greatest Commandment

³⁴But when the Pharisees heard that he had silenced the Sadducees, they gathered together. ³⁵Then one of them, a lawyer, asked him in order to test him, ³⁶"Teacher, which is the greatest commandment in the law?" ³⁷He said to him, "'You shall love the Lord your God with all your heart, with all your soul, and with all your mind.' ³⁸This is the greatest and first commandment. ³⁹And a second is like it: 'You shall love your neighbor as yourself.' ⁴⁰On these two commandments hang the whole law and the prophets."

The Question about the Christ

⁴¹While the Pharisees were gathered together, Jesus asked them, ⁴²saying, "What do you think about the Christ? Whose son is he?" They said to him, "David's." ⁴³He said to them, "How then does David, speaking by the Spirit, call him Lord, saying,

⁴⁴'The Lord said to my Lord,
Sit at my right hand, until I put
your enemies beneath your feet'?

⁴⁵If then David calls him Lord, how is he his son?" ⁴⁶And no one was able to answer him a word, and from that day on no one dared to ask him any more questions.

Whoever Exalts Himself Will Be Humbled

23 ¹Then Jesus spoke to the crowds and to his disciples, ²saying, "The scribes and Pharisees sit on the seat of Moses. ³Therefore, do and observe everything they tell you, but do not imitate their works. For they do not practice what they preach. ⁴They bind burdens heavy and difficult to carry and lay them on others' shoulders, but they themselves are not willing to lift a finger to move them. ⁵They do all their works to be seen by others. For they make their phylacteries wide and their fringes long, ⁶and they love the places of honor at banquets, the most prominent seats in the synagogues, ⁷the salutations in the markets, and to be called Rabbi by others. ⁸But you shall not be called Rabbi, for you have one teacher, and you are all brothers. ⁹And call no one your father on earth, for you have one Father, who is in heaven. ¹⁰Nor should you be called teachers, for you have one teacher, the Christ. ¹¹The greatest among you must be your servant. ¹²For whoever exalts himself will be humbled, and whoever humbles himself will be exalted.

Woes Against the Scribes and Pharisees

¹³"But woe to you, scribes and Pharisees, hypocrites! For you lock others out of the kingdom of heaven. You neither enter yourselves, nor do you allow those who would go in to enter.

¹⁵"Woe to you, scribes and Pharisees, hypocrites! For you travel across sea and dry land to make a single proselyte, and when he becomes one, you make him twice as much a son of Gehenna as yourselves.

¹⁶"Woe to you, blind guides, who say, 'If anyone swears by the temple, it is nothing. But if anyone swears by the gold of the temple, he is obligated by his oath.' ¹⁷You blind fools! Which is greater, the gold or the temple that makes the gold holy? ¹⁸And you say, 'If anyone swears by the altar, it is nothing, but if anyone swears by the gift upon the altar, he is obligated by his oath.' ¹⁹You blind men! Which is greater, the gift or the altar that makes the gift holy? ²⁰So whoever swears by the altar, swears by it and by everything on it; ²¹and whoever swears by the temple, swears by it and by him who dwells in it; ²²and whoever swears by heaven, swears by the throne of God and by him who sits upon it.

²³"Woe to you, scribes and Pharisees, hypocrites! For you tithe mint and dill and cumin, but have neglected the weightier matters of the law: justice, mercy, and faith. It was necessary to do the former, but without omitting the latter. ²⁴You blind guides! You strain out a gnat but swallow a camel!

²⁵"Woe to you, scribes and Pharisees, hypocrites! For you cleanse the outside of the cup and the dish, but inside you are full of greed and self-indulgence. ²⁶You blind Pharisee! First cleanse the inside of the cup, so that its outside may also become clean.

²⁷"Woe to you, scribes and Pharisees, hypocrites! For you are like whitewashed tombs that appear beautiful on the outside, but inside are filled with the bones of the dead and every uncleanness. ²⁸So you also on the outside appear righteous to others, but inside you are full of hypocrisy and lawlessness.

²⁹"Woe to you, scribes and Pharisees, hypocrites! For you build the graves of the prophets and decorate the tombs of the righteous, ³⁰and say, 'If we had lived in the days of our fathers, we would have had no part with them in shedding the blood of the prophets.' ³¹Thus you bear witness against yourselves that you are the sons of those who murdered the prophets. ³²Fill up, then, the measure of your fathers. ³³You serpents, you brood of vipers! How will you escape from the judgment of Gehenna? ³⁴Therefore behold, I send you prophets and wise men and scribes. Some of them you will kill and crucify, and some of them you will flog in your synagogues and pursue from city to city, ³⁵so that upon you may come all the righteous blood poured out upon the earth—from the blood of Abel the just to the blood of Zechariah, the son of Barachiah, whom you murdered between the temple and the altar. ³⁶Amen, I say to you, all these things shall come upon this generation.

Jesus Laments Over Jerusalem

³⁷"O Jerusalem, Jerusalem, who kills the prophets and stones those who are sent to her! How often I would have gathered your children like a hen gathers her young beneath her wings, but you would not. ³⁸Behold, your house is left to you, desolate. ³⁹For I

say to you, you will not see me again until you say, 'Blessed is he who comes in the name of the Lord!'"

The Destruction of the Temple

24 [1]And Jesus left the temple and was going away, when his disciples came to point out to him the buildings of the temple. [2]But he answered and said to them, "Do you not see all these things? Amen, I say to you, there will not be left here one stone upon another that will not be thrown down." [3]And as he sat on the Mount of Olives, the disciples came to him privately, saying, "Tell us, when will these things take place? And what will be the sign of your coming and of the end of the age?"

The Beginning of the Birth Pangs

[4]And Jesus answered and said to them, "See that no one deceives you, [5]for many will come in my name, saying, 'I am the Christ,' and they will deceive many. [6]You will hear of wars and rumors of wars; see that you are not alarmed. For all this must take place, but the end is not yet. [7]For nation will rise against nation, and kingdom against kingdom, and there will be famines and earthquakes in various places. [8]All these things are the beginning of the birth pangs. [9]Then they will hand you over to tribulation and kill you, and you will be hated by all nations because of my name. [10]Then many will fall away, and they will betray one another and hate one another. [11]Many false prophets will arise and deceive many. [12]And because lawlessness will increase, the love of many will grow cold. [13]But the one who endures to the end shall be saved. [14]And this gospel of the kingdom will be preached in the whole world, as a witness to all the Gentiles, and then the end will come.

The Great Tribulation

[15]"Therefore, when you see the abomination of desolation spoken of through Daniel the prophet standing in the holy place, let the reader understand. [16]Then let those who are in Judea flee to the mountains. [17]Let the one who is on his housetop not go down to take what is in his house, [18]and let the one who is in his field not turn back to take his cloak. [19]Woe to those who are pregnant and nursing in those days! [20]"But pray that your flight may not take place in winter or on a Sabbath. [21]For then there will be great tribulation such as has not taken place from the beginning of the world until now, nor ever will take place again. [22]And if those days had not been shortened, no one would be saved. But for the sake of the elect, those days will be shortened. [23]Then if anyone says to you, 'Look, here is the Christ!' or 'There he is!' do not believe it. [24]For false christs and false prophets will arise, and they will perform great signs and wonders in order to deceive, if possible, even the elect. [25]Behold, I have foretold this to you. [26]Therefore, if they say to you, 'Look, he is in the desert!' do not go out. Or, 'Look, he is in the inner rooms!' do not believe it. [27]For as the lightning comes from the east and flashes as far as the west, so will be the coming of the Son of Man. [28]Wherever the corpse is, there the eagles will gather.

The Coming of the Son of Man

[29]"And immediately after the tribulation of those days, the sun will be darkened and the moon will not give her light, and the stars will fall from heaven and the powers of heaven will be shaken. [30]Then the sign of the Son of Man will appear in heaven, and all the tribes of the earth will mourn, and they will see the Son of Man coming upon the clouds of heaven with power and great glory. [31]And he will send forth his angels with the sound of a great trumpet, and they will gather his elect from the four winds, from one end of the heavens to the other.

[32]"From the fig tree learn the parable: when its branch becomes tender and puts forth leaves, you know that summer is near. [33]So likewise, when you see all these things, know that he is near, even at the gates. [34]Amen, I say to you, this generation shall not pass away until all these things take place. [35]Heaven and earth shall pass away, but my words shall never pass away. [36]But about that day and hour no one knows, neither the angels of heaven, nor the Son, but only the Father.

[37]"For just as it was in the days of Noah, so it will be at the coming of the Son of Man. [38]For as in those days before the flood, they were eating and drinking, marrying and giving in marriage, until the day that Noah entered the ark, [39]and they did not know until the flood came and swept them all away, so too will be the coming of the Son of Man. [40]Then two men will be in the field; one will be taken, and one will be left. [41]Two women will be grinding at the mill; one will be taken, and one will be left.

The Thief in the Night

[42]"Stay awake, therefore, for you do not know what day your Lord is coming. [43]But know this, that if the master of the house had known in what watch of the night the thief would come, he would have stayed awake and not have let his house be broken

into. ⁴⁴Therefore, you also must be ready, for the Son of Man is coming at an hour you do not expect.

The Faithful Servant

⁴⁵"Who then is the faithful and wise servant, whom his master has appointed over his household to give them food at the proper time? ⁴⁶Blessed is that servant whom his master will find so doing when he comes. ⁴⁷Amen, I say to you, he will appoint him over all his possessions. ⁴⁸But if that evil servant says in his heart, 'My master is delayed,' ⁴⁹and he begins to strike his fellow servants and to eat and drink with the drunken, ⁵⁰the master of that servant will come on a day when he does not expect and at an hour that he does not know, ⁵¹and he shall cut him in two and put him with the hypocrites, where there shall be weeping and gnashing of teeth.

The Ten Virgins

25 ¹"Then the kingdom of heaven will be compared to ten virgins who took their lamps and went out to meet the bridegroom. ²Five of them were foolish, and five were wise. ³For the foolish took their lamps but did not take oil with them, ⁴while the wise took flasks of oil with their lamps. ⁵While the bridegroom was delayed, they all became drowsy and slept. ⁶At midnight, there was a shout, 'Behold, the bridegroom! Go out to meet him.' ⁷Then all those virgins rose and lit their lamps. ⁸The foolish said to the wise, 'Give us some of your oil, since our lamps have gone out.' ⁹But the wise answered and said, 'No, for there will not be enough for us and for you. Rather, go to the merchants and buy some for yourselves.' ¹⁰And while they were going to buy some, the bridegroom came, and those who were ready went in with him to the wedding feast, and the door was locked. ¹¹Afterward the rest of the virgins also came, saying, 'Lord, Lord, open to us!' ¹²But he answered and said, 'Amen, I say to you, I do not know you.' ¹³Stay awake, therefore, for you do not know the day or the hour.

The Talents

¹⁴"For it is like a man going away on a journey, who called his servants and entrusted his possessions to them. ¹⁵To one he gave five talents, to another, two talents, and to another, one talent—to each according to his ability. Immediately he set out on his journey. ¹⁶The one who had received the five talents went and traded with them and made five more. ¹⁷Likewise, the one who had received the two talents made two more. ¹⁸But the one who had received the one talent went away, dug a hole in the ground, and hid his master's money. ¹⁹Now after a long time, the master of those servants came and settled accounts with them. ²⁰And the one who had received the five talents came and brought five more talents, saying, 'Master, you entrusted five talents to me. See, I have made five more talents.' ²¹His master said to him, 'Well done, good and faithful servant. You have been faithful with a few things; I will put you in charge of many. Enter into the joy of your master.' ²²The one who had received the two talents also came and said, 'Master, you entrusted two talents to me. See, I have made two more talents.' ²³His master said to him, 'Well done, good and faithful servant. You have been faithful with a few things; I will put you in charge of many. Enter into the joy of your master.' ²⁴Then the one who had received the one talent came and said, 'Master, I knew you were a hard man, reaping where you have not sown, and gathering where you have not scattered. ²⁵So I was afraid and went and hid your talent in the ground. Here, have what is yours.' ²⁶His master answered and said to him, 'You evil and lazy servant! You knew that I reap where I have not sown and gather where I have not scattered? ²⁷Then you should have given my money to the lenders, and at my coming I would have recovered what was mine with interest. ²⁸Therefore, take the talent away from him and give it to the one who has ten talents. ²⁹For to everyone who has, more will be given, and he will have in abundance. But from the one who does not have, even what he has will be taken away. ³⁰And cast the unprofitable servant into the outer darkness, where there shall be weeping and gnashing of teeth.'

The Sheep and the Goats

³¹"When the Son of Man comes in his glory and all the angels with him, then he will sit upon his throne of glory. ³²And all nations will be gathered before him, and he will separate them one from another, like a shepherd separates the sheep from the goats. ³³And he will place the sheep at his right hand and the goats at his left. ³⁴Then the King will say to those at his right hand, 'Come, you blessed of my Father, inherit the kingdom prepared for you from the foundation of the world. ³⁵For I was hungry and you gave me food, I was thirsty and you gave me drink, I was a stranger and you took me in, ³⁶I was naked and you clothed me, I was sick and you visited me, I was in prison and you came to me.' ³⁷Then the righteous will answer him, saying, 'Lord, when did we see you hungry and feed

you, or thirsty and give you drink? ³⁸When did we see you a stranger and take you in, or naked and clothe you? ³⁹And when did we see you sick or in prison and visit you?' ⁴⁰And the King will answer and say to them, 'Amen, I say to you, whatever you did to one of the least of these my brothers, you did it to me.' ⁴¹Then he will also say to those at his left hand, 'Depart from me, you accursed, into the eternal fire prepared for the devil and his angels. ⁴²For I was hungry and you gave me no food, I was thirsty and you gave me no drink, ⁴³I was a stranger and you did not take me in, I was naked and you did not clothe me, I was sick and in prison and you did not visit me.' ⁴⁴Then they will also answer him, saying, 'Lord, when did we see you hungry or thirsty or a stranger or naked or sick or in prison, and not minister to you?' ⁴⁵Then he will answer them, saying, 'Amen, I say to you, whatever you did not do to one of the least of these, you did not do to me.' ⁴⁶And these will go away to eternal punishment, but the righteous to eternal life."

The Passion of Jesus Christ

26 ¹Now when Jesus had finished all these words, he said to his disciples, ²"You know that after two days Passover is coming, and the Son of Man will be handed over to be crucified."

³Then the chief priests and the elders of the people gathered together in the courtyard of the high priest, who was called Caiaphas. ⁴And they took counsel that they might arrest Jesus by deceit and kill him. ⁵But they said, "Not at the feast, lest there be a riot among the people."

The Anointing at Bethany

⁶Now when Jesus was in Bethany in the house of Simon the leper, ⁷a woman came to him with an alabaster jar of very costly ointment. And she poured it on his head as he reclined at table. ⁸But when his disciples saw it, they were indignant, saying, "Why this waste? ⁹For this ointment could have been sold for a large sum and given to the poor." ¹⁰When Jesus perceived it, he said to them, "Why do you trouble the woman? She has done a good work for me. ¹¹For you always have the poor with you, but you will not always have me. ¹²When she poured this ointment on my body, she did it for my burial. ¹³Amen, I say to you, wherever this gospel is preached in the whole world, what she has done will be spoken of, in memory of her."

Judas and the Thirty Pieces of Silver

¹⁴Then one of the twelve, who was called Judas Iscariot, went to the chief priests ¹⁵and said, "What are you willing to give me if I hand him over to you?" And they agreed to give him thirty pieces of silver. ¹⁶And from that time, he sought an opportunity to betray him.

The Last Supper

¹⁷Now on the first day of Unleavened Bread, the disciples came to Jesus, saying, "Where do you want us to prepare for you to eat the Passover?" ¹⁸And he said, "Go into the city to a certain person and say to him, 'The Teacher says, My time is at hand. I will keep the Passover at your house with my disciples.'" ¹⁹And the disciples did as Jesus had directed them, and they prepared the Passover.

²⁰Now when it was evening, he reclined at table with the twelve. ²¹And while they were eating, he said, "Amen, I say to you, one of you will betray me." ²²And they were exceedingly sorrowful, and each one of them began to say to him, "Surely not I, Lord?" ²³And he answered and said, "The one who dips his hand in the dish with me will betray me. ²⁴The Son of Man goes as it is written of him, but woe to that man by whom the Son of Man is betrayed! It would have been better for that man if he had never been born." ²⁵Then Judas, his betrayer, answered and said, "Surely not I, Rabbi?" He said to him, "You have said it."

²⁶And as they were eating, Jesus took bread, said the blessing, broke it, and gave it to the disciples, and said, "Take, eat; this is my body." ²⁷And he took a cup, and giving thanks, he gave it to them, saying, "Drink from it, all of you. ²⁸For this is my blood of the covenant, which is poured out for many for the forgiveness of sins. ²⁹But I say to you, from now on, I will not drink of this fruit of the vine until that day when I drink it new with you in the kingdom of my Father."

Strike the Shepherd and the Sheep Will Be Scattered

³⁰And after singing a hymn, they went out to the Mount of Olives. ³¹Then Jesus said to them, "This very night you will all fall away because of me. For it is written, 'I will strike the shepherd, and the sheep of the flock will be scattered.' ³²But after I am raised up, I will go before you into Galilee." ³³But Peter answered and said to him, "If all fall away because of you, I will never fall away." ³⁴Jesus said to him, "Amen, I say to you, on this very night, before the cock crows, you will deny me three times." ³⁵Peter said to him, "Even

if I must die with you, I will never deny you." And all the disciples said likewise.

The Agony in Gethsemane

³⁶Then Jesus came with them to a place called Gethsemane and said to the disciples, "Sit here, while I go over there and pray." ³⁷And he took Peter and the two sons of Zebedee with him, and he began to be sorrowful and distressed. ³⁸Then he said to them, "My soul is very sorrowful, even unto death. Remain here, and keep watch with me." ³⁹And going a short distance away, he fell on his face and prayed, saying, "My Father, if it is possible, let this cup pass from me; yet, not as I will, but as you will." ⁴⁰And he came to the disciples and found them sleeping, and he said to Peter, "So you could not keep watch with me one hour? ⁴¹Watch and pray that you may not enter into temptation. The spirit is willing, but the flesh is weak." ⁴²He went away again a second time and prayed, saying, "My Father, if it is not possible for this cup to pass from me unless I drink it, your will be done." ⁴³And he came and found them sleeping again, for their eyelids were heavy. ⁴⁴And he left them and went away once more and prayed a third time, saying the same words. ⁴⁵Then he came to the disciples and said to them, "Are you still sleeping and taking your rest? Behold, the hour has come, and the Son of Man is betrayed into the hands of sinners. ⁴⁶Rise, let us be going. See, my betrayer is at hand."

Jesus Is Arrested

⁴⁷While he was still speaking, behold, Judas, one of the twelve, came with a great crowd with swords and clubs, from the chief priests and elders of the people. ⁴⁸Now his betrayer gave them a sign, saying, "Whoever I kiss is the one; arrest him." ⁴⁹And immediately he came to Jesus, and said, "Hail, Rabbi!" And he kissed him. ⁵⁰And Jesus said to him, "Friend, why are you here?" Then they came and laid hands on Jesus and arrested him. ⁵¹And behold, one of those with Jesus stretched out his hand, drew his sword, struck the servant of the high priest, and cut off his ear.

⁵²Then Jesus said to him, "Put your sword back in its place! For all who take up the sword will perish by the sword. ⁵³Do you think I am not able to call upon my Father, and he will at once send me more than twelve legions of angels? ⁵⁴But how would the scriptures be fulfilled, which say that it must happen this way?" ⁵⁵In that hour Jesus said to the crowds, "Have you come out with swords and clubs to seize me, as though I were a robber? Day after day I sat teaching in the temple, and you did not arrest me. ⁵⁶But all this has taken place so that the writings of the prophets might be fulfilled." Then all the disciples deserted him and fled.

Jesus Before the Sanhedrin

⁵⁷Then those who arrested Jesus led him away to Caiaphas the high priest, where the scribes and the elders were gathered. ⁵⁸But Peter followed him from a distance as far as the courtyard of the high priest, and he went inside and sat with the servants, to see the end.

⁵⁹Now the chief priests and the whole Sanhedrin were seeking false testimony against Jesus in order to put him to death, ⁶⁰but they found none, though many false witnesses came forward. Finally, two came forward ⁶¹and said, "This man said, 'I am able to destroy the temple of God and to build it in three days.'" ⁶²And the high priest rose up and said to him, "Have you no answer to what these men testify against you?" ⁶³But Jesus was silent. And the high priest said to him, "I adjure you by the living God, tell us if you are the Christ, the Son of God." ⁶⁴Jesus said to him, "You have said it. But I say to you,

> From now on, you will see the Son of Man
> seated at the right hand of Power
> and coming on the clouds of heaven."

⁶⁵Then the high priest tore his garments, saying, "He has blasphemed! Why do we still need witnesses? See now, you have heard his blasphemy. ⁶⁶What is your verdict?" They answered and said, "He deserves death." ⁶⁷Then they spat in his face, and beat him, and struck him, ⁶⁸saying, "Prophesy to us, you Christ! Who is it that struck you?"

Peter Denies Jesus Three Times

⁶⁹Now Peter was sitting outside in the courtyard. And a servant girl came to him, saying, "You also were with Jesus the Galilean." ⁷⁰But he denied it before them all, saying, "I do not know what you are talking about." ⁷¹And when he went out to the gateway, another servant girl saw him and said to those who were there, "This man was with Jesus the Nazarene." ⁷²And again he denied it with an oath, "I do not know the man!" ⁷³After a little while, those who were standing by came and said to Peter, "Truly you also are one of them, for your accent gives you away!" ⁷⁴Then he began to curse and to swear, "I do not know the man!" And immediately the cock crowed. ⁷⁵Then Peter remembered the word Jesus had spoken, "Before the cock crows, you will deny me three times." And he went out and wept bitterly.

The Sanhedrin Meets Again

27 ¹When it was morning, all the chief priests and elders of the people took counsel against Jesus to put him to death. ²And when they had bound him, they led him away and handed him over to Pilate the governor.

The Death of Judas

³When Judas, his betrayer, saw that he was condemned, he regretted what he had done and returned the thirty pieces of silver to the chief priests and elders, ⁴saying, "I have sinned by betraying innocent blood." And they said, "What is that to us? See to it yourself!" ⁵And he threw down the pieces of silver in the temple and departed, and he went away and hanged himself. ⁶And the chief priests took the silver pieces and said, "It is not lawful to put this in the temple treasury, since it is blood money." ⁷So they took counsel and used them to buy the Potter's field as a burial place for strangers. ⁸Therefore that field has been called the Field of Blood to this day. ⁹Then was fulfilled what was spoken through Jeremiah the prophet, "And they took the thirty pieces of silver, the price of him on whom a price had been placed by some of the sons of Israel. ¹⁰And they gave them for the Potter's field, just as the Lord ordered me."

Pilate Questions Jesus

¹¹Now Jesus stood before the governor, and the governor asked him, saying, "Are you indeed the King of the Jews?" And Jesus said to him, "You say so." ¹²And when he was accused by the chief priests and elders, he gave no answer. ¹³Then Pilate said to him, "Do you not hear how many things they testify against you?" ¹⁴But he gave no answer to him, not even to one word, so that the governor marveled greatly.

Barabbas and Jesus

¹⁵Now at the feast the governor was accustomed to release one prisoner for the crowd, whomever they wanted. ¹⁶And they had at that time a notorious prisoner called Barabbas. ¹⁷So when they were gathered together, Pilate said to them, "Whom do you want me to release for you? Barabbas? Or Jesus, who is called Christ?" ¹⁸For he knew they had handed him over because of envy.

¹⁹While he was sitting on the judgment seat, his wife sent word to him, saying, "Have nothing to do with that righteous man, for I have suffered many things today in a dream because of him." ²⁰But the chief priests and elders persuaded the crowds to ask for Barabbas and destroy Jesus. ²¹The governor answered and said to them, "Which of the two do you want me to release for you?" They said, "Barabbas!" ²²Pilate said to them, "What then shall I do with Jesus who is called Christ?" They all said, "Let him be crucified!" ²³But the governor said, "Why, what evil has he done?" But they shouted all the louder, saying, "Let him be crucified!"

²⁴When Pilate saw that he was accomplishing nothing, but rather that a riot was breaking out, he took water and washed his hands in front of the crowd, saying, "I am innocent of this man's blood. See to it yourselves!" ²⁵Then all the people answered and said, "His blood be upon us and upon our children." ²⁶Then he released Barabbas to them. And after he had Jesus scourged, he handed him over to be crucified.

The Crowning with Thorns

²⁷Then the soldiers of the governor took Jesus into the praetorium and gathered the whole cohort to him. ²⁸They stripped him and put a scarlet robe around him. ²⁹And weaving a crown of thorns, they placed it on his head and put a reed in his right hand. And they knelt before him and mocked him, saying, "Hail, King of the Jews!" ³⁰And they spit on him and took the reed and struck him on the head. ³¹And after they had mocked him, they stripped him of the robe, put his own garments on him, and led him away to crucify him.

The Crucifixion

³²As they came out, they found a man of Cyrene named Simon. This man they forced to carry his cross. ³³And when they came to a place called Golgotha, which means "the Place of the Skull," ³⁴they gave him wine mixed with gall to drink. But when he tasted it, he would not drink it. ³⁵And when they had crucified him, they divided his garments by casting lots. ³⁶And they sat down and kept watch over him there. ³⁷And they placed over his head the charge against him, which read, "This is Jesus, the King of the Jews."

³⁸Then two robbers were crucified with him, one on his right hand and one on his left. ³⁹And those who passed by blasphemed him, wagging their heads ⁴⁰and saying, "You who would destroy the temple and build it in three days, save yourself! If you are the Son of God, then come down from the cross!" ⁴¹In the same way, the chief priests also mocked him along with the scribes and elders, saying, ⁴²"He saved others; he cannot save himself! If he is the King of Israel, let him come down from the cross now, and we will

believe in him. ⁴³He trusted in God; let him deliver him now, if he wants him! For he said, 'I am the Son of God.'" ⁴⁴The robbers who were crucified with him also reviled him in the same way.

The Death of Jesus

⁴⁵Now from the sixth hour, there was darkness over all the earth until the ninth hour. ⁴⁶And about the ninth hour, Jesus cried out with a loud voice, saying, *"Eli, Eli, lema sabachthani?"* that is, "My God, my God, why have you forsaken me?" ⁴⁷When some of those standing there heard it, they said, "This man is calling for Elijah." ⁴⁸And immediately one of them ran and took a sponge, filled it with sour wine, put it on a reed, and gave it to him to drink. ⁴⁹But the rest said, "Wait! Let us see if Elijah will come to save him." ⁵⁰And when Jesus had cried out again with a loud voice, he gave up his spirit.

⁵¹And behold, the veil of the temple was torn in two from top to bottom. The earth shook, and the rocks were split. ⁵²The tombs were also opened, and many bodies of the saints who had fallen asleep were raised. ⁵³And after his resurrection, they came out of the tombs and went into the holy city and appeared to many. ⁵⁴Now when the centurion and those with him, who were keeping watch over Jesus, saw the earthquake and what took place, they were terrified and said, "Truly this was the Son of God!"

⁵⁵And many women who had followed Jesus from Galilee and ministered to him were there, looking on from a distance. ⁵⁶Among them were Mary Magdalene, Mary the mother of James and Joseph, and the mother of the sons of Zebedee.

The Burial of Jesus

⁵⁷When it was evening, there came a rich man of Arimathea named Joseph, who was himself a disciple of Jesus. ⁵⁸This man went to Pilate and asked him for the body of Jesus. Then Pilate commanded it to be given. ⁵⁹And taking the body, Joseph wrapped it in a clean linen shroud ⁶⁰and placed it in his own new tomb, which he had cut in the rock. And he rolled a great stone to the door of the tomb and departed. ⁶¹And Mary Magdalene was there, and the other Mary, sitting opposite the tomb.

The Sealing of the Tomb

⁶²On the next day, after the day of Preparation, the chief priests and the Pharisees gathered before Pilate, ⁶³saying, "We remember, lord, how that deceiver said while he was still living, 'After three days I will rise.' ⁶⁴Therefore command that the grave be made secure until the third day, lest his disciples come and steal the body and say to the people, 'He is risen from the dead.' Then the last deception will be worse than the first." ⁶⁵Pilate said to them, "You have a guard of soldiers. Go, and make it as secure as you can." ⁶⁶So they went with the guard and secured the tomb, putting a seal on the stone.

The Resurrection of Jesus

28 ¹Now after the Sabbath, at dawn on the first day of the week, Mary Magdalene and the other Mary came to see the tomb. ²And behold, there was a great earthquake; for an angel of the Lord, descending from heaven, came and rolled away the stone and sat on it. ³His appearance was like lightning, and his clothing was white as snow. ⁴For fear of him, the guards were shaken and became like dead men. ⁵But the angel said to the women, 'Do not fear, for I know that you seek Jesus who was crucified. ⁶He is not here; for he is risen, just as he said. Come, see the place where he lay. ⁷Then go quickly and tell his disciples, 'He is risen from the dead. And behold, he is going before you into Galilee. There you will see him.' Behold, I have told you." ⁸And they departed quickly from the tomb with fear and great joy, and they ran to tell his disciples. ⁹And behold, Jesus met them, saying, "Greetings!" And they came and embraced his feet and worshiped him. ¹⁰Then Jesus said to them, "Do not fear. Go, tell my brothers to go to Galilee. There they will see me."

The Story Told by the Soldiers

¹¹Now as they were going, behold, some of the guard went into the city and told the chief priests everything that had taken place. ¹²And when they gathered with the elders and had taken counsel, they gave a large sum of money to the soldiers ¹³and said, "Say this, 'His disciples came by night and stole the body while we were sleeping.' ¹⁴And if the governor hears of this, we will satisfy him and keep you free from worry." ¹⁵So they took the silver and did as they were instructed. And this story has been spread among Jews to this day.

The Great Commission

¹⁶Then the eleven disciples went into Galilee to the mountain to which Jesus had directed them. ¹⁷And when they saw him, they worshiped him, but some doubted. ¹⁸And Jesus came and spoke to them, saying, "All authority in heaven and on earth has been given to me. ¹⁹Go therefore and make disciples of

all nations, baptizing them in the name of the Father, and of the Son, and of the Holy Spirit, [20]and teaching them to observe everything I have commanded you. And behold, I am with you always, even until the end of the age."

Unit 1

The Good News

Who is Jesus? The Gospel of Matthew answers this crucial question. The opening chapters of Matthew tell of Jesus' origins and reveal Jesus to be the Divine Son of God, who came as the Messiah (the Christ) of God's people. Matthew's account of Jesus' public ministry focuses on his teachings and many deeds of power. The climax of Matthew's Gospel is the Paschal Mystery—Jesus' Passion, Death, Resurrection, and Ascension. Through the Paschal Mystery, Jesus saved us from the powers of sin and death.

God is the Author of all Scripture, but he speaks to us through human authors who were inspired by the Holy Spirit. In his providence, God guided not only the people and events of salvation history but also the inspired accounts of salvation history recorded in the Bible. Through the inspired books of both the Old Testament and New Testament, God reveals that he is a Blessed Trinity of Persons and that we are called to share in his divine life.

The Old Testament Scriptures foreshadowed the saving work of Jesus Christ, who continues to give himself to us today through both Word and sacrament.

Chapters 1-5

Chapter 1: Jesus, Who Is Called the Christ
Chapter 2: The Gospel of the Kingdom
Chapter 3: The Crucified Lord of Glory
Chapter 4: Sacred Scripture, the Inspired Word
Chapter 5: Jesus Christ, the Incarnate Word

Grade 6 Road Map

Unit 1
The Good News
The Gospel of Matthew reveals who Jesus is through both his deeds and words. God speaks to us in Sacred Scripture through human authors inspired by the Holy Spirit.

Unit 2
In the Beginning
Genesis describes the beginning of the universe and humanity, the beginning of sin, and the beginning of God's plan to restore mankind's relationship with himself through the covenant with Abraham and his descendants. In Jesus, God's covenant with Abraham is fulfilled.

Unit 3
You Shall Be My People
Through Moses, God delivered his people from slavery in Egypt and made a covenant with them at Mount Sinai. Despite their unfaithfulness, God brought his people into the Promised Land after they wandered for forty years in the desert. Jesus is the New Moses, who gives the New Law.

Unit 4
The Kingdom of the Lord
The Lord made a covenant with King David and swore to give him an everlasting kingdom. The sins of God's people led to the division and downfall of the kingdom, eventually leading to the destruction of the Temple and the Babylonian exile. In Jesus, God's covenant with David is fulfilled.

Unit 5
The Coming of the Anointed One
God brought his people back from exile to the Promised Land, where they rebuilt the Temple in Jerusalem. The prophets foretold of the coming of the Messiah, who would rebuild the kingdom of David. Jesus, the Son of Man, brings the kingdom through his suffering and Death.

Unit 6
God with Us
The Gospel of Matthew provides reliable testimony that Jesus is the Divine Son of God made man, who delivered us from sin through his Paschal Mystery. Jesus continues to be present to his Church through Word and sacrament—above all, the Holy Eucharist.

Saint Jerome

Mt 6:19-21

6 ¹⁹Do not store up for yourselves treasures on earth, where moth and rust consume, and where thieves break in and steal. ²⁰But store up for yourselves treasures in heaven, where moth and rust do not consume, and where thieves do not break in and steal. ²¹For where your treasure is, there will your heart be also.

Jerome's Dream

What is your greatest treasure? What do you value more than anything else?

If somebody asked you these questions, what would you say? As Christians, we might answer: "God, of course." But are we telling the truth? Is God *really* what we treasure most? We might *think* God is number one in our lives, but what if our hearts are secretly somewhere else? Saint Jerome made an uncomfortable discovery in his late twenties. He realized he was not the holy Christian he thought he was. He treasured something more than Christ.

Jerome was born in an area of the Roman Empire called Dalmatia around A.D. 345. He was raised by Catholic parents. Jerome was very smart and an excellent student. He did so well that his father sent him to one of the best schools in Rome. Jerome loved school, and he especially loved to read. In Jerome's day, if you wanted to own your own books, they needed to be copied out by hand. This was very difficult and expensive, but Jerome enjoyed learning so much that he soon had his own small library. Jerome loved to study the ancient Roman poets and philosophers. One of his favorites was a pagan philosopher named Cicero.

As a young man in Rome, Jerome found himself living a sinful life. Yet inside he knew he needed to change. He wanted to live an authentic Christian life. So, he chose to leave Rome, leaving behind his comfortable life, his teachers, and his friends. He knew his sinful habits would be hard to break.

Therefore, he decided to take radical action: he went out into the desert. There he spent many days fasting and in prayer, drawing closer to Christ and growing in self-discipline.

Some might find Jerome's decision strange or extreme. Yet Jerome's choice was not all that different from that of a great athlete. Excellence in sports requires bodily discipline through intense workouts, strength training, and a special diet. The freedom to excel requires many restrictions. This is also true of the spiritual life. If we do not discipline our bodies and minds, we will not excel in the fight against sin and temptation.

Jerome was making progress rapidly. But he still struggled. As a lover of learning, Jerome could not help but drag his library of books with him into the desert. While up late at night praying or fasting, he would enjoy reading Cicero and other pagan thinkers. But when he tried to read the Bible, he found it boring and unsophisticated. He continued to put off reading Scripture, preferring to read Cicero instead. Then one day Jerome became very sick. He was so sick that some of his Christian friends thought he was going to die. At this moment, Jerome experienced a dream that would change his life.

In his dream, he felt himself rise to Heaven, where he stood before the throne of Christ to be judged for his life on earth. The light from the throne was so bright that Jerome fell to the ground and hid his face. Surrounding the throne, saints and angels stood watching him, waiting to see how Jesus would judge him. Jesus asked Jerome about himself, and Jerome responded, *"I am a Christian." "You lie,"* Jesus said sternly. *"You are a follower of Cicero and not of Christ. For 'where your treasure is, there will your heart be also.'"* (Matthew 6:21).[1]

Immediately, Jerome realized Jesus was speaking the truth. He loved Christ. But he loved Cicero more. His heart and treasure were with pagan wisdom, not God. At this point, it would have been easy for Jerome to get defensive. He could have said to Jesus: "What about all my fasts? My long nights of prayer in the desert? Aren't I holy enough?" But Jerome didn't do that. Instead, he said: "Have mercy on me, Lord, have mercy upon me!" As soon as he humbly asked for forgiveness, the saints and angels also fell on their knees before the throne, begging Jesus to have mercy on Jerome. Jerome swore an oath to God saying that he would, from that moment on, make Jesus the center of his life and study. He would dedicate his life to studying Scripture.

Jerome Wakes Up

Jerome put down Cicero and picked up Scripture. As Jerome dedicated himself to reading the Scriptures, he made a discovery. In the words of an earlier Christian thinker, Jerome realized that the "treasure of divine wisdom" is hidden in "poor and humble words."[2] Scripture seems boring only on the outside. Inside is wisdom greater than anything found in the world. Why didn't Jerome realize this before? He soon learned the answer: his own pride. He needed to become humble—just like the words of Scripture—to become wise in the spiritual life. His pride in his own intelligence blocked out divine wisdom. Jerome also realized he needed the help of the Holy Spirit. All Scripture is inspired by God. To unlock its meaning, we need to pray with humility for the Holy Spirit to guide us.

With the help of the Holy Spirit, Jerome focused his intellectual gifts on the study of Scripture. He spent years learning the original languages of the Bible: Hebrew and Greek. The more he studied, the more he loved Scripture. But Jerome was not just loving a text. He was loving a Person: Christ. Jerome realized that Christ is the true treasure hidden within the humble words of Scripture. As Jerome said in one of his letters, when you read Scripture, "it is [Christ] who speaks to you."[3] Similarly, Jerome famously wrote, "Ignorance of the Scriptures is ignorance of Christ."[4] If we want to be Christians, we must grow to love Scripture.

When a person sees a beautiful sunset, what does she often do? Take a picture of it. Why? When we experience something true and beautiful, we do not want it to fade away. We want to "capture it" and have it forever. So, we take pictures. After a person takes a picture, what does he often do next? He shares the picture with his friends. When we experience something beautiful and true, we want to share it with others.

Jerome experienced this with Scripture: the more he studied, the more he wanted to capture and share its beauty and truth with others. Yet there was a big problem. At that time, the common person in the Roman Empire spoke Latin. But a reliable Latin translation of the entire Bible did not exist. With support from the pope, Jerome decided to fix this problem. He translated the entire Bible into Latin from the original languages. This took him nearly twenty-three years! Eventually, his translation became known as the Vulgate (from the Latin word *vulgatus*, meaning "common" or "commonly known"). Now everyone could encounter Christ through reading Scripture.

Jerome also shared his love of Scripture with people he met. While living in Rome, Jerome met a wealthy widow named Paula and her daughter Eustochium. Both women wanted to dedicate their lives to Jesus and asked Jerome to teach them about Scripture. Jerome not only taught them how to read the Word

of God, but he also helped them learn Greek and Hebrew so they could read the Bible in its original languages. Paula eventually became better at Hebrew than Jerome! With the financial support of Paula and others, he formed a community of people to study Scripture and grow in their spiritual lives. Later, Jerome founded two monasteries in the Holy Land. In these monasteries, men and women could grow in their spiritual lives in a supportive community. These monasteries also served as places where pilgrims could stay as they visited the Holy Land and encountered the actual places where Jesus lived and taught. Amid all this work, Jerome constantly wrote letters to people, giving them spiritual advice and teaching them about Scripture.

At the end of his life, there was no more confusion: Jerome was a Christian, not a Ciceronian. His heart was with Christ. His treasure was the humble words of Scripture, not the lofty words of pagan wisdom. He could now truthfully echo the words of Saint Paul: "When I came to you, brethren, I did not come proclaiming to you the testimony of God in lofty words or wisdom. For I decided to know nothing among you except Jesus Christ and him crucified" (1 Cor 2:1–2).

Journal Reflection

1. Early in his life, Saint Jerome found Scripture to be boring and unsophisticated. **What about Scripture do you think led him to see it this way?**
2. Suppose someone followed you around for a week and kept track of how you spent your free time. **Based on this information, what might he think is your most important treasure?**
3. **Once Jerome came to love Sacred Scripture, how did he share that love with others?**
4. **What's your current relationship with Scripture? What's the biggest obstacle that prevents you from reading Scripture more?**

CHAPTER 1

Jesus, Who Is Called the Christ

> **Words to Know**
>
> > *Christ*
>
> > *evangelist*
>
> > *Jesus*

Proclaiming the Good News

"Be not afraid; for behold, I bring you good news of a great joy which will come to all the people; for to you is born this day in the city of David a Savior, who is Christ the Lord." —Luke 2:10–11

 ## Jesus Who?

Imagine that new neighbors moved in just before the start of school this year. They stop by to introduce themselves to your family and you realize that they have a daughter about your age. She casts her eyes around from your family's front door and notices a crucifix hanging on the wall in your home. Turning to you with a puzzled expression on her face, she gestures at the crucifix and asks you, "Who's that?"

This question catches you off guard. After your initial surprise, you respond somewhat cautiously, "That's Jesus, of course." This reply leaves her looking even more confused. Not unkindly, but with a real curiosity to know more, she asks another question: "Jesus? Jesus *who*?"

If this happened to you today, how would you answer her question? Who is Jesus?

_____

_____

_____

The Good News

"Who Do You Say That I Am?"

In the Bible, we read about Jesus asking his disciples the very same question:

Mt 16:13-16

16 ¹³[Jesus] asked his disciples, "Who do people say that the Son of Man is?" ¹⁴And they said, "Some say John the Baptist, others Elijah, still others say Jeremiah or one of the prophets." ¹⁵He said to them, "But you, who do you say that I am?" ¹⁶Simon Peter answered and said, "You are the Christ, the Son of the living God."

In this passage, many people were confused about Jesus' identity. But Peter knew who Jesus really is and identified Jesus by two important titles, **"the Christ"** and **"the Son of the living God."** What do these titles tell us about Jesus?

The word "*Christ*" means "anointed one." In the Bible, anointing with oil symbolizes the Holy Spirit. Jesus is filled with the power of the Holy Spirit.

The royal line of Israel's kings began with the great king David. God promised that one day he would raise up one of David's descendants to be the greatest of all kings. This king would also be a savior and bring salvation to the world. This long-expected savior was known as the "anointed one," as the *Messiah* in Hebrew or as the *Christ* in Greek. By calling Jesus "the Christ," Peter was saying that Jesus is the long-awaited heir of David, the king and savior.

Peter went on to say that Jesus is the "Son of the living God." Jesus is not just a human king of the line of David; Jesus is God's own eternal Son! Jesus is God. Peter's confession captured the two amazing elements of Jesus' identity: he is human (of the line of David), and he is divine (God's own Son).

Even Jesus' name reveals to us who Jesus is. The name *Jesus* means "God saves." Jesus is God himself, who saves us from the powers of sin and death. Saint Matthew began the story of Jesus with a list of his ancestors that includes the great king David, confirming Peter's claim that Jesus is the long-expected anointed king. Saint Matthew also recounted that Jesus was conceived of the Holy Spirit in Mary's womb, showing that Jesus is not only human (born from Mary) but also divine (the eternal Son of God the Father).

Isaiah with Saint Matthew on His Shoulders. French School, 13th century

The Good News of Jesus Christ

The Bible tells us the Good News of Jesus Christ. The Good News is that Jesus, who is God, came as our Savior so that we might share in God's own eternal life. Jesus wants each of us to experience personally the happiness of God's friendship forever.

The Greek word for "good news" or "gospel" is *euangelion* (you-an-GELL-ee-on). From this word we get the English word "evangelist." An evangelist is someone who proclaims the Good News of Jesus Christ. The four Gospels in the New Testament—Matthew, Mark, Luke, and John—are written by evangelists. The Gospels give an account of the words and deeds of Jesus the Christ. The Gospels are the heart of the Bible because Jesus is at the center of the Gospels.

To begin our study of Sacred Scripture, we will turn first to the Good News itself, the Gospel of Jesus Christ. We will explore how the evangelist Saint Matthew answers the question, Who is Jesus? Our goal is not just to learn *about* Jesus but to deepen our personal relationship *with* Jesus. We will begin by exploring Matthew's account of Jesus' infancy and the start of his public ministry in Matthew 1–4.

Chapter 1 Summary

1. We come to know Jesus in the Bible, particularly in the Gospels written by the four Evangelists: Matthew, Mark, Luke, and John.

2. Jesus is the Beloved Son of God the Father. He was conceived by the Holy Spirit in the womb of the Blessed Virgin Mary. Jesus is fully divine and fully human.

3. Jesus is the Christ (the Anointed One, the Messiah), who came to save us from sin.

Knowing Christ Jesus

 Look back over the passages in Matthew 1-4 that you've read.

Passages	Optional Passages
The Birth of Jesus Christ *(Mt 1:18–25)*	The Genealogy of Jesus Christ *(Mt 1:1–17)*
The Preaching of John the Baptist *(Mt 3:1–6)*	The Magi from the East *(Mt 2:1–12)*
The Baptism of Jesus *(Mt 3:13–17)*	The Flight to Egypt *(Mt 2:13–15)*
Jesus Begins to Preach in Galilee *(Mt 4:17–25)*	The Return from Egypt *(Mt 2:19–23)*
	The Temptations of Jesus *(Mt 4:1–11)*

If you could pick *one verse* out of all of these to help your neighbor know better who Jesus is, which verse would you choose? Copy the verse and its reference below:

Mt ___1___ : ___21___
    (Chapter)   *(Verse)*

_____
_____
_____

What does this verse reveal about Jesus? How would you use this verse in telling others about Jesus?

_____
_____
_____
_____
_____

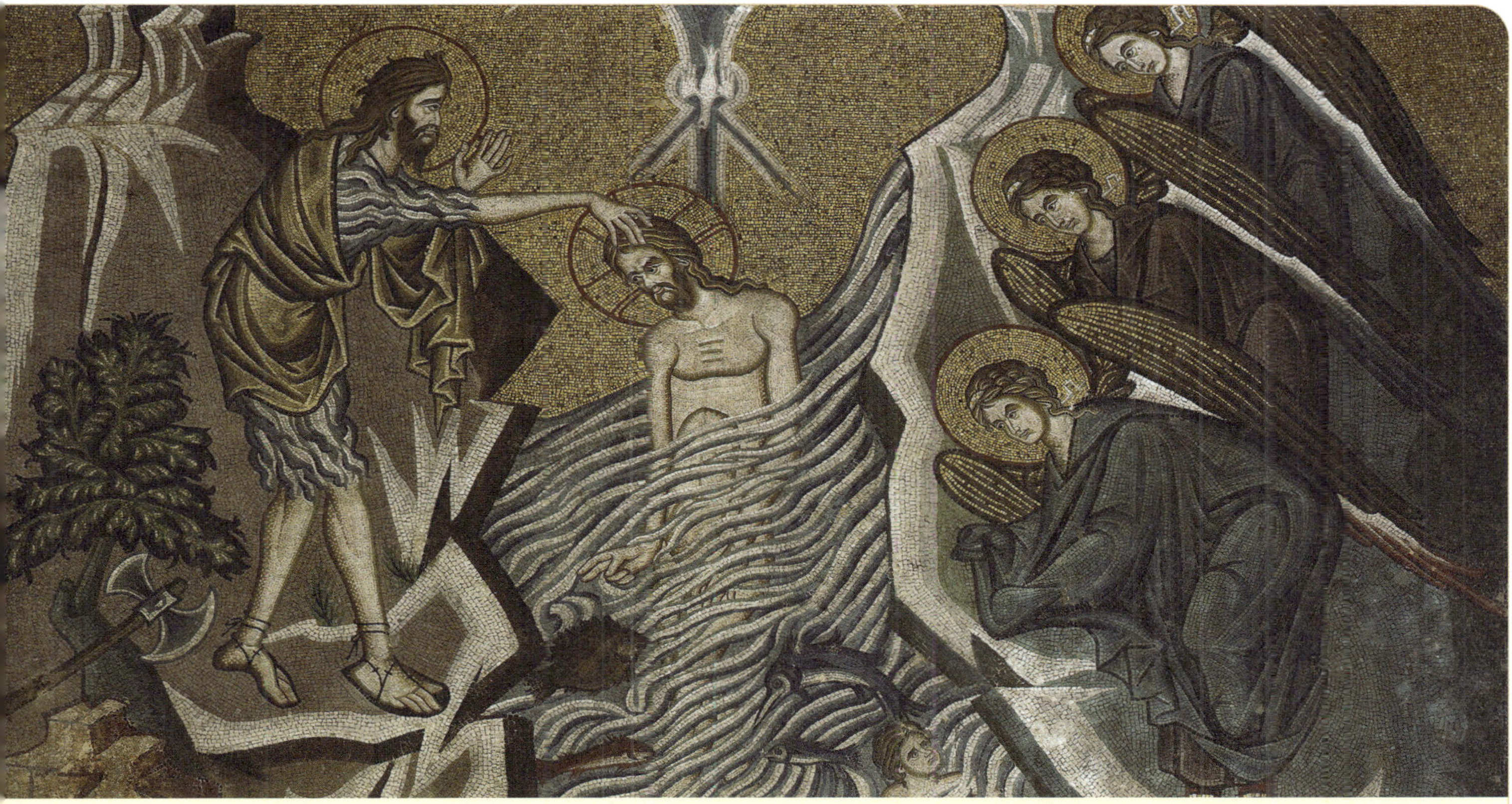

The Baptism of Christ, Byzantine School, 13th century

Let Us Pray—Psalm 1

The Church understands the Book of Psalms as the "masterwork of prayer in the Old Testament" (*CCC* 2585). In the Psalms, "the Word of God becomes man's prayer" (*CCC* 2587). God's words truly become our own when we pray the Psalms, as we do at every Mass. As we begin to study Sacred Scripture, let us reflect on the first psalm, which describes the happiness of those who study God's Word.

Ps 1:1-6

1 ¹Blessed is the man
    who walks not in the counsel of the wicked,
  nor stands in the way of sinners,
    nor sits in the seat of scoffers;
²but his delight is in the law of the LORD,
    and on his law he meditates day and night.
³He is like a tree
    planted by streams of water,
  that yields its fruit in its season,
    and its leaf does not wither.
  In all that he does, he prospers.

⁴The wicked are not so,
    but are like chaff which the wind drives away.
⁵Therefore the wicked will not stand in the judgment,
    nor sinners in the congregation of the righteous;
⁶for the LORD knows the way of the righteous,
    but the way of the wicked will perish.

Chapter 1 Review:
Jesus, Who Is Called the Christ

Refer to the reading from this chapter and passages from Matthew 1–4 in the front of your book to answer the following questions.

1. What is the meaning of the name Jesus? _____

2. According to the angel, from what does Jesus save us? (See Mt 1:21.) _____

3. Jesus of Nazareth is called the "Christ." What does the title "Christ" (Messiah) mean?
   _____

4. Someone who proclaims the Gospel (the Good News) of Jesus Christ is known as an
   _____.

5. The very first verse of Matthew's Gospel identifies Jesus as the "son of David." This shows us that Jesus is _____.

6. Peter said that Jesus is the "Son of the living God." This shows us that Jesus is
   _____.

7. How does the voice of God the Father identify Jesus at his baptism? (See Mt 3:17.)
   _____

8. Who are the first four disciples that Jesus calls to follow him? (See Mt 4:18–22.)
   _____

9. How do the following verses from Matthew 1 reveal that Jesus' father is God the Father (and that Saint Joseph is his foster father): verses 16, 18, 20?
   _____
   _____
   _____

The Power of Jesus' Name

There are many names and titles we can use to address Jesus. These include Son of God, Lamb of God, King, Lord, Savior, Redeemer, and Good Shepherd. But there is one name that is privileged above all. It is the name the angel announced to Saint Joseph that he was to give to Mary's child: the name Jesus. Note the singular power of this name as described by the Church:

> But the one name that contains everything is the one that the Son of God received in his incarnation: JESUS. The divine name may not be spoken by human lips, but by assuming our humanity The Word of God hands it over to us and we can invoke it: "Jesus," "YHWH saves." . . . To pray "Jesus" is to invoke him and to call him within us. His name is the only one that contains the presence it signifies. Jesus is the Risen One, and whoever invokes the name of Jesus is welcoming the Son of God who loved him and who gave himself up for him. (*CCC* 2666)

Friar's Badge with the Nativity, José de Páez

There is amazing power in the name of Jesus. When you speak that name in faith, whether silently or out loud, you are calling upon God to be present with you. This is the only name that works in this way. I can say the name Joy, but it does not necessarily make me joyful, nor does it make my friend Joy appear. But Jesus comes to us every time we call his name in faith.

As we learned, the name Jesus means "God saves." When you call on Jesus' name in faith, you will discover his saving power. The simplest and yet most powerful way to pray, then, is to invoke the holy name of Jesus throughout the day and realize that God is present. When you do that, it will transform the way you pray and speak to God. Like a password entrusted to us to access a great treasure, the name of Jesus gives us access to God's presence and saving power.

Journal Reflection

Names often have meaning—for example, Hope or Joy, or even Peter (which means "rock") or Timothy (which means "one who honors God"). Reflect on the meaning of Jesus' name. **Knowing that to speak Jesus' name with faith makes him present, how does that change the way you think about Jesus' name and how you speak his name when you pray?**

Baptized into Christ

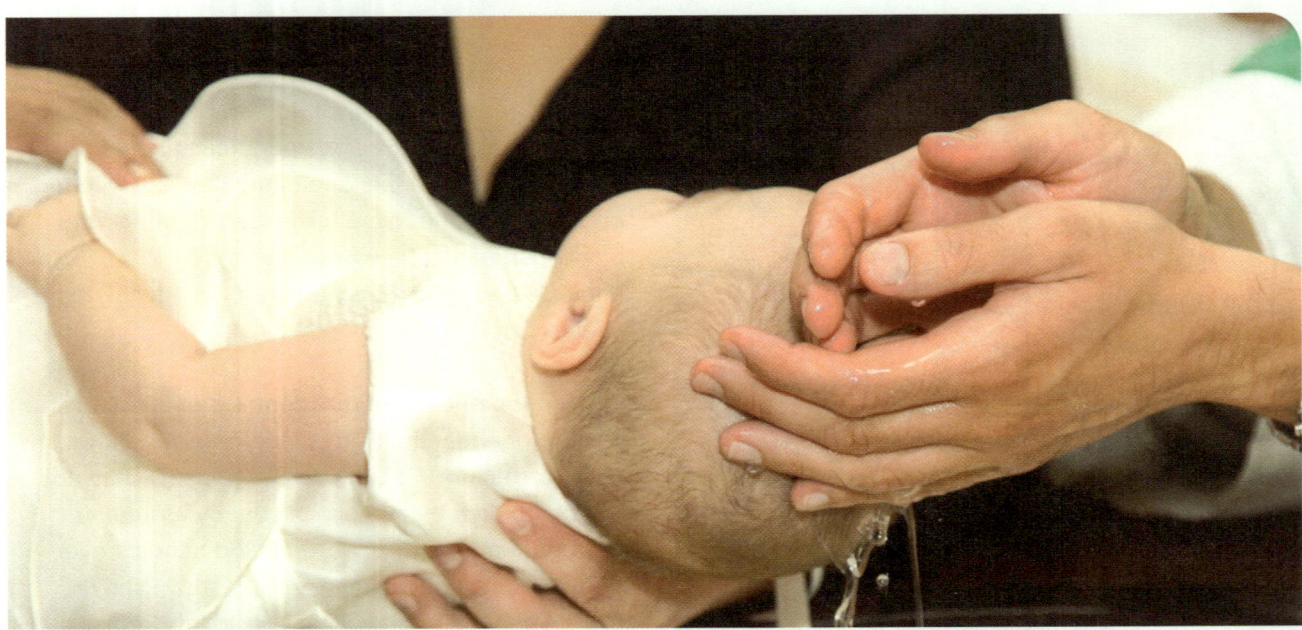

Read

Recall that the voice of the Father sounded forth at Jesus' baptism, saying, "This is my beloved Son" (Mt 3:17). In the passage to the right, Saint Paul reminds us that in our own Baptism we became sons and daughters of the Heavenly Father.

Reflect

Spend 5–10 minutes reflecting on the following:

- How do I relate to God?
- Do I act as if I am part of God's family, as if God is my loving Father and I am his beloved child?

Pray

In a spirit of humility and great trust, turn now to the Lord and pray the prayer of God's children, the Our Father, found on page 335.

Act

Pray the Our Father each night this week before you go to bed.

Gal 3:26-27; 4:4-7

3 [26] For in Christ Jesus you are all sons of God, through faith. [27] For as many of you as were baptized into Christ have put on Christ. . . .

4 [4] But when the time had fully come, God sent forth his Son, born of woman, born under the law, [5] to redeem those who were under the law, so that we might receive adoption as sons. [6] And because you are sons, God has sent the Spirit of his Son into our hearts, crying, "Abba! Father!" [7] So through God you are no longer a slave but a son, and if a son then an heir.

Catechism of the Catholic Church, 2774

"'The Lord's Prayer is truly the summary of the whole gospel,'[1] the 'most perfect of prayers.'[2] It is at the center of the Scriptures."

CHAPTER 2

The Gospel of the Kingdom

Words to Know

> repent

> Sermon on the Mount

Proclaiming the Good News

"He has delivered us from the dominion of darkness and transferred us to the kingdom of his beloved Son, in whom we have redemption, the forgiveness of sins."
—Colossians 1:13–14

"The Kingdom of Heaven Is at Hand"

Sermon on the Mount, Carl Bloch

Jesus began his public ministry with a call to repentance: "Repent, for the kingdom of heaven is at hand!" (Mt 4:17). To enter the kingdom, we must repent. The word "*repent*" means "a change of mind or heart." We repent by turning away from sin.

The Kingdom of Heaven, sometimes called the Kingdom of God, is something Jesus talked about often. Spreading the Kingdom of Heaven on earth was the focus of his mission. So, what is this kingdom? Where can we find it?

The first thing about the Kingdom of Heaven, or any kingdom, is the king who rules it. In Israel's history, the kings from the line of David ruled the Kingdom of Israel. Since those kings were anointed by God's prophets and enforced God's laws, Israel belonged to God. Thus, Israel was God's kingdom because it lived under God's covenant and law. The kings of Israel represented God and ruled on his behalf. Jesus, the Son of David, is King of the Kingdom of Heaven.

The Sower, James Tissot

Laws shape the way a kingdom or nation lives. After beginning his public ministry, Jesus went up a mountain and gave an extended teaching about how those who want to be part of his new kingdom should live. This teaching is known as the *Sermon on the Mount* and is found in chapters 5–7 of Matthew's Gospel. In this teaching, Jesus teaches us the New Law. This New Law of love is written on our hearts by God. Through grace, the Holy Spirit transforms us to love God and others. When we read about Jesus giving a New Law on a mountain, we are reminded of Moses, who received the Old Law, the Ten Commandments, on Mount Sinai. Jesus is a New Moses.

In Matthew's Gospel, Jesus teaches about the Kingdom of Heaven by using parables. Jesus uses images and events that we are familiar with to teach us truths about God and his kingdom. For example, many of Jesus' parables use images from farming or family life. Jesus uses these common life experiences to make the mysteries of God's kingdom easier for us to understand.

After his Sermon on the Mount, Jesus went out and performed ten deeds of power, or miracles, like healing a leper and curing the blind (Mt 8–9). Jesus brings a new authority as King, a power that comes from Heaven. Jesus' miracles reveal that he has the authority not only to give a New Law but also to heal and forgive sins. No king of David's line could perform miracles by his own power, which shows that Jesus is more than human; he is the "Son of the living God" (Mt 16:16)

Through his words and deeds, Jesus teaches that if we are to belong to the Kingdom of Heaven, we must turn from sin and obey God's will. Jesus models this perfect obedience to God the Father. Jesus tells us to pray for the strength to imitate his obedience. In his Sermon on the Mount, Jesus teaches us to pray the Our Father. In this prayer, we pray with Jesus' own words for God's will to be done in all things. If we do God's will and love as he loves, we will enjoy the rewards and blessings of God's kingdom forever.

Chapter 2 Summary

1. Jesus is the King of God's kingdom.

2. Jesus teaches the New Law, a law of love, in the Sermon on the Mount.

3. Jesus teaches that to enter the Kingdom of Heaven, we must repent from sin and do the will of God the Father in all things.

Knowing Christ Jesus

 In Chapter 1, you selected a single verse from Matthew 1-4 that you thought would best explain to your neighbor who Jesus is. Consider the passages you've read in Matthew 5-16 and the many ways they continue to fill out Matthew's portrait of Jesus.

Select *one verse* from the passages we read in Matthew 5-16 that reveals a *different* aspect of Jesus' identity from the verse you chose in the last chapter. Copy the verse below.

Mt _____ : _____
    (Chapter)   *(Verse)*

_____

_____

_____

Passages	Optional Passages
The Beatitudes *(Mt 5:1–12)*	The Wise Man and the Foolish Man *(Mt 7:24–29)*
Hatred and Love of Enemies *(Mt 5:43–48)*	The Faith of the Centurion *(Mt 8:5–13)*
Jesus Stills a Storm *(Mt 8:23–27)*	Jesus and John the Baptist *(Mt 11:1–6)*
Jesus Heals Two Demon-Possessed Men *(Mt 8:28–34)*	The Father and the Son *(Mt 11:25–30)*
Jesus Heals a Paralytic *(Mt 9:1–8)*	The Feeding of the Five Thousand *(Mt 14:13–21)*
Jesus, Peter, and the Keys of the Kingdom *(Mt 16:13–28)*	

The Handing Over of the Keys, Pietro Perugino

What does this verse reveal about Jesus? How would you use this verse in telling others about Jesus?

_____
_____
_____
_____
_____

Let Us Pray—Psalm 145

In Psalm 145, we give thanks to God for his kingdom and praise him for his words and deeds.

Ps 145:1-2, 8-13

145 ¹I will extol you, my God and King,
and bless your name for ever and ever.
²Every day I will bless you,
and praise your name for ever and ever. . . .
⁸The LORD is gracious and merciful,
slow to anger and abounding in mercy.
⁹The LORD is good to all,
and his compassion is over all that he has made.
¹⁰All your works shall give thanks to you, O LORD,
and all your saints shall bless you!

¹¹They shall speak of the glory of your kingdom,
and tell of your power,
¹²to make known to the sons of men your mighty deeds,
and the glorious splendor of your kingdom.
¹³Your kingdom is an everlasting kingdom,
and your dominion endures throughout all generations.
The LORD is faithful in all his words,
and gracious in all his deeds.

Chapter 2 Review:
The Gospel of the Kingdom

Refer to the reading from this chapter and passages from Matthew 5–16 in the front of your book to answer the following questions.

1. To __Repent__ is to turn away from sin.

2. What do we call Jesus' extended teaching in Matthew 5-7 in which he teaches the New Law?
   __Sermon on the mount__

3. Jesus calls us to __love__ our enemies and __Pray__ for our persecutors. (See Mt 5:44.)

4. Which prayer did Jesus teach his disciples to pray in the middle of the Sermon on the Mount? (See Mt 6:9-13.) __Our father__.

5. What words did Jesus first speak to the paralytic who was brought to him? (See Mt 9:2.)
   __"Your sins are forgiven"__

6. How did Peter identify Jesus when he asked his disciples, "Who do you say that I am?" (See Mt 16:16.) __He has divine power.__

7. What did Jesus' miracle of calming the storm reveal about him? (See Mt 8:23-27.)

   _____
   _____
   _____
   _____
   _____

The Ladder of Prayer

Detail from *The Ladder of Divine Ascent*, Sucevita Monastery, Moldavia

For centuries, many people in the Church have used the image of a ladder to explain how we can pray with Sacred Scripture. This process is called *lectio divina* ("holy reading"). In *lectio divina*, we pray with a short passage of Scripture.

The first step of the ladder is called in Latin **lectio** ("**reading**"). We begin this step with the Sign of the Cross and a moment of silence. Then we slowly *read* the passage. As we read, we focus on learning what the passage says. We may pause on certain words or phrases that stand out to us. After this, we spend another moment in silence, recognizing God is present and speaking to us in the passage.

The second step of the ladder is **meditatio** ("**meditation**"). In this step, we think about the passage. We spend a few moments silently pondering what God is saying to us. We pay attention to any words, pictures, or thoughts that come into our minds as we read the passage.

Once we have heard God's Word, we then ask ourselves what we say in response to the Lord. The third step of the ladder is called **oratio** ("**prayer**"). During this step, we respond to God in prayer. We talk with God, who is our Heavenly Father. We may offer praise to God, give him thanks for his Word and all the blessings in our lives, tell him we are sorry for our sins, and ask him for his help and grace.

The fourth and final step of the ladder is **contemplatio** ("**contemplation**"). Contemplation is a gift of the Lord by which we rest in the joy of his presence. Our goal is to calm ourselves and simply be with God during this time. We should sit quietly and listen for God's voice in our hearts. Over time, we should challenge ourselves to sit quietly for longer periods of time.

Catechism of the Catholic Church, 2654

"The spiritual writers, paraphrasing Matthew 7:7, summarize in this way the dispositions of the heart nourished by the word of God in prayer: 'Seek in **reading** and you will find in **meditating**; knock in mental **prayer** and it will be opened to you by **contemplation**.'"[1]

Journal Reflection

How does *lectio divina* help us avoid focusing too much on ourselves when we pray?

The Light of the World

Read

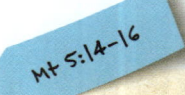
Mt 5:14-16

⁵ ¹⁴"You are the light of the world. A city set on a hill cannot be hidden. ¹⁵Nor does anyone light a lamp and put it under a bushel basket, but on a lampstand, and it gives light to all in the house. ¹⁶In the same way, let your light shine before others, so that they may see your good works and glorify your Father in heaven."

Jesus calls us to be "the light of the world." This means to be an example to others of the way to live. As a light can help someone see in the darkness, so we should be an example to others so they can see how to do good.

Oftentimes, we don't take Jesus' words to heart. We think that he is preaching only to the people of his time. Yet Jesus' call to be light in the world applies just as much to us as it did to his first disciples two thousand years ago. Now, you may be thinking, *I'm only in middle school . . . How can I be the light of the world?! How can I be a disciple like Saint Peter or Saint Matthew?!*

God consistently calls people who do not feel qualified or seem capable of fulfilling their calling. Remember that Jesus called Simon Peter, *a fisherman*, to lead his Church. He called Matthew, a tax collector, to be one of his first disciples and record the Gospel. God always gives us the grace to answer his call.

The saints are great models of holiness, but this does not mean we are called to be just like them in every way. God has a unique plan for you. He is calling you to be a witness of Jesus Christ to those people around you, especially your friends and family.

Reflect

Spend 5–10 minutes reflecting on the following:

- Am I open about being a Christian or do I try to hide it from others?
- Can people tell that I am a Christian by the way I live, talk, and act?
- Do I treat others with charity or am I rude and short to them when I get in a bad mood?

Pray

Spend a few minutes in silent prayer meditating on Jesus' words from the Sermon on the Mount above (Mt 5:14–16).

Act

Make a resolution to be a light to those around you this week. Find one specific way to witness to the Good News of Jesus Christ by your words and actions.

CHAPTER 3

The Crucified Lord of Glory

> **Words to Know**
>
> > *Great Commission*
> > *Paschal Mystery*
> > *Resurrection*

Proclaiming the Good News

"We beg you on behalf of Christ, be reconciled to God. For our sake he made him to be sin who knew no sin, so that in him we might become the righteousness of God."
—2 Corinthians 5:20–21

Christ on the Cross, Diego Velázquez

Jesus: "God Saves"

Saint Peter declared that Jesus is the Messiah and Son of the living God. Afterward, Jesus foretold that he would die by crucifixion and then be raised to life on the third day. The final chapters of Matthew's Gospel provide an extended account of the *Paschal Mystery*, through which Jesus brings salvation from the powers of sin and death by his Passion, Death, Resurrection, and Ascension.

The evening before his Passion, Jesus gathered his twelve Apostles to celebrate the Feast of Passover. Here, at the Last Supper, Jesus instituted the Sacrament of the Eucharist. He took bread, saying, "Take, eat; this is my body" (Mt 26:26). Then he took a cup of wine, saying, "Drink from it, all of you. For this is my blood of the covenant, which is poured out for many for the forgiveness of sins" (Mt 26:28). Jesus' name means "God saves." Now, at the climax of the Gospel we discover how Jesus saves us from sin: by shedding his blood and dying for us.

From the Saints

"Authority has been given to him who a little earlier was crucified, who was buried in a tomb, who lay there dead, who afterward was resurrected. But authority has been given 'in heaven and on earth.' Thus he who was previously reigning in heaven reigns on earth through the faith of believers."[1]
—Saint Jerome

At the heart of the early Church's proclamation of the Gospel is the historical event in which Jesus, having died on the Cross and been buried in the tomb, truly rose from the dead on the third day and appeared to his disciples. As the Church teaches, "The *Resurrection* of Jesus is the crowning truth of our faith in Christ" (*CCC* 638; emphasis added). The Gospel itself stands or falls on the truth of Jesus being raised from the dead. Jesus' Resurrection gives us the promise that through him we, too, can experience new life. His Resurrection is a sign that the powers of sin and death are defeated.

Christ Glorified in the Court of Heaven, Fra Angelico

The Appearance of Christ on Mountain in Galilee, Duccio di Buoninsegna

In the final scene of Matthew's Gospel, the Risen Christ appeared to his eleven Apostles and gave them their mission: go and make disciples of all nations (see Mt 28:16–20). This is the **Great Commission** that Jesus gives his Church. The Great Commission is directed to everyone who follows Jesus. We are all called to evangelize, to share the Good News of Jesus through our words and deeds.

Chapter 3 Summary

1. Through the Paschal Mystery, Jesus saves us from our sins.

2. Jesus of Nazareth died by crucifixion outside the city of Jerusalem.

3. After his Resurrection from the dead, Jesus sent his Apostles to proclaim the Good News to all nations.

Knowing Christ Jesus

 In both Chapters 1 and 2, you selected a single verse from Matthew's Gospel that you thought would best help you to explain to your neighbor who Jesus is. You will now do this one last time for the final section of Matthew's Gospel.

Passages	Optional Passages
The Transfiguration (Mt 17:1–13)	Jesus Cleanses the Temple (Mt 21:12–17)
Jesus Enters into Jerusalem (Mt 21:1–11)	The Greatest Commandment (Mt 22:34–40)
The Last Supper (Mt 26:17–29)	The Sheep and the Goats (Mt 25:31–46)
The Crucifixion (Mt 27:32–50)	
The Resurrection (Mt 28:1–10)	
The Great Commission (Mt 28:16–20)	

Select *one* verse in these passages that reveals an essential aspect of Jesus' identity. Copy the verse below.

Mt _____ : _____
    (Chapter)   *(Verse)*

_____

_____

_____

What does this verse reveal about Jesus? How would you use this verse in telling others about Jesus?

_____

_____

_____

_____

Let Us Pray—Psalm 16

Psalm 16 is a great prayer of trust in God's merciful love. The early Church found in this psalm a foreshadowing of Jesus' Resurrection from the dead (see Acts 2:31; 13:35). As we pray this psalm, let us do so confident in God's desire to deliver us all from the power of death.

Ps 16:1-2, 6-11

16 ¹Preserve me, O God, for in you I take refuge.
   ²I say to the Lord, "You are my Lord;
    I have no good apart from you." . . .
⁶The lines have fallen for me in pleasant places;
   yes, I have a goodly heritage.
⁷I bless the Lord who gives me counsel;
   in the night also my heart instructs me.
⁸I keep the Lord always before me;
   because he is at my right hand, I shall not be moved.
⁹Therefore my heart is glad, and my soul rejoices;
   my body also dwells secure.
¹⁰For you do not give me up to Sheol,
   or let your godly one see the Pit.
¹¹You show me the path of life;
   in your presence there is fulness of joy,
   in your right hand are pleasures for evermore.

Chapter 3 Review:
The Crucified Lord of Glory

Refer to the reading from this chapter and passages from Matthew 17–28 in the front of your book to answer the following questions.

1. Jesus delivers us from the powers of sin and death through his Passion, Death, Resurrection, and Ascension. This is called the _Paschal mystery_.

2. Which two figures from the Old Testament appeared alongside Jesus at his Transfiguration? (See Mt 17:1-13.) _Moses and elijah_

3. When Jesus entered Jerusalem riding on a donkey and a colt, the crowds proclaimed him to be whose son? (See Mt 21:1-11.) _Son of david_

4. What feast did Jesus celebrate with his twelve Apostles the night before he was killed? (See Mt 26:17-29.) _Passover_

5. Where was Jesus crucified? (See Mt 27:32-44.) _Golgotha "The place of the School"_

6. On what day of the week did Jesus rise from the dead? (See Mt 28:1.)

7. Summarize in three to four sentences Saint Matthew's account of the Paschal Mystery as told in chapters 26–28 in his Gospel.

56 Chapter 3

Can We Trust the Gospels?

Imagine walking down the street and seeing a newspaper lying on the ground. You pick it up and read the headline: "FIRE-BREATHING DRAGONS DESTROY THE CITY OF ATLANTIS." You read the article and at the end it says, "Written by Anonymous."

Now, to test whether this document is reliable, you may ask yourself three questions:

1. *Do I know who the author is?*
2. *Is the author an eyewitness, or does he have access to the testimony of eyewitnesses?*
3. *Is there evidence outside the document that can help verify its claims?*

When we ask these questions of this newspaper article, we learn that it is not a trustworthy document:

1. We do not know who the author is.
2. Therefore, we cannot say if the author was an eyewitness or had access to eyewitnesses.
3. Fire-breathing dragons and the city of Atlantis are myths. There is no evidence to prove they ever existed.

Some claim that the Gospels are no more trustworthy than an article about dragons and Atlantis. So, let's ask the same three questions of the Gospels and see what we learn.

1. **Who are the authors of the Gospels?**

Every copy of the Gospels in history is attributed to one of the four Evangelists: Matthew, Mark, Luke, or John. No historical evidence exists that these Gospels were ever attributed to anyone else.

2. **Are the authors eyewitnesses, or do they have access to the testimony of eyewitnesses?**

Two of the Gospel authors were eyewitnesses to Christ's life: Matthew and John. These two Apostles lived with Jesus for three years and received daily instruction from him.

Can we not trust Mark and Luke's Gospels, then? Mark and Luke were not eyewitnesses to Christ's life, but they relied on the testimony of eyewitnesses. According to early historical testimony, Mark wrote his Gospel with the help of Saint Peter the Apostle, and Luke was a companion of Saint Paul and also knew some of the Apostles. There are even some traditions that suggest Luke interviewed the Blessed Virgin Mary!

3. **Is there evidence outside the Gospels that can help verify their claims?**

Archaeologists have discovered evidence to support the Gospels. For example, in the nineteenth century, scientists found the Pool of Bethesda mentioned in John 5. Archaeological findings also have proven that figures mentioned in the Gospels, such as Pontius Pilate and the several kings named Herod, truly existed. Additionally, non-Christian writings refer to many of the same people and events in the Gospels, including Jesus himself.

Looking at how the Gospels hold up against these three questions, we can reasonably say that they are reliable and contain true historical accounts of Jesus' life, Death, and Resurrection.

Journal Reflection

How does knowing the Gospels are reliable change how you see your faith and mission as an evangelist?

Praying to Jesus as a Friend

Read

We learn a lot about Christ from reading the Gospels. We know that he is the Divine Son of God, who became man, suffered, died, and rose again so that we may receive the forgiveness of our sins and share in the eternal life of the Blessed Trinity. But Jesus is not just some remote figure who won our salvation and disappeared. Rather, he is a friend that we can come to know and love through prayer.

When we pray, we lift our minds and hearts to God. We tell him our hopes and joys as well as our fears and sorrows. He listens to what we have to say and wants to comfort, guide, and love us. He is a real person and the most perfect friend who loves you. Like any friend, we should talk to him daily, and we should listen for his voice.

Yet prayer is not always easy because we often feel like we are too busy or too tired. Oftentimes, we become distracted in our prayer, and we focus on other things instead of Christ. In this way, we are acting like a friend who comes to visit but is distracted by his phone.

Jesus remains patient with us even when we are distracted. Therefore, no matter how often we get distracted or how busy we get, we should continue to pray consistently and seek to grow in our knowledge and love for Jesus.

Light of the World, William Holman Hunt

Reflect

Spend 5–10 minutes reflecting on the following:

- Do I relate to Christ as my friend as well as my Lord?
- How much time do I spend with Jesus in prayer?
- How do I react when I find myself distracted in prayer?

Pray

Spend a minute in prayer, speaking to Jesus in your own words. End by reciting the Lord's Prayer (the Our Father).

Act

This week, set aside a consistent time to pray with God alone every day. Take an icon or image of Christ and reflect on the face of Jesus during your prayer.

CHAPTER 4
Sacred Scripture, the Inspired Word

Words to Know

> *canon*

> *inspiration*

Proclaiming the Good News

"In many and various ways God spoke of old to our fathers by the prophets; but in these last days he has spoken to us by a Son, whom he appointed the heir of all things, through whom also he created the ages." —Hebrews 1:1–2

The Sermon on the Mount, Fra Angelico

The God Who Speaks

The Word of God

God has spoken. This startling claim might give us pause. How has God spoken? When? And to whom? The Letter to the Hebrews opens by answering these very questions. The first verse says that God "spoke of old to our fathers *by the prophets*" (1:1; emphasis added). The Old Testament contains many accounts of God speaking to important figures such as Moses and King David, as well as prophets like Isaiah and Jeremiah.

But the next verse reveals a far more profound way God speaks to us: "In these last days he has spoken to us *by a Son*" (1:2; emphasis added). In Jesus Christ, God speaks his Word in the flesh. God has spoken through the Incarnation, life, Death, Resurrection, and Ascension of Jesus Christ.

In the Scriptures, God gives the Church a reliable record of this twofold speaking in history, when he spoke both "by the prophets" and then "by a Son." God speaks to us in a way we can hear and understand so that we will know his great love for us and his plan for our lives in Christ.

Inspired by God

What sets the books of Sacred Scripture apart? What makes the books collected in the Bible different from every other book written throughout human history? All 73 books of the Bible were written through the *inspiration* of the Holy Spirit. The word "inspired" is borrowed from one of the books of the New Testament:

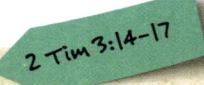
2 Tim 3:14-17

3 ¹⁴But as for you, continue in what you have learned and have firmly believed, knowing from whom you learned it ¹⁵and how from childhood you have been acquainted with the Sacred Writings which are able to instruct you for salvation through faith in Christ Jesus. ¹⁶All Scripture is inspired by God and profitable for teaching, for reproof, for correction, and for training in righteousness, ¹⁷that the man of God may be complete, equipped for every good work.

The phrase "inspired by God" in verse 16 could be translated more literally as "God-breathed." The Sacred Scriptures are those books that God breathed forth through the Holy Spirit. What makes all 73 books of the Bible into one single book is they have God as their Author. But what does this mean about the human authors? How should we understand the role people like Saint Matthew or Saint Paul had in writing the Scriptures?

Inspiration is not a mechanical process. God did not take control of the human authors and manipulate them into writing word for word what he said to them. The human authors were true authors who through the grace of the Holy Spirit wrote the books of the Bible. Each wrote with freedom and creativity what God wanted to reveal for our salvation. In order to interpret correctly what the human authors have written, we must ask the Holy Spirit to guide us. We can turn to the saints, who show us by their lives what happens when we allow ourselves to be led by the Spirit and shaped by God's Word.

Dei Verbum, 21
"In the sacred books, the Father who is in heaven meets His children with great love and speaks with them."

How Sacred Scripture Is like Jesus Christ

There are a few helpful ways of explaining the Church's teaching about inspiration. One way is by comparing Sacred Scripture with the Incarnation of Jesus Christ. Remember, the Incarnation refers to the mystery of the Divine Son of God (the Word) becoming man. We saw this in the opening chapter of Matthew's Gospel. The angel told Joseph, "Do not fear to take Mary your wife, for the child conceived in her is of the Holy Spirit" (1:20). Jesus is the eternal Son of God, who became fully human in the womb of the Blessed Virgin Mary.

Jesus is both fully God *and* fully man. Similarly, the Sacred Scriptures are truly the words of God and the words of men. We can further compare Jesus Christ (the incarnate Word) and Sacred Scripture (the inspired Word). Jesus is like us in all things except sin. Similarly, Sacred Scripture is without error although it was written by men. So, it is necessary to interpret it properly.

Jesus Christ *The Incarnate Word*	Sacred Scripture *The Inspired Word*
Fully divine	The Word of God
Fully human	The words of men
Without sin	Without error

To help us understand the Church's teaching on inspiration, we will compare two paintings by Caravaggio. Both depict the inspiration of Saint Matthew.

The image on the left is Caravaggio's original painting. This first painting was rejected because it presents a mistaken understanding of inspiration. It gives the impression that the angel is controlling what Matthew writes down.

The image on the right is the revised painting of Caravaggio. This painting better reflects the Church's teaching on inspiration. It displays Matthew's openness to the grace of God and his freedom in writing his Gospel.

How does the second version of this scene (painting on the right) succeed in depicting the mystery of inspiration in ways that the original painting failed?

_____

_____

_____

_____

Divine Revelation

Who Is God?

God speaks to us through Scripture. But why does he speak at all? What does he want to tell us? God speaks through Scripture to reveal himself and his plan for us.

By reading a novel, we can often learn something about its author. God is the Author of the entire universe. By observing creation, we can learn things about its Creator. For example, the complexity of the universe tells us its Creator must be intelligent and very powerful. Yet if we can know and experience God through creation, why do we need Scripture?

Can a person see the sunlight if his eyes are closed? Of course not. Similarly, sin "darkens our eyes" to the light of God that shines through his creation. God speaks to us through creation. But sin casts a shadow over our eyes and prevents us from clearly seeing God's handiwork around and within us. We make idols of created things and forget the Creator of all things. One reason God speaks to us in Scripture is to overcome our blindness to his presence.

There is another reason: God speaks in Scripture to reveal things that go far beyond what we could ever know through creation. Jesus reveals to us the mystery of the Blessed Trinity. God is a Trinity of Persons: Father, Son, and Holy Spirit. Scripture teaches us that "God is love" (1 Jn 4:8). There is in God's very being an "eternal exchange" of love between the Father, the Son, and the Holy Spirit (*CCC* 221). Creation can tell us some things about the Creator. But Scripture gives us a glimpse into the very heart of God.

What Is God's Plan for Us?

A dropped pen falls to the ground. An acorn grows into an oak. Ice melts at 32°F. We live in a predictable universe. We live in a universe with rules, with laws of nature. God is a lawgiver. God creates an orderly universe where everything—including us—has a purpose. God has a plan for everything, especially our lives. In Scripture, God reveals to us our deepest purpose: to share in the life of the Blessed Trinity. The Son became man so that—united to him—we can become adopted children of the Father through the Holy Spirit. We are called to participate in the eternal exchange of love between Father, Son, and Holy Spirit. This divine love fulfills the deepest desires of our hearts. We all desire to love and be loved. Only God can give us a love that lasts forever.

But unlike pens obeying the law of gravity, we have the freedom to choose to love God. The decision to break that law is called sin. Sin separates us from God and prevents us from achieving our purpose. In Scripture, God reveals his plan to rescue mankind from sin. No matter what sin we have committed, we can find salvation in Jesus, the Son. The Good News of the Gospel is that God does not abandon us. Through repentance and faith in Christ Jesus, we can be reunited with the God who is Love.

THE NEW TESTAMENT

Matthew.....1005	1 Timothy.....1306
Mark.....1063	2 Timothy.....1313
Luke.....1090	Titus.....1318
John.....1135	Philemon.....1321
...tles 1169	Hebrews.....1323
	1341

The Canon of Scripture

God speaks to us in Scripture. But how did Scripture come together? How was it decided which books are God's inspired Word?

In the early Church, many writings were written or read, but not all of them became part of the Bible. The Church's official list of books in the Bible is called the *canon*. In the early Church, many writings were produced. The term "canon" means "rule" or "measure." The Church's canon of Scripture provides a measure when it comes to which writings should be taken as Scripture and which should not. We can think of the canon as the Bible's table of contents.

The canon of Scripture is divided into two parts: the Old Testament and the New Testament. In Catholic Bibles, the Old Testament has 46 books, and the New Testament has 27 books. (For a complete list of the books found in the Bible, see page 331.) It took a long time for the Church to discern which writings were inspired by God and should be part of the Bible. The first official declaration of the 73-book canon occurred at the Council of Rome in A.D. 382. Since this time, the Church has consistently recognized only these 73 books as inspired by God.

Jesus promises to guide and protect his Church no matter what. At the end of Matthew's Gospel, Jesus made this promise to his Church: "Behold, I am with you always, even until the end of the age" (28:20). Similarly, in Matthew's Gospel, Jesus declared to Saint Peter, "You are Peter, and upon this rock I will build my Church, and the gates of hell shall not prevail against it" (16:18). Through the Holy Spirit, Jesus guided the Church in forming the canon of Scripture. He continues to guide her in interpreting the inspired Word.

Chapter 4 Summary

1. All 73 books of the Bible were inspired by the Holy Spirit. They have God as their Author.

2. Scripture is the Word of God in the words of men.

3. God speaks to us in Scripture to reveal himself and his plan for us to share in the life of the Blessed Trinity.

Scripture: A Stream of Living Water

The Jordan River

Mt 8:1-4

8 ¹When [Jesus] came down from the mountain, many crowds followed him. ²And behold, a leper came and worshiped him, saying, "Lord, if you will it, you can make me clean." ³And he stretched out his hand and touched him, saying, "I will it; be made clean." And immediately his leprosy was cleansed. ⁴And Jesus said to him, "See that you tell no one. But go, show yourself to the priest and offer the gift that Moses commanded, for a testimony to them."

Suppose you have a friend who knows nothing about Jesus or Christianity. He opens a Bible to the passage above and asks you about it. What are some of the things you would talk about?

_____
_____
_____
_____

Pope Saint Gregory the Great once wrote that Scripture is like a stream of water that is both shallow and deep. It is shallow enough for a lamb to stand in but deep enough for an elephant to float.¹

What he means is that Scripture is for everyone. A person who has little experience with Scripture (a lamb) can still learn something from it. Even for those who have studied Scripture for years (an elephant), there is always more to be learned. There are many levels or "depths" to Scripture, like a stream that is both shallow and deep.

As an example of the depths of Scripture, let us return to Matthew 8. On the surface, this passage teaches us that Jesus is a healer who can perform deeds of power. If we look a little deeper, we notice hints of Jesus' divine identity. The leper *worships* Jesus. The leper refers to Jesus as "Lord." Those familiar with Matthew's Gospel will know the word "Lord" often is used to refer to God. Those who know the Old Testament well might notice the connection between how Jesus acts in this passage and how God acts in creating the universe in the Book of Genesis. In Genesis 1, God wills something, and it *immediately* happens. Here, Jesus *wills* the leper to be healed, and *immediately* he is healed. Jesus is acting as only God can!

This is just a brief example. There is much more that can be said about Matthew 8, and there is always more to be learned! This is why the Church uses cycles of readings in the liturgy. We hear the same Scripture passages proclaimed every year or every several years at Mass. The Church knows there is no end to what we can learn, even if we have heard the same passage a hundred times.

Let us—also remember the words of Saint Jerome, who said that every time you read Scripture, "it is Christ who speaks to you." There is always something new Christ can teach us. This is why listening carefully to the readings at Mass is so important. Christ speaks to each of us personally through the inspired Scriptures. Are we listening?

Do you listen carefully to the readings at Mass? If not, what tends to get in the way?

_____

_____

What are one or two specific things you can do to hear Christ better when he speaks to you in the readings at Mass?

_____

_____

Let Us Pray—Psalm 119

Psalm 119 is the longest of all 150 psalms in the Old Testament. This psalm provides an extended meditation on God's Word as a source of light and joy in our lives. As you pray these verses from Psalm 119, make these inspired words your own, asking the Lord to give you a greater love for the Scriptures.

Ps 119:105-112

119 ¹⁰⁵Your word is a lamp to my feet
  and a light to my path.
¹⁰⁶I have sworn an oath and confirmed it,
  to observe your righteous ordinances.
¹⁰⁷I am sorely afflicted;
  give me life, O LORD, according to your word!
¹⁰⁸Accept my offerings of praise, O LORD,
  and teach me your ordinances.
¹⁰⁹I hold my life in my hand continually,
  but I do not forget your law.

¹¹⁰The wicked have laid a snare for me,
  but I do not stray from your precepts.
¹¹¹Your testimonies are my heritage for ever;
  yes, they are the joy of my heart.
¹¹²I incline my heart to
  perform your
  statutes
 for ever,
  to the end.

Chapter 4 Review:
Sacred Scripture, the Inspired Word

1. God "spoke of old to our fathers by the ___Prophets___" (Heb 1:1).

2. Through the Incarnation, life, Death, Resurrection, and Ascension of Jesus Christ, God "has spoken to us by a ___Son___" (Heb 1:2).

3. All 73 books of the Bible were written through the ___Inspiration~~Author or Prophets~~___ of the Holy Spirit.

4. The mystery of the ___Incarnation___ can help us understand how Scripture is both the Word of God *and* the words of men.

5. Scripture reveals our deepest purpose in life. What is that? ___to share in the life of the blessed trinity.___

6. The Church's official list of 73 books that make up the Bible is called the ___Canon___.

7. Take a moment to look back at the two paintings of Saint Matthew. What are these two paintings describing? ___Insperation of Scipture___

   Why is the first painting flawed?

   _____
   _____
   _____
   _____
   _____
   _____
   _____
   _____

The Deuterocanonical Books

Saint Jerome Writing, Caravaggio

How many books are in the Bible?

The answer depends on which Christian group you ask. All Christians agree to the same 27-book New Testament. However, there is disagreement on the Old Testament. Catholics recognize 46 books, whereas some non-Catholic Christians recognize only 39 books. The 7 disputed Old Testament books are called the deuterocanonical books.

Why is there disagreement on the Old Testament? First, we must realize that even Jews at the time of Jesus did not agree on what books were inspired Scripture. Debates within Judaism about the canon continued for many years. However, by the second and third centuries A.D., most Jews accepted a Hebrew version of the Old Testament that leaves out the deuterocanonical books. Yet beginning with the Council of Rome in A.D. 382, the Church affirmed a canon that includes the deuterocanonical books. Why?

A few hundred years before Christ, the Old Testament was translated from Hebrew to Greek. This famous translation is known as the Septuagint. The Septuagint includes *all* the deuterocanonical books. The Septuagint was used widely among Jews before and during the time of Christ. It was also quoted frequently by New Testament writers, including Matthew. The Septuagint was the primary translation used by the early Church. Therefore, the Church's decision at the Council of Rome to keep the deuterocanonical books makes sense.

The Church's decision was unquestioned until the Protestant Reformation, over eleven hundred years later. The Protestant Reformer Martin Luther broke away from the Catholic Church. He created a version of the Bible that excludes the deuterocanonical books. He argued for the same 39-book version of the Hebrew Old Testament used by later Jews. Other Protestant Reformers followed Luther's lead. In response to the Protestant Reformation, the Church reaffirmed and defended her 46-book Old Testament canon at the Council of Trent (A.D. 1545–1563).

Deuterocanonical Books

- *Tobit*
- *Judith*
- *Baruch*
- *Sirach*
- *1 Maccabees*
- *2 Maccabees*
- *Wisdom*

Journal Reflection

Martin Luther famously argued that the Bible is the only real authority that can determine what Christians believe. Yet the canon of Scripture—the Church's official list of books that should be in the Bible—is not itself part of the Bible. **Why might this be a problem for Luther's view?**

Reverence for Sacred Scripture

Read
Saint Jerome wrote,

> We are reading the sacred Scriptures. For me, the Gospel is the Body of Christ; for me, the holy Scriptures are his teaching. And when he says: *whoever does not eat my flesh and drink my blood* (Jn 6:53), even though these words can also be understood of the [Eucharistic] Mystery, Christ's body and blood are really the word of Scripture, God's teaching. When we approach the [Eucharistic] Mystery, if a crumb falls to the ground we are troubled. Yet when we are listening to the word of God, and God's Word and Christ's flesh and blood are being poured into our ears yet we pay no heed, what great peril should we not feel?[2]

As Catholics, we are used to being reverent in receiving the Eucharist. We know not to let "a crumb fall to the ground." But Saint Jerome also reminds us we should approach the Scriptures with reverence, for Christ is present in the inspired Word.

In her celebration of the Mass, the Church helps us grow in reverence for Scripture. Here are a few examples:

- The Book of the Gospels is raised up and carried into the Church at the beginning of Mass.
- The Book of the Gospels is placed on the altar, the same place where the Liturgy of the Eucharist occurs.
- We stand for the Gospel reading as a sign of our readiness to encounter Christ in his Word.

Reflect
Spend 5–10 minutes reflecting on the following:

- When the readings are proclaimed at Mass, am I prepared to meet Christ?
- Do I spend time reading Scripture on a regular basis? Is there a 5-minute period each day that I could dedicate to reading Scripture?

Pray
Pray the following in preparation for Mass:

> Lord Jesus, you are the Bread of Life. You feed us both through the Scriptures and the Eucharist. You offer yourself to us at the table of your Word and Body. Help me receive you worthily in both Word and sacrament so that I might in turn bring the Good News to all whom I meet. I ask this in your most holy name. Amen.

Act
Prayerfully read through the Gospel passage for this upcoming Sunday prior to Mass. Be open to receive whatever Christ wants to say to you. You can access the readings at www.bible.usccb.org.

Pope Francis elevating the Book of the Gospels

CHAPTER 5

Jesus Christ, the Incarnate Word

Words to Know

> charity

> divine providence

> salvation history

Proclaiming the Good News

"Ignorance of the Scriptures is ignorance of Christ." —Saint Jerome

Jesus Appearing to Two Disciples on the Road to Emmaus, William Brassey Hole

God's Plan for Us

On the Road to Emmaus

Does God have a plan for history? Does he have a plan for your life? Everyone wonders at some point if God is involved in history and everyday life. Luke's Gospel tells of two of Jesus' disciples wrestling with these same questions after Jesus died on the Cross:

24 ¹³That very day two of them were going to a village named Emmaus, about seven miles from Jerusalem, ¹⁴and talking with each other about all these things that had happened. ¹⁵While they were talking and discussing together, Jesus himself drew near and went with them. ¹⁶But their eyes were kept from recognizing him. ¹⁷And he said to them, "What is this conversation which you are holding with each other as you walk?" And they stood still, looking sad. ¹⁸Then one of them, named Cleopas, answered him, "Are you the only visitor to Jerusalem who does not know the things that have happened there in these days?" ¹⁹And he said to them, "What things?" And they said to him, "Concerning Jesus of Nazareth, who was a prophet mighty in deed and word before God and all the people, ²⁰and how our chief priests and rulers delivered him up to be condemned to death, and crucified him. ²¹But we had hoped that he was the one to redeem Israel. Yes, and besides all this, it is now the third day since this happened. ²²Moreover, some women of our company amazed us. They were at the tomb early in the morning ²³and did not find his body; and they came back saying that they had even seen a vision of angels, who said that he was alive. ²⁴Some of those who were with us went to the tomb, and found it just as the women had said; but him they did not see." ²⁵And he said to them, "O foolish men, and slow of heart to believe all that the prophets have spoken! ²⁶Was it not necessary that the Christ should suffer these things and enter into his glory?" ²⁷And beginning with Moses and all the prophets, he interpreted to them in all the Scriptures the things concerning himself.

Road to Emmaus, Resurrection Appearances of Jesus, Giovanni and Francesco Cagnola

On the road to Emmaus, Jesus interpreted the Old Testament Scriptures for his disciples. Beginning with Moses and the Prophets, he took them through Scripture's story to show them God's plan.

As the one Divine Author, God wrote one storyline throughout Scripture. This storyline provides us with the big picture of God's plan for all history and each one of us. God's plan to save us from sin and unite the Church to himself in love is called *salvation history*. (An outline of salvation history can be found on page 334.)

Jesus helped his disciples on the road to Emmaus see how Jesus himself is the center of salvation history. Every action of Jesus' life was a fulfillment of God's plan—his silences, his miracles, his gestures, his prayer, his love for people, his total gift of himself on the Cross for our salvation, and his final victory over death in his Resurrection and Ascension.

In his wisdom, God guides the people and events of salvation history. God's guidance of salvation history according to his wisdom and love is known as his *divine providence*. As we read the story of salvation history, we see God guiding his people to cooperate with his help so that they reach fulfillment and perfection.

Scripture Builds Up Our Charity

God's plan for each of us is to be united with him in the special kind of love known as charity. *Charity* is love of God above all else, and the love of our neighbor as ourselves for the love of God. Charity is one of the three theological virtues (faith, hope, and charity). These virtues empower Christians to share in the life of the Blessed Trinity. Jesus teaches that charity is the greatest virtue:

> Mt 22:37-40
>
> **22** ³⁷"'You shall love the Lord your God with all your heart, with all your soul, and with all your mind.' ³⁸This is the greatest and first commandment. ³⁹And a second is like it: 'You shall love your neighbor as yourself.' ⁴⁰On these two commandments hang the whole law and the prophets."

Detail from *Adoration of the Trinity*, Albrecht Dürer

Charity is the greatest virtue and the fulfillment and perfection of the Christian life (see Col 3:14). It is a gift of God's grace. Scripture shows us what true charity is. When we read God's Word and see his actions in history, we learn how to love him and others more perfectly.

In Scripture, we learn the difference between right love versus wrong love. If we love something evil or untrue, it is a false or wrong love. Loving murder, stealing, lying, or false gods are examples. Sometimes, we can love the right things but in the wrong way. According to the virtue of justice, we owe some people love more than others. Since God created us and saved us by the Death and Resurrection of Jesus, we should love him more than anyone else. So, if we love ice cream more than God, we could call that a disordered love. It's fine to love ice cream, but to love it more than God is wrong.

What is disordered love? When we love something too much or too little. For example, if someone loves video games or social media more than parents or siblings, that is a love that is out of order, or disordered. If you love sports more than God, that is a disordered love. If you love an animal or pet more than the homeless person begging on the street corner, that is disordered.

We learn about Israel's struggle to love well in the Old Testament. God's people sometimes worshipped false gods and idols instead of loving the one true God above all else. Sin is usually rooted in loving something (like money) or someone (like a celebrity) more than God. Sin can also be rooted in loving ourselves more than others, which happens when we do things like stealing or telling lies. The Bible teaches us how to love the right things in the right way so that we find true peace and happiness and fulfill God's will.

The more we prayerfully read and study God's Word in the Bible, the more we learn about God's desire to be united with us in love. As Scripture teaches, "God is love, and he who abides in love abides in God, and God abides in him" (1 Jn 4:16). Knowing and loving God is the ultimate purpose of our lives.

The Word of God and the Church

The Three Kinds of Books in Scripture

Remember, the canon of Scripture contains 73 sacred books: 46 in the Old Testament and 27 in the New Testament. The Old Testament can be divided into three categories.

In the Old Testament, we find the Pentateuch [PEN-tuh-took] and other historical books. The Pentateuch is the first five books of the Bible: Genesis, Exodus, Leviticus, Numbers, and Deuteronomy. Other historical books include Joshua, 1 and 2 Samuel, and 1 and 2 Kings, among others. These books tell of the people and events of salvation history.

The second kind of books we see in the Old Testament is wisdom literature. These books teach how to pray and grow in holiness and virtue. Wisdom literature in the Bible includes the Book of Psalms, the Book of Proverbs, and the Book of Wisdom, among others.

The third category is the prophetic books. These books contain the words of numerous prophets sent by God to prepare his people for the coming Messiah. Prophetic books include Isaiah, Jeremiah, and Ezekiel.

There is a similar, threefold way of thinking about the books of the New Testament. The Gospels and the Book of Acts tell the history of Christ and his Church. The New Testament letters from Saint Paul and others, which we call the Epistles, teach much about Christian wisdom. The Book of Revelation, the last book of the Bible and a kind of prophetic book, tells of the future glory awaiting the faithful after Christ's Second Coming.

Old Testament	New Testament
Pentateuch/Historical Books	Gospels/Acts
Psalms/Wisdom Literature	Epistles
Prophetic Books	The Book of Revelation

Word and Sacrament

24 ²⁸So they drew near to the village to which they were going. He appeared to be going further, ²⁹but they constrained him, saying, "Stay with us, for it is toward evening and the day is now far spent." So he went in to stay with them. ³⁰When he was at table with them, he took the bread and blessed and broke it, and gave it to them. ³¹And their eyes were opened and they recognized him; and he vanished out of their sight. ³²They said to each other, "Did not our hearts burn within us while he talked to us on the road, while he opened to us the Scriptures?" ³³And they rose that same hour and returned to Jerusalem; and they found the Eleven gathered together and those who were with them, ³⁴who said, "The Lord has risen indeed, and has appeared to Simon!" ³⁵Then they told what had happened on the road, and how he was known to them in the breaking of the bread.

Lk 24:28-35

Jesus' two disciples listened as he taught about the Scriptures, but they still did not recognize him. They did not yet understand that he had risen from the dead and was the one walking with them. But one important action opened their eyes to his presence.

The disciples recognized Jesus when he sat with them, took bread, blessed it, broke it, and gave it to them to eat. Saint Luke used the same language to describe Jesus' actions in this passage as he did to describe Jesus' actions at the Last Supper. With Jesus' words, this bread became the Eucharist, just as it did at the Last Supper.

Jesus did two important things for the disciples that day. First, Jesus explained how the Scriptures were fulfilled in his dying and rising. Second, Jesus gave himself to them in the breaking of the bread—the Eucharist. The Church relives these two key experiences at every Mass. The Mass is divided into two main parts, each one corresponding to the experience of the disciples on the road to Emmaus.

The Mass begins with the Liturgy of the Word, in which we hear readings from the Old Testament, with an additional reading from the Psalms, and after which there may be a reading from a New Testament epistle. Finally, we stand to hear the Gospel read because it tells of Jesus' words and deeds that bring the Old Testament to fulfillment. In the Homily, the priest or deacon explains the Scriptures just as Jesus did on the road to Emmaus.

The second part of the Mass is the Liturgy of the Eucharist, where the priest, who has received the Sacrament of Holy Orders, stands in the Person of Jesus and takes, blesses, and breaks the bread. He then gives us the Eucharist so that we may be united to Christ in Holy Communion.

Supper at Emmaus, Resurrection Appearances of Jesus, Giovanni and Francesco Cagnola

The Liturgy of the Word and Liturgy of the Eucharist together form one act of worship. The *Catechism* teaches, "The Eucharistic table set for us is the table both of the Word of God and of the Body of the Lord" (*CCC* 1346). The eucharistic celebration always includes the following:

- The proclamation of the Word of God
- Thanksgiving to God the Father for all his benefits, above all, the gift of his Son
- The consecration of bread and wine
- Participation by receiving the Lord's Body and Blood

The road to Emmaus and the table at Emmaus show us that Jesus seeks to share with every disciple his Word and his very Body. Jesus shows us we need both the Word of God and the Sacrament of the Eucharist. Both Word and sacrament become our spiritual nourishment. If we understand the events of salvation history, we will better understand and experience that same mystery at each Mass. Then our hearts will be set on fire by understanding the Scriptures, and our eyes can be opened to see Jesus in the Eucharist.

Chapter 5 Summary

1. God has a plan of love for all of history; we learn to see this providential plan by reading the storyline of Scripture.

2. Reading Scripture helps us grow in charity, which is the fulfillment and perfection of the Christian life.

3. Jesus gives himself to us in both Word and sacrament at every Mass as our spiritual nourishment.

Scripture Gives Us Hope

Saint Paul wrote that "whatever was written in former days was written for our instruction, that by steadfastness and by the encouragement of the Scriptures we might have hope" (Rom 15:4).

The theological virtue of hope gives us supernatural confidence in God's plan. With hope, we can trust that God will carry out this plan in our lives and lead us to fulfillment and perfection. As Saint Paul reminds us, we have hope by the "encouragement of the Scriptures."

As we read in Luke 24:13–27, two of Jesus' disciples were walking from Jerusalem (where Jesus was killed) to the town of Emmaus. Jesus responded to the disciples' despair as if they should know better! He called them "foolish" and "slow of heart to believe" (24:25). Jesus' reaction suggests that the Scriptures have clearly foretold these events, and they should have had no reason to lose hope.

To restore their hope, Jesus gave them encouragement through the Scriptures. He showed how the Scriptures, which were written hundreds and sometimes a thousand years earlier, reveal that Jesus is the one who would redeem Israel. God has kept his promises.

Since God has fulfilled the promises he made to Moses and the prophets, he can be trusted to fulfill all his promises. Therefore, we can have hope and trust he will do the other things he promised. We can trust he will save us from our sin, make us his children, and give us his divine life through grace.

The opposite of hope is despair. We despair when we do not trust that God will carry out his plan. Sometimes we despair by thinking we are not loved enough by God: *Certainly, he is not really planning to do all that for me*. Perhaps we despair of God's mercy: *I am too sinful for God to forgive me*.

There are many Scriptures that help fight off despair. The Psalms are especially good at reminding us of God's love and kindness so that we have confidence in him.

Psalm 78 is a great prayer for anyone who lacks hope in God's mercy. In fact, it was written to encourage people to "set their hope in God" (78:7). How does it do this? Psalm 78 tells about all the ways God's people were unfaithful to him; yet God is still faithful to them. This psalm is a good reminder that even if we are unfaithful, God remains faithful and will still love us and help us if we ask for his mercy.

If we ever struggle with hope, the Scriptures remind us that God has a plan to save us and he wants us to cooperate with him as he carries out this plan in our lives.

What events in Scripture give you hope?

_____
_____
_____

Why do you think some people lose hope in God's love and mercy? What advice would you have for them?

_____
_____
_____
_____
_____

Let Us Pray—Psalm 103

Psalm 103 begins by praising our God, who is faithful to his promises. As you pray this psalm, consider the ways that you have encountered God's mercy in your life.

Ps 103:1-8

103 ¹Bless the LORD, O my soul;
and all that is within me, bless his holy name!
²Bless the LORD, O my soul,
and forget not all his benefits,
³who forgives all your iniquity,
who heals all your diseases,
⁴who redeems your life from the Pit,
who crowns you with mercy and compassion,
⁵who satisfies you with good as long as you live
so that your youth is renewed like the eagle's.
⁶The LORD works vindication
and justice for all who are oppressed.
⁷He made known his ways to Moses,
his acts to the people of Israel.
⁸The LORD is merciful and gracious,
slow to anger and abounding in mercy.

Chapter 5 Review:
Jesus Christ, the Incarnate Word

1. In the final chapter of his Gospel, Luke the Evangelist tells us about the Risen Jesus' encounter with two disciples on the road to __Emmaus__. (See Lk 24:13.)

2. When did the two disciples recognize Jesus? (See Lk 24:28-35.) __When he broke bread__

3. Scripture has one storyline because it has one Divine Author, who is __God__.

4. What do we call God's plan throughout history, as told in the Bible, to save us from our sins and unite the Church to himself in love? __God Salvation__

5. What do we call God's guidance of salvation history according to his wisdom? __Divine Providence__

6. Complete the sentence: Charity is love of __God above all else and love our neighbor as our selves__.

7. Scripture shows us what true __Charity__ is.

8. Describe how the account of the disciples on the road to Emmaus reflects how Jesus gives himself to us in the Mass in Word and sacrament.

_____
_____
_____
_____
_____
_____

Our Story

1 Cor 10:1-4

10 ¹I want you to know, brethren, that our fathers were all under the cloud, and all passed through the sea, ²and all were baptized into Moses in the cloud and in the sea, ³and all ate the same supernatural food ⁴and all drank the same supernatural drink. For they drank from the supernatural Rock which followed them, and the Rock was Christ.

In this passage from his First Letter to the Corinthians, Saint Paul teaches us that the story of salvation history is our story. Saint Paul looked at the events in the Old Testament Book of Exodus and compared them to God's work in our lives through the sacraments.

In the Exodus, God delivered the people of Israel from slavery in Egypt. He appeared to them as a pillar of smoke and fire and miraculously led Moses and the people through the Red Sea (see Ex 13:21; 14:22, 29). In the crossing of the Red Sea, Saint Paul saw the prefiguring of the Sacrament of Baptism.

After they crossed the Red Sea, God led Israel through the wilderness. He provided them with supernatural food in the form of miraculous bread from Heaven called manna (see Ex 16:4, 35). He gave them supernatural drink in the form of water that flowed from a rock (see Ex 17:6). Saint Paul saw that the manna in the desert and the miraculous water from the rock foreshadowed the Eucharist. Jesus Christ, whom Saint Paul called the "Rock," gives us supernatural food in his Body and Blood in the Eucharist.

What does this passage teach us about salvation history? It teaches us that the story of salvation history is our family story. God delivered our ancestors from their trials and tribulations. He will do the same for us if we follow him.

Our "fathers," as Saint Paul said, were "baptized" into Moses and received the same supernatural food and drink. But in Jesus, we are saved by the New Moses, Jesus Christ, who delivers us not from earthly bondage but from sin and death.

Moses Striking the Rock, Corrado Giaquinto

We enter into our family story through Baptism. We are strengthened to live out our part in salvation history through the other sacraments, especially the Holy Eucharist.

Journal Reflection

How does knowing that the story of salvation history is your own story change how you read the Bible and participate in the sacraments?

Challenges in Reading Scripture

Read

Reading Scripture can be difficult. Saint Jerome struggled for years before he grew to love Scripture. Here are six tips inspired by Saint Jerome to help us read Scripture.

1. **Pray to the Holy Spirit.** Saint Jerome prayed before reading Scripture and frequently asked others to pray for him. All of Scripture is inspired by the Holy Spirit. It makes sense to pray to the same Spirit to guide us in reading Scripture!

2. **Ask for help.** Jerome once wrote, "I have never ever trusted in my own powers to study the divine volumes."[1] We should take Jerome's advice. If we are having a hard time understanding Scripture, we should seek help from people and resources that can teach us from the wisdom of the Church.

3. **Learn Church teaching.** In a letter, Jerome wrote, "Remain firmly attached to the traditional doctrine that you have been taught."[2] Jerome knew that the true understanding of Scripture can never go against the Church's Tradition. The more we learn from Church teaching, the better we can understand Scripture.

4. **Be consistent.** Jerome once wrote a letter to a priest, saying, "Read the divine Scriptures frequently; rather, may your hands never set the Holy Book down."[3] We will not grow to love Scripture unless we read it consistently. Start by setting aside 5 minutes each day.

5. **Be patient when something is confusing.** Jerome was a student of Scripture for many years. Even near the end of his life, he was still learning new things! Be patient if something doesn't make sense at first.

6. **Go to confession.** Jerome once wrote, "Provided our bodies are not the slaves of sin, wisdom will come to us."[4] Jerome's own sin of pride caused him to avoid Scripture. Regular confession can help us grow in humility and be prepared to learn from God in Scripture.

Reflect

Spend 5–10 minutes reflecting on the following:

- Do I currently struggle with reading the Bible? What challenges do I face?

- Do I ask God for the grace to understand his inspired Word, or do I rely only on myself?

Pray

Spend a few minutes telling Jesus about the challenges and difficulties you face in your life. Then ask him to send his Spirit upon you to help you encounter him in Scripture. End by praying an Our Father.

Act

This week, spend 5 minutes each day reading Scripture. Before reading, pray to the Holy Spirit for guidance. Go to confession sometime this month.

Unit 2

In the Beginning

The Book of Genesis is a book of beginnings. Genesis 1–2 describes the beginning of the universe and humanity. God created the universe through a peaceful command. Humans were made in God's image as the high point of the act of Creation. Genesis 3–11 describes the beginning of sin on earth. Out of pride, Adam and Eve disobeyed God's command and broke their relationship with the Creator. The accounts of Cain and Abel, the Flood, and the Tower of Babel reveal how sin continued to deepen and spread. Despite man's sin, God sought to rescue fallen humanity and reunite mankind with himself.

The remaining chapters in the Book of Genesis describe how God chose a single family—Abraham and his descendants—to become the source of restoring humanity's relationship with himself. Through his covenant with Abraham and his faithfulness to the Old Testament patriarchs, God built up his Chosen People. Throughout salvation history, God remained faithful to his covenant with Abraham's descendants.

The Gospel of Matthew reveals Jesus as the Son of Abraham, the New Isaac, through whom God's covenant with Abraham is fulfilled.

Chapters 6–9

Chapter 6: Creator of Heaven and Earth
Chapter 7: "Through the Devil's Envy"
Chapter 8: The God of Abraham, Isaac, and Jacob
Chapter 9: Jesus, the Son of Abraham

Grade 6 Road Map

Unit 1
The Good News
The Gospel of Matthew reveals who Jesus is through both his deeds and words. God speaks to us in Sacred Scripture through human authors inspired by the Holy Spirit.

Unit 2
In the Beginning
Genesis describes the beginning of the universe and humanity, the beginning of sin, and the beginning of God's plan to restore mankind's relationship with himself through the covenant with Abraham and his descendants. In Jesus, God's covenant with Abraham is fulfilled.

Unit 3
You Shall Be My People
Through Moses, God delivered his people from slavery in Egypt and made a covenant with them at Mount Sinai. Despite their unfaithfulness, God brought his people into the Promised Land after they wandered for forty years in the desert. Jesus is the New Moses, who gives the New Law.

Unit 4
The Kingdom of the Lord
The Lord made a covenant with King David and swore to give him an everlasting kingdom. The sins of God's people led to the division and downfall of the kingdom, eventually leading to the destruction of the Temple and the Babylonian exile. In Jesus, God's covenant with David is fulfilled.

Unit 5
The Coming of the Anointed One
God brought his people back from exile to the Promised Land, where they rebuilt the Temple in Jerusalem. The prophets foretold of the coming of the Messiah, who would rebuild the kingdom of David. Jesus, the Son of Man, brings the kingdom through his suffering and Death.

Unit 6
God with Us
The Gospel of Matthew provides reliable testimony that Jesus is the Divine Son of God made man, who delivered us from sin through his Paschal Mystery. Jesus continues to be present to his Church through Word and sacrament—above all, the Holy Eucharist.

Saint Teresa Benedicta of the Cross *(Edith Stein)*

Discovering God

Edith Stein (later known as Saint Teresa Benedicta of the Cross) was born in Germany on October 12, 1891. She was the youngest of eleven children in a faithful Jewish family. They strictly observed the laws of God because of their mother, Auguste Stein. The family's faithfulness continued even after Edith's father died when she was two years old, and her mother had to take over the family business.

From a young age, Edith loved to learn. She had incredible intelligence and was far more advanced than others her age. Edith even refused to go to kindergarten after realizing how much she surpassed her fellow students in understanding the subjects. Throughout her early school years, she enjoyed spending time in silent thought.

Although she lived in a faithful Jewish household, she began to believe that there was no evidence for what her family believed. Most of all, she found it difficult to believe in God's existence. So, when she was about fourteen years old, she chose to give up praying. She lived this way until she was almost twenty-one; however, she never stopped pursuing the truth about God.

In 1911, Edith began to attend a famous university in Germany to study philosophy under a renowned professor, Edmund Husserl. The challenge she had was to see beyond mere opinions and feelings to discover what was true in the world. Edith began grappling with whether anyone could know God or his truth.

The outbreak of World War I (1914–1918) put Edith's studies on hold. Countries across Europe were part of the fighting, including her home country of Germany. She could not stand by while so many were hurt in the war. So, in 1915, with her philosophy studies on pause because of the war, Edith volunteered to become a military nurse. They stationed her at a military hospital to serve those dying of infectious diseases. During this time, she said, "I no longer have a life of my own."[1] Her life was at the service of others.

Sadly, one of her dear friends, Reinach, died during the war, leaving behind a wife. When Edith visited her, she expected her to be depressed and inconsolable. Instead, Edith was surprised to encounter a woman who was full of hope derived from her Christian faith. This encounter was crucial in Edith's search for seeing God in the world. She began to see that suffering has meaning. Christ and his Cross strengthen us in our sufferings.

After being a military nurse for a year, Edith returned to her studies and finished her doctorate with the highest honor. In 1916, she continued to work hard assisting Professor Husserl. More than anything, Edith wanted to be a professor at the university. However, at this time, she was unable to become one since she was a woman. She didn't let this discourage her from searching for the truth.

Throughout this time, Edith struggled with bouts of depression. It was only made worse by her long hours of research and study. Nothing seemed to give her the rest she desperately needed. Unafraid to discover the truth, Edith began to try prayer. She sat in silence and thought of God and his truth. To her surprise, she found that this time in silence was fruitful. But she continued to have doubts about God. That all changed in 1921.

Edith would regularly spend time with her friend's family out of town to escape the stress of academic work. One night during a visit, she couldn't sleep and grabbed Saint Teresa of Avila's autobiography from her friend's bookshelf. Saint Teresa of Avila was a saint from the 1500s who taught others about the depths of prayer and God's love. Edith read her biography all in one sitting. "When I finished the book," she recalled later, "I said to myself: This is the truth."[2] Saint Teresa of Avila's life and writings about the spiritual life introduced Edith to God more profoundly. She began to understand better who God is and the truth and happiness she had been seeking.

Edith bought a Bible and a catechism and began to learn more. The teachings of the Catholic faith convinced her that this was the truth about God. She spoke to the local Catholic priest and was baptized into the Catholic Church on January 1, 1922. Her life as a disciple was only beginning.

The Weight of the Cross

After her Baptism, Edith wanted to become a Carmelite nun like Saint Teresa of Avila. The Carmelites are a religious order that focuses on living a life of poverty and prayer in the community. The sisters live in a cloister, a convent that they never leave once they enter. They do this to stay focused on God in prayer without the world's distractions.

Edith's spiritual directors—faithful priests—encouraged her to wait until she had been a Catholic longer. They also thought Edith was called to use her intellectual gifts to serve the Church publicly. Edith took their advice and accepted a teaching position at a Catholic school in Speyer, Germany, to teach German and history.

For the next eleven years (1922–1933), Edith was called to continue being in the public eye—a very different way of life than she hoped to have one day. She realized that "other things are expected of us in this world" and "that the deeper someone is drawn to God, the more he has to 'get beyond himself'" and "go into the world and carry divine life into it."[3] When she wasn't in the classroom, writing academic papers, or spending hours in front of the tabernacle without moving, she was giving lectures at Catholic events all over Germany.

Her primary task as a lecturer was to confront the popular ideas of her time that claimed there was no God or things that are true regardless of whether people believe them. The twentieth century brought about some of the most significant advancements in technology and science. With these leaps forward, people began to see science as the *only* source of truth. Edith, however, spoke against this trend, especially when it came to the dignity of the human person and the existence of moral truths. When she spoke, her words possessed a quiet power that influenced her listeners.

In the early 1930s, the Nazi party, led by Adolf Hitler, was on the rise in Germany, and Edith began to see how much danger Jews were in and, thus, her family. The Nazis hated the Jews and treated them as less than other people and races. Employment for Jews and those of Jewish origins was increasingly difficult. Edith then realized that "human activity cannot help us, but only the Passion of Christ—my desire is to share in that."[4] She knew it was possible to help those persecuted by the Nazis only if she finally devoted her life to prayer as a Carmelite. Her work as a teacher and speaker was not going to be enough.

She entered the Carmelites on her birthday, October 12, 1933. Later she took the name Teresa Benedicta of the Cross. The phrase "of the Cross" symbolized that Edith accepted any future suffering like Christ had accepted his death on the Cross. She knew that entering the convent would not preserve her from the Nazis. "[The Nazis] will surely get me out of here. In any case, I cannot count on being left in peace here,"[5] she said. She was right, but that didn't stop her from writing books and articles about God, his existence, and the truths he has revealed.

In 1938, the general election for German Parliament took place. Either the Carmelite sisters could vote for Nazi party control or against it. They knew their ballots weren't anonymous. Thus, the Nazis would see if they voted against them. Their votes against the Nazis would place the sisters in danger. Even knowing this, Edith did not vote for the Nazis. She chose to do the right thing rather than remain safe. When the German officer collected their ballots at the convent, he noted that she was of Jewish origin.

Once the Nazis gained complete control of the country later that year, the Nuremberg Laws went into effect. These laws were outright persecution of the Jewish population. Attacks on Jewish homes, businesses, and synagogues erupted in Germany. Edith had to leave. She was a danger to her convent because they could be arrested or killed for protecting a Jew.

She was sent secretly to another Carmelite convent in Echt, Netherlands, for the next three years as World War II (1939–1945) was underway in Europe. Her new convent wasn't preserved from the approaching danger. Edith had multiple chances to go somewhere safe, but she either refused or circumstances kept her from leaving. In all things, Edith remembered the name she had taken and accepted the cross of suffering. God blessed Edith by having her biological sister, Rosa, who was also newly Catholic, come and live with her at the convent.

On August 2, 1942, the Nazis began their "subtle" attack on the Catholic Church by rounding up all Catholics of Jewish background. Edith and her sister Rosa were brought to a holding camp with many others. She was able to write back to her Carmelite sisters during those few days. She wrote, "I am content about everything. One cannot acquire [an understanding of the Cross] unless one begins by really suffering the weight of the cross."[6] Her words revealed that she had truly accepted her suffering like Christ for the good of others. Her final days demonstrated this. Witnesses recounted seeing her when she arrived at the Auschwitz concentration camp, where an estimated one million Jews were murdered. She was more concerned with the well-being of others than her own, right up to the moment of her death.

The German philosopher and theologian Edith Stein, who died in Auschwitz

Saint Teresa Benedicta of the Cross died as a martyr on August 9, 1942. We celebrate her feast day on the same day.

Journal Reflection

1. Edith Stein had doubts about God's existence. **Why do you think some people do not believe that God exists?**

2. **If someone does start to doubt God's existence, how can he be like Edith Stein in addressing his doubts?**

3. God created everything good. **From our understanding of Genesis, the Fall of Adam and Eve, and Original Sin, why did the evils Edith experienced occur?**

4. We read about Joseph's trust in God's providence and how God brought about a great good out of the sufferings and evil Joseph experienced. In a similar way, Edith faced great evils and suffering at the hands of the Nazis. **How can we be like Joseph and Edith Stein when confronting suffering and evil in the world?**

CHAPTER 6

Creator of Heaven and Earth

Words to Know

> covenant

> ex nihilo

> image of God

Proclaiming the Good News

"God created man for incorruption, and made him in the image of his own eternity." —Wisdom 2:23

Creation of Adam, Michelangelo

"In the Beginning"

In this chapter, we begin exploring the first book of the Old Testament: Genesis. The word "genesis" means "origin" or "beginning." Genesis describes many beginnings: the beginning of the heavens and earth, the beginning of humans, and the beginning of God's Chosen People, the Israelites.

Creation

Genesis begins with the creation of the universe. Through his almighty power, God brought into existence a good and orderly universe. God created everything in "seven days."

Giving Form . . .		Filling the Void . . .		Divine Rest
Day 1: Light and darkness	→	**Day 4:** Sun, moon, and stars	→	
Day 2: Sky and seas	→	**Day 5:** Birds of the air and sea animals	→	**Day 7:** God rests
Day 3: Dry land and vegetation	→	**Day 6:** Land animals and humans	→	

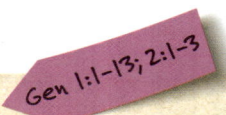
Gen 1:1-13; 2:1-3

1 ¹In the beginning God created the heavens and the earth. ²The earth was without form and void, and darkness was upon the face of the deep; and the Spirit of God was moving over the face of the waters.

³And God said, "Let there be light"; and there was light. ⁴And God saw that the light was good; and God separated the light from the darkness. ⁵God called the light Day, and the darkness he called Night. And there was evening and there was morning, one day.

⁶And God said, "Let there be a firmament in the midst of the waters, and let it separate the waters from the waters." ⁷And God made the firmament and separated the waters which were under the firmament from the waters which were above the firmament. And it was so. ⁸And God called the firmament Heaven. And there was evening and there was morning, a second day.

⁹And God said, "Let the waters under the heavens be gathered together into one place, and let the dry land appear." And it was so. ¹⁰God called the dry land Earth, and the waters that were gathered together he called Seas. And God saw that it was good. ¹¹And God said, "Let the earth put forth vegetation, plants yielding seed, and fruit trees bearing fruit in which is their seed, each according to its kind, upon the earth." And it was so. ¹²The earth brought forth vegetation, plants yielding seed according to their own kinds, and trees bearing fruit in which is their seed, each according to its kind. And God saw that it was good. ¹³And there was evening and there was morning, a third day. . . .

2 ¹Thus the heavens and the earth were finished, and all the host of them. ²And on the seventh day God finished his work which he had done, and he rested on the seventh day from all his work which he had done. ³So God blessed the seventh day and hallowed it, because on it God rested from all his work which he had done in creation.

God or Gods?

Genesis may seem like a strange text. Words and phrases are frequently repeated. There are "days" before the sun was even created! What's going on?

In the ancient Near East, there were many myths about the gods and Creation. In one famous myth, Creation happened through a violent, chaotic struggle. One of the gods was murdered, and out of her corpse, the earth was created. Humans were created from the blood of another murdered god. Humans were created to be the slaves of the gods.

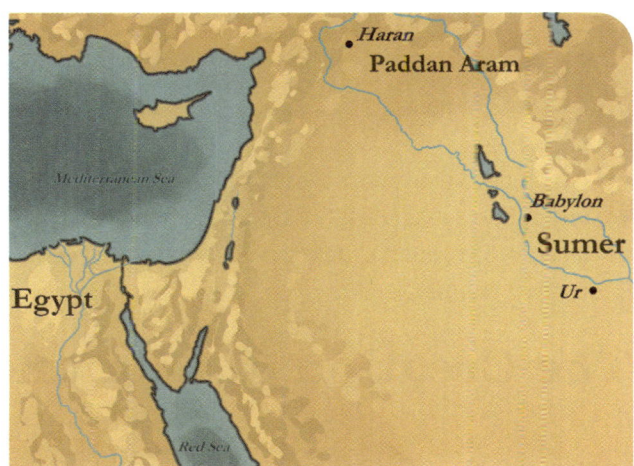

Genesis presents a very different picture. There are not *many* gods, just God. God did not create through violence but freely and directly through a peaceful command. God is good, and everything God creates is good. By contrast, the gods of ancient pagan mythology were evil, murderous, and enslavers.

The repetition in Genesis 1 draws our attention to the *differences* between Genesis and these myths. For example, "and God said" is repeated to remind us there is only one God doing everything. There are not *many* gods. The repeated line "and it was good" teaches us that God and everything God creates is good. God is *unlike* the gods of ancient pagan myth.

We begin to see "what's going on" in Genesis. One of the goals of the inspired human author of Genesis was to write against the myths of the gods. Genesis wants to teach the truth about God's creation of the world.

The Seven Days

God created everything ex nihilo, a Latin expression meaning "out of nothing." The universe was brought from not existing into existence by God. When God created the universe, the problem was that it was "without form and void" (Gen 1:2). In the first three days, God gave *form* to the "formlessness." He created light and darkness, the skies and seas, dry land and vegetation. In the next three days, God *filled* the "void." The light and darkness were populated by the sun and moon. The sky, sea, and land were filled with various creatures. Day 7 is unique because it has no end. There is no "evening" and "morning." On this day, God rests.

When the human author wrote about "seven days" of Creation, he was not likely talking about seven 24-hour periods. He was using symbolic and poetic language to make a point. In Scripture, the number seven is connected to the biblical idea of a covenant. By saying the act of Creation took place over *seven* days, the human author was using poetic language to teach us an important truth: God created us to form *a covenant* with us.

A covenant is an agreement between God and humans that forms a sacred bond. Think of a covenant bond like becoming part of a family. A person who is not blood-related can become part of a family either through adoption or marriage. Like an adoption or marriage, a covenant is an agreement where humans become part of God's family.

God created us to be members of the divine family, to be his adopted sons and daughters. We are created to share in God's own life. We are *not* made to be slaves of the gods, as the pagan myths say. God's rest on the "seventh day" symbolizes eternal life. The seventh day has no end because eternal life in God has no end.

"Let Us Make Man in Our Image"

We now turn to Genesis' account of the creation of man. "Man" here means both male and female human beings. We were God's last creation. God saved the best for last. While God declared all things he created "good," he declared the creation of man to be *very* good (emphasis added). Unlike the rest of creation, man is made in God's own image.

The Creation of Humans

Gen 1:26-28, 31

1 ²⁶Then God said, "Let us make man in our image, after our likeness; and let them have dominion over the fish of the sea, and over the birds of the air, and over the cattle, and over all the earth, and over every creeping thing that creeps upon the earth." ²⁷So God created man in his own image, in the image of God he created him; male and female he created them. ²⁸And God blessed them, and God said to them, "Be fruitful and multiply, and fill the earth and subdue it; and have dominion over the fish of the sea and over the birds of the air and over every living thing that moves upon the earth." . . . ³¹And God saw everything that he had made, and behold, it was very good. And there was evening and there was morning, a sixth day.

Gen 2:7-9, 15-25

2 ⁷Then the LORD God formed man of dust from the ground, and breathed into his nostrils the breath of life; and man became a living soul. ⁸And the LORD God planted a garden in Eden, in the east; and there he put the man whom he had formed. ⁹And out of the ground the LORD God made to grow every tree that is pleasant to the sight and good for food, the tree of life also in the midst of the garden, and the tree of the knowledge of good and evil. . . .

¹⁵The LORD God took the man and put him in the garden of Eden to till it and keep it. ¹⁶And the LORD God commanded the man, saying, "You may freely eat of every tree of the garden; ¹⁷but of the tree of the knowledge of good and evil you shall not eat, for in the day that you eat of it you shall die."

¹⁸Then the LORD God said, "It is not good that the man should be alone; I will make him a helper fit for him." ¹⁹So out of the ground the LORD God formed every beast of the field and every bird of the air, and brought them to the man to see what he would call them; and whatever the man called every living creature, that was its name. ²⁰The man gave names to all cattle, and to the birds of the air, and to every beast of the field; but for the man there was not found a helper fit for him. ²¹So the LORD God caused a deep sleep to fall upon the man, and while he slept took one of his ribs and closed up its place with flesh; ²²and the rib which the LORD God had taken from the man he made into a woman and brought her to the man. ²³Then the man said,

"This at last is bone of my bones
 and flesh of my flesh;
she shall be called Woman,
 because she was taken out of Man."

²⁴Therefore a man leaves his father and his mother and clings to his wife, and they become one flesh. ²⁵And the man and his wife were both naked, and were not ashamed.

The Image of God

God said, "Let us make man in our image" (Gen 1:26). Why did the one true God refer to himself using the plural "us"? One view is that this hints at the Blessed Trinity. Within the oneness of God are *three* Divine Persons: Father, Son, and Holy Spirit. Though Creation is commonly thought of as the work of God the Father, *all three* Divine Persons together created the universe and man.

In some ancient myths, kings were considered "in the image" of the gods and "sons" of the gods. Once again, Genesis goes against these pagan myths. *All* human persons are made in the *image of God*. We are all kings and queens of creation, not just the elite few. We are all called to be God's adopted children. Being made in God's image reveals important truths about who we are. The following table provides a summary of some of these truths:

Because we are made in God's image . . .

. . . we are, in a sense, like God.
- We share with God certain abilities: the ability to reason, to act freely, and to love.
- We have these abilities because of the soul God breathes into each of us (see Gen 2:7).

. . . we are created to share in God's own divine life.

. . . we are kings and queens of creation.
- God gave Adam and Eve "dominion" over all creation (Gen 1:26). Humans are to imitate God's loving care of creation.

"Male and Female He Created Them"

As we read above, both men and women are created in God's image. Men and women are equal in worth. When Eve was created, Adam declared, "This at last is bone of my bones and flesh of my flesh" (Gen 2:23). Adam viewed his wife as an equal. He saw they were made for each other.

God intentionally created us male and female. Being male or female is an unchangeable aspect of our identity. Genesis teaches us that our gender and identity are not something we *create* but something we *receive* from our wise and loving Creator.

The Creation account in Genesis ends with a statement about marriage. Genesis is clear that marriage is not a human invention. God created marriage when he created man and woman for each other. It is through the "one-flesh" union between a man and a woman that new life is formed. Marriage allows humans to fulfill God's command to "be fruitful and multiply, and fill the earth and subdue it" (Gen 1:28).

Chapter 6 Summary

1. God created the world out of nothing by his own power.

2. God entered a covenant with mankind to share his divine life with us.

3. Human persons are made in God's image as male and female.

Genesis and Science

Think about the last time you visited a library. What sections did you visit? History? Poetry? Literature? It makes sense that we categorize different kinds of books. We know that different books are written for different *purposes*. For example, some books are written to tell us about history, and others to express beautiful poetry. So, to what section does the Bible belong? History? Poetry? Literature?

This is a trick question! The Bible does not belong in any *single* place in a library. In a way, the Bible *is* a library! The entire Bible was inspired by God. God revealed divine truth through many different human authors over a long period of time. These human authors wrote for *different purposes*. For example, sometimes, the human author wrote to record historical events as they happened. Sometimes, the human author wrote beautiful poetry to praise God. Sometimes, the human author wrote about real events *using* poetry.

Genesis 1–2 would be a good example of this last case. In Genesis 1–2, the human author is teaching us about real events: God *did* create the whole universe; there really *was* a first human couple; everything God created really *was* good. Yet the human author teaches us these things *using poetic and symbolic language*. For example, when the author said God created in "seven days," he likely did not mean seven 24-hour periods. "Seven days" is a poetic way of teaching us that God created humans to make us part of his family.

When we pick up the Bible, it is helpful to have some understanding of *the sort of text* we are reading and *the purposes* the human author had in writing it. Without this understanding, we will probably misinterpret what we are reading!

For example, some people read about the "seven days" of Creation and say, "Doesn't science theorize that it took *millions* of years for humans to evolve from their ancestors? Didn't it take *billions* of years for the universe to form? Scripture is just wrong!"

A person who says this has misunderstood *what sort of text* they are reading. They are reading Genesis 1–2 as if it were a purely historical record or some kind of early science textbook. The human author of Genesis 1–2 *was* teaching us about real events. But he did so using poetic language. He was not trying to write a modern history book or a science textbook.

Scripture is not always easy to understand. There are many reasons for this, including the following:

1. Scripture was written a long time ago in several different ancient languages.
2. Scripture was written by people living in cultures very different from our own.
3. Scripture used styles of writing that are unfamiliar to many modern readers.

As Catholics, we believe that if Scripture is properly understood, it will never go against scientific truth. The reason is that all truth—whether from Scripture or science—comes from God.

Suppose someone handed you a random book written in English that you had never read before. What are some things you would do to try to figure out *what sort of text* you have been given?

_____

_____

_____

_____

What do you think are some things a person would have to study if he wanted to be good at interpreting and understanding the Bible?

_____

_____

_____

Let Us Pray—Psalm 8

In Psalm 8, the psalmist reflects on the vastness of the universe and cannot help but feel small and insignificant by comparison. Yet he marvels at how God views each of us as the high point of his creation. Let us join in the psalmist's wonder and praise of God our Creator as we pray Psalm 8.

Ps 8:1–9

8 ¹O Lord, our Lord,
   how majestic is your name in all the earth!
You whose glory above the heavens is chanted
   ²by the mouth of babes and infants,
you have founded a bulwark because of your foes,
   to still the enemy and the avenger.
³When I look at your heavens, the work of your fingers,
   the moon and the stars which you have established;
⁴what is man that you are mindful of him,
   and the son of man that you care for him?

⁵Yet you have made him little less than the angels,
   and you have crowned him with glory and honor.
⁶You have given him dominion over the works of your hands;
   you have put all things under his feet,
⁷all sheep and oxen,
   and also the beasts of the field,
⁸the birds of the air, and the fish of the sea,
   whatever passes along the paths of the sea.
⁹O Lord, our Lord,
   how majestic is your name in all the earth!

Chapter 6 Review:
Creator of Heaven and Earth

1. The universe was brought from not existing into existence by God. The term "ex _____" refers to this idea.

2. A _____ is an agreement between God and humans that forms a sacred bond.

3. Because we are made in God's image, we share certain abilities with God: _____, _____, _____, and the ability to love.

4. On Days 4–6, God filled the "_____."

5. Being male or female is an _____ aspect of our identity.

6. Humans are created to share in _____ divine life.

7. How is Genesis different from the pagan myths of the gods? Give two examples to support your answer.

_____

_____

_____

_____

_____

_____

_____

_____

The Dignity of the Human Person

Scripture and the Church teach that humans have immense dignity. The word "dignity" means "worth."

Human persons have so much worth because they are made in God's image. Genesis teaches that while we have physical bodies, we also have spiritual souls breathed into us by God. Part of us is not physical (i.e., our souls). It is our souls that especially make us like God. It is because we have souls that we can reason, act freely, and love. We are a unity of body *and soul.*

When it comes to physical things, we are used to estimating their worth and using them for our own purposes. For instance, we might buy a pair of running shoes worth seventy-five dollars to use in a track competition. However, the value of human persons cannot be reduced to any dollar amount. As the *Catechism* puts it, humans possess the dignity "of a person," *not* the dignity of a physical "something." We must not treat persons as we would physical objects that we use to fulfill our purposes.

Spend a few moments silently reflecting on this question: In your experience, where have you seen a person treated as an object rather than as a person with dignity?

Journal Reflection

What do you think is one thing in our culture that causes people to treat others as objects?

What is one practical thing a person can do to avoid treating another person as an object?

Catechism of the Catholic Church, 357

"Being in the image of God the human individual possesses the dignity of a person, who is not just something, but someone. He is capable of self-knowledge, of self-possession and of freely giving himself and entering into communion with other persons. And he is called by grace to a covenant with his Creator, to offer him a response of faith and love that no other creature can give in his stead."

Finding God in Creation

Read

We sometimes say that an artist "pours himself" into his art. Every great work of art reflects something of the artist who created it. The Book of Wisdom states,

> From the greatness and beauty of created things comes a corresponding perception of their Creator. (13:5)

God is like an artist, and the world is his art. We can catch a glimmer of God in the beauty of his creation.

It is easy to become disconnected from the natural world. One common way we become distracted from the beauty of the natural world and the world of real relationships is through an unhealthy attachment to the online world. The online world often gives us false impressions of reality. Consider social media, where photos are edited to give the impression of a perfect, flawless life. We also might begin to prefer interacting with people from the "safe" distance of our phones and computers rather than fostering real and fruitful relationships in person. Reconnecting with the natural world and real-life relationships can help us reconnect with God, the Divine Artist who created this beautiful world.

Reflect

Spend 5–10 minutes reflecting on the following:

- Do I spend time in nature on a regular basis? Have I ever experienced God in nature?
- Does the time I spend on social media make me feel better about myself? Does it bring me closer to God?
- Do I ever feel the urge to check my phone, even if I don't know why?

Pray

The Holy Spirit helps us pray and is the artisan of God's works. Pray the following:

> Come, Creator Spirit, visit the souls of your people; fill with grace from on high the hearts which you have created. Amen.

Act

Find a quiet place alone in nature. Let the beauty of nature draw you closer to its Creator. Pray for 5–10 minutes.

CHAPTER 7

"Through the Devil's Envy"

Words to Know

> *Original Sin*

> *sin*

Proclaiming the Good News

"As by one man's disobedience many were made sinners, so by one man's obedience many will be made righteous." —Romans 5:19

The Expulsion of Adam and Eve from Paradise, Benjamin West

"The Eyes of Both Were Opened"

God created a universe filled with good things. He created human beings in his own image and offered to share his own life with them. Yet Adam and Eve chose to reject God's love. Their friendship with God fell apart, and the world fell with them.

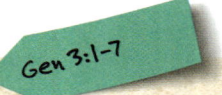
Gen 3:1-7

3 ¹Now the serpent was more subtle than any other wild creature that the LORD God had made. He said to the woman, "Did God say, 'You shall not eat of any tree of the garden'?" ²And the woman said to the serpent, "We may eat of the fruit of the trees of the garden; ³but God said, 'You shall not eat of the fruit of the tree which is in the midst of the garden, neither shall you touch it, lest you die.'" ⁴But the serpent said to the woman, "You will not die. ⁵For God knows that when you eat of it your eyes will be opened, and you will be like God, knowing good and evil." ⁶So when the woman saw that the tree was good for food, and that it was a delight to the eyes, and that the tree was to be desired to make one wise, she took of its fruit and ate; and she also gave some to her husband, and he ate. ⁷Then the eyes of both were opened, and they knew that they were naked; and they sewed fig leaves together and made themselves aprons.

The Fall

God commanded Adam and Eve not to eat from the Tree of the Knowledge of Good and Evil (see Gen 2:17). Instead of obeying, Adam and Eve sinned (see Gen 3:6). *Sin* is a free choice to disobey God's law and reject his love. Adam and Eve's sin is known as the Original Sin.

"The serpent" is elsewhere called "Satan" or "the Devil." Satan was an angel who rebelled against God. Why? The Old Testament Book of Wisdom says it was because of *envy*: "Through the devil's envy death entered the world" (2:24). Satan was envious because God gave humans a high place in creation. He and his followers fell away from God. Their goal has always been to lead humans to fall away too.

Adam and Eve's sin began with *distrust*. God told Adam and Eve that if they ate from the forbidden tree, they would die (see Gen 2:17). Satan tempted them to doubt God's words. They believed his lie. Then they gave in to pride. They were not satisfied with being made in God's image. Even sharing in God's own life was not enough. They wanted to "be like God" (Gen 3:5) on their own terms, apart from God's plan. They wanted *to take God's place*. They wanted to determine *for themselves* what was right and wrong.

Every sin we commit is like this first sin of Adam and Eve. In every sin, we distrust God. We believe his law will not make us happy. Out of pride, we do what *we* want instead of what *God* wants.

After the Fall

Gen 3:8-15

3 ⁸And they heard the sound of the LORD God walking in the garden in the cool of the day, and the man and his wife hid themselves from the presence of the LORD God among the trees of the garden. ⁹But the LORD God called to the man, and said to him, "Where are you?" ¹⁰And he said, "I heard the sound of you in the garden, and I was afraid, because I was naked; and I hid myself." ¹¹He said, "Who told you that you were naked? Have you eaten of the tree of which I commanded you not to eat?" ¹²The man said, "The woman whom you gave to be with me, she gave me fruit of the tree, and I ate." ¹³Then the LORD God said to the woman, "What is this that you have done?" The woman said, "The serpent beguiled me, and I ate." ¹⁴The LORD God said to the serpent,

"Because you have done this,
  cursed are you above all cattle,
  and above all wild animals;
upon your belly you shall go,
  and dust you shall eat
  all the days of your life.
¹⁵I will put enmity between you and the woman,
  and between your seed and her seed;
he shall bruise your head,
  and you shall bruise his heel."

Sin causes wounds. Adam and Eve's sin, called the Original Sin, wounded their relationship with God. They became *afraid* of God. Their loving friendship with God was lost. They lost God's grace in their souls. The Church calls this wound the loss of original holiness.

The loss of original holiness led to three other wounds. First, Adam and Eve experienced wounds *within themselves*. For example, they felt shame. Second, sin wounded their relationship *with each other*. Notice how Adam *blamed* Eve for their situation. Third, their relationship *with creation* was wounded. God said to Adam, "Cursed is the ground because of you" (Gen 3:17). Adam and Eve no longer lived in harmony with themselves, each other, and creation. The Church calls this disharmony the loss of original justice.

The Church uses the term "Original Sin" to describe two things: (1) the first sin of Adam and Eve, and (2) the effects their sin has on us. By committing the Original Sin, Adam and Eve fell from grace. They lost the gifts of original holiness and original justice. We inherit their wounded human nature. We now experience the following effects because of our wounded human nature:

- **Death**—Humans now experience death.
- **Concupiscence**—Humans feel *inclined*, or *drawn*, to do what we know is wrong.
- **Weakened will**—It is harder to choose what is truly good.
- **Darkened intellect**—It is harder to know what is truly good.

Despite Adam and Eve's actions, God did not stop loving humanity. In Genesis 3:15, the Good News of God's plan to save us from sin was foreshadowed. God said that Eve's "seed" would bruise Satan's head. That "seed," or descendant, of Eve is Jesus. Jesus became the New Adam. He conquered Satan and the forces of sin and death.

Vanitas Still Life with a Tulip, Skull and Hour-Glass, Philippe de Champaigne

"It Grieved Him to His Heart"

After Adam and Eve were exiled from the garden, sin continued to increase and spread over the earth. We see this in the passages on Cain and Abel, Noah, and the Tower of Babel.

Cain and Abel

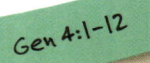
Gen 4:1-12

4 ¹Now Adam knew Eve his wife, and she conceived and bore Cain . . . ²And again, she bore his brother Abel . . . ³In the course of time Cain brought to the LORD an offering of the fruit of the ground, ⁴and Abel brought of the firstlings of his flock and of their fat portions. And the LORD had regard for Abel and his offering, ⁵but for Cain and his offering he had no regard. So Cain was very angry, and his countenance fell. ⁶The LORD said to Cain, "Why are you angry, and why has your countenance fallen? ⁷If you do well, will you not be accepted? And if you do not do well, sin is lurking at the door; its desire is for you, but you must master it." ⁸Cain said to Abel his brother, "Let us go out to the field." And when they were in the field, Cain rose up against his brother Abel, and killed him. ⁹Then the LORD said to Cain, "Where is Abel your brother?" He said, "I do not know; am I my brother's keeper?" ¹⁰And the LORD said, "What have you done? The voice of your brother's blood is crying to me from the ground. ¹¹And now you are cursed from the ground, which has opened its mouth to receive your brother's blood from your hand. ¹²When you till the ground, it shall no longer yield to you its strength; you shall be a fugitive and a wanderer on the earth."

God accepted Abel's offering but not Cain's (see Gen 4:4–5). Why? The value of an offering lies not in *what* is given but *in the love with which it is given*. Abel loved God. Cain's heart was far from God. It is not *what* Cain offered that was the problem. *Cain* was the problem: "For *Cain* and his offering he had no regard" (Gen 4:5; emphasis added).

Adam and Eve's Original Sin caused wounds. Cain's personal sins *deepened* these wounds in him. Cain suffered the consequences of his own evil choice: he had to wander the earth as a fugitive. Yet God did not abandon him. He protected Cain from others (see Gen 4:15). God wanted Cain to turn from evil and return to him. God still loved Cain.

Noah and the Flood

Gen 6:5-6, 8, 13-14, 18-19, 22

6 ⁵The LORD saw that the wickedness of man was great in the earth, and that every imagination of the thoughts of his heart was only evil continually . . . . ⁶and it grieved him to his heart . . . . ⁸But Noah found favor in the eyes of the LORD . . . . ¹³And God said to Noah, "I have determined to make an end of all flesh; for the earth is filled with violence through them; behold, I will destroy them with the earth. ¹⁴Make yourself an ark of gopher wood . . . . ¹⁸But I will establish my covenant with you; and you shall come into the ark, you, your sons, your wife, and your sons' wives with you. ¹⁹And of every living thing of all flesh, you shall bring two of every sort into the ark, to keep them alive with you; they shall be male and female . . . . ²²Noah did this; he did all that God commanded him.

In the generations after Cain, sin and division quickly spread. Human hearts desired "evil continually" (Gen 6:5). The earth was filled with murderous "Cains." The exception was a righteous man named Noah.

Notice how God reacted to all this evil: "It grieved him to his heart" (Gen 6:6). God loves humanity. His heart ached because of the evil and violence he saw on earth. God flooded the earth with water to end this wickedness and violence.

The Flood brought about a new creation. God wanted humans to fill the earth once again. After the Flood, God repeated the command he gave to Adam and Eve: "Be fruitful and multiply" (Gen 9:1). God said to Noah, "I will establish my covenant with you" (Gen 6:18). In this covenant, God promised never to flood the whole world again. God gave the rainbow as a sign of this covenant. Despite human sin, God would be merciful and continue to love humanity.

The Tower of Babel

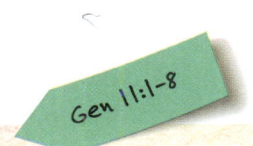
Gen 11:1-8

11 ¹Now the whole earth had one language and few words. ²And as men migrated from the east, they found a plain in the land of Shinar and settled there. ³And they said . . . ⁴"Come, let us build ourselves a city, and a tower with its top in the heavens, and let us make a name for ourselves, lest we be scattered abroad upon the face of the whole earth." ⁵And the LORD came down to see the city and the tower, which the sons of men had built. ⁶And the LORD said, "Behold, they are one people, and they have all one language; and this is only the beginning of what they will do; and nothing that they propose to do will now be impossible for them. ⁷Come, let us go down, and there confuse their language, that they may not understand one another's speech." ⁸So the LORD scattered them abroad from there over the face of all the earth, and they left off building the city.

A few generations after Noah, people built a tower "with its top in the heavens" to "make a name" for themselves (Gen 11:4). They wanted what Adam and Eve wanted: *to take God's place*. They wanted to build a city apart from God.

God knew their pride and ambition would lead them to destruction. He responded by confusing their language and scattering them. This prevented humans from cooperating to carry out their evil plans. Yet God's solution was only temporary. Because he loves humanity, his plan is to reunite all nations with himself.

Tower of Babel,
Pieter Brueghel the Elder

Chapter 7 Summary

1. Through their distrust of God and their pride, Adam and Eve sinned against God. Every sin we commit is like the sin of Adam and Eve.

2. Adam and Eve's sin caused wounds: the loss of original holiness and original justice. We inherit this loss of original holiness and original justice.

3. God continually seeks to draw sinners back to himself because he loves us.

The Sin of Pride

The people of Babel made a tower "with its top in the heavens" so they could "make a name" for themselves (Gen 11:4). We, too, can seek to tower over others and even over God. We call this the sin of *pride*.

Saint Thomas Aquinas defined pride as the effort *to be above what we are*. A person who is smart and knows she is smart is not committing the sin of pride. She is being truthful about who she is. A person who is a star basketball player and admits he is good at basketball is not being prideful. He is being honest about who he is. Pride is a *false* view of ourselves. Pride is when we see ourselves as *higher or better* than we really are.

A common form of pride is when we exaggerate our talents. For instance, a person might try to act smarter than she is to impress someone. Or a person might refuse to admit his mistakes to appear more perfect than he really is.

Another way pride sneaks into our lives is when we become too focused on ourselves or our accomplishments. Examples of this include the following:

- Wanting to be the center of attention
- Seeking popularity or praise for ourselves
- Gossiping and bullying to feel better about ourselves
- Thinking we do not need to learn from others
- Bragging

In these situations, we make ourselves or our talents too important, often at the expense of the needs and feelings of others.

A third form of pride is when we do not recognize God in our lives. We might treat the talents we have as totally our own, rather than as gifts from God. We might neglect our prayer lives, thinking we do not really need God's help. The truth is that *everything* we possess is a gift from God. At *every* moment, we depend upon God. To act as if we do not need God is to have a *false* view of ourselves.

The solution to pride is the virtue of humility. Humility is a truthful view of ourselves. A humble person does not exaggerate or downplay her talents. She recognizes God as the source of her gifts. Nor is she too preoccupied with herself. A humble person tends to "forget" himself. He is much more focused on God and other people.

Where do I see the sin of pride in my life?

_____
_____
_____
_____

What is a specific way I can become more "self-forgetful" and focused on God and others?

_____
_____
_____

Let Us Pray—Psalm 51

In Psalm 51, the psalmist reflects on his own sins. But he also recalls God's love and mercy, reminding us that God is always willing to forgive us if we turn to him with a humble heart.

Ps 51:3-6, 12-13, 17

51 ³For I know my transgressions,
and my sin is ever before me.
⁴Against you, you only, have I sinned,
and done that which is evil in your sight,
so that you are justified in your sentence
and blameless in your judgment.
⁵Behold, I was brought forth in iniquity,
and in sin did my mother conceive me.
⁶Behold, you desire truth in the inward being;
therefore teach me wisdom in my secret heart. . . .

¹²Restore to me the joy of your salvation,
and uphold me with a willing spirit.
¹³Then I will teach transgressors your ways,
and sinners will return to you. . . .
¹⁷The sacrifice acceptable to God is a broken spirit;
a broken and contrite heart,
O God, you
will not
despise.

Chapter 7 Review:
"Through the Devil's Envy"

1. _____ is a free choice to disobey God's law and reject his love.

2. Adam and Eve's sin wounded their relationship with God. What are the three wounds that Adam and Eve experienced from the loss of original justice? _____
   _____
   _____

3. What term does the Church use to describe the first sin of Adam and Eve and the effects their sin has on us? _____

4. Who is the serpent? _____

5. What was the forbidden tree that Adam and Eve ate from called? _____
   _____

6. *Every sin we commit is like the sin of Adam and Eve.* In every sin, we _____ God. We believe his law will not make us _____. Out of _____, we do what we want instead of what *God* wants.

7. God does not abandon us when we sin. He seeks to draw us back to himself because he loves us. Give an example of God's love for sinners using one of the Scripture passages in this chapter.

   _____

   _____

   _____

   _____

   _____

Sin, Punishment, and God's Mercy

One of the themes in this chapter's readings from Genesis is *sin and punishment*. For instance, Adam and Eve sinned and their punishment was exile from the garden. Cain sinned and his punishment was wandering the earth as a fugitive.

There is another theme in our readings that is easier to miss: *punishment and mercy*. God punishes because he is *merciful*. How was Adam and Eve's punishment of exile merciful? The answer is in Genesis 3:22–23:

Gen 3:22-23

> **3** ²²Then the LORD God said, "Behold, the man has become like one of us, knowing good and evil; and now, lest he put forth his hand and take also of the tree of life, and eat, and live for ever"— ²³therefore the LORD God sent him forth from the garden of Eden, to till the ground from which he was taken.

Adam and Eve rebelled against God. If they were to then eat from the Tree of Life—the tree that gives eternal life—they would *forever* be in a state of rebellion from God. Eternal separation from God is the worst possible fate. It means forever losing the source of all goodness and happiness: God.

So, God removed Adam and Eve from the garden. They no longer had access to the Tree of Life. They would now experience death. But it also meant they were not doomed to be rebels forever. They could *change their ways* before they died. God's punishment of exile was itself a mercy.

God created us so that we might share in his own life. No matter how much we sin, God does not stop trying to reunite us with himself. Yet God will not force us into a relationship with him. We are free to reject God's mercy.

Thankfully, God gives us our entire lives to accept his mercy and turn away from our sins. Yet we never know when God will call us from this life. We should turn to God today and live in the true happiness and peace for which we were created.

Journal Reflection

Is there something keeping you from seeking God's mercy in the Sacrament of Reconciliation?

> "Have I any pleasure in the death of the wicked, says the Lord GOD, and not rather that he should turn from his way and live?"
> —Ezekiel 18:23

> "[God] desires all men to be saved and to come to the knowledge of the truth."
> —1 Timothy 2:4

Loving Father or Divine Dictator?

Read

Jesus once said, "Amen, I say to you, unless you turn and become like little children, you will never enter the kingdom of heaven" (Mt 18:3). Have you ever seen a little kid play with his parents? He will wildly leap into his mom's or dad's arms without hesitation. The thought that he could be dropped is not even on his mind.

Adam and Eve had a childlike trust in God. God was their Father, and they were his beloved children. They loved God and trusted in his commandments. Why? Because God was their loving Father and would never command something that was bad for them.

The Devil attacked this childlike trust by introducing doubt into their minds. For the Devil said to Eve, "You will not die. For God knows that when you eat of it your eyes will be opened, and you will be like God, knowing good and evil" (Gen 3:4–5).

As Adam and Eve gave in to their doubts, their entire view of God and God's commands changed. They no longer saw God as the loving Father who commanded things for their own good. God was now a Divine Dictator trying *to control* them and to prevent them from stealing *his power*. A relationship of love was replaced by a relationship of power and fear. Adam and Eve were ashamed of their sin; they became afraid of God and tried to hide from him (see Gen 3:10).

Jesus called the Devil the Father of Lies (see Jn 8:44). The first lie from the Father of Lies was to tempt Adam and Eve into thinking God is not a loving Father.

Reflect

Spend 5–10 minutes reflecting on the following:

- Is my relationship with God based on *fear*? Do I worry that God cannot really love me? Or he will not forgive me? Do I worry that God is out to get me if I mess up?

- Do I trust in God's loving plan for me, even when I am suffering or going through difficulty?

- Do I view God's commandments and the teachings of the Church more as restrictions on my freedom or more as loving commands to keep me safe and happy?

Pray

Pray the Our Father.

Act

Begin and end each day this week by saying this simple prayer: "Jesus, I trust in you."

CHAPTER 8
The God of Abraham, Isaac, and Jacob

Words to Know

> Chosen People

> patriarch

> twelve tribes of Israel

Proclaiming the Good News

"The LORD said to Abram, . . . in you all the families of the earth shall be blessed." —Genesis 12:1, 3

Continuing the Story of Salvation

List key events that show that Adam and Eve's sin led to more sins in the human family.

_____

_____

_____

_____

_____

_____

_____

Abraham's Journey from Ur to Canaan, József Molnár

God's Covenant with Abraham

The Call of Abram

Following the Tower of Babel, mankind was scattered and divided. But God had a plan to reconcile the world with himself. God chose one man and his family line to continue his plan. He made a covenant to form a sacred bond with a man named Abram. Through this covenant, God grew his family and formed his Chosen People.

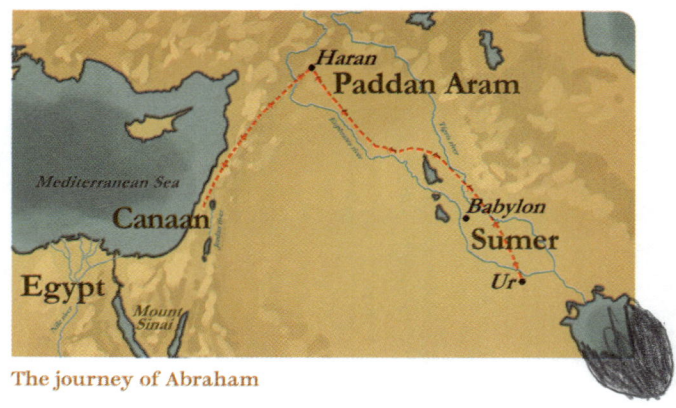

The journey of Abraham

Gen 12:1-4

12 ¹Now the LORD said to Abram, "Go from your country and your kindred and your father's house to the land that I will show you. ²And I will make of you a great nation, and I will bless you, and make your name great, so that you will be a blessing. ³I will bless those who bless you, and him who curses you I will curse; and in you all the families of the earth shall be blessed." ⁴So Abram went, as the LORD had told him; and Lot went with him. Abram was seventy-five years old when he departed from Haran.

Abram was comfortable in his homeland of Ur. But then God called Abram. He told Abram to leave his home, belongings, and family. Imagine how difficult this would be! But Abram responded with faith and obedience. To obey in faith is to accept God's Word as truth and to live according to his will.

In the Garden of Eden, we saw Adam's example of disobedience. But now, Abram provides an example of obedience in faith. Abram obeyed God's will, even when he was called to leave his homeland, possessions, and family behind. He set out, not knowing where he was going. But Abram faithfully believed God would care for him.

As part of his covenant with Abram, God made a threefold promise to him:

1. **God promised Abram, "I will make of you a great nation" (Gen 12:2).** God called Abram to leave his homeland. But God promised to provide the Promised Land to Abram and his descendants. They grew into a great nation in this fruitful land that flowed with "milk and honey" (Ex 3:8).

2. **God promised Abram, "I will bless you, and make your name great" (Gen 12:2).** God promised to make Abram's family line into a royal dynasty of kings who would rule over God's people. From Abram's line came the great kings of God's Chosen People, including King David, King Solomon, and eventually Jesus Christ, the King of God's eternal kingdom.

3. **God promised Abram, "You will be a blessing" (Gen 12:2).** God called Abram to leave his family behind. But God promised Abram many descendants. He changed Abram's name to Abraham, meaning "father of a multitude" (Gen 17:5). God's *Chosen People* are Abraham and his descendants. Through Abraham's descendants, God sent the Savior, his Son, Jesus. God offers salvation to all people through Jesus Christ, a descendant of Abraham.

Abraham became the father of God's people through his faith and obedience. We honor Abraham as the "father of all who believe" (Rom 4:11). Abraham is our father in faith because he modeled how to listen to God's Word and follow his will.

A Son Promised and Born

God promised Abraham descendants as numerous as the stars (see Gen 15:5). But Abraham and his wife, Sarah, did not have any children, and both were past the age of having children. Despite this challenge, God miraculously kept his promise. God came to Abraham and Sarah and promised them a son:

> **18** ¹And the LORD appeared to [Abraham] by the Oaks of Mamre, as he sat at the door of his tent in the heat of the day. ²He lifted up his eyes and looked, and behold, three men stood in front of him.... ⁹They said to him, "Where is Sarah your wife?" And he said, "She is in the tent." ¹⁰The LORD said, "I will surely return to you in the spring, and Sarah your wife shall have a son." And Sarah was listening at the tent door behind him. ¹¹Now Abraham and Sarah were old, advanced in age;... ¹²So Sarah laughed to herself, saying, "After I have grown old, and my husband is old, shall I have pleasure?" ¹³The LORD said to Abraham, "Why did Sarah laugh, and say, 'Shall I indeed bear a child, now that I am old?' ¹⁴Is anything too hard for the LORD? At the appointed time I will return to you, in the spring, and Sarah shall have a son."

Sarah laughed at God's plan! She was barren, so she thought it was impossible for God to bless them with a child. She failed to believe that all things are possible for God. But God remained faithful to his promise. Sarah conceived and gave birth to a son, whom they named Isaac, which means "he laughs" (see Gen 21:1–6).

God kept his promise to bless Abraham and Sarah with a son. In Scripture, we see that God is consistently faithful to his promises. As God's people, we should imitate Abraham and others in Scripture who listened to God's Word, accepted it, and lived according to his will.

But what does God promise to us? He promises to transform us with his grace and to satisfy completely our desires for truth, love, and happiness. We may sometimes think that God is not faithful to these promises, but this is untrue. God is always faithful, as we see in Scripture. The God of Abraham is truly worthy of our faith and belief.

God's Chosen People

Jacob and Esau

After Abraham's death, God continued to grow his Chosen People through Isaac. Isaac married a woman named Rebekah, and she conceived twins. The two boys struggled together in her womb. God explained to her that each boy would lead a nation and that these nations would be divided.

God promised Rebekah that the younger brother's nation would rule the older brother's nation. But Rebekah did not believe that God would keep this promise.

In those times, it was customary for a father to bless his firstborn son. The son who received this blessing would rule over his siblings. When Isaac was near death, he called for Esau, the firstborn, to give him this blessing. Instead of believing that God would keep his promise to have Jacob rule over his older brother, Rebekah grasped this opportunity. She helped Jacob trick his father into giving him the firstborn blessing instead.

Rebekah sent Jacob into Isaac's room instead of Esau. Isaac, being almost blind, blessed Jacob. Esau found out about the trick and was angry with Jacob. Jacob had to flee for his life from his brother. Jacob fled and started his family in a foreign land.

While in this foreign land, Jacob had a mysterious encounter with an angel of God. One night, an angel came to Jacob as a man and wrestled with him until morning. In the morning, Jacob asked the man for a blessing. The man blessed him and told him he would be called Israel from then on, which means "he who strives with God" (see Gen 32:28).

Joseph Cast into the Well by His Brothers, Anonymous

Joseph's Rise to Power in Egypt

Through Abraham's descendant Israel, God continued to keep his promise to bless all the families of the earth. Israel had twelve sons: Reuben, Simeon, Levi, Judah, Dan, Naphtali, Gad, Asher, Issachar, Zebulun, Joseph, and Benjamin. Israel's sons and their families became the *twelve tribes of Israel*.

Israel loved Joseph more than any of his other children. Sadly, Joseph's eleven brothers grew jealous of Israel's love for him. His brother Judah convinced the other brothers to sell Joseph into slavery for twenty pieces of silver. Joseph was forced to go to Egypt. The brothers let their father, Israel, think wild animals killed Joseph.

God remained with Joseph throughout his life. God communicated his will and plan to Joseph through dreams. Because Joseph was open to God, God enabled Joseph to interpret these dreams. While imprisoned in Egypt, Joseph interpreted Pharaoh's dreams that revealed an upcoming famine. Joseph helped Pharaoh devise a plan to store food in preparation for the famine. As part of God's plan, Pharaoh raised Joseph to a position of power to reward him for saving Egypt. Pharoah made Joseph responsible for distributing food to the people during the famine.

Israel Brings His Family to Egypt

Israel and his family were hungry and suffering during the famine. He sent his sons, except the youngest, Benjamin, to Egypt to purchase food. Upon arriving, the brothers came upon Joseph but did not recognize him. Joseph recognized them but pretended not to.

Instead, Joseph accused them of being spies plotting Egypt's destruction. He demanded that one brother, Simeon, remain imprisoned in Egypt while the other brothers returned to Canaan and brought their youngest brother, Benjamin, to Egypt. Joseph told them that if they did this, they would prove themselves trustworthy.

Joseph filled his brothers' bags with grain and sent them home. His brothers returned and told their father what had happened. They told Israel that they must take Benjamin to Egypt. But Israel refused. He had already lost one son (Joseph), while another was imprisoned in Egypt (Simeon). He did not want to lose yet another son!

The famine worsened, and their food ran out again. Judah promised his father that he would take care of Benjamin to the point of offering his own life to protect him. Israel reluctantly agreed and sent them back to Egypt with Benjamin.

When they arrived, they bowed down to Joseph, who pretended not to recognize his brothers again. When it came time for them to return to Canaan, Joseph secretly had a silver cup placed in Benjamin's sack. While the brothers were a short distance from the city, Joseph had their bags searched for his missing cup. Joseph found the cup and accused them of stealing! As punishment, he commanded that Benjamin remain in Egypt as a slave.

Judah, the same brother who long ago convinced the others to sell Joseph into slavery, stepped forward and pleaded with Joseph. Judah offered to take Benjamin's place as a slave. Amazed, Joseph tearfully responded:

Gen 45:4-5, 8, 15; 50:18-20

45 ⁴"I am your brother, Joseph, whom you sold into Egypt. ⁵And now do not be distressed, or angry with yourselves, because you sold me here; for God sent me before you to preserve life. . . . ⁸So it was not you who sent me here, but God . . . ¹⁵And he kissed all his brothers and wept upon them. . . .

50 ¹⁸His brothers also came and fell down before him, and said, "Behold, we are your servants." ¹⁹But Joseph said to them, "Fear not, for am I in the place of God? ²⁰As for you, you meant evil against me; but God meant it for good, to bring it about that many people should be kept alive, as they are today."

Joseph faithfully believed in God's providence. Joseph saw that God allowed him to be sold into slavery so that he would become influential in Egypt. Through Joseph's influence, God saved many people from starvation.

Like Joseph, we must learn to believe faithfully in God's providence no matter what evils we experience. Just as God remained with Joseph in every situation, God is with us in every difficulty and evil we experience. He strengthens us with his grace to believe and obey him. While we may not see how God will bring good out of the evil we experience, we must still learn to believe in him and his plan.

Through Joseph's faithfulness, God continued to keep his promise to make Abraham's descendants a blessing to the nations. God saved his Chosen People, and many others, from the famine. After Joseph reconciled with his brothers, Israel brought his family to Egypt.

God's Faithfulness to the Patriarchs

In his providence, God remained faithful to his promises in his covenant with Abraham. God made Abraham, Isaac, and Jacob (Israel) into the *patriarchs*, or the fathers and rulers, of his Chosen People. God called his Chosen People to prepare the world for when he would invite all people and nations into his family, the Church. In Jesus Christ and the Church, God fulfilled his promise to bless the entire world through Abraham's descendants.

Chapter 8 Summary

1. God chose Abraham and made a covenant with a threefold promise to him.

2. Abraham, Isaac, and Jacob (Israel) became the patriarchs of God's Chosen People.

3. In Jesus Christ and the Church, God fulfilled his promise to make Abraham's descendants a source of blessing for all families of the earth.

Faithfulness and Obedience

Read the passages below from the Book of Genesis and the Letter to the Hebrews and answer the questions.

Gen 15:1-6

15 ¹The word of the LORD came to Abram in a vision, "Fear not, Abram, I am your shield; your reward shall be very great." ²But Abram said, "O Lord GOD, what will you give me, for I continue childless, and the heir of my house is Eliezer of Damascus?" ³And Abram said, "Behold, you have given me no offspring; and a slave born in my house will be my heir." ⁴And behold, the word of the LORD came to him, "This man shall not be your heir; your own son shall be your heir." ⁵And he brought him outside and said, "Look toward heaven, and number the stars, if you are able to number them." Then he said to him, "So shall your descendants be." ⁶And he believed the LORD; and he reckoned it to him as righteousness.

In verse 5, God brought Abram outside and told Abram to count the stars. Abram's descendants would be as countless as the stars. At first glance, we may assume that this event happened at night, when the stars are visible. But later we read that the sun set after this occurred (see Gen 15:12). God told Abram to "look toward heaven, and number the stars" when no stars were visible. God called Abraham to believe in something that he could not see.

What do you think this detail reveals about Abraham's faithfulness to God?

_____

_____

Because of Abram's faithfulness, God changed his name to Abraham, meaning "father of a multitude." Abraham is known as our father in faith or the "father of all who believe." Saint Paul quoted Genesis 15:6 in his Letter to the Romans: "What does the Scripture say? 'Abraham believed God, and it was reckoned to him as righteousness'" (4:3). Righteousness signifies a right relationship with God. Abraham was brought into a right relationship (righteousness) with God through faith. He believed what God said was true and relied on it.

Detail from *Abraham*, Joseph Schonman

The Letter to the Hebrews also highlights Abraham's great faithfulness in obeying God.

Heb 11:8-9, 11-12, 17-19

11 ⁸By faith Abraham obeyed when he was called to go out to a place which he was to receive as an inheritance; and he went out, not knowing where he was to go. ⁹By faith he sojourned in the land of promise, as in a foreign land, living in tents with Isaac and Jacob, heirs with him of the same promise.... ¹¹By faith Sarah herself received power to conceive, even when she was past the age, since she considered him faithful who had promised. ¹²Therefore from one man, and him as good as dead, were born descendants as many as the stars of heaven and as the innumerable grains of sand by the seashore.... ¹⁷By faith Abraham, when he was tested, offered up Isaac, and he who had received the promises was ready to offer up his only-begotten son, ¹⁸of whom it was said, "Through Isaac shall your descendants be named." ¹⁹He considered that God was able to raise men even from the dead; hence he did receive him back and this was a symbol.

This passage from the Letter to the Hebrews focuses on three key moments in the life of Abraham that exemplify his faith. What are those three moments?

1. _____
2. _____
3. _____

Just as he called Abraham, God calls us to follow his will even when we don't always know where we are going. What are some things that God may be calling you to do in your life?

_____
_____

Like Abraham, we must believe that God will remain faithful to his promises. When have you struggled to believe in God's presence or his promises?

_____
_____

Like Abraham, we should be willing to sacrifice some good things that we care about. What are some good things that we offer as a sacrifice to God?

_____
_____

Let Us Pray—Psalm 77

As we pray with Psalm 77, we praise God for his mighty deeds in growing and caring for his Chosen People. May we learn to be always faithful to God, who also loves and cares for us.

Ps 77:1, 11-15

77 ¹I cry aloud to God,
 aloud to God, that he may hear me.
¹¹I will call to mind the deeds of the LORD;
 yes, I will remember your wonders of old.
¹²I will meditate on all your work,
 and muse on your mighty deeds.
¹³Your way, O God, is holy.
 What god is great like our God?
¹⁴You are the God who works wonders,
 who have manifested your might among the peoples.
¹⁵With your arm you redeemed your people,
 the sons of Jacob and Joseph.

Chapter 8 Review:
The God of Abraham, Isaac, and Jacob

1. God called a particular family line to be his Chosen People and to be the source of restoring man's relationship with him. Who were God's Chosen People?
   Abraham and his decendants

2. Who was the patriarch who had twelve sons whose families became twelve tribes? _Israel_

3. What is a patriarch? _Fathers and rulers_

4. Who are the patriarchs of God's people in the Old Testament?
   Abraham, Isaac and Jacob

5. List the parts of God's threefold promise to Abraham and explain the meaning of each:
   Great nation, Great name, a blessing

6. Describe ways that Abraham modeled faith and obedience to God.

7. Identify one event from this chapter and, in your own words, explain how it demonstrates God's providential care and faithfulness to the promised line of Isaac and Jacob.

What's in a Name?

In Scripture, we read about times when God changed people's names. For example, in Genesis 17, God changed Abram's name, which means "exalted father," to Abraham, which means "father of a multitude."

Later, we read about God giving Jacob, Abraham's grandson, the name Israel. God gave Jacob this name after a mysterious event in which Jacob wrestled with an angel of God. Israel means "he who strives/struggles with God."

Take a moment to look at Matthew 16:13–20 on page 15. Jesus continued this same pattern when he changed Simon's name to Peter. In Greek, *petros* means "rock."

So, what is with all this name changing? When someone receives a new name in Scripture, it reveals the specific role this person has in God's plan.

Original Name	New God-Given Name	New God-Given Role
Abram ("exalted father")	Abraham ("father of a multitude")	Abraham and his descendants became instruments of worldwide blessing.
Jacob	Israel ("he who strives/struggles with God")	Israel became the father of the twelve tribes of Israel, the people with whom God wrestled, in order to make them into a holy nation and priestly kingdom.
Simon	Peter (Greek: *petros* = "rock")	Peter became the foundation on which Jesus established his Church. Jesus made Peter the first pope.

In the chart above, we see how the names God gave to Abram, Jacob, and Simon each reveal their important roles in God's plan of salvation. Abram became Abraham, through whose descendants God blessed all peoples and nations. Abraham is our father in faith. Jacob became Israel, through whom God established the twelve tribes of Israel and later the nation and Kingdom of Israel. The people of Israel often struggled against God's will and sinned against him.

Lastly, Simon became Peter. Jesus made Peter the rock and foundation of the Church he established here on earth. Peter became the visible foundation of Christ's Church and the first pope. Peter and all his successors throughout history shepherd the entire "flock," or people, of Christ.

Journal Reflection

Name changes in the Bible signify that God is calling someone to a new role in his plan. In Baptism, we receive a sort of name "change." Our parents announce our name to the Church. From this moment, we share in the mission of Jesus and his Church. **What role do you think God is calling you to have in his plan?**

Forgiving Family Members

Read

In this chapter, we saw an incredible example of forgiveness. Joseph forgave his brothers after they sold him into slavery. We should strive to imitate Joseph in our lives. Even though it may be difficult, we should love and forgive as God does.

Forgiving someone who has hurt us is often difficult, especially when it is one of our family members. We may feel that the people who are supposed to love us most have injured or betrayed us through their words or deeds. Sometimes even after they have asked for forgiveness, we hold on to past injuries and form grudges. Without forgiveness, deep wounds can be created between family members.

Forgiveness means letting go of resentment of someone who has hurt us and willing his good. When we forgive someone, it does not mean we should allow him to hurt us repeatedly. Forgiveness does not excuse the other person's sinful actions. But God does call us to let go of any anger or hatred we have toward that person and to desire what is best for him.

The *Catechism* reminds us that it "is not in our power not to feel or to forget an offense; but the heart that offers itself to the Holy Spirit turns injury into compassion and purifies the memory in transforming the hurt into intercession" (CCC 2843). In other words, we may be unable to control the hurt we feel. However, if we allow God to work in our hearts, even the hurt we feel can move us to forgive and pray for the person who has hurt us.

Reflect

Spend 5–10 minutes reflecting on the following:

- What has someone in my family recently done that has been hurtful? Have I forgiven this person? Do I want to forgive this person?

- Have I prayed for those who have hurt me and asked God to grant me the grace of forgiveness?

- Have I asked for forgiveness when I have hurt someone in my family through my words or actions?

Pray

Spend time in prayer before a crucifix and contemplate how Jesus forgives us of our sins and gives us a share in his own divine life.

Act

This week, go to the Sacrament of Reconciliation and ask for God's mercy for your sins and the grace to help you forgive others.

CHAPTER 9

Jesus, the Son of Abraham

Words to Know

> *type*

> *typology*

Proclaiming the Good News

"If God is for us, who is against us? He who did not spare his own Son but gave him up for us all, will he not also give us all things with him?" —Romans 8:31–32

Arrest of Christ, Fra Angelico

"Take Your Son ... Whom You Love"

The Old and the New

Saint Augustine once wrote, "The New Testament lies hidden in the Old, and the Old Testament is unveiled in the New."[1] By this, he summarized an important aspect of how the Church reads Sacred Scripture, known as typology. *Typology* is the way we discern how deeds and words in the Bible foreshadow the fulfillment of God's plan in Jesus Christ.

At times during our study of the Old Testament, we will pause and return to the Gospel of Matthew to see examples of the New Testament being hidden in the Old, and the Old Testament being revealed in the New. You may remember that Saint Matthew began his Gospel by identifying Jesus as "the son of Abraham" (Mt 1:1). Having read about God's covenant with Abraham and his son Isaac in the last chapter, we are able to understand better what Matthew meant when he declared Jesus to be "the son of Abraham."

Isaac, the Beloved Son of Abraham

Some years after God blessed Abraham and his wife Sarah with their son Isaac, God came to Abraham and gave him a heart-piercing command:

Gen 22:1-8

> **22** ¹After these things God tested Abraham, and said to him, "Abraham!" And he said, "Here am I." ²He said, "Take your son, your only-begotten son Isaac, whom you love, and go to the land of Moriah, and offer him there as a burnt offering upon one of the mountains of which I shall tell you." ³So Abraham rose early in the morning, saddled his donkey, and took two of his young men with him, and his son Isaac; and he cut the wood for the burnt offering, and arose and went to the place of which God had told him. ⁴On the third day Abraham lifted up his eyes and saw the place afar off. ⁵Then Abraham said to his young men, "Stay here with the donkey; I and the lad will go yonder and worship, and come again to you." ⁶And Abraham took the wood of the burnt offering, and laid it on Isaac his son; and he took in his hand the fire and the knife. So they went both of them together. ⁷And Isaac said to his father Abraham, "My father!" And he said, "Here am I, my son." He said, "Behold, the fire and the wood; but where is the lamb for a burnt offering?" ⁸Abraham said, "God will provide himself the lamb for a burnt offering, my son." So they went both of them together.

Isaac was Abraham's "only-begotten son" (22:2) because he was the son of promise. Isaac was the son through whom God swore to give Abraham descendants as many "as the stars of heaven" (22:17). And yet, God commanded Abraham to take his beloved son Isaac and offer him as a sacrifice!

Catechism of the Catholic Church, 140

"The unity of the two Testaments proceeds from the unity of God's plan and his Revelation. The Old Testament prepares for the New and the New Testament fulfills the Old; the two shed light on each other; both are true Word of God."

Despite the difficulty of what God was asking of Abraham, he responded with silent obedience. When Abraham and Isaac arrived at the mountain, Isaac was confused. He knew that to make a burnt offering to God, they needed to kill a lamb and then burn its remains as a sacrifice. But there was no lamb. When questioned, Abraham gave an incomplete response: God will provide the lamb. He did not yet tell his son Isaac that *he* was to be the sacrificial lamb.

The Sacrifice of Isaac, Giovanni Domenico Tiepolo

The Binding of Isaac

22 ⁹When they came to the place of which God had told him, Abraham built an altar there, and laid the wood in order, and bound Isaac his son, and laid him on the altar, upon the wood. ¹⁰Then Abraham put forth his hand, and took the knife to slay his son. ¹¹But the angel of the LORD called to him from heaven, and said, "Abraham, Abraham!" And he said, "Here am I." ¹²He said, "Do not lay your hand on the lad or do anything to him; for now I know that you fear God, seeing you have not withheld your son, your only-begotten son, from me." ¹³And Abraham lifted up his eyes and looked, and behold, behind him was a ram, caught in a thicket by his horns; and Abraham went and took the ram, and offered it up as a burnt offering instead of his son. . . .

¹⁵And the angel of the LORD called to Abraham a second time from heaven, ¹⁶and said, "By myself I have sworn, says the LORD, because you have done this, and have not withheld your son, your only-begotten son, ¹⁷I will indeed bless you, and I will multiply your descendants as the stars of heaven and as the sand which is on the seashore. And your descendants shall possess the gate of their enemies, ¹⁸and by your descendants shall all the nations of the earth bless themselves, because you have obeyed my voice."

Gen 22:9-13, 15-18

We should probably not think of Isaac as a little child. Jewish tradition saw Isaac as a strong young man. Isaac carried the heavy wood for the sacrifice all the way up a mountain. If Isaac had wanted, it seems he could have overpowered his much older father. Instead, Isaac willingly obeyed his father's commands even after discovering that *he* was to be the sacrificial lamb.

Abraham proved his faith to God. God provided a ram to sacrifice in place of Abraham's beloved son, Isaac. In response to Abraham's faithfulness, God renewed his covenant with him and swore to bless all nations through Abraham's descendants.

"God Will Provide Himself the Lamb"

The God of Life

God's command to sacrifice Isaac may seem unthinkable. How could a good God command such a thing? How could Abraham obey? To answer these questions, we must consider again Abraham's faith.

In the last chapter, we read a passage from the Letter to the Hebrews in the New Testament that spoke about Abraham's faith (see page 110). Abraham's faith was not a blind obedience to some unknown God. His faith was a trusting response to the God who had revealed his truthfulness and goodness many times over the course of Abraham's life.

God would never command anything without an important reason. If God commanded the sacrifice of Isaac, then with faith, Abraham believed in God's loving plan, even if he could not see it or fully understand it. Abraham's faith led him to trust that "God was able to raise men even from the dead" (Heb 11:19).

Abraham believed that God could bring life out of death because Abraham remembered that God had brought forth a child for Abraham and Sarah, even though they were both well past childbearing age. Hebrews even called Abraham "as good as dead" (11:12) on account of his old age. Surely, Abraham thought, this same God who blessed him with his son would restore Isaac to life even if he was offered as a burnt offering. Abraham had faith in the good God of life.

From the Saints

"Just as the Lord carried his own cross, so Isaac himself carried to the place of sacrifice the wood on which he was to be placed. And in the end . . . when Abraham noticed the ram, it was caught in a thicket by its horns. Of whom, then, was the ram a figure if not Jesus, who was crowned with . . . thorns before he was sacrificed?"[2]

—Saint Augustine

Jesus, the Beloved Son of God

At the end of the passage from Hebrews, it says that "[Abraham] did receive [Isaac] back and this was a symbol" (11:19). This suggests that Abraham's sacrifice of Isaac was not just an event in the past. It was also a symbol, or type, of an event to come—the sacrifice of Jesus. Remember that typology is the way we discern how deeds and words in the Bible foreshadow the fulfillment of God's plan in Jesus Christ. We use the word "*type*" to speak about the person or event that foreshadows this future fulfillment. Thus, we can say that the sacrifice of Isaac is a type of Jesus' sacrifice on the Cross.

Furthermore, Isaac can be understood as a type of Jesus. At two pivotal moments in the Gospel of Matthew, Jesus is referred to as "the beloved Son" of God. At both Jesus' baptism and his Transfiguration, God the Father's voice declared from Heaven, "This is my beloved Son" (3:17; 17:5). Saint Matthew seems to be inviting those who hear his Gospel to consider the ways in which Jesus, the Beloved Son of God, is like Isaac, the beloved son of Abraham.

A close reading of Genesis 22 reveals more parallels between Isaac and Jesus. Isaac, the beloved son, carried the wood of his sacrifice up a mountain. Jesus, the Beloved Son, willingly carried the wood of the Cross up a mountain. Isaac offered himself willingly as a sacrifice in obedience to his father, Abraham. Jesus willingly offered himself as a sacrifice in obedience to God the Father. Abraham told Isaac, "God will provide himself the lamb" (Gen 22:8). Jesus is identified as "the Lamb of God" (Jn 1:36). Abraham received his beloved son, Isaac, back. God the Father received his Beloved Son, Jesus, back from the dead when he was raised to life in the Resurrection.

Jesus Fulfilled God's Covenant with Abraham

Jesus was foreshadowed in another way in Genesis: in God's covenant with Abraham. When Matthew called Jesus "the son of Abraham" (Mt 1:1), he was doing more than saying that he was a New Isaac. He was showing that Jesus is one of Abraham's descendants. In fact, Jesus is the promised descendant. God promised Abraham that through his descendants, all the nations of the world would be blessed. In Jesus, that promise is fulfilled.

Jesus, the Son of Abraham, blessed the whole world by offering himself as the New Isaac on the Cross. Through the Paschal Mystery—his suffering, Death, Resurrection, and Ascension—Jesus offers salvation to the whole world. His sacrifice on the Cross is the blood of the new and everlasting covenant that God makes with all people (see Mt 26:28). Jesus' Resurrection reveals that God has defeated the powers of sin and death.

After his Resurrection, Jesus commanded his Apostles to go make disciples of *all nations* (see Mt 28:16–20). Through Jesus, the Son of Abraham, the gift of the Holy Spirit is made available to all nations.

Crucifixion, Benozzo Gozzoli

Chapter 9 Summary

1. God commanded Abraham to sacrifice his beloved son, Isaac, to test Abraham's faith.

2. The sacrifice of Isaac is a type of the sacrifice of Jesus Christ, the Beloved Son of God the Father.

3. Through Jesus' Paschal Mystery, God fulfilled his promise to bless the entire world through Abraham's descendants.

Praying with Obedience

Jesus is the Son of Abraham—a New Isaac. Jesus is perfectly obedient to God the Father's will. He was willing to offer himself as the perfect sacrifice, "the Lamb of God, who takes away the sin of the world" (Jn 1:29). Just before he was arrested and led off to be killed, Jesus gave us an example of perfect obedience in prayer.

Spend time in silent prayer, thinking about Jesus' agony in the Garden of Gethsemane. Follow the prompts below.

1. Begin by making the Sign of the Cross. Calm your mind and focus your attention on God. Slowly read Saint Luke the Evangelist's account of Jesus' prayer in the garden:

Agony in the Garden, El Greco

Lk 22:39-46

22 ³⁹And he came out, and went, as was his custom, to the Mount of Olives; and the disciples followed him. ⁴⁰And when he came to the place he said to them, "Pray that you may not enter into temptation." ⁴¹And he withdrew from them about a stone's throw, and knelt down and prayed, ⁴²"Father, if you are willing, remove this chalice from me; nevertheless not my will, but yours, be done." ⁴³And there appeared to him an angel from heaven, strengthening him. ⁴⁴And being in an agony he prayed more earnestly; and his sweat became like great drops of blood falling down upon the ground. ⁴⁵And when he rose from prayer, he came to the disciples and found them sleeping for sorrow, ⁴⁶and he said to them, "Why do you sleep? Rise and pray that you may not enter into temptation."

2. Read this passage again. Then close your eyes and use your imagination to enter this moment in history. Imagine the garden itself as if you were actually there. See the moon and the stars. Hear the wind blowing through the trees. Is it warm or cold outside? What else can you see in the garden? *After a few moments in silence, move on to the next section.*

3. With your eyes closed, imagine the Person of Jesus kneeling in prayer in the garden. See him looking up to Heaven in distress and sadness. Consider the anxiety and fear he is facing. Imagine seeing his sweat becoming drops of blood, falling to the ground. *After a few moments in silence, move on to the next section.*

4. Now reread Jesus' words in verse 42 above. Close your eyes and listen to Jesus' voice praying these words to his Father. Think of his amazing trust. Consider his perfect obedience in the face of suffering and death. Think of his courage and perseverance. *After a few moments in silence, move on to the next section.*

5. Spend a few moments in silent prayer, thinking about how you can imitate Christ's obedience. End with a prayer to Jesus in your own words. Thank him for his sacrifice. Ask him for the grace to imitate his obedience in your life, especially when you face difficult and challenging times.

6. Answer the following questions:

What stood out to you most during this time of prayer?

_____
_____
_____

How has this time of meditation and prayer changed how you think about Jesus' obedience to God the Father?

_____
_____
_____

Let Us Pray—Psalm 56

Many lines in Psalm 56 sound like what Jesus, as a New Isaac, could have said during his suffering on the Cross. The psalmist sings of a person who trusts in God the Father while he is suffering. As you pray this psalm, ask our Heavenly Father to give you the grace to endure whatever suffering and burdens you are experiencing in your own life.

Ps 56:1-5, 8-13

56 ¹Have mercy on me, O God, for men trample upon me;
all day long foes oppress me;
²my enemies trample upon me all day long,
for many fight against me proudly.
³When I am afraid,
I put my trust in you.
⁴In God, whose word I praise,
in God I trust without a fear.
What can flesh do to me?
⁵All day long they seek to injure my cause;
all their thoughts are against me for evil. . . .
⁸You have kept count of my tossings;
put my tears in your bottle!
Are they not in your book?
⁹Then my enemies will be turned back
in the day when I call.
This I know, that God is for me.
¹⁰In God, whose word I praise,
in the LORD, whose word I praise,
¹¹in God I trust without a fear.
What can man do to me?
¹²My vows to you I must perform, O God;
I will render thank offerings to you.
¹³For you have delivered my soul from death
yes, my feet from falling,
that I may walk before God
in the light of life.

Chapter 9 Review:
Jesus, the Son of Abraham

1. In order to test Abraham, God commanded him to offer his beloved son _____ as a burnt offering.

2. What do we call the discernment of how deeds and words in the Bible foreshadow the fulfillment of God's plan in Jesus Christ? _____

3. Since Jesus fulfilled God's promise to bless the entire world through Abraham, Matthew the Evangelist identified Jesus as "the son of _____" (Mt 1:1).

4. The sacrifice of Isaac is a _____ of the sacrifice of Jesus Christ.

5. Saint Augustine famously expressed that the "New Testament _____ in the Old, and the Old Testament is _____ in the New."

6. At the Great Commission, Jesus commanded his Apostles to "make disciples of all nations" (Mt 28:19). How does this fulfill the third promise God swore to Abraham?

   _____
   _____
   _____

7. List three similarities between Isaac and Jesus from this chapter that reveal the sacrifice of Isaac as a type of Jesus' perfect sacrifice on the Cross.

   _____
   _____
   _____
   _____
   _____

God, the Author of History

An old saying states, "History never repeats itself, but it does often rhyme." There are "rhymes" in history and in the Bible because God is the Author of all history. In his providence, God writes one storyline throughout history and includes "rhymes" or "patterns" that hint at his divine plan. In this chapter, we referred to these "rhymes" of salvation history as *types*.

Remember that typology helps us see how God uses the people and events spoken about in the Bible to point toward the fulfillment of his plan in Christ and the Church. In this chapter, we saw how the sacrifice of Isaac foreshadows Jesus' sacrifice on the Cross. This is one example of typology. The following chart shows other examples of types in the Bible:

Details from *Abraham and Isaac Climbing Mount Moriah*; *Christ Bearing the Cross with Veronica Receiving the Veil Imprinted with the Face of Christ*, Biblia Pauperum

Adam as a Type of Jesus Christ

Through Adam's *disobedience*, *sin* and *death* entered the world.	Through Jesus Christ's *obedience*, *grace* and *righteousness* entered the world.

Joseph as a Type of Jesus Christ

Joseph, the most *beloved son of his father*, was *betrayed* by one of his *twelve* brothers, *Judah*, for *silver*.	Jesus, the *Beloved Son of the Father*, was *betrayed* by one of his *twelve* Apostles, *Judas*, for *silver*.

The Flood as a Type of the Sacrament of Baptism

In the Flood, God used water to *cleanse* the world from *evil* and renew his *creation*.	In Baptism, God *cleanses* us from *sin* and brings us to newness of *life* through his grace.

These "rhymes" show that God is actively involved with the people and events of salvation history. He actively cares for his creation and brings it toward its perfection.

Journal Reflection

How does understanding types and the ways that the Old Testament foreshadows the New Testament influence how you see the Bible, the Church, and the sacraments?

The Litany of Humility

Read

Abraham was obedient to God, even when asked to sacrifice Isaac. Isaac was obedient to God by following Abraham's command. Jesus, the New Isaac, was obedient to the Father. As Saint Paul said, "[Jesus] humbled himself and became obedient unto death, even death on a cross" (Phil 2:8).

Obedience requires humility. It means putting God's plan before our own, even if God's plan involves suffering or difficulty. Praying the Litany of Humility can help us grow in obedience to God's will. In each line of the prayer below, we are asking to be delivered, or freed, from things that may prevent us from doing God's will.

Reflect

Spend 5–10 minutes reflecting on the following:

- What might be preventing me from doing God's will in my life right now?

Pray

Pray the following Litany of Humility.

O Jesus, meek and humble of heart, hear me.

From the desire of being esteemed, deliver me, O Jesus.
From the desire of being loved, deliver me, O Jesus.
From the desire of being extolled, deliver me, O Jesus.
From the desire of being honored, deliver me, O Jesus.
From the desire of being praised, deliver me, O Jesus.
From the desire of being preferred to others, deliver me, O Jesus.
From the desire of being consulted, deliver me, O Jesus.
From the desire of being approved, deliver me, O Jesus.
From the fear of being humiliated, deliver me, O Jesus.
From the fear of being despised, deliver me, O Jesus.
From the fear of suffering rebukes, deliver me, O Jesus.
From the fear of being calumniated, deliver me, O Jesus.
From the fear of being forgotten, deliver me, O Jesus.
From the fear of being ridiculed, deliver me, O Jesus.
From the fear of being wronged, deliver me, O Jesus.
From the fear of being suspected, deliver me, O Jesus.

Christ Crowned with Thorns, Filipino School, 20th century

That others may be loved more than I, Jesus, grant me the grace to desire it.
That others may be esteemed more than I, Jesus, grant me the grace to desire it.
That, in the opinion of the world,
    others may increase and I may decrease, Jesus, grant me the grace to desire it.
That others may be chosen and I set aside, Jesus, grant me the grace to desire it.
That others may be praised and I go unnoticed, Jesus, grant me the grace to desire it.
That others may be preferred to me in everything, Jesus, grant me the grace to desire it.
That others may become holier than I,
    provided that I may become as holy as I should, Jesus, grant me the grace to desire it.

Act

This week, make a small sacrifice for someone you love.

Unit 3

You Shall Be My People

The Book of Exodus contains an account of Moses leading God's Chosen People out of slavery in the land of Egypt. God revealed his name to Moses and empowered him to work signs and wonders in Egypt before Pharaoh. God delivered his people out of Egypt and entered into a covenant with them at Mount Sinai. Through Moses, God gave the Israelites his Law to teach them how to remain faithful to their covenant.

The Book of Numbers shows that time and again after the Lord brought them out of Egypt, the Israelites were unfaithful to their covenant. They did not trust in God's plan. As punishment, they wandered in the wilderness for forty years before they could enter the land of Canaan, the Promised Land. The Book of Joshua tells how God's people finally entered the Promised Land under the leadership of Joshua, who called the people to reject the false gods of the other nations and renew their covenant with the Lord.

The Gospel of Matthew reveals Jesus as the New Moses, the leader of the new Exodus out of slavery to sin and the lawgiver of the New Law.

Chapters 10–12

Chapter 10: Out of Egypt

Chapter 11: A Land Flowing with Milk and Honey

Chapter 12: Jesus, the New Moses

Grade 6 Road Map

Unit 1
The Good News
The Gospel of Matthew reveals who Jesus is through both his deeds and words. God speaks to us in Sacred Scripture through human authors inspired by the Holy Spirit.

Unit 2
In the Beginning
Genesis describes the beginning of the universe and humanity, the beginning of sin, and the beginning of God's plan to restore mankind's relationship with himself through the covenant with Abraham and his descendants. In Jesus, God's covenant with Abraham is fulfilled.

Unit 3
You Shall Be My People
Through Moses, God delivered his people from slavery in Egypt and made a covenant with them at Mount Sinai. Despite their unfaithfulness, God brought his people into the Promised Land after they wandered for forty years in the desert. Jesus is the New Moses, who gives the New Law.

Unit 4
The Kingdom of the Lord
The Lord made a covenant with King David and swore to give him an everlasting kingdom. The sins of God's people led to the division and downfall of the kingdom, eventually leading to the destruction of the Temple and the Babylonian exile. In Jesus, God's covenant with David is fulfilled.

Unit 5
The Coming of the Anointed One
God brought his people back from exile to the Promised Land, where they rebuilt the Temple in Jerusalem. The prophets foretold of the coming of the Messiah, who would rebuild the kingdom of David. Jesus, the Son of Man, brings the kingdom through his suffering and Death.

Unit 6
God with Us
The Gospel of Matthew provides reliable testimony that Jesus is the Divine Son of God made man, who delivered us from sin through his Paschal Mystery. Jesus continues to be present to his Church through Word and sacrament—above all, the Holy Eucharist.

Saint Josephine Bakhita

Love in Suffering

Saint Josephine Margaret Bakhita was born in 1869 in Darfur, a region of Sudan in Africa. She was born into a prominent family. Her uncle was a tribal leader. Her early childhood was happy and free from suffering. But that changed when she was eight years old. Bakhita was kidnapped and sold into the Arab slave trade.

The trauma and suffering that followed caused her to forget much of her early childhood. She even forgot her own name! The Arab slave traders renamed her Bakhita, from the Arab word for "blessed." They hoped this name would attract buyers.

Sadly, the years that followed were far from blessed for Bakhita. She was sold several times and suffered extreme abuse at the hands of her masters. One of her owners, a Turkish general, was especially cruel. She later recounted that she could not remember a single day while in that household that did not involve a beating. As soon as her wounds would start to get better, she would receive more beatings. The general's wife brought in a woman who was an expert at this cruel art of branding. She cut Bakhita 114 times with a razor, then rubbed salt into each wound. Bakhita later recounted, "It seemed I was dying at every moment, especially when they rubbed in the salt. . . . The scars are still with me. I can honestly say that the reason I did not die was that the Lord miraculously destined me for better things."[1]

Bakhita was eventually sold to an official of the Italian government, Callisto Legnani. Callisto did not harm Bakhita. It was the first time since her early childhood that she experienced kindness. When he had to leave the Sudan to return to Italy, she asked to go with him. Upon their arrival, he entrusted her to a wealthy Italian family. She served as a nanny to their daughter Mimmina.

Bakhita loved Mimmina as her own daughter. When the Italian family had to travel to Sudan for an extended time on business, they sent Mimmina and Bakhita to live with the Canossian Sisters, a group of religious sisters in Venice.

It was there that Bakhita came to know who God was for the first time. She had experienced God as a child but had never been told about him. "Seeing the sun, the moon and the stars, I said to myself: Who could be the Master of these beautiful things? And I felt a great desire to see him, to know him and to pay him homage."[2] Now the sisters were teaching her about God. She was learning about this Master of the sun and stars. He was a Master unlike any she had ever known. He was gentle and loving.

When she saw pictures of Jesus' Crucifixion and learned how he suffered, Bakhita realized that God had suffered as she had. He knew pain. He bore permanent marks of suffering just like she did. Bakhita fell in love with this Master. She understood that she was truly free with this Master. In this freedom, she was able to forgive her enemies. Even though she was physically scarred, she knew she was strong, beautiful, and loved by God. She wanted to live forever for him. "When I am with him wherever he wants me to be, I feel so good inside and out: he is the Master, and I am his poor little creature."[3]

As Bakhita later looked back on the sufferings of her early life, it was difficult for her to speak about them. But she found the strength to share her life story to show how the Lord protected her and strengthened her, even before she knew his name. She always began her stories of these years by saying, "For the glory of God, to exalt the power of God, who showed me his salvation . . ."[4]

Josephine's New Beginning

When Mimmina's family came home to Italy, they announced they would return to Sudan and take Bakhita with them. Bakhita wanted to stay with the sisters. She had come to know God as a good and loving Master. She knew that returning to Sudan would make becoming a Christian difficult. She did not want to leave this new Master who loved her. She wanted to live for him. She refused to go.

The sisters and the patriarch of Venice supported Bakhita. The case went to the Italian courts, which ruled she was a free woman. She was no longer a child, and slavery was illegal in Italy and Sudan. She did not have to go with Mimmina's family.

Just a few months later, in January of 1890, Bakhita was baptized and took the name Josephine Margaret. She entered the Canossian Sisters, the religious order she was living with, and dedicated her life to serving her loving Master. She lived a life of humble simplicity, spending her days cooking, doing the laundry, and working as the portress, the sister who answers the door for visitors. Her reputation for holiness quickly spread throughout the town of Schio, and people came to ask for her prayers and advice.

One mother came to Sister Josephine begging for prayers for her son who was a seminarian. He had fallen sick with tuberculosis, and one of his lungs had collapsed. Sister Josephine assured the mother that her son would be ordained. She offered her prayers and sufferings for the young man. He recovered and was ordained. When he went to the doctor several years later, they could find no indication that he had ever suffered from tuberculosis.

Sister Josephine sometimes traveled throughout Italy to tell her story to help the cause of missionaries going to Africa. But most of her life was spent in the convent, witnessing to the people of Schio with love and gentleness.

During World War II, the people of Schio were convinced that the holy presence of Sister Josephine would protect the city from violence. She consoled them, telling them the bombs would not strike their homes. Only twice throughout the war did bombs hit any buildings in the city, and never did they damage any house. Once they hit a factory. Another time fifty bombs were dropped outside the city, but none exploded.

Sister Josephine suffered numerous health problems at the end of her life but never complained. Instead, she offered up her sufferings and remained cheerful, looking forward to Heaven. Sister Josephine Margaret Bakhita died on February 8, 1947. The townspeople immediately began to beg that she be canonized. She was canonized on October 1, 2000, by Pope Saint John Paul II, becoming the first saint from Sudan.

Journal Reflection

1. Like the Israelites, Bakhita was enslaved and forced to work under cruel masters. But God was with her during this time. In seeing the beauty of nature, she knew there was a good Master. **What are some ways God reminds you that he loves you even when life is hard?**

2. When Bakhita saw pictures of Jesus' suffering, she understood God's love even better. **How might this have helped her forgive those who hurt her?**

3. The Israelites could have victory in the Promised Land only when they trusted the Lord. **How does Bakhita's life show her trust in the Lord?**

4. As Christians, we believe that our earthly life is a journey that prepares us for eternal life. Saint Josephine Bakhita accepted all the trials in this life as opportunities to grow in her love and trust in God. **How does Josephine Bakhita's example influence how you see the difficulties you face?**

CHAPTER 10
Out of Egypt

Words to Know

> Decalogue
> idolatry
> theophany

Proclaiming the Good News

"Christ, our Paschal Lamb, has been sacrificed." —1 Corinthians 5:7

Continuing the Story of Salvation

List six or seven key events from the Book of Genesis that we read about in Unit 2. Begin with Creation and end with God's people in Egypt.

Jesus' Miracles
Noahs Ark
Adam and eve
Cain and Abel
tower of babel
Sacrifice Isaac

Moses and the Burning Bush, Sébastien Bourdon

Moses, the Servant of the Lord

The Burning Bush

The Book of Exodus begins with the account of events that occurred after the death of Joseph and his brothers. God's Chosen People remained in Egypt for over four hundred years. They became known as the Israelites. When a new pharaoh came into power, he enslaved the Israelites for fear of their growing strength.

Following many attempts to control their growth, the pharaoh commanded every newborn Israelite boy be drowned in the Nile River. After hiding her baby boy for three months, an Israelite mother saved her baby by floating him down the river in a basket. Pharaoh's daughter found him and adopted him as her own son. She gave him the name Moses and raised him in the royal household.

Fresco in the cupola with the name of God in Saint Clement's Church, Eastcheap

As a grown man, Moses fled Egypt into the land of Midian after killing an Egyptian taskmaster who was beating an Israelite. There the Lord revealed himself to Moses in the burning bush. This is called a *theophany*, which is a visible appearance of God in the world. On Mount Sinai, the Lord spoke to Moses from a bush that was burning but was not consumed by the flame:

Ex 3:6-8, 10-15

3 ⁶[The LORD] said, "I am the God of your father, the God of Abraham, the God of Isaac, and the God of Jacob. . . .

⁷"I have seen the affliction of my people who are in Egypt, and have heard their cry because of their taskmasters; I know their sufferings, ⁸and I have come down to deliver them out of the hand of the Egyptians, and to bring them up out of that land to a good and broad land, a land flowing with milk and honey. . . . ¹⁰Come, I will send you to Pharaoh that you may bring forth my people, the sons of Israel, out of Egypt." ¹¹But Moses said to God, "Who am I that I should go to Pharaoh, and bring the sons of Israel out of Egypt?" ¹²He said, "But I will be with you; and this shall be the sign for you, that I have sent you: when you have brought forth the people out of Egypt, you shall serve God upon this mountain."

¹³Then Moses said to God, "If I come to the sons of Israel and say to them, 'The God of your fathers has sent me to you,' and they ask me, 'What is his name?' what shall I say to them?" ¹⁴God said to Moses, "I AM WHO I AM. . . . ¹⁵This is my name for ever, and thus I am to be remembered throughout all generations."

God revealed his name to Moses. God's name, "I AM WHO I AM" (3:14), revealed his presence with Moses. Moses could now call on God using his name. When Moses called on God's name, he called on God's presence and power. With God's presence and power, Moses could lead God's Chosen People out of slavery in Egypt.

God chose Moses to lead Israel out of Egypt. But Moses did not immediately accept this mission from God. Moses tried to explain to God that *he was not worthy* of this incredible mission. Moses doubted *anyone would believe him* when he said God sent him. Moses also tried to persuade God to send someone else because he was not *eloquent in speaking*. Despite these excuses, God promised to be with Moses and empower him to lead his people out of Egypt.

132 | Chapter 10

We often feel that we are not worthy or capable of making a difference in the world. But God promises to be with us as well. God empowered Moses to complete his mission, and if we choose to believe in God and open ourselves to his grace, he will empower us to accomplish great things in his name.

The First Passover

Trusting that God was with him, Moses returned to Egypt with his brother, Aaron. They brought the Lord's message to Pharaoh, but he refused to let the Israelites go. Because of Pharaoh's hardness of heart, the Lord brought judgment on the Egyptians through a series of ten plagues.

In the first of these plagues, Moses turned the waters of the Nile River into blood. Following other great wonders, the Lord rescued the Israelites through the tenth and final plague, the death of the firstborn. To protect their firstborn children, God instructed Moses and the Israelites to celebrate a feast that became known as Passover, as it was the night God passed over the Israelites who kept this feast:

Ex 12:21-23, 28-31

12 ²¹Moses called all the elders of Israel, and said to them, "Select lambs for yourselves according to your families, and kill the Passover lamb. ²²Take a bunch of hyssop and dip it in the blood which is in the basin, and touch the lintel and the two doorposts with the blood which is in the basin; and none of you shall go out of the door of his house until the morning. ²³For the LORD will pass through to slay the Egyptians; and when he sees the blood on the lintel and on the two doorposts, the LORD will pass over the door, and will not allow the destroyer to enter your houses to slay you. . . ."

²⁸Then the sons of Israel went and did so; as the LORD had commanded . . . , so they did.

²⁹At midnight the LORD struck all the firstborn in the land of Egypt. . . . ³⁰And Pharaoh rose up in the night, he, and all his servants, and all the Egyptians; and there was a great cry in Egypt, for there was not a house where one was not dead. ³¹And he summoned Moses and Aaron by night, and said, "Rise up, go forth from among my people, both you and the sons of Israel; and go, serve the LORD, as you have said."

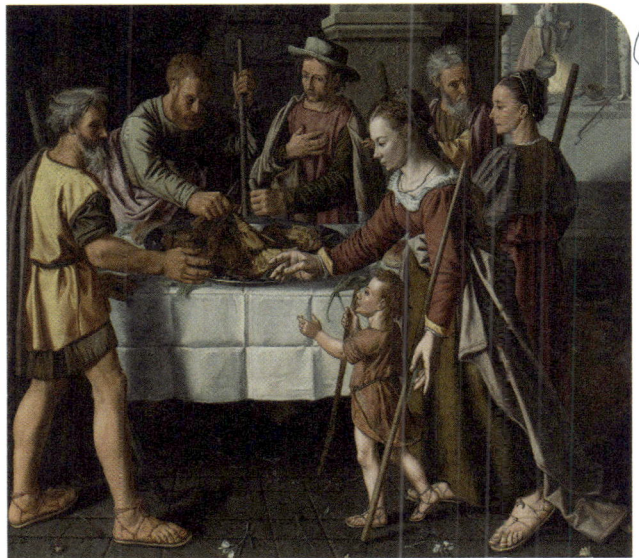

The First Passover Feast,
Peinture d' Huybrecht Beuckelaer

God proved his power to Pharoah and Egypt through the plagues. But Pharoah never repented. Instead, he pridefully ignored God's commands. With this choice, Pharoah brought the suffering of the final plague upon himself and his nation.

The Israelites, on the other hand, obeyed God. At God's command, they listened to Moses and followed the instructions for the Passover. God instructed the Israelites to celebrate the Passover meal with sandals on their feet and staffs in their hands (see Ex 12:11). God wanted his people to be ready to follow him at a moment's notice.

We must choose whom we will imitate: Pharoah in his pride or Israel in their obedience and willingness to follow God's will.

Israel Went Forth from Egypt

Crossing the Red Sea

Pharaoh let the Israelites leave Egypt, but he quickly regretted this decision and sent his army after Israel. The Egyptian army trapped the fleeing Israelites against the Red Sea, but a giant pillar of fire and cloud came between the Egyptians and the Israelites, protecting Israel all night:

Ex 14:13-14, 21-23, 26-28, 30-31

14 ¹³And Moses said to the people, "Fear not, stand firm, and see the salvation of the LORD. . . . ¹⁴The LORD will fight for you, and you have only to be still." . . .

²¹Then Moses stretched out his hand over the sea; and the LORD drove the sea back by a strong east wind all night, and made the sea dry land, and the waters were divided. ²²And the sons of Israel went into the midst of the sea on dry ground. . . . ²³The Egyptians pursued, and went in after them into the midst of the sea, all Pharaoh's horses, his chariots, and his horsemen. . . .

²⁶Then the LORD said to Moses, "Stretch out your hand over the sea, that the water may come back upon the Egyptians, upon their chariots, and upon their horsemen." ²⁷So Moses stretched forth his hand over the sea. . . . ²⁸The waters returned and covered the chariots and the horsemen and all the host of Pharaoh that had followed them into the sea; not so much as one of them remained. . . .

³⁰Thus the LORD saved Israel that day. . . . ³¹And Israel saw the great work which the LORD did against the Egyptians, . . . and they believed in the LORD and in his servant Moses.

The Decalogue

After parting the Red Sea, God led the Israelites to Mount Sinai, the same mountain where he spoke to Moses in the burning bush. The Lord fed them on their way with manna, a daily miraculous food that was called "bread from heaven" (Ex 16:4).

At Mount Sinai, God gave his laws to Moses, who delivered them to the Israelites. The twelve tribes declared they would be obedient to the Lord. Moses then took the blood of sacrificial animals and threw half of it on the altar and half on the people. This ritual symbolized the relationship God wanted to have with his people—they are bound by blood, like family, in a covenant. God made a covenant with his people again through Moses as he had done through Noah and Abraham.

As part of this covenant, the Lord gave Moses the *Decalogue* (from the Greek for "ten words"). We often refer to these "ten words" as the Ten Commandments. These "ten words" of God lead his people to freedom in living as God designed.

God delivered his people and gave them his law so they could be united with him in the sacred bond of a covenant. If Israel disobeyed God's law, they would break their covenant with him and remove themselves from his protection. They would risk being conquered by other nations and enslaved once again.

If we open ourselves to the grace of Christ and obey God's laws, we will remain free from sin and under his protection. We will stay in a loving covenant relationship with God.

The Ten Commandments are a gift from God that teach us how to be faithful to our covenant relationship with God. We respond in love by being obedient to God. Consider the First Commandment:

> **20** ²"I am the LORD your God, who brought you out of the land of Egypt, out of the house of bondage. ³You shall have no other gods before me. ⁴You shall not make for yourself a graven image, or any likeness of anything that is in heaven above, or that is in the earth beneath, or that is in the water under the earth; ⁵you shall not bow down to them or serve them."

Ex 20:2–5

The First Commandment forbids *idolatry*, which is worshipping any created thing in place of the Creator. The only right and just worship is the worship of the living God, who revealed himself to Moses in the burning bush. If we worship God alone, we will remain in a loving covenant relationship with him.

The Covenant Broken and Renewed

Sadly, the Israelites were not faithful to God's law. While Moses was on the mountain for forty days and forty nights, they grew impatient, waiting for him to return. They demanded that Moses' brother, Aaron, make gods for them out of gold, as they had worshipped in Egypt. The people committed idolatry and worshipped a golden calf. They broke their covenant relationship with God.

Moses descended the mountain and saw the idol. He shattered the two tablets containing the Decalogue and destroyed the golden calf. As a consequence of their sin, God told Moses that God would not go with the Israelites to the Promised Land. Moses interceded for the Israelites and sought to restore their relationship with the Lord. God came to Moses in another theophany on Mount Sinai:

Moses and the Tablets of the Law, Laurent de La Hyre

The Lord was merciful. His glory descended on Mount Sinai. He forgave his people's sin and restored them into the covenant. He again delivered his law to Moses. Moses wrote down the "words of the covenant, the ten commandments" on new stone tablets (Ex 34:28) and brought them down the mountain.

> **34** ⁵And the LORD descended in the cloud, . . . ⁶and proclaimed, "The LORD, the LORD, a God merciful and gracious, slow to anger, and abounding in mercy and faithfulness. . . . ¹⁰"Behold, I make a covenant."

Ex 34:5–6, 10

God also instructed Moses to build a tabernacle, which was a portable tent for the worship of God. After it was built, "the cloud covered the tent of meeting, and the glory of the LORD filled the tabernacle" (Ex 40:34). Through this cloud, God would remain present to his Chosen People as they journeyed from Mount Sinai to the Promised Land.

Chapter 10 Summary

1. God revealed his name to Moses and empowered him to perform mighty works.

2. God delivered his people from slavery in Egypt and gave them his law so they could be united with him in the sacred bond of a covenant.

3. After Israel's sin of idolatry, God showed mercy on them and restored his covenant with them.

You Shall Have No Other Gods before Me

Anyone who reads the Old Testament notices quickly that the worship of false gods is a regular temptation and frequent sin of God's people. When we read about the Israelites worshipping the golden calf, it is easy to judge them. The Book of Psalms reveals to us the consequences of false worship:

Ps 115:3-8

115 ³Our God is in the heavens;
he does whatever he pleases.
⁴ Their idols are silver and gold,
the work of men's hands.
⁵They have mouths, but do not speak;
eyes, but do not see.
⁶They have ears, but do not hear;
noses, but do not smell.
⁷They have hands, but do not feel;
feet, but do not walk;
and they do not make a sound in
their throat.
⁸Those who make them are like them;
so are all who trust in them.

The Golden Calf and the First Commandment, Anonymous

This suggests that we become more and more like what we worship.

Saint Paul cautioned the Christians in Rome about man's tendency to devote ourselves to something other than the living God:

Rom 1:22-23, 25

1 ²²Claiming to be wise, they became fools, ²³and exchanged the glory of the immortal God for images resembling mortal man or birds or animals or reptiles.... ²⁵They exchanged the truth about God for a lie and worshiped and served the creature rather than the Creator, who is blessed for ever!

But do we have to bow down physically and worship a statue in order to break the First Commandment of the Decalogue?

Echoing the words of Saint Paul, the *Catechism* reminds us that "idolatry not only refers to false pagan worship. . . . Idolatry consists in divinizing what is not God. Man commits idolatry whenever he honors and reveres a creature in place of God" (*CCC* 2113). We commit the sin of idolatry whenever we love a created thing as the ultimate source of our happiness instead of the Creator. Anyone or anything we put ahead of God is a kind of "idol."

What are three idols that take the place of God in our culture?

1. _____
2. _____
3. _____

Which of these idols do you think is most dangerous to people your age? Why?

_____
_____
_____
_____

Let Us Pray—Exodus 15

As we read about God's mighty works in leading his people out of slavery in Egypt, we pray the hymn of thanksgiving known as the Song of Moses. We praise God for the salvation he has made ours in Jesus Christ.

Ex 15:1-6, 18

15 ¹I will sing to the Lord, for he has triumphed gloriously;
  the horse and his rider he has thrown into the sea.
²The Lord is my strength and my song,
  and he has become my salvation;
this is my God, and I will praise him,
  my father's God, and I will exalt him.
³The LORD is a man of war;
  the LORD is his name.
⁴Pharaoh's chariots and his host he cast into the sea;
  and his picked officers are sunk in the Red Sea.
⁵The floods cover them;
  they went down into the depths like a stone.
⁶Your right hand, O LORD, glorious in power,
  your right hand, O LORD, shatters the enemy. . . .
¹⁸The LORD will reign for
  ever and ever.

Chapter 10 Review:
Out of Egypt

1. What is a visible appearance of God in the world called? **theophany**

   Give one example from this chapter. _____

   _____

2. What word is translated as "ten words" and is often used to refer to the Ten Commandments? **Decalogue**

3. The First Commandment forbids the sins of worshipping any created thing in place of the Creator. What is this sin called? **Idolatry**

4. Retell the story of the Exodus in your own words. Be sure to explain both what happened and why God brought his people out of Egypt.

   _____
   _____
   _____
   _____
   _____

5. Explain how God's law relates to his covenant with his people.

   _____
   _____

6. Identify a verse from the passages we read in which we learn something important about who God is from what he says or does. Copy down the reference (chapter and verse) below.

   Ex ____ : ____

   What does this verse reveal to us about God?

   _____
   _____
   _____

A New Eden: The Tabernacle of Moses

The Book of Exodus concludes with a detailed account of the building of the tabernacle. The tabernacle was a portable place of worship where the Lord promised to be with his people. Careful readers will notice similarities between the building of the tabernacle under the direction of Moses and the creation of the world by God in Genesis 1–2. How the tabernacle was built intentionally recalls God's "building" of all creation. Consider the chart below:

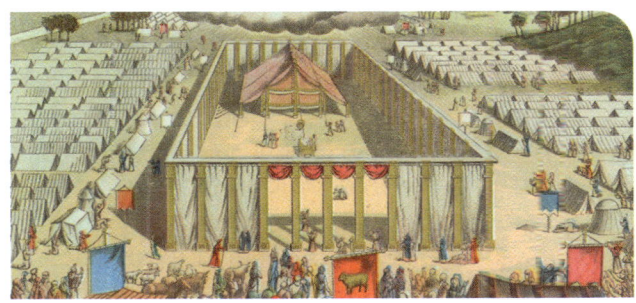

The Tabernacle in the Wilderness, English School, 19th century

Creation *Genesis 1-2*	**The Tabernacle** *Exodus 39-40*
"God saw everything that he had made, and behold, it was very good" (Gen 1:31).	"Moses saw all the work, and behold, they had done it; as the LORD had commanded, so had they done it" (Ex 39:43).
"The heavens and the earth were finished, and all the host of them" (Gen 2:1).	"Thus all the work of the tabernacle of the tent of meeting was finished" (Ex 39:32).
"On the seventh day God finished his work which he had done" (Gen 2:2).	"Moses finished the work" (Ex 40:33).
"God blessed the seventh day and hallowed it" (Gen 2:3).	"Moses blessed them" (Ex 39:43).

There are further connections between the Creation story and the tabernacle that reveal the tabernacle of Moses as a kind of new Eden, the place where God dwelt with his people. The tabernacle was decorated in ways that remind us of the Garden of Eden: it used precious metals such as gold and onyx, which are both mentioned in Genesis 2. The golden lampstand was made to look like a flowering tree, of which there were many in Eden, especially the Tree of Life. A river flowed out from Eden to water the whole earth, and in the tabernacle, there was a bronze basin referred to as a "sea" (1 Kings 7:25) that held a great quantity of water for ritual washings.

All this suggests that the tabernacle was a new Eden for God's people. Just as Adam and Eve walked in the presence of God, Israel lived with the presence of God in the tabernacle. Israel enjoyed a closeness to the Lord that other nations did not yet have. On the other hand, the account of the building of the tabernacle also reveals to us that the world, especially the Garden of Eden, is a place of communion and worship of the Creator. God is continually trying to restore the relationship between man and himself that was lost in the Fall.

Journal Reflection

God was present to our first parents in Eden. Later, he dwelt in the midst of Israel in the tabernacle. Now he is with us in a remarkable way in the Most Blessed Sacrament—his Body, Blood, Soul, and Divinity—which is kept in the tabernacles of our churches. **What could you do to be more aware and appreciative of the gift of Jesus' presence in the Holy Eucharist?**

Keep Holy the Lord's Day

Read

On Mount Sinai, the Lord promised Moses that he would free the Israelites from slavery in Egypt. In escaping Egypt and its false gods, the people of Israel would now be free to worship the one true God. As the Book of Exodus states, "When you have brought forth the people out of Egypt, *you shall serve God on this mountain*" (3:12; emphasis added). The Israelites often failed to be obedient to God. Soon after crossing the Red Sea, they began worshipping an idol.

The Third Commandment of the Decalogue states, "Remember the sabbath day, to keep it holy" (Ex 20:8). To be holy means *to be set apart for God's service*. The Sabbath was the day of the week the Israelites were supposed to stop working and instead rest and spend time worshipping the Lord. The Sabbath was supposed to remind the Israelites of the seventh day of Creation (when God rested after creating all things) and their liberation from slavery in Egypt. It was a holy day because it was a day that was supposed *to be set apart or treated differently* from every other day of the week in order *to serve* God.

From the time of the early Church, Christians have set apart Sunday, the day of the week that Jesus rose from the dead. Catholics fulfill the Third Commandment on Sunday, the Lord's Day. Catholics "keep holy" Sunday by attending Mass and avoiding any work or activities that get in the way of worshipping God. Catholics are also encouraged to spend time resting with family and helping those in need.

Instead of making the day holy, it is easy to forget God entirely and treat Sunday as simply another day to get work done or to fill it up with other activities. Like the Israelites before us, Catholics can easily substitute worshipping God with worshipping idols of our own making.

Reflect

Spend 5–10 minutes reflecting on the following:

- If somebody were to follow me the whole week and saw everything I did, could he tell based on my actions that there is any difference between how I treat Sunday and how I treat the other days of the week?

- Is there anything I do on Sunday that I treat *as more important* than spending time with God at Mass?

- Am I spending time with my family on Sunday? If not, can I think of ways to increase family time? Some suggestions:
  - *Having all meals with my family instead of eating by myself or with friends*
  - *Organizing a family movie night or game night*

Pray

Silently read through the Ten Commandments on page 339. Ask God to show you ways to keep and obey these commandments in your life.

Act

This week, keep Sunday holy by attending Mass and spending time with your family.

140 Chapter 10

CHAPTER 11
A Land Flowing with Milk and Honey

Words to Know

> Ark of the Covenant

> magnanimity

Continuing the Story of Salvation

List five or six key events that took place in Moses' life after God revealed himself and his name to Moses at the burning bush.

_____

_____

_____

_____

_____

Proclaiming the Good News

"It is the LORD who goes before you; he will be with you, he will not fail you or forsake you; do not fear or be dismayed."

—Deuteronomy 31:8

Moses and the Messengers from Canaan, Giovanni Lanfranco

In the Wilderness

They Soon Forgot His Works

When the Lord called Moses to lead the Israelites out of Egypt, he promised to bring them to the land of Canaan. This land was a place of rich material abundance, "a land flowing with milk and honey" (Ex 3:8). But even after the Lord had freed the Israelites, they failed to trust in him. They turned away from the freedom God offered them and became slaves through idolatry, worshipping the golden calf. Yet God had mercy and remained faithful to the covenant he had made with his Chosen People.

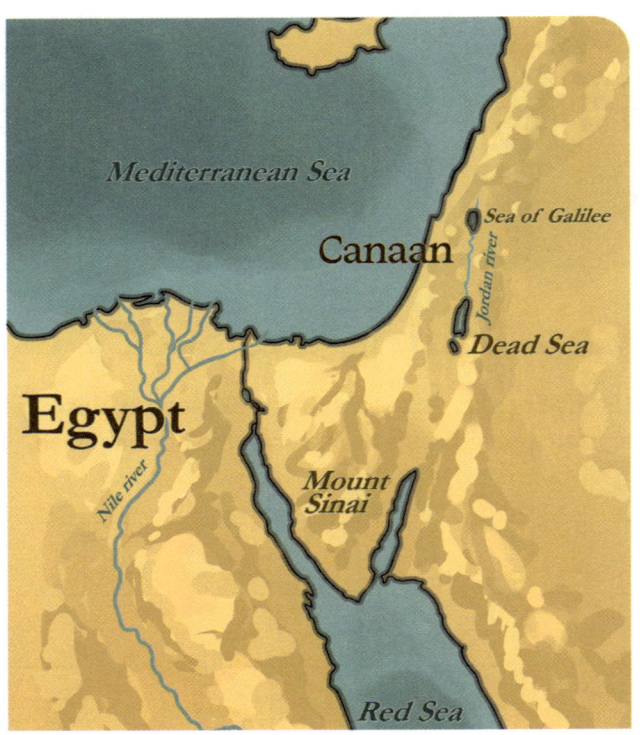

The Book of Numbers records what happened when the Israelites left Mount Sinai. They journeyed many miles in the wilderness before they came to the land of Canaan. When they reached the border of the Promised Land, Moses sent out twelve spies, one from each of the twelve tribes of Israel, to explore the land. Among these twelve chosen spies were Joshua, from the tribe of Ephraim, and Caleb, from the tribe of Judah.

Num 13:25-28, 30-32

13 ²⁵At the end of forty days they returned from spying out the land. ²⁶And they came to Moses and Aaron and to all the congregation of the sons of Israel in the wilderness of Paran, at Kadesh; they brought back word to them and to all the congregation, and showed them the fruit of the land. ²⁷And they told him, "We came to the land to which you sent us; it flows with milk and honey, and this is its fruit. ²⁸Yet the people who dwell in the land are strong, and the cities are fortified and very large...."

³⁰But Caleb quieted the people before Moses, and said, "Let us go up at once, and occupy it; for we are well able to overcome it." ³¹Then the men who had gone up with him said, "We are not able to go up against the people; for they are stronger than we." ³²So they brought to the sons of Israel an evil report of the land which they had spied out, saying, "The land, through which we have gone to spy it out, is a land that devours its inhabitants; and all the people that we saw in it are men of great stature."

The twelve spies confirmed they had reached the Promised Land. The fruit they brought back proved Canaan was a land of abundance, a land flowing with milk and honey. However, the land was occupied and well-defended by strong people.

Caleb and Joshua placed their trust in the Lord and argued that the Israelites should immediately seize the land. But the other ten spies disagreed with them. They believed the inhabitants of the Promised Land couldn't be conquered. These ten faithless spies spread an "evil report of the land" (13:32) to discourage the Israelites from trying to take the land God had promised.

Both Caleb and Joshua had courage because they knew the Lord would give his people the strength to take the Promised Land. They had faith that God could do great things through them. The other spies gave in to fear because they thought only of their own weaknesses and not of the strength that comes from God alone.

Magnanimity is the virtue that allows us to do great and noble things confidently for God and others. A magnanimous person does not trust only in her own abilities. She has faith that God will give her the strength she needs to accomplish great things.

They Despised the Promised Land

Ten of the spies lacked the virtue of magnanimity and so were afraid to take the Promised Land. Their fear spread among the people of Israel.

Num 14:1-4, 7-11

14 ¹Then all the congregation raised a loud cry; and the people wept that night. ²And all the sons of Israel murmured against Moses and Aaron; the whole congregation said to them, "Would that we had died in the land of Egypt! Or would that we had died in this wilderness! ³Why does the LORD bring us into this land, to fall by the sword? Our wives and our little ones will become a prey; would it not be better for us to go back to Egypt?"

⁴And they said to one another, "Let us choose a captain, and go back to Egypt." . . .

⁷[Joshua and Caleb] said to all the congregation of the sons of Israel, . . . ⁸"If the LORD delights in us, he will bring us into this land and give it to us. . . . ⁹Only, do not rebel against the LORD; and do not fear the people of the land, for . . . the LORD is with us, do not fear them." ¹⁰But all the congregation said to stone them with stones.

Then . . . ¹¹the LORD said to Moses, "How long will this people despise me? And how long will they not believe in me, in spite of all the signs which I have wrought among them?"

Desert wilderness on the Sinai Peninsula

Adam and Eve's sin began with distrust. Our first parents doubted God's truth and goodness. They thought they would be happier by disobeying God's commands. The Israelites also placed their trust in themselves and not in the Lord. They assumed God was leading them to their deaths and they would all "fall by the sword" (14:3).

The Israelites' faithlessness ran deep. They believed Pharaoh and his false gods would provide for them better than the Lord, who had brought them out of Egypt. But Caleb and Joshua were faithful and trusted in God. They called the Israelites to trust in the Lord, who continued to be with his people despite their sin.

God punished the Israelites for their lack of faith. He prevented those who did not trust in him from entering the Promised Land. The Israelites had to wander in the wilderness for forty years—one year for each day the spies had explored the land of Canaan. Only after forty years would the children of those who came out of Egypt be allowed to enter the Promised Land.

They Shall Inherit the Land

At the Waters of Meribah

During their forty-year journey in the wilderness, the Israelites continued to distrust God and the leaders he had appointed for them—Moses and his brother, Aaron. At one point, God instructed Moses how he, the Lord, would supply his people with water in the desert:

> *Num 20:7-8, 10-13*
>
> **20** ⁷The LORD said to Moses, ⁸"Take the rod, and assemble the congregation, you and Aaron your brother, and tell the rock before their eyes to yield its water." . . .
>
> ¹⁰And Moses and Aaron gathered the assembly together before the rock, and he said to them, "Hear now, you rebels; shall we bring forth water for you out of this rock?" ¹¹And Moses lifted up his hand and struck the rock with his rod twice; and water came forth abundantly, and the congregation drank, and their cattle. ¹²And the LORD said to Moses and Aaron, "Because you did not believe in me, to sanctify me in the eyes of the sons of Israel, therefore you shall not bring this assembly into the land which I have given them." ¹³These are the waters of Meribah, where the sons of Israel contended with the LORD.

It might be surprising to read that the Lord accused Moses of lacking faith: "You did not believe in me" (20:12). But the Scripture gives two reasons for this accusation:

- Moses said to the people, "Shall we bring forth water for you?" (20:10). Moses spoke as if the strength of he and Aaron alone would bring forth water, and not the strength of God working through them. He was more interested in proving his own power before the people than in leading the people to trust in God's power, "to sanctify [God] in the eyes of the sons of Israel" (20:12).

- Moses did not follow God's instructions. God told Moses to speak to the rock to bring water forth (see 20:8). The Lord said nothing about striking the rock. Moses took things into his own hands instead of obeying God.

Taking Possession of the Land

As punishment for his lack of faith, Moses was not allowed to enter the Promised Land. After his death, the faithful spy Joshua led the Israelites into the land of Canaan. The book of the Bible named after Joshua tells of these events.

God wanted to teach the Israelites not to rely on their own strength but to trust in God's power and faithfulness. The Lord parted the waters of the Jordan

The Fall of Jericho, Jean Fouquet

River so that the Israelites could cross on dry ground and enter the land promised to the descendants of Abraham. Then the Lord revealed how they would conquer the heavily guarded city of Jericho:

Josh 6:1-7

6 ¹Now Jericho was shut up from within and from without because of the sons of Israel; none went out, and none came in. ²And the LORD said to Joshua, "See, I have given into your hand Jericho, with its king and mighty men of valor. ³You shall march around the city, all the men of war going around the city once. Thus shall you do for six days. ⁴And seven priests shall bear seven trumpets of rams' horns before the ark; and on the seventh day you shall march around the city seven times, the priests blowing the trumpets. ⁵And when they make a long blast with the ram's horn, as soon as you hear the sound of the trumpet, then all the people shall shout with a great shout; and the wall of the city will fall down flat, and the people shall go up every man straight before him." ⁶So Joshua . . . called the priests and said to them, "Take up the ark of the covenant, and let seven priests bear seven trumpets of rams' horns before the ark of the LORD." ⁷And he said to the people, "Go forward; march around the city, and let the armed men pass on before the ark of the LORD."

The Israelites did as God commanded, and the walls of Jericho came crumbling down. God gave Jericho to his people. We see this especially in the role of the Ark of the Covenant in the defeat of Jericho. The [Ark of the Covenant] was a wooden chest plated with gold where God made himself present to his people.

God commanded the Ark of the Covenant to be brought before the armies of Israel when they marched around Jericho. He had Israel do this to teach his people that it was by his presence and power that they would have victory, and not their own strength.

They Inclined Their Hearts to the Lord

God's power and faithfulness to the covenant with Israel enabled his people to defeat their enemies and inherit the land he had promised them. After the victory, Joshua gathered all the tribes of Israel and called them to renew their trust in the Lord:

Josh 24:2, 14-18

24 ²And Joshua said to all the people, . . . ¹⁴"Fear the LORD, and serve him in sincerity and in faithfulness; put away the gods which your fathers served beyond the River, and in Egypt, and serve the LORD. ¹⁵And if you be unwilling to serve the LORD, choose this day whom you will serve . . . ; but as for me and my house, we will serve the LORD." ¹⁶Then the people answered, "Far be it from us that we should forsake the LORD, to serve other gods; ¹⁷for it is the LORD our God who brought us and our fathers up from the land of Egypt, out of the house of bondage . . . ; ¹⁸therefore we also will serve the LORD, for he is our God."

The Israelites promised to remember all God had done for them. They rejected the false gods of other nations and swore that they would worship the one Lord, the God of Israel.

Chapter 11 Summary

1. The Israelites often failed to trust in the Lord because they were fearful instead of faithful.

2. Joshua and Caleb demonstrated the virtue of magnanimity when they did great things by trusting in God's strength and not their own.

3. After forty years in the wilderness, God raised up Joshua to lead his people into the Promised Land where they renewed their covenant with the Lord.

The Virtue of Meekness

Meekness is often misunderstood. For many, to be meek means being weak or a pushover. But consider what Sacred Scripture reveals about meekness:

- "The man Moses was very meek, more than all men that were on the face of the earth" (Num 12:3).

- "Take my yoke upon you, and learn from me, for I am meek and humble in heart, and you will find rest for your souls" (Mt 11:29).

- "Blessed are the meek, for they shall inherit the earth" (Mt 5:5).

The first verse above describes Moses as a meek man. In the second verse, Jesus describes himself as meek. And in the third verse, Jesus teaches us that meekness is required to enter the Kingdom of Heaven.

Neither Moses nor Jesus were pushovers. Moses confronted the corrupt, powerful pharaoh. Jesus boldly preached the Good News, even when it led others to hate him. Meekness is a calm strength, not a weakness. Rather than our being controlled by anger, meekness is the virtue that strengthens us to control our anger and direct it toward doing good.

Anger is a natural reaction when we see an evil or injustice. At times, Moses got angry. For example, Moses "went out from Pharoah in hot anger" after warning Pharoah about the final plague (Ex 11:8). Jesus also got angry. Recall that he drove out the money changers from the Temple and flipped over their tables (see Mt 21:12). Anger is good when it helps us confront evil or injustice. Moses' anger helped him confront the wicked pharaoh. Jesus' anger caused him to stop those who were disrespecting God's holy Temple.

Yet anger easily can become sinful. Anger becomes sinful when we lose control of our temper. Meek people are slow to anger and not easily offended. They show patience and understanding. They carefully consider the right course of action.

Anger also becomes sinful when it leads us to hate others and to want their harm. Meek people keep their anger from becoming sinful. Moses, for example, was angry at the Israelites' faithlessness. Yet he did not hate the people. Instead, he interceded for them constantly. He begged God to be merciful and forgive their many sins.

Jesus calls each of us to control our anger through the virtue of meekness. This can be a difficult task. However, Jesus can do great things in us if we allow his grace to work in our lives. Going to the Sacrament of Reconciliation is a great way to allow Christ to give us the strength of meekness.

When does your anger tend to get out of control? When do you find it tempting to hate someone?

_____
_____

What are some specific ways you can avoid these situations?

_____
_____
_____

Name a time when you were quick to anger but you had wrongly judged the situation and did not need to be angry. What did you learn from the experience?

_____
_____
_____

Let Us Pray—Psalm 114

In Psalm 114, the psalmist recalls God's faithfulness to Israel. God delivered the Israelites out of Egypt and led them into the Promised Land across the Jordan River. As you pray this psalm, ask the Father to help you trust in his strength and faithfulness.

Ps 114:1-8

114
¹When Israel went forth from Egypt,
　the house of Jacob from a people of strange language,
²Judah became his sanctuary,
　Israel his dominion.
³The sea looked and fled,
　Jordan turned back.
⁴The mountains skipped like rams,
　the hills like lambs.
⁵What ails you, O sea, that you flee?
　O Jordan, that you turn back?
⁶O mountains, that you skip like rams?
　O hills, like lambs?
⁷Tremble, O earth, at the presence of the LORD,
　at the presence of the God of Jacob,
⁸who turns the rock into a pool of water,
　the flint into a spring of water.

Chapter 11 Review:
A Land Flowing with Milk and Honey

1. How many spies did Moses send into the Promised Land? _____

2. What were the names of the two faithful spies? _____

3. How long did the Israelites wander in the desert as punishment before entering the Promised Land? _____

4. What was the name of the wooden box covered in gold where God made himself present to his people? _____

5. Why were most of the Israelites at first afraid to enter the Promised Land?
   _____
   _____

6. Who took Moses' place and led the people of Israel into the Promised Land? _____

7. From this chapter, give three or more specific examples that show how the Israelites were sinful and failed to trust in the Lord.
   _____
   _____
   _____
   _____
   _____

8. How did Caleb and Joshua live out the virtue of magnanimity?
   _____
   _____
   _____

The Bronze Serpent

We find an important example of God's mercy in the Book of Numbers. During Israel's forty years wandering in the wilderness, the people grew rebellious and complained about God's blessings:

Num 21:5-9

21 ⁵And the people spoke against God and against Moses, "Why have you brought us up out of Egypt to die in the wilderness? For there is no food and no water, and we loathe this worthless food." ⁶Then the LORD sent fiery serpents among the people, and they bit the people, so that many sons of Israel died. ⁷And the people came to Moses, and said, "We have sinned, for we have spoken against the LORD and against you; pray to the Lord, that he take away the serpents from us." So Moses prayed for the people. ⁸And the LORD said to Moses, "Make a fiery serpent, and set it up as a sign; and every one who is bitten, when he sees it, shall live." ⁹So Moses made a bronze serpent, and set it up as a sign; and if a serpent bit any man, he would look at the bronze serpent and live.

Shockingly, the "worthless food" (21:5) they complained about was nothing other than the manna, the miraculous daily "bread from heaven" (Ex 16:4). The people who sinned by their poisonous words were punished by snakes with poisonous tongues. But Moses again interceded for the people, and the Lord again showed himself to be "abounding in mercy" (Ex 34:6). The bronze serpent became a source of healing. Those who looked upon it with faith lived. At the same time, the bronze serpent was also a reminder of the people's sin.

Jesus compared himself to the bronze serpent when speaking to one of his disciples about his Crucifixion in John's Gospel:

Jn 3:13-16

3 ¹³"No one has ascended into heaven but he who descended from heaven, the Son of man. ¹⁴And as Moses lifted up the serpent in the wilderness, so must the Son of man be lifted up, ¹⁵that whoever believes in him may have eternal life."
¹⁶For God so loved the world that he gave his only-begotten Son, that whoever believes in him should not perish but have eternal life.

Crucifixion, from a missal, French School, 13th century

The bronze serpent lifted up on a pole foreshadowed Jesus being lifted up on the Cross. When the Israelites looked upon the bronze serpent with faith, they were saved from the deadly bites of the fiery serpents. Similarly, it is through faith in Christ Crucified that we are saved from the powers of sin and death. The Cross of Christ reminds us not only of the grave consequences of our sins but also much more of the depth of God's mercy and love for us.

Journal Reflection

**In what ways does the crucifix remind you of the consequences of your sins?
In what ways does it remind you of God's mercy and love?**

Letting God In

Read

Jesus said, "Ask, and it shall be given to you; seek, and you shall find; knock, and it shall be opened to you" (Mt 7:7).

Jesus promises us that he will be there for us, to give us what is always best for us. We just need *to ask* him. We need *to seek* him. We need *to knock* at his door.

However, too often we try to take our lives into our own hands. We try to fix our own problems and keep God far away. We can be just like the Israelites, who trusted in themselves rather than in God's power. Because of their self-reliance, they were too afraid to enter the Promised Land. They quickly realized they did not have enough strength to face the dangers that awaited them.

The same is true for us. We cannot flourish simply by our own strength. We cannot face the dangers and obstacles life throws at us by ourselves. We need to let God in. We need to trust in his goodness and power. We need *to ask* him, *to seek* him, and *to knock* at his door.

If we do this, we can face any challenge in our lives and say, as Caleb did, "We are well able to overcome it" (Num 13:30).

Reflect

Spend 5–10 minutes reflecting on the following:

- In what areas of my life do I need to give up control and let God in?
- What is preventing me from trusting in God right now?

Pray

Pray the Our Father.

Act

This week, think about a decision you need to make in your life. It can be either a decision you are facing now or one you may possibly face in the future. Ask God to strengthen you and to help you know and do his will.

CHAPTER 12

Jesus, the New Moses

Words to Know

> *Beatitudes*

> *New Law*

Proclaiming the Good News

"The law was given through Moses; grace and truth came through Jesus Christ." —John 1:17

Scene of the Massacre of the Innocents, Leon Cogniet

A Prophet like Moses

Moses with the New Tablets of the Law on Mount Sinai, Anonymous

Moses, the Servant of the Lord

In the centuries leading up to the Birth of Jesus, God's people were waiting for a new Moses. This hope for a new Moses rose out of the Scriptures themselves. In the Book of Deuteronomy, Moses foretold that the Lord would one day raise up a prophet like him to lead God's Chosen People:

Deut 18:15-18

18 ¹⁵"The LORD your God will raise up for you a prophet like me from among you, from your brethren—him you shall heed—¹⁶just as you desired of the LORD your God at Horeb on the day of the assembly, when you said, 'Let me not hear again the voice of the LORD my God, or see this great fire any more, lest I die.' ¹⁷And the LORD said to me, 'They have rightly said all that they have spoken. ¹⁸I will raise up for them a prophet like you from among their brethren; and I will put my words in his mouth, and he shall speak to them all that I command him.'"

This prophet like Moses would speak God's own words, so Moses told the people that they must "heed" him (18:15). In other words, they must listen to him. The final verses of the Book of Deuteronomy revisit the promise of a new Moses and reveal something further about him:

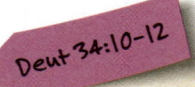

Deut 34:10-12

34 ¹⁰And there has not arisen a prophet since in Israel like Moses, whom the LORD knew face to face, ¹¹none like him for all the signs and the wonders which the LORD sent him to do in the land of Egypt, to Pharaoh and to all his servants and to all his land, ¹²and for all the mighty power and all the great and terrible deeds which Moses wrought in the sight of all Israel.

What would truly set apart this prophet like Moses was not the miracles he would perform but his unique relationship with God: "The LORD used to speak to Moses face to face, as a man speaks to his friend" (Ex 33:11). Eventually, this hope for a new Moses came to be associated with the hope for the Messiah, the anointed King who would save God's people through a new Exodus.

Jesus Is Revealed as the New Moses

Recall the words of Saint Augustine: "The New Testament lies hidden in the Old, and the Old Testament is unveiled in the New."[1] Saint Matthew unveiled Jesus as the New Moses by focusing on ways that Jesus' life echoed Moses' life. He wrote his Gospel in this way to show that Jesus fulfilled the hopes of God's people for a new Moses. Consider some of the parallels between Moses and Jesus in the Book of Exodus and the Gospel of Matthew, respectively.

Moses *Book of Exodus*	Jesus *Gospel of Matthew*
Threatened by the murderous command of Pharaoh, king of Egypt (see 1:15–16)	Threatened by the murderous command of Herod the king (see 2:16)
Rescued from death as a young child by the actions of his mother (see 2:1–3)	Rescued from death as a young child by the actions of Saint Joseph, his foster father (see 2:13–14)
Safely brought up in Egypt as a young child, having been adopted by Pharaoh's daughter (see 2:5–10)	Safely brought up in Egypt as a young child (see 2:14–15)
Called back to Egypt, the place of his birth, years after having fled from Pharaoh (see 4:19–20)	Called back to Israel, the place of his Birth, years after having fled from Herod (see 2:19–21)
Fasted for forty days and forty nights on Mount Sinai (see 34:28)	Fasted for forty days and forty nights in the wilderness (see 4:2)
Delivered the Old Law (the Decalogue) received from God on Mount Sinai to the people of Israel (see 19:2–3)	Taught the New Law to his disciples on a mountain (see 5:1–2)
Fed thousands in the wilderness with miraculous "bread from heaven"—the manna (16:4)	Fed thousands in the wilderness with miraculous bread when he multiplied the five loaves (see 14:13–21)

When we are attentive to these connections between the Old and New Testaments, we deepen our understanding of who Jesus is and what he came to do. God preserved Moses from danger as a young child so that he could lead God's people out of slavery in Egypt in the Exodus. So, too, God ensured Jesus' safety as a young child so that he could lead us out of spiritual slavery to the powers of sin and death in a new Exodus.

The New Exodus

The Hope for a New Law

Moses went up Mount Sinai to receive the Decalogue from the Lord. The Old Law, which was summed up in the Ten Commandments, was good and holy and prepared the way for the New Law of the Gospel. The Old Law helped the Israelites know how to love God and their neighbor but did not have the power to transform their hard hearts. The Israelites often fell prey to idolatry and other sins as they hardened their hearts and turned away from the Lord.

But God remained faithful to his covenant and did not abandon his people. He promised to redeem his people from their sins and give them a New Law. We find this New Law promised in the Book of Jeremiah:

> **Jer 31:31-34**
>
> **31** ³¹"Behold, the days are coming, says the LORD, when I will make a new covenant with the house of Israel and the house of Judah, ³²not like the covenant which I made with their fathers when I took them by the hand to bring them out of the land of Egypt, my covenant which they broke. . . . ³³But this is the covenant which I will make with the house of Israel after those days, says the LORD: I will put my law within them, and I will write it upon their hearts; and I will be their God, and they shall be my people. ³⁴And no longer shall each man teach his neighbor and each his brother, saying, 'Know the LORD,' for they shall all know me, from the least of them to the greatest, says the LORD; for I will forgive their iniquity, and I will remember their sin no more."

Just as the Old Law was given when God made a covenant with his people at Mount Sinai, so the New Law would come as part of a promised New Covenant. But the New Law was unlike the Old Law God gave to Moses and the Israelites in an important way: it would be written not on stone tablets but *upon the hearts* of God's people. The New Law would draw people into an intimate relationship with God and bring about the forgiveness of sins.

Jesus Gives the New Law

Jesus fulfilled the prophecy of Jeremiah by giving the *New Law*. The New Law given by Jesus is the grace of the Holy Spirit given to us through faith in Christ and the sacraments, beginning with Baptism. As Saint Paul wrote, "God's love has been poured into our hearts through the Holy Spirit who has been given to us" (Rom 5:5). The New Law is a law of grace that transforms our hearts so that we might love as Christ loves.

The New Law is expressed above all in Jesus' Sermon on the Mount (see Mt 5–7). As the New Moses, Jesus went up a mountain to teach the New Law. The Sermon on the Mount can be understood as a sort of instruction manual for how to live out the New Law in our lives.

At the beginning of Jesus' Sermon on the Mount, we find the Beatitudes. The *Beatitudes* are Jesus' teachings about how to achieve eternal happiness with God in Heaven. The word "beatitude" means "happiness." The Beatitudes remind us that God calls us to share in his own life. In inviting his disciples to embrace the Beatitudes, Jesus calls us to imitate him in love, resulting in true happiness.

Jesus' New Law gives us the strength to obey God's commandments, especially the twofold commandment to love God above all things and to love our neighbor as ourselves. It is a law of love that reflects the very life of the Blessed Trinity, the God who is love. This is why Jesus instructs his disciples, "Love one another as I have loved you" (Jn 15:12).

The New Covenant

Through the prophet Jeremiah, the Lord promised not only a New Law but also a New Covenant. Moses led God's Chosen People out of Egypt in the Exodus so that they could enter into a covenant with God at Mount Sinai:

Sermon on the Mount, Henrik Olrik

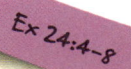

24 ⁴Moses . . . rose early in the morning, and built an altar at the foot of the mountain. . . . ⁵And he sent young men of the sons of Israel, who offered burnt offerings and sacrificed peace offerings of oxen to the LORD. ⁶And Moses took half of the blood and put it in basins, and half of the blood he threw against the altar. ⁷Then he took the book of the covenant, and read it in the hearing of the people; and they said, "All that the LORD has spoken we will do, and we will be obedient." ⁸And Moses took the blood and threw it upon the people, and said, "Behold the blood of the covenant which the LORD has made with you in accordance with all these words."

Notice that the bond uniting God (symbolized by the altar) with his people was called "the blood of the covenant" (24:8). At the Last Supper, Jesus echoed these words to describe what he would accomplish through his sacrifice on the Cross and the whole Paschal Mystery. When he took the cup of wine, he said, "This is my blood of the covenant, which is poured out for many for the forgiveness of sins" (Mt 26:28).

Jesus' blood was "poured out" when he was crucified. Through his Death and Resurrection, Jesus established the New Covenant that freed us from slavery to sin and reconciled us to God (see Jer 31:34). At every Mass, we participate in the saving work accomplished by Jesus Christ, the New Moses, who freed us from slavery to sin in the new Exodus.

Chapter 12 Summary

1. God taught his people through the prophets to look forward to a new Exodus that would be led by a new Moses.

2. Saint Matthew presented Jesus as the New Moses, who brought about a new Exodus and established the New Covenant through his Paschal Mystery.

3. Jesus gave the New Law, the law of the Gospel, which is a law of grace that frees us from the powers of sin and death to love as God loves.

The New Law of Freedom

Jesus, the Divine Physician

When was the last time you went to the doctor? We typically go to a doctor to make sure our bodies are healthy. A body is healthy when everything in it is fulfilling its purpose. For example, a heart is healthy if it serves its purpose of pumping blood throughout the body.

To be healthy, we need to get enough exercise and sleep, eat the right foods, and take care of our mental health. Yet we also need something more. As we learned in Chapter 6, humans are a unity of body and soul. If we want to flourish, we need more than healthy bodies; we need healthy souls.

A healthy soul, just like a healthy body, is one that can fulfill its purpose. As the Church teaches, "Man is made to live in communion with God in whom he finds happiness" (*CCC* 45). God made us to share in his own blessed life. We will flourish and be happy if we fulfill this purpose, but we will suffer if we do not. Sin prevents us from achieving our purpose because it draws us away from God, the source of our happiness.

When our bodies are unhealthy, we see a doctor. Sometimes a doctor must give a patient "tough love." The patient may have to be told to go on a serious diet and get more exercise. The doctor may give what seems like hard instructions, but it is done out of care for the patient.

When our souls are unhealthy, we also need to see a doctor. Jesus is the Divine Physician. As he taught, "Those who are well have no need of a physician, but those who are sick; I came not to call the righteous, but sinners" (Mk 2:17). Jesus came to free us from our slavery to sin and to heal us.

Like a good doctor, Jesus sometimes gives his patients "tough love." In his Sermon on the Mount in Matthew's Gospel, Jesus' commands can seem strict or unreasonable. Jesus commands us to be merciful and just (see 5:6–7), to endure persecution for our faith (see 5:10–11), to control our anger (see 5:21–26), and even to love our enemies (see 5:43–47). But in the New Law, Christ gives not just new commands but the grace of the Holy Spirit to live according to his commands.

True Freedom

Following Jesus requires lots of discipline. We often think of freedom as doing whatever we want. A person is free to eat junk food all day. But he will suffer as a result. True freedom is doing what will make us truly happy. True freedom enables us to live a life of self-giving love.

Living a life of self-giving love requires much self-discipline. Loving God, others, and even ourselves means not always doing what we want and sometimes saying no to our worldly desires. Because of Original Sin, all humans experience an inclination to do what is wrong. We must fight a war within ourselves against our sinful desires to achieve our deepest desire: happiness.

Jesus does not command the impossible. Like an antibiotic, the New Law heals our sin-hardened hearts from the inside. In the New Law, the grace of the Holy Spirit is poured into our hearts through faith in Christ and the sacraments. The New Law empowers us to carry out Jesus' commands and resist temptation. Because we have received God's love, we can fulfill Jesus' Greatest Commandment: to love God above all things and to love our neighbor as ourselves.

 The more we love, the freer we become. Given what you just read, why do you think this is?

_____

_____

_____

Let Us Pray—Psalm 77

Psalm 77 is a psalm of lament. Yet, instead of merely crying out in hopeless despair, the psalmist meditates on God's past saving work in the Exodus. Through contemplating the freedom God gave his people by the hand of Moses, we can nourish our hope that God will ultimately deliver us from the evils that confront us in this life.

Ps 77:1-2, 11-16, 19-20

77 ¹I cry aloud to God,
   aloud to God, that he may hear me.
²In the day of my trouble I seek the Lord;
   in the night my hand is stretched out
      without wearying;
   my soul refuses to be comforted. . . .
¹¹I will call to mind the deeds of the LORD;
   yes, I will remember your wonders of old.
¹²I will meditate on all your work,
   and muse on your mighty deeds.
¹³Your way, O God, is holy.
   What god is great like our God?
¹⁴You are the God who works wonders,
   who have manifested your might among the
      peoples.
¹⁵With your arm you redeemed your people,
   the sons of Jacob and Joseph.
¹⁶When the waters saw you, O God,
   when the waters saw you, they were afraid,
   yes, the deep trembled. . . .
¹⁹Your way was through the sea,
   your path through the great waters;
   yet your footprints were unseen.
²⁰You led your people like a flock
   by the hand of Moses and Aaron.

Chapter 12 Review:
Jesus, the New Moses

1. Before the coming of Christ, the Scriptures taught God's people to look forward to a prophet like _____ who would lead a new _____.

2. Jesus reminded us of Moses when he went up on a mountain to teach his disciples in Matthew 5–7. This extended teaching is known as the _____.

3. In the New Covenant that God foretold through the prophet Jeremiah, where would his law be written? _____

4. The grace of the Holy Spirit that is given to us by God through faith in Christ and the sacraments is known as the _____.

5. Jesus' teachings about how to achieve eternal happiness with God in Heaven that are found at the beginning of the Sermon on the Mount are known as the _____.

6. At the Last Supper, Jesus echoed the words of Moses at Mount Sinai when he used what words? _____

7. The *Catechism* teaches that "the New Law is a law of love, a law of grace, a law of freedom" (*CCC* 1985). Briefly explain what each of these means.

_____
_____
_____
_____
_____
_____

Bread from Heaven

In the Sermon on the Mount, Jesus taught his disciples to pray, "Give us this day our daily bread" (Mt 6:11). This petition for daily bread calls to mind the manna of the Exodus. Psalm 78 speaks of this great gift that the Lord gave daily to his people: "He rained down upon them manna to eat, and gave them the bread of heaven" (78:24). The hope that God would one day raise up a prophet like Moses brought with it the hope that this new Moses would feed God's people with a new manna.

It is against the background of such hope for a new manna that Saint John recorded one of Jesus' most memorable teachings in his Gospel. Following the Feeding of the Five Thousand, Jesus identified himself as the new manna:

The Communion of the Apostles, James Tissot

Jn 6:48–51, 54, 58

6 ⁴⁸"I am the bread of life. ⁴⁹Your fathers ate the manna in the wilderness, and they died. ⁵⁰This is the bread which comes down from heaven, that a man may eat of it and not die. ⁵¹I am the living bread which came down from heaven; if any one eats of this bread, he will live for ever; and the bread which I shall give for the life of the world is my flesh. . . .

⁵⁴"He who eats my flesh and drinks my blood has eternal life, and I will raise him up at the last day. . . . ⁵⁸This is the bread which came down from heaven, not such as the fathers ate and died; he who eats this bread will live for ever."

At the Last Supper, when Jesus established the memorial of the New Covenant by instituting the Eucharist, he gave this gift of the new manna to his Church. The new manna is greater than the manna of the Exodus, for it gives us a share in the eternal life of God himself. When we pray the Our Father, we should do so mindful of the daily bread that Jesus, the New Moses, invites us to eat.

Journal Reflection

The manna sustained the Israelites during the forty years they wandered in the wilderness until they entered the Promised Land. **Why do we need the new manna of the Eucharist to sustain us on our journey through this life?**

From the Saints

"The Father in heaven urges us, as children of heaven, to ask for the bread of heaven. [Christ] himself is the bread who, sown in the Virgin, raised up in the flesh, kneaded in the Passion, baked in the oven of the tomb, reserved in churches, brought to altars, furnishes the faithful each day with food from heaven."²
—Saint Peter Chrysologus

"Do Not Be Anxious"

Read

There is a difference between fear and anxiety. Fear is based on something real and specific. If you do not study for a difficult test, you *fear* not doing well. If you have not practiced for the play, you *fear* forgetting your lines on stage. In both examples, fear is based on something real: not preparing well enough.

Anxiety is different. It is based on *what ifs*, not *what is*. You might study well and still think, *What if I fail?* You might have memorized your lines but still think, *What if I forget everything on stage?* There is no reason to think you will fail the test or forget your lines. You are experiencing *anxiety*, not fear. In the Sermon on the Mount, Jesus taught,

> Mt 6:25, 33–34
>
> **6** ²⁵"I say to you, do not be anxious about your life, what you will eat, or about your body, what you will wear. Is not life more than food and the body more than clothing? . . . ³³But seek first the kingdom of God and his righteousness, and all these things will be added to you. ³⁴Therefore, do not be anxious about tomorrow, for tomorrow will be anxious for itself. Today's trouble is enough for today."

Jesus tells us not to be anxious about our lives. We must let go of the what-ifs. Jesus reminds us that we have *enough* real troubles to deal with each day. Jesus teaches us to "seek first the kingdom" (6:33). This means we must make God number one in our lives and love God above all else. If we have a strong relationship with God, everything else will fall into place. We will still face our daily troubles. But we can approach this suffering and difficulty with faith, trusting that God will give us the strength to face each day.

Reflect

Spend 5–10 minutes reflecting on the following:

- What is causing me fear or anxiety in my life right now?
- Have I talked with God about it?

Pray

Ask the Lord for his help with this simple prayer taken from the *Liturgy of the Hours*:

> God, come to my assistance. Lord, make haste to help me.
> Glory to the Father, and to the Son, and to the Holy Spirit:
> As it was in the beginning, is now, and will be for ever. Amen.

Act

Whenever you feel anxious this week, pray silently, "Jesus, I give this worry to you."

Unit 4

The Kingdom of the Lord

After the Israelites settled in the Promised Land, they continued to fall prey to sin and commit idolatry in the time of the judges. Eventually, the Lord called forth David, a man after God's heart, to be the king over all Israel and made a covenant with him. Then David's son Solomon ruled over the kingdom. At first he ruled with wisdom, but later his sins resulted in the kingdom being divided in two the Kingdom of Israel (North) and the Kingdom of Judah (South).

In the centuries that followed, the Lord raised up prophets—such as Elijah, Elisha, Hosea, Amos, Isaiah, Jeremiah, and Ezekiel—to call his people to repentance, warn them of judgment, and give them hope for restoration. For a time, God permitted the sin of his people but punished them with exile from the Promised Land, as he had foretold. The city of Jerusalem and the Temple were destroyed by the Babylonians as they brought the people into exile.

The Gospel of Matthew reveals Jesus as the Son of David, the New Solomon, through whom God's covenant with David was fulfilled.

Chapters 13-18

Chapter 13: The Lord Raised Up Judges

Chapter 14: David the King

Chapter 15: The House of David

Chapter 16: The Mission of the Prophets

Chapter 17: Into Exile

Chapter 18: Jesus, the Son of David

Grade 6 Road Map

Unit 1
The Good News

The Gospel of Matthew reveals who Jesus is through both his deeds and words. God speaks to us in Sacred Scripture through human authors inspired by the Holy Spirit.

Unit 2
In the Beginning

Genesis describes the beginning of the universe and humanity, the beginning of sin, and the beginning of God's plan to restore mankind's relationship with himself through the covenant with Abraham and his descendants. In Jesus, God's covenant with Abraham is fulfilled.

Unit 3
You Shall Be My People

Through Moses, God delivered his people from slavery in Egypt and made a covenant with them at Mount Sinai. Despite their unfaithfulness, God brought his people into the Promised Land after they wandered for forty years in the desert. Jesus is the New Moses, who gives the New Law.

Unit 4
The Kingdom of the Lord

The Lord made a covenant with King David and swore to give him an everlasting kingdom. The sins of God's people led to the division and downfall of the kingdom, eventually leading to the destruction of the Temple and the Babylonian exile. In Jesus, God's covenant with David is fulfilled.

Unit 5
The Coming of the Anointed One

God brought his people back from exile to the Promised Land, where they rebuilt the Temple in Jerusalem. The prophets foretold of the coming of the Messiah, who would rebuild the kingdom of David. Jesus, the Son of Man, brings the kingdom through his suffering and Death.

Unit 6
God with Us

The Gospel of Matthew provides reliable testimony that Jesus is the Divine Son of God made man, who delivered us from sin through his Paschal Mystery. Jesus continues to be present to his Church through Word and sacrament—above all, the Holy Eucharist.

Saint Gregory the Great

A Humble Leader

Saint Gregory the Great was born into a wealthy Roman family in the sixth century A.D., after the fall of the Roman Empire. He was well educated, and as a young man, he worked in law and administration in the city of Rome. By the age of thirty-three, he was prefect of Rome. This was essentially like being mayor of the city.

Soon after, he heard the call of God to become a monk. Monks are members of a religious community who take vows of poverty, chastity, and obedience. They live together in a place called a monastery and dedicate their lives to prayer and work. Gregory left his career behind, gave his wealth away, and became a Benedictine, a member of the community founded by Saint Benedict. He turned his family home in Rome into a Benedictine monastery. He later said that these years of prayer and work in the monastery were the happiest days of his life. He founded six other Benedictine monasteries and later would write a biography of Saint Benedict.

Gregory would have been happy living a quiet life of prayer and work as a monk. But God had other plans for him. First, the pope sent him to Constantinople to be his ambassador to the emperor and his court. Then in A.D. 590, when the pope died from a plague, the priests and people of Rome begged Gregory to lead the Church as pope. Gregory tried to turn down the election. Some accounts even describe him running away from the city! But he finally agreed. Despite wanting to live a quiet life of prayer, Gregory became the first monk to be elected pope.

The city of Rome had been ruined by famine, floods, attacks, and invasions, as well as the plague. One of the first things Pope Gregory did was lead everyone in a procession around the city, carrying an icon of the Blessed Mother and Jesus, known as *Salus Populi Romani*, which is Latin for "Protectress of the Roman People." This icon can still be seen in the Basilica of Saint Mary Major in Rome. He and the people made this procession to ask for forgiveness of their sins and for God to save them from the plague. As the procession got close to Saint Peter's Basilica, Saint Michael the Archangel appeared on top of a nearby building. Saint Michael was holding a flaming sword high up in the air. Pope Gregory saw him put it in its sheath. The plague was over.

Even though Gregory had wanted to live a quiet life of prayer in his monastery, he humbly obeyed the call to lead the Church and did everything he could to serve the People of God. It was Gregory who first used the phrase "Servant of the Servants of God" to describe the role of the pope. Even while pope, he remained a humble monk at heart.

One day, Gregory saw young boys from the north in the Roman marketplace. He asked someone who these blond-haired, blue-eyed young men were. Compared to the dark-haired, dark-eyed Romans, these boys stood out. He was told that they were Angles from Angleland (modern-day England). "Not Angles, but angels," Gregory said.[1] When he realized they did not know the Gospel, he resolved to send missionaries up to the north. Britain had been part of the Roman Empire, so Christianity had been brought there in the first centuries of the Church. Saint Alban, who is considered the first Christian martyr in England, lived in the third century. But by the time of Gregory, the Anglo-Saxon tribes had plundered the land. Roman law, language, and culture had disappeared. While there were some Christians still in the land we know as England or Great Britain, much of the area was pagan again.

In A.D. 596, Pope Gregory sent forty Benedictine monks to evangelize Britain, led by a monk named Augustine. Augustine established churches and monasteries, including a monastery in Canterbury that stands today. Saint Augustine of Canterbury would not see much of his success before he died in A.D. 605, but the Catholic faith spread throughout the region. Now he and Gregory are together known as the Apostles to England. The Christian faith in Great Britain is due to the hard work and vision of Gregory and Augustine.

A Pope at Work

When Gregory became pope in A.D. 590, Rome and the surrounding cities were suffering. In addition to the plagues and natural disasters, the area had also been attacked by barbarian tribes. These were people who lived in areas north of the borders of the Roman Empire. Groups called the Visigoths and the Vandals were not Christian and did not live like the Romans. They attacked and invaded Rome, taking prisoners, destroying buildings, and stealing the riches of the city. They left the city in ruins.

There was no law or order. No one was in charge, so the region had fallen into disorder. Gregory wrote, "Sights and sounds of the war meet us on every side. The cities are destroyed; the military stations broken up; the land devastated; the earth depopulated. No one remains in the country; scarcely any inhabitants in the towns."[2] He recalled that the Roman Empire was once glorious, strong, and the center of the world, but now "some places are laid waste by pestilence, others are depopulated by the sword, others are tormented by famine, and others are swallowed up by earthquakes."[3]

Gregory stepped up to the task to strengthen and rebuild both the Church and Rome. His experience in administration and governance, since his early days as prefect of Rome, was one reason the people had begged him to become pope. The other reason was his humility. The people knew that he would use all his gifts to serve the Church and the city, which he did.

Saint Gregory realized that one of the biggest threats to both Rome and the Catholic Church was disunity. He immediately set to work healing divisions. Some people ruling countries that called themselves Catholic said they did not need to obey the pope. Other countries were fighting with one another. Some bishops and priests were not teaching correct doctrine. Gregory worked to bring bishops and emperors back into union with the papacy. When the Lombards, a people in northern Italy, were attacking Rome, it was Gregory who negotiated peace with them on behalf of the city.

Pope Saint Gregory wrote more than 840 letters. He wrote to everyone, from bishops and priests to kings and queens. The letters were the work of a pastor who loved his flock. They were full of advice, correction, and support. He worked to stop the spread of errors and misunderstandings concerning the true faith. He wanted to bring those who had separated themselves from the Church back into union with her.

Gregory loved Sacred Scripture, and we have many of his Homilies and writings about Scripture. He also wanted to help people fall in love with the liturgy, so he added revised parts of the Mass and also added some prayers. Part of his work with the liturgy included assembling various chants and establishing

a uniformity in what was sung at Mass. His love for sacred music and chant led to Gregorian chant being named in his honor.

He also worked to make sure the clergy were living good, holy lives; caring for the poor; and serving their people. When the city of Rome was hit by a famine, Gregory fed the people from land that the Church owned outside the city. While that farmland previously had been used to grow food to sell to support the work of the Church, now Gregory ordered that the food be given away. Gregory sent priests out to distribute food, and he would not eat until they had returned. He would often invite the poor to eat at his own table with him.

One of Gregory's many written works is his *Pastoral Rule*. It was a four-part work for bishops and Church leaders. In this work, Gregory outlined characteristics of a good bishop. He wrote about how the bishop should order his life, how the bishop should teach, and the importance of humility in leadership. The Pastoral Rule became one of the most important texts in the Church in the Middle Ages. In France, bishops began taking their oath of office on a copy of the work. Saint Alfred the Great, king of the Anglo-Saxons in the ninth century, translated the work into the Saxon language and sent a copy to every bishop.

Protectress of the Roman People icon

Saint Gregory the Great died in A.D. 604 after successfully leading the Church into the Middle Ages. He was declared a saint and a Doctor of the Church. Saint Bede wrote the inscription on his tomb that spoke of his achievements in evangelizing the Anglo-Saxons, his care for the poor and suffering in Rome, and his wise teaching. It says, "In this tomb are laid the limbs of a great pontiff. . . . Hunger and cold he overcame with food and raiment, and shielded souls from the enemy by his holy teaching. And whatsoever he taught in word, that he lived in deed, that he might be a pattern. . . . By his guiding love he brought the Angles to Christ, gaining armies for the faith from a new people."[4]

Journal Reflection

1. Both Gregory and King David were called to leadership while they were content doing other humble things. **In what area of your life is the Lord calling you to take on a more active role as a leader? What hesitations do you have about this call? How will God's grace be necessary to help you embrace and live out this calling?**

2. **Even though we are not kings or popes, how can we imitate Saint Gregory and King David in spreading the Kingdom of God?**

3. Unity and disunity are important in the stories of both Gregory and Solomon. **What are some differences between King Solomon and Saint Gregory the Great?**

4. **How can we imitate Gregory's humility and service to the poor?**

CHAPTER 13
The Lord Raised Up Judges

Words to Know
> Baal

> Canaanites

> judges

Proclaiming the Good News

"What if some were unfaithful? Does their faithlessness nullify the faithfulness of God? By no means! Let God be true though every man be false." —Romans 3:3–4

Continuing the Story of Salvation

List four or five key events from the Exodus out of Egypt and journey to the Promised Land that show God's faithfulness to his Chosen People, Israel.

_____

_____

_____

_____

_____

_____

Othniel, James Tissot

167

Israel among the Inhabitants of the Land

Israel Settled the Promised Land

Following the death of Joshua, the Lord commanded the Israelites to settle Canaan, the Promised Land. They were to drive out the people already dwelling in the land, who were known as the Canaanites. The Lord knew that if the Canaanites remained in the Promised Land, they would tempt Israel to break God's law by worshipping their false gods and idols.

The Lord wanted to protect Israel from temptations to break the First Commandment. However, the Israelites did not drive out all the Canaanites and instead became superstitious like them. Superstition can cause us to depart from the worship that is due to the one true God and to commit idolatry. The Israelites sought knowledge and insights through forms of magic and communication with evil spirits. Because the Israelites failed to remain faithful to the Lord, they would be conquered by their enemies.

Judg 2:1-3

2 ¹Now the angel of the LORD . . . said, "I brought you up from Egypt, and brought you into the land which I swore to give to your fathers. I said, 'I will never break my covenant with you, ²and you shall make no covenant with the inhabitants of this land; you shall break down their altars.' But you have not obeyed my command. What is this you have done? ³So now I say, I will not drive them out before you; but they shall become adversaries to you, and their gods shall be a snare to you."

The Lord allowed Israel to experience suffering and oppression as the consequences of their sins. He did this to teach Israel they needed his protection and help to flourish. When we sin by turning away from God and rely instead on our own power, we open ourselves to be conquered by sin and suffer its consequences. Like Israel, we must learn to love God above all else.

Israel's Cycle of Sin

Because they relied on their own power instead of trusting in God, the Israelites fell into a repeating cycle of sin. The Book of Judges tells of this cycle:

Judg 2:11-12, 14, 16-19

2 ¹¹The sons of Israel did what was evil in the sight of the LORD . . . ; ¹²and they forsook the LORD, the God of their fathers, who had brought them out of the land of Egypt; they went after other gods, from among the gods of the peoples who were round about them, and bowed down to them; . . . ¹⁴So the anger of the LORD was kindled against Israel, and he gave them over to plunderers, who plundered them; and he sold them into the power of their enemies. . . .

¹⁶Then the LORD raised up judges, who saved them out of the power of those who plundered them. ¹⁷And yet they did not listen to their judges; . . . they soon turned aside from the way in which their fathers had walked, who had obeyed the commandments of the LORD, and they did not do so. ¹⁸Whenever the LORD raised up judges for them, the LORD was with the judge, and he saved them from the hand of their enemies all the days of the judge; . . . ¹⁹But whenever the judge died, they turned back and behaved worse than their fathers, going after other gods, serving them and bowing down to them.

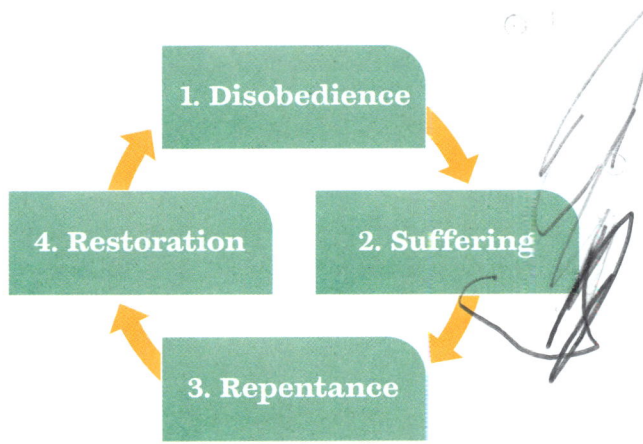

would deliver God's people during times of great distress. These judges did not sit in courtrooms and wear robes, but they were called upon to render just judgments. At times, they led armies. Through God's power, these judges brought *restoration* to God's people by saving them from their enemies and restoring their loving covenant relationship with the Lord. This cycle repeated itself over many years.

The chart above visualizes Israel's repeated cycle of sin and repentance. The Israelites would forget the Lord and grow lazy about keeping his law. This laziness often led them to sinful *disobedience*, primarily idolatry, when they worshipped the false gods of the Canaanites. Because of their disobedience, God allowed the Canaanites to conquer and oppress Israel, leading to great *suffering*.

When Israel showed *repentance* for their sins, the Lord—who is always faithful—showed mercy and delivered them. God raised up *judges*, leaders who

The storm god Baal with a thunderbolt, from Ugarit (Ras Shamra), c. 1350-1250 B.C.

Othniel, the First Judge

God chose a man named Othniel to become the first judge. In his story, we see Israel's cycle of sin in action. Israel turned from God by worshipping the false Canaanite gods. One of these false gods was named *Baal*.

Judg 3:7-11

3 ⁷The sons of Israel did what was evil in the sight of the LORD, forgetting the LORD their God, and serving the Baals.... ⁸Therefore the anger of the LORD was kindled against Israel, and he sold them into the hand of [the] king of Mesopotamia; and the sons of Israel served [him] eight years. ⁹But when the sons of Israel cried to the LORD, the LORD raised up a deliverer for the sons of Israel, who delivered them, Othniel the son of Kenaz, Caleb's younger brother. ¹⁰The Spirit of the LORD came upon him, and he judged Israel; he went out to war, and the LORD gave [the] king of Mesopotamia into his hand.... ¹¹So the land had rest forty years. Then Othniel the son of Kenaz died.

God poured his Holy Spirit upon Othniel to strengthen him. Through God's power, Othniel restored the nation of Israel. When Israel trusted the Lord and relied on his power, they defeated their enemies and found peace. But when they relied on their own power, they fell into sin and suffered at the hands of their enemies.

Gideon the Judge

The Call of Gideon

The Israelites continued to fall into idolatry. The Lord allowed the Midianites, a Canaanite nation, to conquer Israel. The Midianites destroyed the Israelites' crops, leaving them no food. God's people repented, and, in his faithfulness, the Lord raised up a judge named Gideon to deliver and restore his people.

Judg 6:11-16

6 ¹¹Gideon was beating out wheat in the wine press, to hide it from the Midianites. ¹²And the angel of the LORD appeared to him and said to him, "The LORD is with you, you mighty man of valor." ¹³And Gideon said to him, "Please, sir, if the LORD is with us, why then has all this befallen us? . . . But now the LORD has cast us off, and given us into the hand of Midian." ¹⁴And the LORD turned to him and said, "Go in this might of yours and deliver Israel from the hand of Midian; do not I send you?" ¹⁵And he said to him, "Please, Lord, how can I deliver Israel? Behold, my clan is the weakest in Manasseh, and I am the least in my family." ¹⁶And the LORD said to him, "But I will be with you, and you shall strike the Midianites as one man."

God often uses the weak to overcome the strong. Gideon was weak in faith and fortitude. Like Moses many years before, Gideon made excuses for why he could not lead God's people. But God promised to be with Gideon and to strengthen him to defeat the Midianites.

Gideon Conquered through God's Power

Gideon raised an army of around thirty-two thousand men to fight the Midianites. But the Lord told Gideon the army was too large. God knew that with a large army, Israel would think they conquered the Midianites by their own power instead of his. God commanded that Gideon go into battle with only *three hundred* men.

Judg 7:16-22

7 ¹⁶[Gideon] divided the three hundred men into three companies, and put trumpets into the hands of all of them and empty jars, with torches inside the jars. ¹⁷And he said to them, "Look at me, and do likewise; when I come to the outskirts of the camp, do as I do. ¹⁸When I blow the trumpet, I and all who are with me, then blow the trumpets also on every side of all the camp, and shout, 'For the LORD and for Gideon.'"

¹⁹So Gideon and the hundred men who were with him came to the outskirts of the camp at the beginning of the middle watch, when they had just set the watch . . . ²⁰And the three companies blew the trumpets and broke the jars, holding in their left hands the torches, and in their right hands the trumpets to blow; and they cried, "A sword for the LORD and for Gideon!" ²¹They stood every man in his place round about the camp, and all the army ran; they cried out and fled. ²²When they blew the three hundred trumpets, the LORD set every man's sword against his fellow and against all the army.

The Angel and Gideon, Gerbrand van den Eeckhout

God was faithful to his promise to Gideon. The Lord was with Gideon and strengthened the small Israelite army to conquer the Midianites. Once again, God used the weak to overcome the strong. God brought peace to Israel. But sadly, Gideon and the rest of Israel again were unfaithful to God and committed idolatry. They continued in their cycle of sin.

What Was Right in Their Own Eyes

The Book of Judges ends with this statement: "In those days there was no king in Israel; every man did what was right in his own eyes" (21:25). Israel had no earthly king to unite the people and call them to obey God's law.

However, Israel *did* have a king. The Lord was supposed to be their King and leader. He had delivered his people and given them his law so they could be united with him in the sacred bond of a covenant. But the people failed to love the Lord and ignored his law. They believed they could determine what was right or wrong for themselves. In this way, the Israelites behaved like Adam and Eve when they disobeyed God and ate of the Tree of the Knowledge of Good and Evil.

Sometimes, like Israel, we may be tempted to disobey God's law and believe that we have the power to determine right and wrong for ourselves. But this belief only leads to danger, chaos, and suffering.

For example, consider if everyone decided which traffic laws were right or wrong for them. If a person was late for work, he could decide he did not have to stop at the stop sign by the school in his neighborhood. Or another person may decide she does not have to drive the speed limit. Laws like these provide order and are meant to protect us. Without them, the roads would become dangerous and chaotic.

God's laws protect us from sin and lead us to happiness and fulfillment. We learn from the Book of Judges that thinking we have the power to determine right and wrong leads to suffering and evil. But when we honor God as our King and obey his laws, we live in harmony with God and one another, conquer our sins with grace, and enjoy the fullness of life.

Chapter 13 Summary

1. The Israelites failed to drive out the Caananites from the Promised Land, so they fell into idolatry, worshipping false gods such as Baal.

2. Israel fell into a cycle of disobedience, suffering, repentance, and restoration. Each time, God raised up judges to lead and deliver his people.

3. During this time, Israel rejected God as their King and believed they had the power to determine right and wrong for themselves, which led to great suffering and evil.

Overcoming the Cycle of Sin

When reading about the Israelites' sinfulness in the Old Testament, we may be tempted to laugh at them for repeating this pattern of the same sins over and over again. However, we must realize that we, too, often have our own patterns of sin.

The Israelites regularly committed the sin of idolatry and fell into the worship of the false gods of other nations. But for us, these patterns of sin may include habits of lying, anger, cheating, laziness, or impurity.

 Consider a character from a book, television show, or movie who is caught in a pattern of sin and then repents. Fill out the cycle diagram below to show (1) how this character disobeys God, (2) what suffering it causes, (3) what form the character's repentance takes, and (4) what restoration follows that repentance.

Character: _____

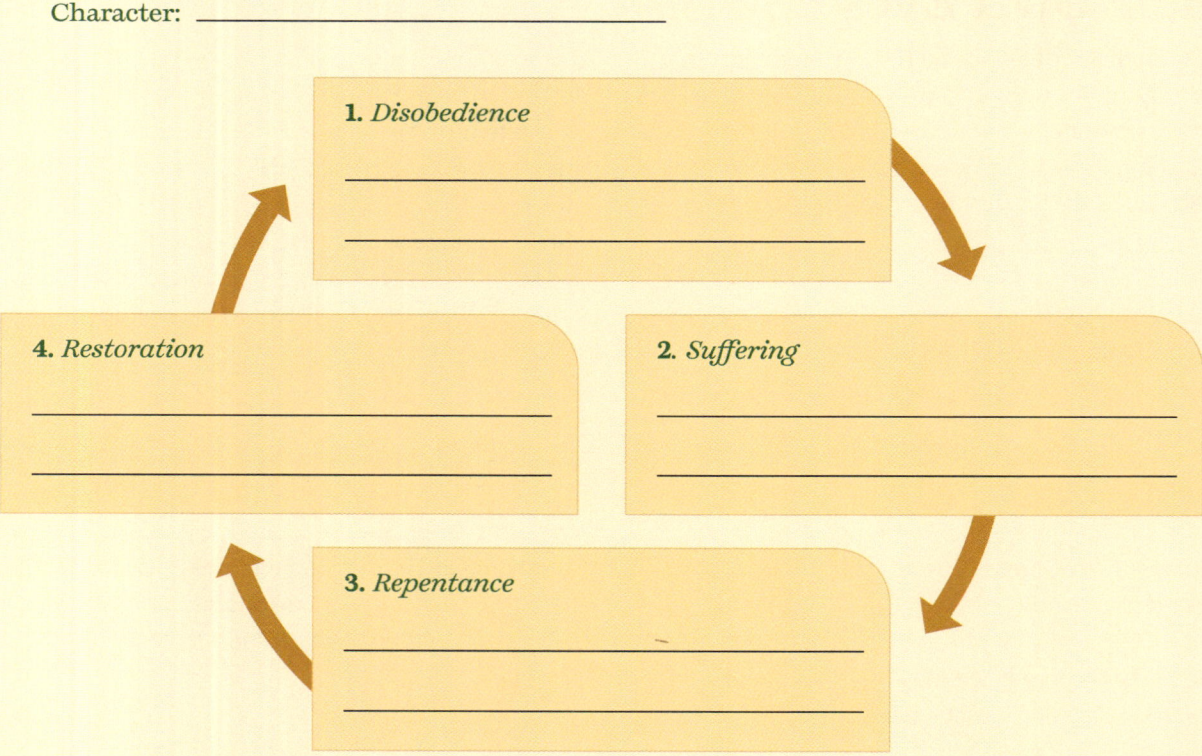

We need God's grace to break habits of sin so we don't repeat the cycle and move from step 4 (restoration) back to step 1 (disobedience). While it may take a long time, we break these patterns of sin with God's grace and repeated action.

To break the pattern of sin, we need to rely on God's grace to *reform* our lives. The following steps are helpful:

1. **R**ecognize the pattern of sin.
2. **E**xamine your conscience each day.
3. **F**ast from sweets, meat, television, or social media.
4. **O**ppose temptation.
5. **R**eceive the Eucharist and the Sacrament of Reconciliation often.
6. **M**editate on God's love for you.

Chapter 13

First, we must recognize that many sins form a pattern, admit that pattern exists, and pray for God's grace to overcome it. What is a pattern of sin that you recognize people your age falling into?

_____

Next, we can take practical steps such as the ones listed in steps 2-6. Take a minute to reflect carefully on the pattern of sin you named above and the suffering it brings to your friends' lives. Based on steps 2-6, what are three specific pieces of advice you would give someone who is falling into this pattern of sin?

_____

_____

_____

Let Us Pray—Psalm 27

In Psalm 27, the psalmist praises God for his faithfulness and protection in times of distress. In the Book of Judges, we see how God always remained faithful to his people, even when they were unfaithful to him. Let us pray with this psalm, giving praise and thanksgiving to God for his loving care and protection.

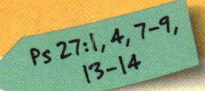

Ps 27:1, 4, 7-9, 13-14

27 ¹The Lord is my light and my salvation;
　　whom shall I fear?
The Lord is the stronghold of my life;
　　of whom shall I be afraid? . . .
⁴One thing have I asked of the Lord,
　　that will I seek after;
that I may dwell in the house of the Lord
　　all the days of my life,
to behold the beauty of the Lord,
　　and to inquire in his temple. . . .
⁷Hear, O Lord, when I cry aloud,
　　be gracious to me and answer me!

⁸You have said, "Seek my face."
My heart says to you,
　"Your face, Lord, do I seek."
　　⁹Hide not your face from me. . . .
¹³I believe that I shall see the goodness of the
　　Lord
　　in the land of the living!
¹⁴Wait for the Lord;
　　be strong, and let your heart take
　　　courage;
　　yes, wait for the Lord!

Chapter 13 Review:
The Lord Raised Up Judges

1. Who were the Canaanites? _____
   _____

2. What was the name of one of the false gods of the Canaanites that the Israelites committed the sin of idolatry by worshipping? _____

3. What was the function of the judges that the Lord raised up for his people?
   _____
   _____

4. In Judges, we read about Israel's cycle of sin. Put the steps of this cycle in order by writing the correct number, 1-4, by each step.

   _____ Restoration   _____ Suffering   _____ Disobedience   _____ Repentance

5. In your own words, explain how this cycle of sin is present in the account of the first judge, Othniel.

   Step 1 _____

   Step 2 _____

   Step 3 _____

   Step 4 _____

6. In what ways did God raise up the weak to overcome the strong in the account of Gideon?
   _____
   _____
   _____
   _____

The Book of Ruth

In the Old Testament, we find a short book called Ruth. This book takes the name of one of its main characters. The book's events occur during the era of Israel's judges.

A woman from Bethlehem named Naomi traveled to the country of Moab with her husband and two sons. Sadly, Naomi's husband died. Her two sons married wives from Moab, one of whom was named Ruth. After ten years, Naomi's sons also died. Naomi decided to return to Bethlehem and told her daughters-in-law they should stay behind in their homeland. But Ruth refused to be separated from her mother-in-law.

Ruth and Naomi, Ary Scheffer

Ruth 1:15–17

1 ¹⁵[Naomi] said, "See, your sister-in-law has gone back to her people and to her gods; return after your sister-in-law." ¹⁶But Ruth said, "Entreat me not to leave you or to return from following you; for where you go I will go, and where you lodge I will lodge; your people shall be my people, and your God my God; ¹⁷where you die I will die, and there will I be buried. May the LORD do so to me and more also if even death parts me from you."

Ruth was a Moabite. Her people did not believe in the one true God of Israel. However, Ruth came to believe in God, and the two women set out for Bethlehem together. While caring for her mother-in-law in Bethlehem, Ruth met a man named Boaz. Boaz saw Ruth's remarkable commitment to caring for her mother-in-law, Naomi, and her faith in the one true God.

Ruth 2:11–12

2 ¹¹"All that you have done for your mother-in-law since the death of your husband has been fully told me, and how you left . . . your native land and came to a people that you did not know before. ¹²The LORD recompense you for what you have done, and a full reward be given you by the LORD, the God of Israel, under whose wings you have come to take refuge!"

Boaz and Ruth later married and had a son named Obed. Obed eventually became the grandfather of David, the great king of Israel and ancestor of Jesus. Through Ruth's faith and commitment to caring for Naomi, God blessed all nations. From her descendants came King David and eventually Jesus Christ, the Son of David.

Ruth modeled the virtue of piety. Piety is the virtue by which we give due honor and service to those to whom we are indebted. We are most indebted *to God* because he gave us everything. Ruth showed piety to God by believing and honoring him over her people's false gods.

We also live with piety by being respectful and loving *toward our parents*. Ruth was respectful and caring to her mother-in-law, Naomi. Ruth could have left Naomi alone and returned to her village to find a husband. But Ruth did not want Naomi to travel back to Bethlehem alone. She continued to care for Naomi as she grew older. She showed Naomi the respect and love that Naomi had shown her.

Journal Reflection

In what ways can you imitate Ruth's piety in your own life by honoring God and your parents?

A Daily Examen

Read

Like the Israelites, we can develop patterns of sin. For example, we may consistently find ourselves lying, gossiping, looking at impure images, or having an outburst of anger. One of the most practical ways to avoid these patterns of sin and become more aware of God's presence in our lives is by praying the Daily Examen. The Daily Examen is a five-step method of prayer that was developed by Saint Ignatius of Loyola; it is meant to be done at the end of the day. It helps us reflect on our day and make practical steps to overcome any pattern of sin with God's grace.

Reflect

Spend 5–7 minutes reflecting on the following five steps of the Daily Examen prayer.

1. **Give thanks to God.** Take a minute to remember that you are in the presence of God. He loves you and wants you to be happy. Thank him for your life, his love, and for another day.

2. **Ask God for light.** Spend a minute asking the Holy Spirit to open your eyes to see how God was working in your life today. Ask that you see your day through God's eyes, not your own.

3. **Review the day.** Over the next 3 minutes, think through your whole day, starting in the morning. Note what you felt and how you reacted to events, people, and places. Consider your thoughts and actions throughout the day. Note times when you acted virtuously and other times when you sinned.

4. **Ask for forgiveness.** Spend a minute asking God for forgiveness for the times you sinned against him this day.

5. **Look toward the next day.** Take a minute to decide on one thing you will do tomorrow to avoid sin or grow in virtue. Ask for God's grace to strengthen you to fulfill this resolution.

Pray

Conclude the five steps of the Daily Examen by praying the Suscipe prayer by Saint Ignatius of Loyola:

> Take, Lord, and receive all my liberty,
> my memory, my understanding, and my entire will,
> all I have and call my own.
> You have given all to me.
> To you, Lord, I return it.
> Everything is yours; do with it what you will.
> Give me only your love and your grace;
> that is enough for me.
> Amen.

Act

Each night this week before you go to bed, take 5–7 minutes to complete the five steps of the Daily Examen prayer.

CHAPTER 14

David the King

Words to Know

> prophet

> pure in heart

Proclaiming the Good News

"He will be great, and will be called the Son of the Most High; and the Lord God will give to him the throne of his father David, and he will reign over the house of Jacob for ever; and of his kingdom there will be no end." —Luke 1:32–33

King David Playing the Lyre, Ethiopian School, 15th century

The Lord and His Anointed

Samuel, the Last Judge of Israel

Following the Book of Judges in the Old Testament are two books that bear the name of the prophet Samuel. The Books of 1–2 Samuel tell the story of the rise of the kingdom in Israel.

The First Book of Samuel begins with an account of Samuel's origins. A woman named Hannah cried out to God in distress. Though she was married, she was childless. As she prayed, she made a vow: "O LORD of hosts, if you will indeed look on the affliction of your maidservant, and remember me, and . . . give to your maidservant a son, then I will give him to the LORD all the days of his life" (1:11). Hannah's vow and prayer bore fruit. She gave birth to a son, whom she named Samuel.

Samuel became both a *prophet* and judge of Israel. A prophet was someone chosen by God to speak God's words and remind people of his promises. Prophets like Samuel called the Israelites to repent of their sins and be faithful to the Lord.

Hannah's Prayer, Julius Schnorr von Carolsfeld

In time, the Israelites demanded that Samuel give them a king. They wanted to be "like all the nations" (1 Sam 8:5). The Israelites were rejecting *the Lord* as their King. They did not think God's love and faithfulness were enough. The Israelites wanted a strong earthly ruler to protect them. Despite Samuel's efforts, the Israelites would not give up their sinful demand. So, the Lord gave them an earthly king.

Saul, the Warrior King

God sent Samuel to anoint as king a strong young man named Saul. Saul was from the tribe of Benjamin and looked the part of a royal leader: "There was not a man among the sons of Israel more handsome than he; from his shoulders upward he was taller than any of the people" (1 Sam 9:2). Saul was also a fearsome warrior and skilled military leader.

One day, Saul led the Israelites to face an army of people called the Philistines. Saul was commanded to wait for Samuel to arrive and offer sacrifice to the Lord. But as the Philistine army came closer, Saul's men grew nervous, and some began to run away. Saul disobeyed the Lord's command and himself offered sacrifices. He failed to trust that the Lord would protect his people without the sacrifice being offered. When Samuel finally arrived, he confronted King Saul:

13 ¹¹Samuel said, "What have you done?" And Saul said, "When I saw that the people were scattering from me, and that you did not come within the days appointed . . . ¹²I said, 'Now the Philistines will come down upon me at Gilgal and I have not entreated the favor of the LORD'; so I forced myself, and offered the burnt offering." ¹³And Samuel said to Saul, "You have done foolishly; you have not kept the commandment of the LORD your God, which he commanded you; for now the LORD would have established your kingdom over Israel for ever. ¹⁴But now your kingdom shall not continue; the LORD has sought out a man after his own heart; and the LORD has appointed him to be prince over his people, because you have not kept what the LORD commanded you."

1 Sam 13:11-14

Saul's disobedience meant that his son would no longer be king after him. Saul continued to disobey the Lord's commands. When confronted about his sins, Saul failed to repent. Instead, he made excuses for his actions. God eventually removed Saul as king. Samuel told Saul, "The LORD has torn the kingdom of Israel from you this day, and has given it to a neighbor of yours, who is better than you" (1 Sam 15:28).

Saul and the Israelites rejected the Lord's kingship and put their trust in earthly power. But the Lord was looking for a king "after his own heart" (1 Sam 13:14) to lead his people. A person who is *pure in heart* seeks to love God above all else and to avoid sin. Such a person puts his trust in God.

ethir one

David, the Son of Jesse

The Lord commanded Samuel to go to the house of a man named Jesse, in Bethlehem. There he would find among Jesse's sons the man who would replace Saul as king.

1 Sam 16:4-7, 10-13

16 ⁴Samuel did what the LORD commanded, and came to Bethlehem. . . . ⁵And he consecrated Jesse and his sons, and invited them to the sacrifice. ⁶When they came, he looked on Eliab and thought, "Surely the LORD's anointed is before him." ⁷But the LORD said to Samuel, "Do not look on his appearance or on the height of his stature . . . for the LORD sees not as man sees; man looks on the outward appearance, but the LORD looks on the heart." . . . ¹⁰And Jesse made seven of his sons pass before Samuel. And Samuel said to Jesse, "The LORD has not chosen these." ¹¹And Samuel said to Jesse, "Are all your sons here?" And he said, "There remains yet the youngest, but behold, he is keeping the sheep." And Samuel said to Jesse, "Send and fetch him; for we will not sit down till he comes here." ¹²And he sent, and brought him in. . . . And the LORD said, "Arise, anoint him; for this is he." ¹³Then Samuel took the horn of oil, and anointed him in the midst of his brothers; and the Spirit of the LORD came mightily upon David from that day forward.

Though Jesse had many strong sons, none of these was to be king of Israel. The Lord chose David not because of his appearance, but because of *his heart*. David was pure in heart. David loved the Lord above all things and put his trust in him. When Samuel anointed David with oil, he received the strength of the Holy Spirit, which would empower him to lead God's people.

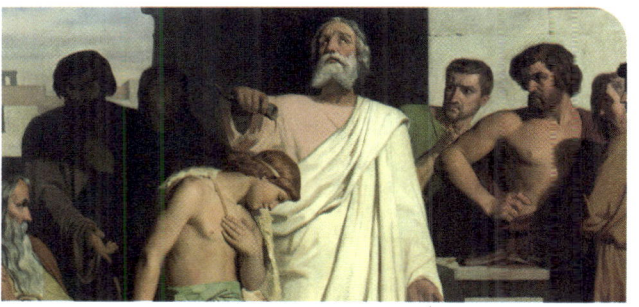
Anointing of David by Samuel, Felix-Joseph Barrias

A King after God's Own Heart

David, Servant of the Lord

After David's anointing, the Philistines attacked Israel. During the battle, a huge Philistine soldier named Goliath cursed the God of Israel and dared one of the Israelites to fight him in a duel. The unarmored young David volunteered.

> *1 Sam 17:45-46, 49-50*
>
> **17** ⁴⁵David said to the Philistine, "You come to me with a sword and with a spear and with a javelin; but I come to you in the name of the LORD of hosts, the God of the armies of Israel, whom you have defied. ⁴⁶This day the LORD will deliver you into my hand, and I will strike you down . . . that all the earth may know that there is a God in Israel." . . .
>
> ⁴⁹David put his hand in his bag and took out a stone, and slung it, and struck the Philistine on his forehead. . . .
>
> ⁵⁰So David prevailed over the Philistine with a sling and with a stone, and struck the Philistine, and killed him.

David proved he was unlike Saul. He trusted that the Lord would protect his people. David's victory over Goliath made him famous. Saul envied David's popularity, which led him to try to kill David. Saul continued to disobey the Lord, and eventually, he lost his own life. David then assumed the kingship over all twelve tribes of Israel.

The Davidic Covenant

The Second Book of Samuel focuses on the rise of David's kingdom. King David made the city of Jerusalem the capital of his kingdom and commanded that the Ark of the Covenant be brought there. Following this, the Lord blessed David and his people with peace and rest from their enemies. At this time, the Lord made a covenant with David.

> *2 Sam 7:11-14*
>
> **7** ¹¹"The LORD declares to you that the LORD will make you a house. ¹²When your days are fulfilled and you lie down with your fathers, I will raise up your offspring after you, who shall come forth from your body, and I will establish his kingdom. ¹³He shall build a house for my name, and I will establish the throne of his kingdom for ever. ¹⁴I will be his father, and he shall be my son."

In this covenant with David, the Lord made three promises concerning David's descendants:

1. **The Lord promised David that he would "establish the throne of his kingdom for ever" (2 Sam 7:13).** God would establish a house (a royal dynasty) descended from David. The Lord would not withdraw his blessing from the descendants of King David; their rule would be everlasting.

2. **The Lord promised that David's son would "build a house for [the Lord's] name" (2 Sam 7:13).** The son of David would construct a house, a permanent place of worship, where sacrifice would be offered to the Lord. David's son Solomon would later build the Temple in Jerusalem.

3. **The Lord promised about David's son, "I will be his father, and he shall be my son" (2 Sam 7:14).** The kings descended from David would be made sons of God by divine adoption. The Lord united the Davidic kings to himself in a unique way through this covenant so that they would share in God's authority to lead his people.

David's Sin and Repentance

David was talented, famous, and powerful. On the outside, he appeared to be an ideal ruler and a virtuous man. Yet a sin of passion would unravel his life.

2 Sam 11:1-5

11 ¹In the spring of the year, the time when kings go forth to battle, . . . David remained at Jerusalem.
²It happened, late one afternoon, when David arose from his couch and was walking upon the roof of the king's house, that he saw from the roof a woman bathing; and the woman was very beautiful. ³And David sent and inquired about the woman. And one said, "Is not this Bathsheba . . . the wife of Uriah the Hittite?" ⁴So David sent messengers, and took her; . . . and he lay with her. . . . ⁵And the woman conceived; and she sent and told David, "I am with child."

David committed serious sins. He committed adultery by behaving with Bathsheba, the wife of Uriah, as if he were married to her. This was a grave sin. David attempted to hide his sin of adultery by commanding that Bathsheba's husband, Uriah, be put on the front lines of a battle so that he would be killed. By murdering Uriah, David avoided the public scandal of fathering a child with another man's wife. This, too, was a grave sin.

The prophet Nathan was sent by the Lord to confront King David about his sins. While Saul had denied wrongdoing and made excuses when confronted by the prophet Samuel, David reacted differently and confessed his sin. He repented and sought God's mercy. In Psalm 51, David expressed his contrition for these sins:

Ps 51:1-2, 10-12

51 ¹Have mercy on me, O God,
according to your merciful love;
according to your abundant mercy
blot out my transgressions
²Wash me thoroughly from my iniquity,
and cleanse me from my sin! . . .

¹⁰Create in me a clean heart, O God,
and put a new and right spirit within me.
¹¹Cast me not away from your presence,
and take not your holy Spirit from me.
¹²Restore to me the joy of your salvation,
and uphold me with a willing spirit.

By repenting, David proved he still loved God above all else. He trusted in God's merciful love and the possibility of being cleansed from his sin. David showed himself to be truly a "man after [God's] own heart" (1 Sam 13:14).

Chapter 14 Summary

1. Saul was appointed the first king of Israel, but he repeatedly disobeyed the Lord's commands. When Saul sinned, he failed to repent.

2. The Lord made a covenant with King David, promising to build him a house (a royal dynasty).

3. David was pure in heart. He sought to love God above all else and to avoid sin. When David did sin, he repented and trusted in the Lord's mercy.

Blessed Are the Merciful

Moses went up Mount Sinai to receive the Ten Commandments. While he was gone, the Israelites committed idolatry by worshipping a golden calf. When Moses returned to witness Israel's sin, he broke the tablets containing the Decalogue. He interceded for the people and prayed that God would forgive the Israelites their sin.

God responded by saying, "The LORD, the LORD, a God merciful and gracious, slow to anger, and abounding in mercy and faithfulness, . . . forgiving iniquity and transgression and sin" (Ex 34:6–7). On Mount Sinai, the Lord revealed himself as the God of mercy.

King David prayed and meditated on God's Word. He was a man after God's own heart. He knew that God was merciful. He trusted that if he repented, God would forgive his sins. Because he loved God, he *wanted* to repent. When King Saul chose to disobey God, he did not repent. When confronted by Samuel about his sins, Saul made excuses for his actions.

Reread the passage from Psalm 51 on the previous page. How do David's *specific words* in this psalm express his trust in the Lord's mercy toward sinners?

_____

_____

_____

_____

Jesus, the New Moses, went up a mountain to teach about the New Law. In his Sermon on the Mount (see Mt 5–7), Jesus did not abolish the Ten Commandments or take back God's revelation of mercy. But he did say something new when he taught his disciples the Beatitudes: "Blessed are the merciful, for they shall receive mercy" (Mt 5:7).

Jesus teaches us something very challenging: we cannot *receive* God's mercy if we do not *show mercy to others*. Each of us is called to imitate God's mercy in our lives.

Read Matthew 18:23-35, where Jesus gives the parable of the unforgiving servant. (Note: a single talent was worth about fifteen years' wages for a worker.) How does this parable reflect Jesus' Beatitude on mercy?

_____

_____

_____

Catechism of the Catholic Church, 2840

"[God's] outpouring of mercy cannot penetrate our hearts as long as we have not forgiven those who have trespassed against us. Love, like the Body of Christ, is indivisible; we cannot love the God we cannot see if we do not love the brother or sister we do see.[1] In refusing to forgive our brothers and sisters, our hearts are closed and their hardness makes them impervious to the Father's merciful love; but in confessing our sins, our hearts are opened to his grace."

What might make it hard to show mercy to others?

_____

_____

_____

What are three specific things you can do to become more merciful?

_____

_____

_____

Let Us Pray—Psalm 25

In Psalm 25, King David calls upon the Lord's mercy and compassion. He asks God to pardon his guilt and not remember his sins. With trust in our loving God, let us pray that the Lord would give us the grace to turn away from our sins and trust in his mercy.

Ps 25:1-2, 4-9

25 ¹To you, O Lord, I lift up my soul.
²O my God, in you I trust,
 let me not be put to shame;
 let not my enemies exult over me. . . .
⁴Make me to know your ways, O Lord;
 teach me your paths.
⁵Lead me in your truth, and teach me,
 for you are the God of my salvation;
 for you I wait all the day long.

⁶Be mindful of your compassion, O Lord,
 and of your merciful love,
 for they have been from of old.
⁷Remember not the sins of my youth, or my transgressions;
 according to your mercy remember me,
 for your goodness' sake, O Lord!
⁸Good and upright is the Lord;
 therefore he instructs sinners in the way.
⁹He leads the humble in what is right,
 and teaches the humble his way.

Chapter 14 Review:
David the King

1. A _____ is someone chosen by God to speak God's words and remind people of his promises.

2. Hannah was the mother of _____ the prophet, the last of the judges of Israel.

3. What does it mean to be "pure in heart"? _____
   _____

4. Which prophet confronted David about his sins? _____

5. What were David's great sins? _____
   _____

6. In which psalm do we find David's prayer of repentance for his sins? _____

7. List the three key promises of the Lord's covenant with David.
   _____
   _____
   _____

8. Scripture describes David as a man after God's own heart. How did David show himself to be pure in heart?
   _____
   _____

9. What is the most notable difference between King David and King Saul?
   _____
   _____

The Psalms

David, Lorenzo Monaco

The Old Testament contains 150 psalms in the Book of Psalms. Nearly half of these are said to be written by King David. The word "psalm" means "praises." Psalms are prayers of praise to God. That does not mean the psalms are always upbeat. In addition to joy and happiness, the psalms express many emotions and struggles most people can relate to, such as fear, anxiety, sadness, loss, persecution, and anger.

There is a psalm that fits any experience anyone might be going through. As the *Catechism* says, "Though a given psalm may reflect an event of the past, it still possesses such direct simplicity that it can be prayed in truth *by men of all times and conditions*" (CCC 2588; emphasis added).

The Church encourages us to pray with the Psalms and make them our own. At every Mass, the Church prays from the Book of Psalms to allow us to lift our minds and hearts to God. This reading from the Book of Psalms comes after the First Reading and is known as the Responsorial Psalm.

The Psalms are also at the heart of the Liturgy of the Hours, the daily prayer of the Church. At certain "hours" of the day (morning, daytime, evening, and night), the faithful take a moment to pray. The prayer consists of Bible readings, petitions, responses, and a heartfelt recitation of the Psalms.

Praying with the Psalms can help us love God and trust him no matter what we are feeling or going through. The Psalms are "the masterwork of prayer in the Old Testament" (CCC 2596).

Joy	Psalm 63; 66; 100
Sadness	Psalm 6; 13; 22
Being criticized by others	Psalm 56; 109; 142
Loneliness	Psalm 23; 25
Physical suffering	Psalm 6; 23; 41
Anger	Psalm 37; 69
Thankfulness	Psalm 40; 67; 95
Feeling distant from God	Psalm 13; 22; 42; 77
Fear	Psalm 23; 91; 121

Journal Reflection

Spend a few minutes writing about what is happening in your life and how you are feeling. Are you happy? Anxious? Suffering?

When you are done, select at least two psalms from the chart above that fit your present experience. Find a Bible and pray these psalms. Offer up whatever you are experiencing to God, trusting in his goodness and love for you.

Sharing in Christ's Kingly Mission

Read

Psalm 89 tells of David having been anointed as king by Samuel the prophet:

Ps 89:19-21

89 ¹⁹Of old you spoke in a vision
to your faithful one, and said:
"I have set the crown upon one who is mighty,
I have exalted one chosen from the people.
²⁰I have found David, my servant;
with my holy oil I have anointed him;
²¹so that my hand shall ever abide with him,
my arm also shall strengthen him."

Empowered by the Spirit of the Lord, David was given the graces he needed *to lead others*. David was a leader in many ways: on the battlefield, in politics, in lawgiving. In all of these, the Lord promised to "abide with him" and "strengthen him" (89:21). The greatest leadership responsibility David had was to lead the people of Israel in serving the Lord.

When we were baptized, we received the gift of the Holy Spirit. A sign of our receiving the Spirit was the anointing with oil (sacred chrism). Baptism unites a person intimately with Christ to share in his mission. Through Baptism, we become kings and queens.

Jesus is the Son of, or descendant of, David. He is the Christ (the Messiah), the Anointed One. Jesus is King of Israel, the King of Kings. When a person is joined to Christ, he shares in Jesus' kingship. He becomes a christ, an anointed one sent by God to share his love and mercy with the world. As God's anointed, we have a responsibility to lead others to God.

Reflect

Spend 5–10 minutes reflecting on the following:

- Am I setting a good example for my friends, siblings, and classmates?
- Is there something I often say or do that might draw people away from God?
- Could a stranger figure out that I am a Christian just by observing my actions?

Pray

To become sharers in Christ's kingly mission, we must first be united to him. Pray the Anima Christi prayer on page 336.

Act

This week, think of one small thing you can change in your life to help you set a better example for others.

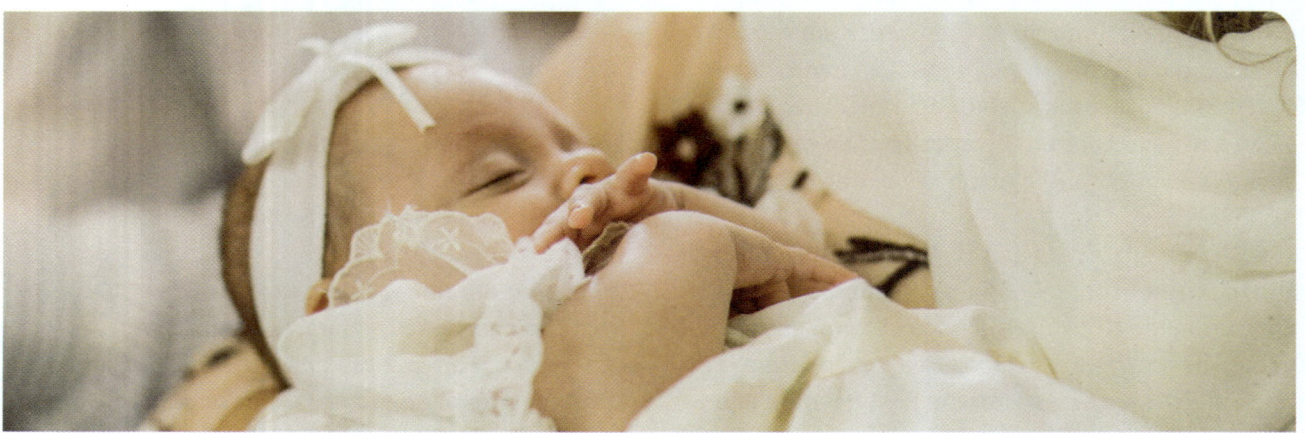

CHAPTER 15
The House of David

Words to Know

> *shalom*

> *Temple*

> *wisdom*

Proclaiming the Good News

"There shall come forth a shoot from the stump of Jesse, and a branch shall grow out of his roots. And the Spirit of the LORD shall rest upon him."
—Isaiah 11:1–2

Continuing the Story of Salvation

List four or five key events from the life of David.

_____
_____
_____
_____
_____
_____
_____

King Solomon, Simeon Solomon

Solomon, the Son of David

Solomon's Anointing

Near the end of King David's life, Bathsheba reminded him that he had promised their son Solomon would rule as king after him. David reassured Bathsheba that he would honor his oath.

1 Kings 1:29-30, 38-40

1 ²⁹And the king swore, saying, "As the LORD lives, who has redeemed my soul out of every adversity, ³⁰as I swore to you by the LORD, the God of Israel, saying 'Solomon your son shall reign after me, and he shall sit upon my throne in my stead'; even so will I do this day." . . .

³⁸So Zadok the priest . . . went down and caused Solomon to ride on King David's mule, and brought him to Gihon. ³⁹There Zadok the priest took the horn of oil from the tent, and anointed Solomon. Then they blew the trumpet; and all the people said, "Long live King Solomon!" ⁴⁰And all the people went up after him, playing on pipes, and rejoicing with great joy.

David had been anointed king by the prophet Samuel. David's son Solomon was anointed king by the priest Zadok at the Gihon River. With Solomon as king, God began to fulfill his promise to build a royal house for David. David's son Solomon would be the first in the royal dynasty of kings descended from David.

The Wisdom of Solomon

Like David, his father, Solomon loved the Lord above all else and desired to follow his commandments. One night, God spoke to Solomon in a dream. In this dream, he offered to give Solomon anything he wanted. Rather than asking for something earthly like wealth or power, Solomon asked for wisdom.

1 Kings 3:9-12

3 ⁹"Give your servant therefore an understanding mind to govern your people, that I may discern between good and evil; for who is able to govern this great people of yours?"

¹⁰It pleased the LORD that Solomon had asked this. ¹¹And God said to him, "Because you have asked this, and have not asked for yourself long life or riches or the life of your enemies, but have asked for yourself understanding to discern what is right, ¹²behold, I now do according to your word. Behold, I give you a wise and discerning mind, so that none like you has been before you and none like you shall arise after you."

Wisdom is a spiritual gift. It allows a person to know God's purpose and plan. It enables a person to see the world from God's perspective. As a wise king, Solomon ruled over Israel. People would come to Solomon to give a judgment when they had disagreements. Even people from other nations journeyed to hear the great wisdom of King Solomon. Many of Solomon's words of wisdom are recorded in the Old Testament Book of Proverbs. For example, Solomon said, "He who trusts in his riches will wither, but the righteous will flourish like a green leaf" (11:28). Solomon thought it foolish to trust in wealth. Riches do not last forever and can easily lead someone away from God. Jesus also warned people

Solomon before the Ark of the Covenant, Blaise Nicolas Le Sueur

about being too attached to possessions. Jesus calls us to be detached from riches in order to enter the Kingdom of Heaven.

Solomon's kingdom enjoyed great peace and prosperity. This was fitting, for the name Solomon comes from the word "*shalom*," which in Hebrew means "peace." Under Solomon's wise rule, "Judah and Israel were as many as the sand by the sea; they ate and drank and were happy" (1 Kings 4:20). The imagery of "sand by the sea" recalls God's promise to Abraham. The Lord swore that Abraham's descendants would be as numerous as "the sand which is on the seashore" (Gen 22:17).

The Temple in Jerusalem

Solomon built the *Temple* of the Lord in Jerusalem. This was the place where God's people could offer sacrifice in worship to the Lord. Building the Temple initially fulfilled God's promise that David's offspring would build a house for God. God promised to be present to his people: "I will dwell among the children of Israel, and will not forsake my people Israel" (1 Kings 6:13). The beauty of the Temple was meant to reflect God's beauty.

6 ²⁹He carved all the walls of the house round about with carved figures or cherubim and palm trees and open flowers, in the inner and outer rooms. ³⁰The floor of the house he overlaid with gold in the inner and outer rooms.

³¹For the entrance to the inner sanctuary he made doors of olivewood; the lintel and the doorposts formed a pentagon. ³²He covered the two doors of olivewood with carvings of cherubim, palm trees, and open flowers; he overlaid them with gold, and spread gold upon the cherubim and upon the palm trees.

The Temple foreshadowed the glory of Heaven. The trees, fruit, and cherubim carved on the walls and doors reminded the Israelites of the Garden of Eden. Adam and Eve enjoyed friendship with God in the Garden of Eden. In a similar way, the Lord was present to his people in the Temple.

Solomon had the Ark of the Covenant brought into the Temple: "The priests brought the ark of the covenant of the LORD to its place, in the inner sanctuary of the house, in the most holy place" (1 Kings 8:6). The Ark now had a formal place of rest. The Temple was truly the house of the Lord.

A Kingdom Divided

Solomon's Idolatry

The Lord told Solomon that his kingdom would flourish if he and his successors followed the Lord. But if they abandoned God, the kingdom would crumble.

The Idolatry of King Solomon, Jacob Hogers

1 Kings 9:4-7

9 ⁴"As for you, if you will walk before me, as David your father walked, with integrity of heart and uprightness, doing according to all that I have commanded you, and keeping my statues and my ordinances, ⁵then I will establish your royal throne over Israel for ever, as I promised David your father. . . . ⁶But if you turn aside from following me, you or your children, and do not keep my commandments and my statutes which I have set before you, but go and serve other gods and worship them, ⁷then I will cut off Israel from the land which I have given them; and the house which I have consecrated for my name I will cast out of my sight."

Despite the Lord's warning, Solomon rejected the gift of wisdom. He failed to keep the Lord's commandments. He broke the laws in the Book of Deuteronomy that forbade kings from selfishly amassing weapons, wives, and wealth.

Laws for Israel's Kings *Deuteronomy*	Solomon's Fall *1 Kings*
"He must not multiply horses for himself or cause the people to return to Egypt in order to multiply horses." (17:16)	"Solomon gathered together chariots and horsemen; he had fourteen hundred chariots and twelve thousand horsemen." (10:26)
"He shall not multiply wives for himself, lest his heart turn away." (17:17)	"[Solomon] had seven hundred wives, princesses, and three hundred concubines; and his wives turned away his heart." (11:3)
"Nor shall he greatly multiply for himself silver and gold." (17:17)	"Now the weight of gold that came to Solomon in one year was six hundred and sixty-six talents of gold." (10:14)

How could the wisest man in the world turn his back on God? Solomon had many wives, a practice known as polygamy. Solomon's polygamy led to *polytheism*—the worship of many gods. He allowed his many foreign wives to worship their false gods. He, too, became drawn to these other gods, and his heart became divided: "His wives turned away his heart after other gods; and his heart was not wholly true to the LORD his God, as was the heart of David his father" (1 Kings 11:4).

Two Kingdoms, Two Kings

Because of Solomon's idolatry, his kingdom would be divided. The Lord sent a prophet to deliver this news to Jeroboam, one of Solomon's servants: "Behold, I am about to tear the kingdom from the hand of Solomon and will give you ten tribes" (1 Kings 11:31). Despite Solomon's sin and because of his father David's purity of heart, God preserved a remnant of the royal house of David.

The split happened as the Lord said it would. When Solomon's son Rehoboam was made king, the ten northern tribes revolted and formed their own nation, with Jeroboam as their king. Only the tribes of Judah and Benjamin remained under the rule of the house of David. The Southern Kingdom, ruled by the Davidic kings, would be known by the name Judah. The ten tribes that revolted formed the Northern Kingdom, which would continue to be known by the name Israel. The Lord promised Jeroboam that the Northern Kingdom of Israel would flourish if he remained faithful to God. However, Jeroboam became fearful of losing power and turned away from the Lord.

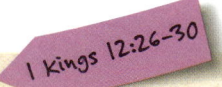

12 ²⁶And Jeroboam said in his heart, "Now the kingdom will turn back to the house of David; ²⁷if this people go up to offer sacrifices in the house of the LORD at Jerusalem, then the heart of this people will turn again to their lord, to Rehoboam king of Judah, and they will kill me and return to Rehoboam king of Judah." ²⁸So the king took counsel, and made two calves of gold. And he said to the people, "You have gone up to Jerusalem long enough. Behold your gods, O Israel, who brought you up out of the land of Egypt." ²⁹And he set one in Bethel, and the other he put in Dan. ³⁰And this thing became a sin, for the people went to the one at Bethel and to the other as far as Dan.

Jeroboam led his people into idolatry to stop them from worshipping the true God in the Jerusalem Temple. Idolatry had led to the division of David's kingdom. Idolatry would remain a grave problem in both the Northern and Southern Kingdoms. But as the Lord had been merciful with Israel at Mount Sinai, so, too, he would send prophets to proclaim a message of repentance and mercy.

Chapter 15 Summary

1. David's son Solomon was crowned king of Israel and ruled the nation in peace with his wisdom.

2. Solomon built the Jerusalem Temple, the place where the Lord would dwell among his people.

3. Solomon and subsequent kings allowed idolatry to flourish, which resulted in the division of the kingdom of David into the Northern Kingdom (Israel) and the Southern Kingdom (Judah).

The Virtue of Temperance

Imagine that a three-year-old boy finds a bag of chocolates. He looks around carefully and sees no one. What will he likely do? Chances are, he will not calmly eat just one chocolate and carefully put the rest of the bag away. He will probably stuff his face with as much chocolate as possible! He might even eat until he gets sick.

The boy knows chocolate is yummy. He might even understand that eating too much chocolate will make him sick. But he eats the chocolate anyway. He lacks the understanding and strength to say no to his cravings.

King Solomon once wrote, "A man without self-control is like a city broken into and left without walls" (Prov 25:28). A city without walls can easily get attacked. Physical desires can quickly overpower a person without self-control.

The cardinal virtue of temperance "moderates the attraction of pleasures and provides balance in the use of created goods. It ensures the will's mastery over instincts and keeps desires within the limits of what is honorable" (*CCC* 1809). In other words, temperance enables us to have self-control over our pursuit of physical pleasures.

Notice the language used: *moderation, balance, limits, mastery*. Physical pleasure ceases to be good for us when we pursue it without moderation, balance, or limits. Too much chocolate makes us sick. An unbalanced diet makes us unhealthy. A person fasting, dieting, or training for a marathon might need to limit his chocolate intake or avoid chocolate altogether. A person who has temperance is not a slave to her physical desires. She has mastery over her instincts. She is free to pursue what is truly good and follow God's commands.

What would be an example of how temperance can help us follow God's commandments?

_____
_____
_____

During periods of his life, King Solomon lacked temperance. His pursuit of earthly pleasures led him to violate God's commands.

What laws of God did Solomon violate because of his pursuit of pleasure?

_____
_____
_____

Chapter 15

What are some things in your life you have trouble limiting?

_____

_____

How might this lack of freedom prevent you from pursuing what is truly good? How might it hurt your ability to follow God?

_____

_____

This week, consider giving up something that you really enjoy (perhaps a particular food or drink, a video game, or social media). Replace the time that you spend on that habit with time in prayer. See how long you can keep this up. Afterward, reflect on the amount of time you went without the habit you gave up. What does this reveal about your mastery over your desires?

Let Us Pray—Psalm 72

God is the God of wisdom and justice. Solomon and the kings of Israel were supposed to imitate God's wisdom and justice in the way they governed the people. As you pray Psalm 72, ask God to help you treat others justly, especially those who are most in need.

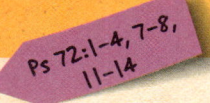

Ps 72:1-4, 7-8, 11-14

72 ¹Give the king your justice, O God,
   and your righteousness to the royal son!
²May he judge your people with righteousness,
   and your poor with justice!
³Let the mountains bear prosperity for the people,
   and the hills, in righteousness!
⁴May he defend the cause of the poor of the people,
   give deliverance to the needy,
   and crush the oppressor! . . .
⁷In his days may righteousness flourish,
   and peace abound, till the moon be no more!

⁸May he have dominion from sea to sea,
   and from the River to the ends of the earth! . . .
¹¹May all kings fall down before him,
   all nations serve him!
¹²For he delivers the needy when he calls,
   the poor and him who has no helper.
¹³He has pity on the weak and the needy,
   and saves the lives of the needy.
¹⁴From oppression and violence he redeems their souls;
   and precious is their blood in his sight.

Chapter 15 Review:
The House of David

1. Solomon became famous for having the gift of _____. This spiritual gift allows a person to know God's purpose and plan and to see the world from God's perspective.

2. When the Lord made a covenant with David, he promised that David's son would "build a house for my name" (2 Sam 7:13). This was initially fulfilled when Solomon built the _____ in Jerusalem.

3. How did Solomon violate the three laws of kings written in the Book of Deuteronomy?
   _____
   _____

4. The ten tribes that broke away from the house of David became known as _____, the Northern Kingdom.

5. Which two tribes remained under the rule of the Davidic kings as the Kingdom of Judah, the Southern Kingdom? _____

6. Who was the son of Solomon who was the first to rule over the Kingdom of Judah?
   _____

7. What does the word "shalom" mean? _____

8. God promised to bless Jeroboam, the king of the Northern Kingdom, as long as he remained faithful. But Jeroboam became afraid. Why was he afraid, and what sinful act did this fear lead him to?
   _____
   _____
   _____

The Temple and Church Architecture

High altar at Saint Peter's Basilica, Rome

The Temple of Solomon was an architectural wonder. It was built as a place for God to dwell on earth. When people came to the Temple, they would encounter God through prayer and offering of sacrifices.

The architecture of many Catholic churches is meant to recall the Temple in Jerusalem. Solomon's Temple contained bronze basins that held water used for cleansing and ritual purposes. When a person first enters a Catholic church, she dips her hand in the holy water font and makes the Sign of the Cross. The holy water reminds us of our Baptism, when we were cleaned from our sins. The Temple had ten golden lampstands that were lit daily. Catholic churches have many candles, including tall candles near the altar. A lit candle is always near the tabernacle as a sign of reverence for the Real Presence of Jesus in the Eucharist and as a reminder that Jesus is the Light of the World.

When Solomon dedicated the Temple, he went before the altar and "knelt with hands outstretched toward heaven; and he stood, and blessed all the assembly of Israel" (1 Kings 8:54–55). Solomon then offered sacrifices to the Lord. Solomon's actions foreshadowed the Catholic Mass, where the priest stands at the altar, offers the eucharistic sacrifice, stretches out his hands, and blesses the assembly of the church.

In the Temple, the bread of the Presence was displayed on a golden table and eaten by the priests weekly. The bread of the Presence was a type of the Eucharist. At the heart of a Catholic church is the tabernacle, where the Blessed Sacrament resides. During the Consecration at Mass, the gifts of bread and wine are transubstantiated into the Body and Blood, Soul and Divinity of Jesus Christ.

The similarities between the Temple and Catholic churches remind us that the worship and sacrifices offered by the people of Israel foreshadowed the ultimate worship and sacrifice that Jesus established in the Eucharist.

Journal Reflection

As humans, we are a unity of body and soul. The Catholic Mass draws our souls into union with God *through* our bodily senses. **What are some ways the Mass engages our five senses? How can you better use your five senses to worship God at Mass?**

A Sanctuary at Home

Read

Solomon built the magnificent Temple so that Israel could experience the presence of God on earth and worship him. The splendor of the Temple reflected only a fraction of the glory and beauty of God. The art and design of the building created a space where the worshipper could be drawn into the mystery of God. Catholic churches today continue the tradition of using art—statues, paintings, and stained glass—to connect us with God.

Sacred art is not just for churches. As Catholics, we are encouraged to decorate our homes with sacred art or objects to remind us of God. Some Catholic families even create an altar in their home, where they can gather in prayerful worship.

Reflect

Spend 5–10 minutes reflecting on the following:

- Why is it important for Catholics to have religious art in their homes?
- Which religious picture or item in my home do I like the most, and why?
- What religious picture or item would I like to add to my home, and why?

Pray

When you have some quiet time at home, pray the following:

> Visit, we beseech thee, O Lord, this dwelling,
> and drive far from it all snares of the enemy;
> let thy holy angels dwell herein,
> to preserve us in peace;
> and let thy blessing be upon us forever.
> Through Christ our Lord.
> Amen.

Act

The next time you are at church, spend a few minutes looking at one of the pieces of religious art. Consider what the art is teaching you about the Catholic faith. As you look at the art, say a brief prayer or make the Sign of the Cross.

CHAPTER 16

The Mission of the Prophets

Words to Know

> hesed

> judgment

Continuing the Story of Salvation

List four key events that happened after Solomon was made king. Conclude your list of events with a brief description of the grave sin of King Jeroboam.

_____

_____

_____

_____

_____

_____

Proclaiming the Good News

"I believe in the Holy Spirit, the Lord, the giver of life, who proceeds from the Father and the Son, who with the Father and the Son is adored and glorified, who has spoken through the prophets."

—Nicene Creed

The Prophet Elias Prays on Mount Carmel, Visigothic-Mozarabic Bible of St. Isidore's, A.D. 960

197

Elijah the Prophet

The Lord Answers by Fire

Around the year 930 B.C., after King Solomon died and the kingdom was divided, Jeroboam led the Kingdom of Israel into idolatry. Like Jeroboam, the kings who came after him also fell into grave sin, "doing evil in the sight of the LORD, walking in the way of Jeroboam, and . . . making Israel to sin" (1 Kings 16:19). One of these sinful kings was Ahab. Ahab married Jezebel, a princess from Sidon. Jezebel's people worshipped the false god Baal, a storm god. The worship of Baal involved horrific rituals, including child sacrifice.

Under Jezebel's influence, Ahab built an altar for Baal and brought in hundreds of Baal's false prophets. To punish Ahab for his sins, the Lord brought a drought upon the land. By sending a drought, the Lord was showing the people that this god of thunder, lightning, and rain was powerless and a fraud. To further discredit Baal, the prophet Elijah challenged the false prophets of Baal at Mount Carmel. There, the Lord would prove that he alone was the living and true God.

The Rival Sacrifices of Elijah and the Priests of Baal, Lucas Cranach the Younger

1 Kings 18:23-24, 26, 29, 31-33, 35-39

18 ²³[Elijah said,] "Let two bulls be given to us; and let them choose one bull for themselves, and cut it in pieces and lay it on the wood, but put no fire to it; and I will prepare the other bull and lay it on the wood, and put no fire to it. ²⁴And you call on the name of your god and I will call on the name of the LORD; and the God who answers by fire, he is God." . . . ²⁶And [the prophets of Baal] took the bull which was given them, and they prepared it, and called on the name of Baal from morning until noon, saying, "O Baal, answer us!" . . . ²⁹And as midday passed, they raved on, . . . but there was no voice; no one answered, no one heeded. . . .

³¹[Then] Elijah took twelve stones, according to the number of the tribes of the sons of Jacob . . . ³²and with the stones he built an altar in the name of the LORD. And he made a trench about the altar. . . . ³³And he put the wood in order, and cut the bull in pieces and laid it on the wood. And he said, "Fill four jars with water, and pour it on the burnt offering, and on the wood." . . . ³⁵And the water ran round about the altar, and filled the trench also with water. . . .

³⁶Elijah the prophet came near and said, "O LORD, God of Abraham, Isaac, and Israel, let it be known this day that you are God in Israel, and that I am your servant, and that I have done all these things at your word. ³⁷Answer me, O LORD, answer me, that this people may know that you, O LORD, are God, and that you have turned their hearts back." ³⁸Then the fire of the LORD fell, and consumed the burnt offering, and the wood, and the stones, and the dust, and licked up the water that was in the trench. ³⁹And when all the people saw it, they fell on their faces; and they said, "The LORD, he is God; the LORD, he is God."

When the Lord answered Elijah's prayer and sent fire upon the sacrifice, the people recognized the truth: the Lord God of Abraham, Isaac, and Jacob is the only true God. Following this dramatic encounter between Elijah and the prophets of Baal, the Lord ended the drought in the land.

In this event, we can recognize that the heavenly fire Elijah called down on the sacrifice "was a 'figure' of the fire of the Holy Spirit, who transforms what he touches" (*CCC* 696). Many of the Church Fathers saw this sacrifice as a type of the Eucharist, where bread and wine are completely transformed by the Holy Spirit into the Body and Blood of our Lord Jesus Christ. At every Mass, we should pray that our hearts be turned back to the Lord, as were those of the people on Mount Carmel.

Elijah Meets God at Mount Horeb

Queen Jezebel went into a rage and sought to kill Elijah because of what happened on Mount Carmel. Elijah fled into the wilderness. The Lord commanded Elijah to journey to Mount Horeb, another name for Mount Sinai.

1 Kings 19:8-9, 11-15, 18

19 ⁸And [Elijah] arose, and ate and drank, and walked in the strength of that food forty days and forty nights to Horeb the mount of God.

⁹And there he came to a cave, and lodged there; and behold, the word of the LORD came to him, and he said to him, . . . ¹¹"Go forth, and stand upon the mount before the LORD." And behold, the LORD passed by, and a great and strong wind tore the mountains, and broke in pieces the rocks before the LORD, but the LORD was not in the wind; and after the wind an earthquake, but the LORD was not in the earthquake; ¹²and after the earthquake a fire, but the LORD was not in the fire; and after the fire a still small voice.

¹³And when Elijah heard it, he wrapped his face in his mantle and went out and stood at the entrance of the cave. And behold, there came a voice to him, and said, "What are you doing here, Elijah?" ¹⁴He said, "I have been very jealous for the LORD, the God of hosts; for the sons of Israel have forsaken your covenant, thrown down your altars, and slain your prophets with the sword; and I, even I only, am left; and they seek my life, to take it away." ¹⁵And the LORD said to him, . . . ¹⁸"Yet I will leave seven thousand in Israel, all the knees that have not bowed to Baal, and every mouth that has not kissed him."

The Israelites in the Northern Kingdom had done the unimaginable. They rejected the Lord and worshipped the bloodthirsty god Baal. Elijah had remained faithful to the Lord even though his life was at risk. But the Lord reminded Elijah that he was not the only true believer left. There was a faithful group of seven thousand Israelites who still worshipped the true God. The Lord would not abandon his people.

Elijah in the Desert of Horeb, William Brassey Hole

The Lord Is Faithful

Elisha the Prophet

The prophet Elijah continued to speak the Word of God to the people. A man named Elisha became one of his followers. One day, Elijah and Elisha went to the Jordan River.

2 Kings 2:8-9, 11-13, 15

> **2** ⁸Then Elijah took his coat, and rolled it up, and struck the water, and the water was parted to the one side and to the other, till the two of them could go over on dry ground.
> ⁹When they had crossed, Elijah said to Elisha, "Ask what I shall do for you, before I am taken from you." And Elisha said, "I beg you, let me inherit a double share of your spirit." . . . ¹¹And as they still went on and talked, behold, a chariot of fire and horses of fire separated the two of them. And Elijah went up by a whirlwind into heaven. ¹²And Elisha saw it and he cried, "My father, my father! the chariots of Israel and its horsemen!" And he saw him no more. . . .
> ¹³And he took up the coat of Elijah that had fallen from him, and went back and stood on the bank of the Jordan. . . .
> ¹⁵Now when the sons of the prophets who were at Jericho saw him over against them, they said, "The spirit of Elijah rests on Elisha." And they came to meet him, and bowed to the ground before him.

Elisha wanted to continue in the prophet Elijah's footsteps. He asked for a "double share" (2:9) in the spirit of Elijah. After Elijah was taken up to Heaven, his request was granted. Elijah had performed several deeds of power during his ministry, such as parting the Jordan River. But Elisha performed *even more* deeds of power than Elijah. Like Elijah, Elisha miraculously multiplied bread to feed people and raised a dead person to life. Elisha also cured a man of leprosy and gave sight to the blind.

Yet Elisha's miracles did not prevent the Northern Kingdom (Israel) from falling into sin. Each of the kings of Israel is described with the same tragic words: "He did what was evil in the sight of the LORD" (2 Kings 3:2). At first, the kings in the Southern Kingdom (Judah) were more faithful to the Lord. Yet by the time of King Ahaz, a descendant of King David, Judah was no better than Israel. Ahaz offered incense and sacrifices to many false gods, and "he even burned his son as an offering" (2 Kings 16:3).

God's Judgment and Israel's Hope

The prophet Hosea lived during the eighth century B.C. In this time after Elisha's death, the kings in the Northern Kingdom continued leading the people into sin. Hosea's mission, like that of other prophets, can be summarized in three basic steps: (1) call the Israelites to repent of their sins; (2) warn the Israelites of God's coming judgment; and (3) offer the Israelites hope for the time after God's judgment. Hosea had much to say about Israel's sins:

Hos 4:1-2, 7, 9

> **4** ¹Hear the word of the LORD, O people of Israel;
> for the LORD has a controversy with the
> inhabitants of the land.
> There is no faithfulness or kindness,
> and no knowledge of God in the land;
> ²there is swearing, lying, killing, stealing, and
> committing adultery;
> they break all bounds and murder follows
> murder. . . .
> ⁷The more they increased,
> the more they sinned against me;
> I will change their glory into shame. . . .
> ⁹I will punish them for their ways,
> and repay them for their deeds.

Here Hosea announces God's judgment on the people. God's *judgment* is an act of justice in which he punishes or rewards people according to their actions. God is the God of justice. Unlike the pagan gods, God distinguishes between the innocent and the guilty, the righteous and the wicked. Hosea did not just speak of God's judgment. He also spread God's message of *mercy* for the people of Israel, and gave them hope:

Hos 2:19-20

2 ¹⁹"And I will espouse you for ever; I will espouse you in righteousness and in justice, in steadfast love, and in mercy. ²⁰I will espouse you in faithfulness; and you shall know the LORD."

God used the image of the love between a husband and wife to describe his love for his people. God's love is not temporary but permanent: "I will espouse you for ever" (2:19). God's love is faithful and loyal. The Hebrew word for this merciful, "steadfast love" is *hesed* (2:19).

Hosea critiqued the people of Israel for their lack of *hesed*: "There is no faithfulness or kindness" (4:1). They rejected God's love. They "cheated" on the Lord with the false gods of other nations. Though the Lord judged the Israelites for their sins, he did not abandon them. God's *hesed* was stronger than the Israelites' acts of betrayal. This is why there was hope for Israel.

As part of God's judgment of Israel's sins, God would allow them to be conquered by foreign powers. They would then be exiled from the Promised Land. Yet this conquest and exile would be only temporary. Hosea promised that the Lord would be faithful and bring his people out of exile:

Hos 14:4, 7

14 ⁴I will heal their faithlessness;
I will love them freely,
for my anger has turned from them. . .
⁷They shall return and dwell beneath my shadow,
they shall flourish as a garden;
they shall blossom as the vine,
their fragrance shall be like the wine of Lebanon.

From the Saints

"The Lord loves Israel with the love of a special choosing, much like the love of a spouse,¹ and for this reason He pardons its sins and even its infidelities and betrayals. When He finds repentance and true conversion, He brings His people back to grace.² In the preaching of the prophets, mercy signifies a special power of love, which prevails over the sin and infidelity of the chosen people."³

—*Pope Saint John Paul II*

Chapter 16 Summary

1. Through the prophet Elijah, the Lord confronted the worship of the false god Baal.

2. The prophets called people to repentance, announced God's judgment, and gave the people hope after judgment.

3. Through the prophet Hosea, the Lord gave his just judgment and reminded the people of his *hesed*— his merciful, steadfast love.

Calling for Justice

The prophets frequently talked about the sin of idolatry. Idolatry was a serious betrayal of the covenant and of God's love. The prophets also knew that idolatry was the root of many other evils. The more Israel turned away from the God of justice, the more its society became unjust.

In the eighth century B.C., the prophet Amos drew attention to injustice against the poor and vulnerable in the Northern Kingdom (Israel). For example, Amos wrote,

Dr. Martin Luther King Jr. addresses an audience in Washington, D.C.

Amos 8:4–6

> **8** ⁴"Hear this, you who trample upon the needy,
>   and bring the poor of the land to an end,
> ⁵saying "When will the new moon be over,
>   that we may sell grain?
> And the sabbath,
>   that we may offer wheat for sale, . . .
> and deal deceitfully with false balances,
> ⁶that we may buy the poor for silver
>   and the needy for a pair of sandals,
>   and sell the refuse of the wheat?"

Here Amos critiques those who care more about earning money than their religious duties. Their greed caused them to exploit the poor and the needy and deal dishonestly with others.

What are some ways our society today is neglecting the poor?

_____

_____

_____

What are some ways the vulnerable or needy are being taken advantage of in our society today?

_____

_____

_____

The corporal works of mercy are an excellent way to help those who are poor and vulnerable. In the Gospel of Matthew, Christ reminds us that those who serve the poor and needy are *serving Christ himself* (see 25:35–40). Christ identifies himself with the poor and afflicted. Christ also reminds us that he will judge each of us on how well we helped those in need (see 25:41–46).

What are some concrete ways you can fulfill one or more of the corporal works of mercy in your community today?

_____

_____

_____

_____

In his famous "I Have a Dream" speech, Martin Luther King Jr. (MLK), quoted the prophet Amos: "We will not be satisfied until 'justice rolls down like waters, and righteousness like a mighty stream' [5:24]."[4] In his fight for civil rights and against racial injustice, MLK was following the tradition of the Jewish prophets who spoke God's message of justice. MLK knew that if he wanted to follow God, he needed to be like Amos and stand up against injustice and defend the poor and vulnerable. As he said in his speech, "Now is the time to make justice a reality for all of God's children."

Let Us Pray—Psalm 37

The prophets spoke God's Word to the people and called them to repentance. The prophets also reminded the people to trust in God's mercy. Psalm 37 reminds us that those who trust in God will find refuge and deliverance from evil.

Ps 37:3–6, 23–24, 39–40

37 ³Trust in the LORD, and do good;
  so you will dwell in the land, and be
    nourished in safety.
⁴Take delight in the LORD,
  and he will give you the desires of your heart.
⁵Commit your way to the LORD;
  trust in him, and he will act.
⁶He will bring forth your vindication as the light,
  and your right as the noonday. . . .
²³The steps of a man are from the LORD,
  and he establishes him in whose way he delights;

²⁴though he fall, he shall not be cast headlong,
  for the LORD is the stay of his hand. . . .
³⁹The salvation of the righteous is from the LORD;
  he is their refuge in the time of trouble.
⁴⁰The LORD helps them and delivers them;
  he delivers them from the wicked, and saves
    them,
  because they take refuge in him.

Chapter 16 Review:
The Mission of the Prophets

1. Who was the false god worshipped by many in the Northern Kingdom during the reign of King Ahab? _____

2. What is God's *hesed*? _____

3. What was the test on Mount Carmel that proved that this god was false and powerless?
   _____
   _____
   _____

4. On what mountain did Elijah encounter the Lord? _____

5. Name some deeds of power that the prophet Elisha performed:
   _____
   _____
   _____

6. What were the three steps in the mission of Hosea and other prophets?
   1. _____
   2. _____
   3. _____

7. What does God's "judgment" refer to?
   _____
   _____

A Virgin Shall Conceive

The Nativity with the Prophets Isaiah and Ezekiel, Duccio di Buoninsegna

In the second half of the eighth century B.C., the prophet Isaiah began his ministry as an official in the court of Uzziah, the king of the Southern Kingdom (Judah). Like many prophets before him, Isaiah called people to repent of their sins. He also gave the people hope for future healing.

During the reign of King Ahaz, Isaiah communicated one of God's messages of hope: "The Lord himself will give you a sign. Behold, a virgin shall conceive and bear a son, and shall call his name Immanuel" (7:14). This future son of a virgin would rescue Israel from its enemies.

Isaiah's prophecy was fulfilled in Jesus Christ. As Saint Matthew records in the opening chapter of his Gospel, Jesus is truly Emmanuel, "God with us" (1:23). Without ceasing to be God, the Divine Son of God became fully human and was born of the Virgin Mary. This virginal conception of Christ means that Jesus was conceived in Mary's womb without a human father. God the Father is fully the Father of Jesus.

Mary did not just give birth to Jesus as a virgin; she remained a virgin her whole life. As the Church teaches, "Mary 'remained a virgin in conceiving her Son, a virgin in giving birth to him, a virgin in carrying him, a virgin in nursing him at her breast, always a virgin:'[5] with her whole being she is 'the handmaid of the Lord'[6]" (CCC 510).

Mary's perpetual virginity is a sign of her complete dedication to God. When the Angel Gabriel told her that she would give birth to the Son of the Most High, she responded, "Behold, I am the handmaid of the Lord; let it be to me according to your word" (Lk 1:38). She remained totally devoted to God her whole life.

Saint Paul once wrote, "God chose what is weak in the world to shame the strong" (1 Cor 1:27). God overthrew Satan and the mighty forces of evil through a humble virgin, Mary of Nazareth.

Journal Reflection

The Virgin Mary devoted her whole life to God. Her whole life can be summarized by the words she said to Gabriel: "Let it be to me according to your word." **What are the obstacles in your life that prevent you from following God fully, like Mary did?**

Living as a Prophet

Read

Even though the people of Israel continued to sin, the Lord never stopped calling them back to himself. One way he sought to call them back to life with him was by sending prophets: "Through the prophets, God calls Israel and all nations to turn to him, the one and only God" (*CCC* 201). There were various prophets with different personalities and messages, but they had a few things in common:

- **They were all *called* to be prophets.** Being a prophet was not a career. In fact, some prophets had day jobs! One prophet, Amos, was a herdsman and a tree caretaker (see Amos 7:14). Some prophets were even unsure about prophesying for the Lord (see Jer 1:6).

- **They proclaimed only what God desired.** While the methods of proclaiming God's message were different, they shared only what God wanted, no matter how difficult.

- **They were often ignored or rejected.** It wasn't easy to be a prophet, but they leaned upon the Lord for support in order to persevere.

God calls us to be prophets through our Baptism into Christ. That doesn't mean that we will receive mystical visions. It means that God asks us to share his Word with others. We, too, are called to invite others to know God through our words and actions. Like the prophets, we must say and do what God wants, even if it will not always be popular with others.

Catechism of the Catholic Church, 2595

"The prophets summoned the people to conversion of heart and, while zealously seeking the face of God, like Elijah, they interceded for the people."

Reflect

Spend 5–10 minutes reflecting on the following:

- Who in my school, family, or friend group needs to see or hear God's love through me?
- What can I say or do that will draw others to the Lord?
- What scares me about being a prophet? Am I reluctant to do so? Why?

Pray

Think of any family members or friends who have turned from the Lord and are far from him. Pray earnestly for them with these words of the prophet Elijah:

> Answer me, O Lord, answer me, that this people may know that you, O Lord, are God, and that you have turned their hearts back. (1 Kings 18:37)

Act

Choose one act of charity to perform for a friend or family member, and have a conversation with a friend about your Catholic faith.

CHAPTER 17

Into Exile

Words to Know

> exile

> presumption

Proclaiming the Good News

"I know the plans I have for you, says the LORD, plans for welfare and not for evil, to give you a future and a hope. . . . You will seek me and find me; when you seek me with all your heart, I will be found by you, says the LORD."

—Jeremiah 29:11, 13–14

The Destruction of Jerusalem by Nebuchadnezzar, William Brassey Hole

The Fall of the Northern Kingdom

Moses' Prophecy

Even before the Israelites entered the Promised Land, Moses warned them about the grave consequences of their sin and idolatry. Moses foretold that the Lord would remove his people from the Promised Land and they would be scattered among other nations. God's Chosen People would go into exile. *Exile* is when people are taken from their homeland and sent to live in a foreign land.

Deut 4:25-31

> **4** ²⁵"When you . . . have grown old in the land, if you act corruptly . . . by doing what is evil in the sight of the LORD your God, so as to provoke him to anger, . . . ²⁶you will soon utterly perish from the land which you are going over the Jordan to possess; you will not live long upon it. . . . ²⁷And the LORD will scatter you among the peoples, and you will be left few in number among the nations where the LORD will drive you. ²⁸And there you will serve gods of wood and stone, the work of men's hands, that neither see, nor hear, nor eat, nor smell. ²⁹But from there you will seek the LORD your God, and you will find him, if you search after him with all your heart and with all your soul. ³⁰When you are in tribulation, and all these things come upon you in the latter days, you will return to the LORD your God and obey his voice, ³¹for the LORD your God is a merciful God; he will not fail you or destroy you or forget the covenant with your fathers which he swore to them."

With this prophecy of a future exile also came a promise of return. The Lord would again reveal his great mercy: "The LORD your God will restore your fortunes, and have compassion upon you, and he will gather you again from all the peoples where the LORD your God has scattered you" (Deut 30:3). The Lord would not forget the covenant he made with Abraham and his descendants. He would prove faithful to his word and his people.

The Assyrian Exile

What Moses had foretold hundreds of years earlier began to be fulfilled during the reign of Hoshea. Hoshea was the last king of the Northern Kingdom (Israel). His reign ended when the Assyrians invaded Israel.

The Assyrians eventually conquered the capital city of Samaria in the year 722 B.C. and sent many of the Israelites into exile. The Second Book of Kings records these events and explains that the cause of the exile of the Northern Kingdom's people was their own evil.

2 Kings 17:13-18

17 **13**The LORD warned Israel and Judah by every prophet and every seer, saying, "Turn from your evil ways and keep my commandments and my statutes, in accordance with all the law which I commanded your fathers, and which I sent to you by my servants the prophets." **14**But they would not listen, but were stubborn, as their fathers had been, who did not believe in the LORD their God. **15**They despised his statutes, and his covenant that he made with their fathers, and the warnings which he gave them. They went after false idols, and became false, and they followed the nations that were round about them, concerning whom the LORD had commanded them that they should not do like them. **16**And they forsook all the commandments of the LORD their God, and made for themselves molten images of two calves; ... and served Baal. **17**And they burned their sons and their daughters as offerings, and used divination and sorcery, and sold themselves to do evil in the sight of the LORD, provoking him to anger. **18**Therefore the LORD was very angry with Israel, and removed them out of his sight; none was left but the tribe of Judah only.

The Lord was very patient with Israel. Time and again he sent prophets to call the Israelites to repent of their sins and to warn them of God's judgment. Yet the Israelites did not listen but became *more* wicked, even offering their own children as sacrifices to false gods. The Lord allowed the Assyrians to send the ten tribes of the Northern Kingdom into exile.

Judah Resists

After conquering Israel, the Assyrians also tried to conquer Judah. Sennacherib [suh-NAK-uh-rib], the king of Assyria, mocked God and threatened to invade Jerusalem with his vast army. The king of Judah, Hezekiah [HEZ-ih-kigh-uh], responded to the threat with prayer:

2 Kings 19:15-16, 19-20, 33-34

19 **15**And Hezekiah prayed before the LORD, and said: "O LORD the God of Israel, ... you are the God, you alone. ... **16**Incline your ear, O LORD, and hear; open your eyes, O LORD, and see; and hear the words of Sennacherib, which he has sent to mock the living God. ... **19**So now, O LORD our God, save us, I beg you, from his hand, that all the kingdoms of the earth may know that you, O LORD, are God alone."

20Then Isaiah [the prophet] sent to Hezekiah, saying, "Thus says the LORD, the God of Israel: Your prayer to me about Sennacherib king of Assyria I have heard. ...

33By the way that he came, by the same he shall return, and he shall not come into this city, says the LORD. **34**For I will defend this city to save it, for my own sake and for the sake of my servant David."

King Hezekiah Spreads His Case before the Lord, English School, 19th century

The Lord answered Hezekiah's prayer. God protected Jerusalem from the Assyrian army, as the prophet Isaiah had foretold. Sennacherib was forced to retreat to his own land. The Kingdom of Judah, ruled by the descendants of King David, would be preserved for a time.

The Fall of the Southern Kingdom

The Spread of Sin

Hezekiah was a righteous king, but his son Manasseh [muh-NASS-uh] was not. When Manasseh became king, he built places in Judah to worship false gods. He even sacrificed his own son to the bloodthirsty god Baal. Manasseh led the whole Kingdom of Judah into sin. The people of Judah became so hardened in their sin that they refused to repent and seek God's mercy and forgiveness.

Part of the reason the people of Judah refused to repent was because of the Temple. The people assumed that because the Lord was present in his Temple in Jerusalem, they were safe. They thought they could do whatever they wanted without consequence. Because of their idolatry, the Lord sent prophets, such as Jeremiah, to confront them about their sins and call them to repent.

The Prophet Jeremiah, Byzantine School

Jer 7:3-4, 8-11

7 ³"Thus says the LORD of hosts, the God of Israel, Amend your ways and your doings, and I will let you dwell in this place. ⁴Do not trust in these deceptive words: 'This is the temple of the LORD, the temple of the LORD, the temple of the LORD.' . . .

⁸"Behold you trust in deceptive words to no avail. ⁹Will you steal, murder, commit adultery, swear falsely, burn incense to Baal, and go after other gods . . . ¹⁰and then come and stand before me in this house . . . and say, 'We are delivered!'—only to go on doing all these abominations? ¹¹Has this house, which is called by my name, become a den of robbers in your eyes?"

When we assume that God will forgive us even if we do not repent, we are guilty of the sin of *presumption*. The people of Judah were guilty of presumption. They assumed that because God's power and mercy were always available to them in the Temple, they did not need to obey God's laws or repent of their sins. The Lord is indeed merciful and forgiving. But to receive his mercy, we must *turn to* him and *turn away* from our sin. An unrepentant sinner does neither. Not surprisingly, when Jeremiah confronted the sinful people of Judah, he often called them to turn to the Lord.

The Babylonian Exile

Still, despite Jeremiah's warnings, the people of Judah continued to steal, commit adultery, worship false gods, and even murder their own children. Therefore, the Lord removed them from the land and scattered them, just as Moses had foretold centuries earlier. God allowed the nation of Babylon, led by King Nebuchadnezzar [NEB-oo-kad-NEZ-uhr], to conquer the Kingdom of Judah.

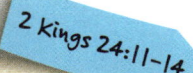
2 Kings 24:11-14

24 ¹¹"Nebuchadnezzar king of Babylon came to the city, while his servants were besieging it; ¹²and . . . the king of Judah gave himself up to the king of Babylon, himself, and his mother, and his servants, and his princes, and his palace officials. The king of Babylon took him prisoner . . . ¹³and carried off all . . . the treasures of the king's house, and cut in pieces all the vessels of gold in the temple of the LORD, which Solomon king of Israel had made, as the LORD had foretold. ¹⁴He carried away all Jerusalem, and all the princes, and all the mighty men of valor, ten thousand captives, and all the craftsmen and the smiths; none remained, except the poorest people of the land.

In 586 B.C., the Babylonians conquered Jerusalem and burned down the Temple Solomon had built. The people of Judah were left without a descendant or "son" of David as king, without the Temple, and without a land of their own. They were exiled in Babylon, and this left them confused and despairing. Had God abandoned his covenants with Abraham and David? Sometimes painful surgery is necessary to heal a deep wound. Exile was the painful surgery required to heal God's people of their self-inflicted wounds of sin. By allowing his people to experience the suffering of exile, the Lord sought to turn their hearts away from evil and back to him.

The prophet Jeremiah did not just remind the people of Judah of their sins and of God's judgment. He also delivered hope for healing and a new life. The Lord had not forgotten his covenants. He would raise up a descendant of David who would restore the kingdom for all time.

Jer 23:5-6, 8; 33:20-21

23 ⁵"Behold, the days are coming, says the LORD, when I will raise up for David a righteous Branch, and he shall reign as king and deal wisely, and shall execute justice and righteousness in the land. ⁶In his days Judah will be saved, and Israel will dwell securely. . . .
⁸Then they shall dwell in their own land." . . .

33 ²⁰"Thus says the LORD: If you can break my covenant with the day and my covenant with the night, so that day and night will not come at their appointed time, ²¹then also my covenant with David my servant may be broken, so that he shall not have a son to reign on his throne."

The Lord would prove himself faithful. His covenant with David and his descendants was as unbreakable as the cycle of day and night. As Moses had foretold, "[The LORD] will not fail you or destroy you or forget the covenant with your fathers" (Deut 4:31). The Lord would one day restore the kingdom of David. A future anointed King—a "son" of David, the "Branch" (Jer 23:5)—would rule with justice over God's people.

Chapter 17 Summary

1. Moses prophesied that God's Chosen People would one day be exiled from the Promised Land because of their sins.

2. The Assyrians conquered the Northern Kingdom (Israel) in 722 B.C. The Babylonians conquered the Southern Kingdom (Judah) in 586 B.C., destroying the Temple in Jerusalem.

3. Jeremiah gave the people in exile hope that the Lord would raise up a new Davidic king who would restore the kingdom.

The Good Shepherd

When we face great suffering, it is easy to fall into despair. We can sometimes feel that there is no way out or no solution. We can feel alone and isolated. Certainly some of the people from Judah felt despair as they lived as exiles in Babylon.

When we experience suffering, we can avoid despair by remembering exactly *who* God is. The Lord is not like the bloodthirsty god Baal, delighting in the suffering and misery of his human victims. God is loving and merciful. Even when the people of Judah strayed from the Lord—becoming a murderous and evil people—the Lord did not forget his people. He sought to heal them and restore them to life. God does not abandon us.

The prophet Ezekiel comforted the exiles in Babylon by reminding them that the Lord was like a good shepherd who cared for the flock of his people:

The Good Shepherd, Philippe de Champaigne

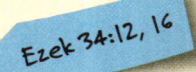

Ezek 34:12, 16

34 ¹²"As a shepherd seeks out his flock when some of his sheep have been scattered abroad, so will I seek out my sheep; and I will rescue them from all places where they have been scattered. . . . ¹⁶I will seek the lost, and I will bring back the strayed, and I will bind up the crippled, and I will strengthen the weak."

Judah had wandered far away from God. Like a good shepherd, the Lord chased after his lost sheep. Jesus applied Ezekiel's words to himself. Jesus said, "I am the good shepherd; I know my own and my own know me, as the Father knows me and I know the Father; and I lay down my life for the sheep" (Jn 10:14). On the Cross, Jesus laid down his life to draw all of us—his lost sheep—back to himself. Jesus is willing to pursue and rescue you, even to the point of offering his life for you on the wood of the Cross.

What does this reveal about your worth in God's eyes?

_____

_____

_____

How might this understanding of God's love and mercy help you trust in his love and mercy in your life?

_____

_____

Because God is a Good Shepherd, we can have hope amid suffering. Hope is the theological virtue that makes it possible for us to trust in God and His plan of love. Hope allows us to trust that we will receive the promise of Heaven if we repent of our sins.

How is despair opposed to the virtue of hope?

_____

_____

The people of Judah were guilty of the sin of presumption. Because they had the Temple, they were certain they could be saved without needing to repent.

How is the sin of presumption opposed to the virtue of hope?

_____

_____

_____

Let Us Pray—Psalm 137

In Psalm 137, the psalmist reflects on life in exile in Babylon. While suffering in exile, the psalmist remembers Jerusalem with hope. May we, too, remember the hope we have in God and in Heaven while we experience exile and suffering on our earthly journey.

Ps 137:1-6

137 ¹By the waters of Babylon,
   there we sat down and wept,
  when we remembered Zion.
²On the willows there
  we hung up our lyres.
³For there our captors
   required of us songs,
  and our tormentors, mirth, saying,
    "Sing us one of the songs of Zion!"

⁴How shall we sing the LORD's song
   in a foreign land?
⁵If I forget you, O Jerusalem,
   let my right hand wither!
⁶Let my tongue cleave to the roof of my mouth,
   if I do not remember you,
  if I do not set Jerusalem
   above my highest joy!

Chapter 17 Review:
Into Exile

1. When people are taken from their homeland and sent to live in a foreign land, it is called **Exile**.

2. Which nation conquered the Northern Kingdom (Israel) in 722 B.C.? **Assyria**

3. According to 2 Kings, what was the cause of the ten tribes of the Northern Kingdom going into exile? **Adultery Sin**

4. What is the sin of presumption? **Believing that God will give us with no repent**

5. Which nation conquered the Southern Kingdom (Judah) in 586 B.C.? **Babylone**

6. Who was the better king of Judah: Hezekiah or his son Manasseh? Why? **God → Manasseh did not bec. he kept believing in God**

7. Why did the Babylonian exile cause many people in Judah to be confused? **bec he burned down the covenant**

8. How did Jeremiah give the people hope for new life after exile? **Bring them another King**

The Sign of Jonah

Read Matthew 12:38–42 on page 11.

The scribes and Pharisees questioned Jesus, demanding a sign. They wanted him to prove himself to them. Jesus had already performed many signs, such as healing a paralyzed man and driving out demons. But the scribes and Pharisees hardened their hearts and refused to accept Jesus. In response to their demand, Jesus said they would be given only "the sign of Jonah the prophet" (12:39).

The Old Testament Book of Jonah recounts the prophet Jonah's call to preach repentance to the people of Nineveh. Nineveh was the capital city of the Assyrians, the people who eventually conquered the Northern Kingdom (Israel). Jonah did not want to go to Nineveh, and so he got on a boat to flee from the Lord. Eventually, Jonah was cast overboard and swallowed by a huge fish. Jonah spent three days in the fish's belly, after which the fish spit Jonah out. The Lord then commanded Jonah to go to Nineveh. Many have read this account as meaning that Jonah actually died and was raised to life by the Lord on the third day.

Jonah called the people of Nineveh to repent of their sins or face destruction. The people obeyed. Even though they did not worship the Lord and were not part of the Chosen People, they turned away from evil. The people of Nineveh were more faithful to God than the Chosen People! They repented after *one* message from a *single* prophet. Israel and Judah received *many* messages from *many* prophets, and still they hardened their hearts.

Jonah was a type of Jesus Christ. Like Jonah, Jesus died and three days later was raised from the dead. Jonah's message of repentance was received with faith by a Gentile (a non-Israelite) nation. This was a sign of a greater conversion of Gentiles to come. Already in Jesus' lifetime, Gentiles began to repent of their sins and believe in him. In the decades following Jesus' Death and Resurrection, great numbers of Gentiles began to worship Jesus Christ

Jonah Preaching to the Ninevites, Gustave Doré

as Lord. Within three hundred years, Christianity became the majority religion of the pagan Roman Empire. Jesus' words and deeds had caused most of the pagan world to abandon their idolatry.

Jesus is the Divine Son of God. Through his teaching and ultimately his Death and Resurrection, all the nations of the world—both Jew and Gentile—came to worship Jesus as Lord.

Journal Reflection

The scribes and Pharisees demanded a sign from Jesus. They wanted Jesus to prove himself to them. **Can you name some times in your life when you have felt God's presence? What signs has God given you to remind you of his presence in your life and his love for you?**

Trusting God amid Suffering

Read

We all suffer—even people we put on pedestals. Suffering does not mean that God doesn't love us! Would we say that God doesn't love his Son even though he underwent the Passion? No, God infinitely loves his Son. At Jesus' baptism, God the Father announced, "This is my beloved Son, in whom I am well pleased" (Mt 3:17). Jesus is the Father's Beloved Son and *still* he underwent great suffering.

Through the grace of Baptism, we, too, became God's beloved sons and daughters. He infinitely loves us. We must remember that God is the *perfect* Father. He is all-powerful and all-loving. This means that he permits, or allows, sufferings to occur only out of love. This is difficult to believe sometimes, especially when our suffering is great.

For example, we may not understand why he'd allow a parent to lose a job or a family member to pass away. In moments like these, we must recall that our Heavenly Father is the perfect Father who infinitely loves us as his beloved children. While we may not have an explanation for our suffering, we can rest in the Father and know that it is all in his hands.

Reflect

Spend 5–10 minutes reflecting on the following:

- How do I respond to suffering? Do I turn to God for help, or do I stop praying?
- Is there any suffering in my life that challenges my faith in our Heavenly Father's goodness?
- How can I learn more about the Heavenly Father's love?

Pray

Pray the Our Father.

Act

When you undergo suffering this week, recite the following: "I am a beloved child of the Heavenly Father."

CHAPTER 18

Jesus, the Son of David

Words to Know

> *Hosanna*
> *Lord*
> *ransom*

Proclaiming the Good News

"I am the good shepherd. The good shepherd lays down his life for the sheep." —John 10:11

The Good Shepherd, Paleo-Christian, 5th century

Son of David and Lord

One Flock, One Shepherd

In Chapter 17, we read a passage from the Book of Ezekiel that foretold the Lord God coming as the shepherd of his people. God promised his exiled people that he would rescue them. He is the Good Shepherd, so he would not let his sheep remain scattered forever. But the prophecy continues and speaks not just of the Lord God as shepherd but also of a new David who would shepherd God's people.

Ezek 34:11-12, 15-16, 22-24

> **34** ¹¹"Thus says the Lord GOD: Behold, I, I myself will search for my sheep, and will seek them out. ¹²As a shepherd seeks out his flock when some of his sheep have been scattered abroad, so will I seek out my sheep; and I will rescue them from all places where they have been scattered.... ¹⁵I myself will be the shepherd of my sheep, and I will make them lie down, says the Lord GOD. ¹⁶I will seek the lost, and I will bring back the strayed, and I will bind up the crippled, and I will strengthen the weak....
>
> ²²"I will save my flock, they shall no longer be a prey; and I will judge between sheep and sheep. ²³And I will set up over them one shepherd, my servant David, and he shall feed them: he shall feed them and be their shepherd. ²⁴And I, the LORD, will be their God, and my servant David shall be prince among them; I, the LORD, have spoken."

David was the king after God's own heart, whom the Lord had called to shepherd all twelve tribes of Israel. Through the prophet Ezekiel, God promised to send another shepherd-king, a new David. This promise of a new David gave rise to hopes for the Messiah, a future anointed king descended from King David. These promises are fulfilled by Jesus Christ, the Son of David.

Saint Matthew recorded numerous times during Jesus' public ministry when people addressed him as "Son of David." For instance, two blind men seeking healing cried out to Jesus, "Have mercy on us, Son of David" (9:27). And a Canaanite woman whose daughter was possessed by a demon begged Jesus, "Have mercy on me, Lord, Son of David!" (15:22). Jesus was fulfilling God's promise that he would "bind up the crippled" and "strengthen the weak" (Ezek 34:16). Jesus revealed himself to be the Christ, the one the prophet Micah had foretold would be born in Bethlehem and would one day shepherd God's people (see Mt 2:4–6).

But Jesus was not just another earthly king in a long line of kings. He is the Divine Son of God made man. During his public ministry, Jesus healed people by his own divine power. When people begged Jesus to have mercy on them, they were seeking God's *hesed*, his merciful love. Jesus could share God's love directly with them because he is the Divine Son.

As Christians, we confess our belief that Jesus is the Divine Son of God when we address him as Lord. The title "*Lord*" is commonly used in the Gospels to show respect to an authority figure. When Christians confess Jesus as Lord, we express our greatest respect and adoration for Jesus, who has been given "all authority in heaven and on earth" (Mt 28:18).

Catechism of the Catholic Church, 570

"Jesus' entry into Jerusalem manifests the coming of the kingdom that the Messiah-King, welcomed into his city by children and the humble of heart, is going to accomplish by the Passover of his Death and Resurrection."

The Entry of Christ into Jerusalem, Louis Felix Leullier

Greater Than Solomon

When David's son Solomon was made king, he rode on a mule to the place where he was anointed (see the passage from 1 Kings 1 on page 188). Centuries later, the prophet Zechariah foretold the coming of a future anointed king who would be a new Solomon. The coming of this future son of David, the Messiah, would be the cause of great joy and would bring peace to all people.

Zech 9:9-11, 16

9 ⁹Rejoice greatly, O daughter of Zion!
   Shout aloud, O daughter of Jerusalem!
Behold, your king comes to you;
   triumphant and victorious is he,
humble and riding on a donkey,
   on a colt the foal of a donkey.
¹⁰I will cut off the chariot from Ephraim
   and the war horse from Jerusalem;
and the battle bow shall be cut off,
   and he shall command peace to the nations;
his dominion shall be from sea to sea,
   and from the River to the ends of the earth.
¹¹As for you also, because of the blood of my
      covenant with you,
   I will set your captives free from the
      waterless pit. . . .
¹⁶On that day the LORD their God will save
      them
   for they are the flock of his people.

The future king would be known for his humility, triumphantly riding not on a great warhorse but on a donkey. The Messiah's reign would bring peace and salvation for all God's people, his flock. Zechariah's words were fulfilled by Jesus. Jesus entered Jerusalem riding on a donkey as the people shouted, "Hosanna to the Son of David!" (Mt 21:9). The word "*Hosanna*" means "Save!" or "Give salvation!" The people celebrated Jesus as the long-awaited Son of David, who would save them.

The salvation Jesus brought was not just freedom from oppression by a foreign power. Rather, Jesus fulfilled the prophecy of Zechariah: "Because of the blood of my covenant with you, I will set your captives free from the waterless pit" (9:11). By his Cross and Resurrection, Jesus saved humanity from the powers of sin and death.

For Freedom Christ Has Set Us Free

A King's Ransom

The triumphal entry of Jesus into Jerusalem is just one way that Jesus fulfilled the words of the prophet Zechariah. There are other prophetic texts in the Book of Zechariah that the Evangelists showed were fulfilled in the Christ. As Jesus told the disciples on the road to Emmaus, "Was it not necessary that the Christ should suffer these things and enter into his glory?" (Lk 24:26). The Paschal Mystery reveals Jesus as the Messiah that the prophets foretold—the Messiah who would ultimately save us from sin.

Foretold by the Prophets *Book of Zechariah*	**Fulfilled in Christ** *The Gospels*
God's shepherd would be detested; thirty pieces of silver would be paid to be rid of him (see 11:8, 12–13).	The chief priests and elders conspired to arrest Jesus and kill him. They bribed Judas Iscariot to betray Jesus for thirty pieces of silver (see Mt 26:3–4, 14–15).
One day, there would be great mourning in Jerusalem as the people looked upon "him whom they have pierced" (12:10).	Jesus was nailed to a Cross by the Romans; a group of women who had followed Jesus looked upon him pierced on the Cross (see Mt 27:55–56; Jn 19:37).
"On that day there shall be a fountain opened for the house of David and the inhabitants of Jerusalem to cleanse them from sin and uncleanness" (13:1).	When a soldier pierced Jesus' side, "at once there came out blood and water" (Jn 19:34), which symbolized the outpouring of the Holy Spirit made available to us through Baptism and the sacraments.

As the Messiah, Jesus did not come just to heal people of physical blindness or sickness, as he healed many in his public ministry. Jesus came to heal us from sin. Before Jesus' Birth, the angel told Joseph that Mary's Son would "save his people from their sins" (Mt 1:21). Jesus' entire life prepared him for his greatest saving act: freely offering himself on the Cross. Jesus declared that he "did not come to be served but to serve, and to give his life as a ransom for many" (Mt 20:28). A *ransom* is a payment required for the release of a captive. Jesus ransomed us from captivity to the powers of sin and death by freely giving his life on the Cross.

Mankind's captivity to sin and death and our need for a savior began with Adam and Eve's Original Sin. They let their trust in God die and freely turned away from him in their sin. As a result of Original Sin, mankind now experiences physical death (see Gen 2:17). We are also born with a human nature deprived of the spiritual life of grace. We, like Adam and Eve, can fail to trust in God and are inclined to commit sin. Even after Baptism, we can commit grave sins that cut us off from our covenant relationship with God, who is the Author of Life.

Chapter 18

Sin is a betrayal of God's love. We owe everything to God, and so he deserves our love in return. Sin is a serious injustice. Since God is *infinitely* good, each sin is an *infinite* injustice. The only thing that could erase an infinite injustice is something infinitely good. But nothing in the created universe is infinitely good. Only God himself is infinitely good. Human sin created a debt to God that we ourselves cannot repay. Since we cannot repay the infinite debt caused by sin, we remain held as captives by the weight of our sins.

Through his Death and Resurrection, Jesus conquered sin and death. While we still experience physical death, Jesus freed us from captivity to spiritual death and eternal separation from God. In Baptism, we become united with Christ and share in his victory over death. With the grace of Baptism and the other sacraments, we can conquer sin in our lives and enjoy eternal life with God in Heaven.

The Crucifixion, follower of Peter Paul Rubens

Jesus Fulfilled God's Covenant with David

Jesus was the long-awaited Son of David, who fulfilled the words of the prophets. Jesus also perfectly fulfilled the three promises God made in his covenant with David. The Lord had promised David that he would "establish the throne of his kingdom for ever" (2 Sam 7:13). After Jesus' Resurrection, he said to his Apostles, "All authority in heaven and on earth has been given to me" (Mt 28:18). Jesus ascended into Heaven, where he reigns as King of God's everlasting kingdom.

The Lord promised that David's son would "build a house for [the Lord's] name" (2 Sam 7:13). Jesus said to Saint Peter, "I say to you, you are Peter, and upon this rock I will build my Church, and the gates of hell shall not prevail against it" (Mt 16:18). The *Church* is the house that Jesus, the Son of David, built. It is the Mystical Body of Christ where God dwells among his people. It is the seed and beginning on earth of the everlasting Kingdom of God.

The Lord promised about David's son, "I will be his father, and he shall be my son" (2 Sam 7:14). Jesus is the Divine Son of God. God the Father is eternally the Father of the Son. God the Son is eternally the Son of the Father. By becoming united to Jesus through Baptism, we become adopted sons and daughters of our Father in Heaven.

Chapter 18 Summary

1. The prophets foretold the coming of a son of David, the Messiah, who would shepherd God's people. Jesus fulfilled the prophets perfectly.

2. Jesus is truly the Divine Son of God made man, whose divinity we confess when we address him as Lord.

3. Through his Death and Resurrection, Jesus ransomed humanity from captivity to sin and death.

"Take My Yoke upon You"

When Solomon was king, he became greedy in his pursuit of riches and power. Solomon forced many people in his kingdom to harsh labor, mining for riches and collecting resources from other lands. When Solomon died, his son Rehoboam became king. The people came to Rehoboam pleading for him to relax the harsh labor his father had forced upon them. Read Rehoboam's response to the Israelites in the passage from 1 Kings below. Then compare his words with those of Jesus from Matthew's Gospel.

1 Kings 12:3-4, 13-14

12 ³All the assembly of Israel came and said to Rehoboam, ⁴"Your father made our yoke heavy. Now therefore lighten the hard service of your father and his heavy yoke upon us, and we will serve you." . . .
¹³And the king answered the people harshly . . . ¹⁴saying, "My father made your yoke heavy, but I will add to your yoke; my father chastised you with whips, but I will chastise you with scorpions."

Mt 11:28-30

11 ²⁸"Come to me, all you who are weary and burdened, and I will give you rest. ²⁹Take my yoke upon you and learn from me, for I am meek and humble in heart, and you will find rest for your souls. ³⁰For my yoke is sweet, and my burden is light."

A yoke is a piece of wood placed on the back of oxen while they plow fields. The people were being crushed under the heavy "yoke" of Solomon's forced labor. But King Rehoboam vowed to lay even harsher burdens on the people. He wanted to make their yoke heavier. By contrast, Jesus, the one true King, promises to give us rest: "My yoke is sweet, and my burden is light" (Mt 11:30). Jesus is a King who lifts burdens. He already has ransomed us from captivity to sin and death.

When we struggle with sin or are suffering, Jesus invites us to "yoke ourselves" to him. Do you spend time with Jesus in prayer? Do you talk to Jesus as a friend, bringing your struggles and worries to him? Jesus is eager to lift our burdens.

Yet we can easily become experts at *not* turning to Jesus. Sometimes we feel we can handle our problems on our own, without Jesus' help. Or we may feel embarrassed or ashamed by our sins, and so we do not want to talk to Jesus about them. Sometimes we prioritize other things over prayer: video games, sports, schoolwork, or spending time with friends.

What is preventing you from spending time every day in prayer, talking to Jesus as a friend?

_____

_____

If we try to carry our burdens ourselves, we will fail. We are weak and cannot save ourselves. If shame or embarrassment holds us back from speaking with Jesus, our King, we must remember the Cross. Jesus knew every sin we would commit. But he was not ashamed of us. Our sins did not stop him from going to the Cross out of love for each one of us. So, we should not be ashamed to turn to him. If we make other things more important than spending time with Jesus, we are falling into the same trap that often ensnared the people of Israel. We are serving other gods. Yet there is only *one* God who can bring us peace and true happiness.

Spend a few minutes prayerfully reflecting on this question: What is weighing you down right now in your life?

_____

_____

Choose one of your burdens. Imagine writing about this burden on a piece of paper and placing it in an envelope. Then imagine Jesus sitting on his heavenly throne. You walk up to Jesus, kneel before him, and hand the envelope to him. When Jesus opens it, what does he say to you? Spend a few minutes prayerfully listening to what Jesus has to say. Then talk to him, as you would a friend.

Conclude by turning to Matthew 7:7–11 on page 5. Read and reread Jesus' words. Spend a few minutes in prayer.

Let Us Pray—Psalm 23

Psalm 23 is perhaps the most well known and beloved of all 150 psalms in the Bible. As we pray this psalm, recall that God is our Shepherd. He will not lead us astray, no matter what suffering or difficulty we are going through. The psalmist encourages us to put all our trust in God.

Ps 23:1-6

23 ¹The LORD is my shepherd, I shall not want;
² he makes me lie down in green pastures.
He leads me beside still waters;
³ he restores my soul.
He leads me in paths of righteousness
    for his name's sake.
⁴Even though I walk through the valley of the shadow of death,
   I fear no evil;
for you are with me;
   your rod and your staff,
   they comfort me.
⁵You prepare a table before me
    in the presence of my enemies;
you anoint my head with oil,
    my cup overflows.
⁶Surely goodness and mercy shall follow me
    all the days of my life;
and I shall dwell in the house of the LORD
    for ever.

Chapter 18 Review:
Jesus, the Son of David

1. What did people call Jesus as he healed them from various illnesses?

2. Which prophet predicted the coming of the future shepherd-king and descendant of David? _____

3. How did Jesus fulfill the prophecy in Zechariah of a new Solomon?

4. Explain how Jesus fulfilled each of the three promises the Lord gave to David when he made a covenant with him.

5. What do we confess when we address Jesus with the title "Lord"? _____

6. What does it mean to say that Jesus' Death on the Cross "ransoms" us? _____

7. The prophet Zechariah foretold that there would be "a fountain opened for the house of David and the inhabitants of Jerusalem to cleanse them from sin and uncleanness" (13:1). How did Jesus fulfill this passage? Which sacrament did this foreshadow above all?

Hosanna!

When Jesus entered Jerusalem, the people cried out, "'Blessed is he who comes in the name of the Lord!' Hosanna in the highest!" (Mt 21:9). The crowds hailed Jesus as the King, the long-awaited Son of David of prophecy. As Jesus entered Jerusalem, the city of kings, people expected him to restore the kingdom of David. The crowds did not expect what happened next. After entering Jerusalem, Jesus indeed mounted a throne—the throne of a Roman cross. Jesus received his royal crown—a crown of thorns. Jesus was hailed the King of the Jews—as pagan soldiers mocked and beat him.

The crowds turned against Jesus. Most of his followers abandoned him. He was treated like a criminal, tortured, and killed. Yet just when it seems like Jesus was a failed Messiah, an imposter to the throne of David, something amazing happened: God raised Jesus from the dead. Jesus' Resurrection proved that he was telling the truth. He truly was the King. After his Resurrection and Ascension into Heaven, Jesus entered his heavenly kingdom—a kingdom that has no end.

At every Mass, we do not just *remember* these events in the past; we *participate* in them. These past events are *made present* to us, here and now. During the Liturgy of the Eucharist, we repeat the words of the crowds when Jesus entered Jerusalem: "'Blessed is he who comes in the name of the Lord!' Hosanna in the highest!" (21:9). We hear anew Jesus' words at the Last Supper: "Take, eat; this is my body. . . . Drink from it, all of you. For this is my blood of the covenant, which is poured out for many for the forgiveness of sins" (26:26–28).

At every Mass, the one perfect sacrifice of Christ on the Cross is made present to us. As the *Catechism* teaches, "In the Eucharist Christ gives us the very body which he gave up for us on the cross, the very blood which he 'poured out for many for the forgiveness of sins'" (*CCC* 1365). In the Eucharist, we really receive our King, living and glorious. Jesus is present to us—Body, Blood, Soul, and Divinity—under the appearances of bread and wine.

The Eucharist is "an anticipation of the heavenly glory" (*CCC* 1402). By being united to Christ through the Eucharist, we receive a taste of Jesus' heavenly glory. We are prepared for sharing one day in the fullness of his heavenly kingdom.

Journal Reflection

What can you do in your life right now to draw closer to Jesus Christ, your King, at Mass?

Christ the King

Read

When Christ entered Jerusalem during the third year of his public ministry, the people treated him like the King he is. But was his triumphal entry the end of the New Testament? We know that it wasn't. He was arrested, tortured, and put to death. Truly, his entrance into Jerusalem was a dangerous entrance into enemy-occupied territory.

In the spiritual sense, this event shows us how we often accept Christ into our hearts to be King but how, too often, we turn against him. We have moments when we refuse to obey him or we ignore him. In a way, he becomes an enemy to us. He threatens our selfish desires or comforts. C. S. Lewis, a famous Christian author and philosopher, spoke about it in this way: "Enemy-occupied territory—that is what this world is. Christianity is the story of how the rightful king has landed, you might say landed in disguise, and is calling us all to take part in a great campaign of sabotage."[2]

When we freely choose to commit serious sin, we lose God's grace in our souls. Our hearts become enemy-occupied territory. But when we repent and seek God's mercy and forgiveness, he restores grace in us through the sacraments. The Lord enters our hearts to rid us of the enemy: sin and selfishness. However, he doesn't do it alone. He invites us to participate in his work of destroying this darkness in our lives.

Reflect

Spend 5–10 minutes reflecting on the following:

- Is Jesus welcome in my heart? Does he find a disciple who desires to be close to him?
- Who or what is the king of my heart? Is it Jesus?

Pray

Pray for Christ to reign in your heart:

> Christ Jesus, I acknowledge you King of the Universe.
> All that has been created has been made for you.
> Make full use of your rights over me.
> Divine Heart of Jesus,
> I offer you my efforts
> in order to obtain that all hearts
> may acknowledge your Sacred Royalty,
> and that thus the kingdom of your peace
> may be established throughout the universe.
> Amen.

Act

Examine your conscience each night this week in order to discover whether Christ was ruling over your heart during the day.

Unit 5

The Coming of the Anointed One

During the Babylonian exile, the prophet Daniel gave witness to the Lord God of Israel and gave his people hope through his prophecies. He foretold the coming of a figure—the Son of Man—who would receive an everlasting kingship. The Lord brought his people back from exile to the Promised Land, where they rebuilt the Temple and the walls of Jerusalem under the leadership of men like Zerubbabel, Ezra, and Nehemiah. But after their return, there was no Davidic king ruling over Israel.

In the centuries leading up to the Birth of Christ, while still awaiting their king, the Israelites were persecuted at the hands of the Greeks, especially Antiochus IV. The Maccabees led a successful Jewish revolt against Antiochus IV, cleansing the Temple and leading to the celebration of the Feast of Hanukkah.

Jesus is the Son of Man, foretold by the prophet Daniel, who received an everlasting kingdom through his Paschal Mystery.

Chapters 19–22

Chapter 19: An Everlasting Kingdom
Chapter 20: I Will Bring Them Back
Chapter 21: Zeal for the Law
Chapter 22: Jesus, the Son of Man

Grade 6 Road Map

Unit 1
The Good News
The Gospel of Matthew reveals who Jesus is through both his deeds and words. God speaks to us in Sacred Scripture through human authors inspired by the Holy Spirit.

Unit 2
In the Beginning
Genesis describes the beginning of the universe and humanity, the beginning of sin, and the beginning of God's plan to restore mankind's relationship with himself through the covenant with Abraham and his descendants. In Jesus, God's covenant with Abraham is fulfilled.

Unit 3
You Shall Be My People
Through Moses, God delivered his people from slavery in Egypt and made a covenant with them at Mount Sinai. Despite their unfaithfulness, God brought his people into the Promised Land after they wandered for forty years in the desert. Jesus is the New Moses, who gives the New Law.

Unit 4
The Kingdom of the Lord
The Lord made a covenant with King David and swore to give him an everlasting kingdom. The sins of God's people led to the division and downfall of the kingdom, eventually leading to the destruction of the Temple and the Babylonian exile. In Jesus, God's covenant with David is fulfilled.

Unit 5
The Coming of the Anointed One
God brought his people back from exile to the Promised Land, where they rebuilt the Temple in Jerusalem. The prophets foretold of the coming of the Messiah, who would rebuild the kingdom of David. Jesus, the Son of Man, brings the kingdom through his suffering and Death.

Unit 6
God with Us
The Gospel of Matthew provides reliable testimony that Jesus is the Divine Son of God made man, who delivered us from sin through his Paschal Mystery. Jesus continues to be present to his Church through Word and sacrament—above all, the Holy Eucharist.

Blessed Franz Jägerstätter

A Devout Life

On May 20, 1907, in the rural town of Saint Radegund in Upper Austria, Franz Jägerstätter was born. Many people did not recognize his saintly life until much later. The memory of him almost disappeared, but his story has gained much attention in the last fifty years.

Little is known about Franz's youth. He was born into a hardworking family of farmers. Sadly, his father died in World War I when Franz was young, but his mother remarried. His stepfather helped greatly with young Franz's education. Even though Franz received a basic education, he became an avid reader and an excellent writer.

Franz was something of an unruly young man. He rode a motorcycle and was known to get in fights. He fathered a daughter out of wedlock. But by the time he got married in 1936 to Franziska, he had settled down as a farmer in Radegund.

We know very little about his conversion of heart to a deep devotion to God. It was perhaps because of the piety of his wife. Some believe his conversion resulted from a powerful encounter with God while visiting Rome during his honeymoon. Surrounded by the beauty and rich history of the Church, something stirred in Franz's heart to live a more devout life. Indeed, he did live a devout married life.

By 1938, Franz and Franziska had two daughters, Rosalie and Marie. They were poor, but that didn't stop Franz from giving to those poorer than themselves. He even refused payment for his additional work caring for the church grounds and burying the dead. His piety and service to the Lord didn't stop there. Franz went to Mass every day. His neighbors claimed that he fasted until the noon Mass. Even though he endured backbreaking labor as a farmer, he refused to eat until he had received the Eucharist. Still, with his busy schedule, Franz took time to read the Bible and perform spiritual works of mercy.

From letters he wrote to his godson, we know that what he did wasn't just an outward show. He wrote, "I can say from my own experience how painful life often is when one lives as a halfway Christian; it is more like vegetating than living."[1] Franz wanted to live a *fully* Christian life devoted to the Lord. He also wrote to his godson, "Since the death of Christ, almost every century has seen the persecution of Christians; there have always been heroes and martyrs who gave their

Wedding photograph of Franz and Franziska, spring 1936

lives—often in horrible ways—for Christ and their faith. If we hope to reach our goal someday, then we too must become heroes of the faith."[2]

Franz's chance to become a "hero of the faith" arrived in the late 1930s. Throughout the decade, the Nazi Party rose to power. Austria came under German rule in 1938, when most citizens voted to be accepted into their expanding empire. Franz was the only local citizen in Radegund to vote *against* being under Nazi rule. He saw the evils of the Nazi Party. In a dream, he saw a train being boarded by young people when a voice warned Franz of this train's destructive path. When Franz awoke from the dream, he realized that the train represented the Nazis and that God had warned him not to participate.

Franz heeded the dream and his conscience. He didn't want to support the evil government in any way, even if it could have benefited him and his family. On one occasion, he refused government money for aid after a fire destroyed his home. He was willing to sacrifice friendships and monetary security to follow Christ. His beliefs would be tested in 1940, when he was called up for mandatory military training to fight for the Nazis. Franz had to choose between loyalty to God, country, and family.

Loyalty and Hope

Franz did everything he could to keep from participating in the Nazi's war. However, he agreed to begin mandatory military training with the Nazis on June 17, 1940, just months after the birth of his third daughter, Aloisia. Military training was as far as Franz was willing to go. He refused to take part in any active fighting.

Franz trained with the Nazis from June 1940 until April 1941. He had a few opportunities to return home to care for his farm and loving family. During the time apart, Franz and Franziska frequently wrote letters. In their writings, they shared their struggles and encouraged each other. Franz missed his family, and Franziska had to care for the farm and the three young girls with little help.

These hardships of marriage gave Franz great insight into suffering. He wrote, "Pour out your heart to me for no one—other than God and our heavenly Mother—can better understand your suffering than your beloved husband. . . . We must go courageously on the way of suffering. . . . They may build many beautiful streets today, but they cannot change the way to heaven. This way will always remain rugged and rocky."[3]

Once training was over, Franz returned home to his family. It would be nearly two years before the Nazis called him to active duty. Until that time, he resumed his everyday life on the farm. But he still held on to the firm belief that the Nazis were evil. He told his friends and family that he would refuse to fight if the time came for him to report for active duty.

Fellow Catholics tried to convince Franz that he *should* fight (at this point, the evils of the Nazi Party weren't completely known). One of the most convincing arguments was that Franz should consider his vocation and his responsibility to his family. If he refused to fight, then he'd be charged with treason and could be imprisoned or killed. Who would care for his family if that happened? To this argument, Franz responded, "I have considered my family. I have prayed and put myself and my family in God's hands.

I know that, if I do what I think God wants me to do, he will take care of my family."[4]

Franz also said in response to those who insisted that he fight for the Nazis, "Everyone tells me, of course, that I should not do what I am doing because of the danger of death. . . . I believe it is better to sacrifice one's life right away than to place oneself in the grave danger of committing sin and then dying."[5]

On February 22, 1943, Franz received a notice to report for active military duty. At the end of the month, Franz said a final goodbye to his family. On March 2, he formally declared his refusal to fight. As they had expected, he was arrested and sent to prison. On July 6, a few short months after he was imprisoned, Franz was condemned to death.

In the days leading up to his execution, he received the sacraments of the Holy Eucharist and Reconciliation. His final letters show a man at peace with himself, his family, and God. Among his last writings to his wife and family, Franz wrote, "Now I'll write down a few words as they come to me from my heart. Although I am writing them with my hands in chains, this is still much better than if my will were in chains."[6] He also wrote, "Dearest wife and mother, it is not possible for me to free both of you from the sorrows that you have suffered for me. . . . I thank our Savior that I could suffer for him and may die for him. . . . If I am soon in heaven, I shall ask the loving God to prepare a place for all of you."[7]

On August 9, the day of his execution, the priest with him said that Franz was calm and uncomplaining. He said of Franz, "I can say with certainty that this simple man is the only saint I have ever met in my lifetime."[8] For his steadfast faith in the Lord, Franz was decapitated by the Nazis. The Church declared him a blessed (one step away from a canonized saint) on October 26, 2007, sixty-four years after his martyrdom. His wife and daughters, along with their families, were all present at the beatification. The Church celebrates his feast day on May 21, the date of his Baptism.

Journal Reflection

1. Many Jews, such as Judas Maccabeus, refused to obey the command of Antiochus IV and participate in pagan Greek religious practices. **How did Franz similarly display fortitude?**

2. **How are you called to be courageous like Judas Maccabeus and Franz? What popular ideas or trends must you resist to remain close to God?**

3. **How did Franz's final days leading up to his martyrdom reveal him as a man of hope?**

4. Franz was strong in his convictions of what was true, good, and holy in the face of grave danger. **What sufferings or obstacles in your life require you to keep your focus trained on God?**

CHAPTER 19

An Everlasting Kingdom

Words to Know

> Son of Man

> witness

Proclaiming the Good News

"From now on, you will see the Son of Man seated at the right hand of Power and coming on the clouds of heaven." —Matthew 26:64

Continuing the Story of Salvation

List six to eight key events in salvation history from the time of the judges to the Babylonian exile.

_____

_____

_____

_____

_____

_____

_____

Daniel the Prophet, Duomo di Santa Maria, Milan, Italy

The Prophet Daniel

Daniel in the Lion's Den, Briton Rivière

Witness in Exile

The prophet Daniel lived in exile in Babylon. As a young man, he was well known for his wisdom and intelligence. He eventually became one of the advisers to Nebuchadnezzar, the king of Babylon. Nebuchadnezzar's court also included many pagan sorcerers. Daniel proved himself to be wiser than these sorcerers. Rather than take credit for his gifts, Daniel gave God all the glory. As a result, Nebuchadnezzar declared to Daniel, "Truly, your God is God of gods and Lord of kings, and a revealer of mysteries" (Dan 2:47).

Daniel was an effective witness to the Lord God of Israel. A *witness* is someone who proclaims God's truth to others through his words and actions. What he declares to others is based on his own experience and knowledge. Daniel used his God-given wisdom to help others know the one true God. Though he was in a foreign land surrounded by people who worshipped many false gods, Daniel had the courage to witness to the one true God.

The Den of Lions

After Nebuchadnezzar's death, Daniel continued to gain respect in Babylon. When Darius became king, he made Daniel his second-in-command over the entire empire. When news of the decision spread, King Darius' pagan advisers grew jealous and came up with a plan to get rid of Daniel. They convinced King Darius to sign a law that outlawed members of his government from praying to anyone but Darius himself. Anyone violating this law would be thrown to the lions.

The advisers knew Daniel prayed to the God of Israel three times each day. It would be easy for them to catch Daniel violating the law. Daniel chose to pray to the Lord anyway. When the advisers caught Daniel breaking this unjust law, they dragged him before King Darius. The king was forced to punish Daniel.

Dan 6:16-17, 19-23, 25-28

6 ¹⁶The king commanded, and Daniel was brought and cast into the den of lions. The king said to Daniel, "May your God, whom you serve continually, deliver you!" ¹⁷And a stone was brought and laid upon the mouth of the den, and the king sealed it with his own signet and with the signet of his lords, that nothing might be changed concerning Daniel. . . .

¹⁹Then, at break of day, the king arose and went in haste to the den of lions. ²⁰When he came near to the den where Daniel was, he cried out in a tone of anguish and said to Daniel, "O Daniel, servant of the living God, has your God, whom you serve continually, been able to deliver you from the lions?" ²¹Then Daniel said to the king, "O king, live for ever! ²²My God sent his angel and shut the lions' mouths, and they have not hurt me, because I was found blameless before him; and also before you, O king, I have done no wrong." ²³Then the king was exceedingly glad, and commanded that Daniel be taken up out of the den. So Daniel was taken up out of the den, and no kind of hurt was found upon him, because he had trusted in his God. . . .

²⁵Then King Darius wrote to all the peoples, nations, and languages that dwell in all the earth: "Peace be multiplied to you. ²⁶I make a decree, that in all my royal dominion men tremble and fear before the God of Daniel,

for he is the living God,
    enduring for ever;
his kingdom shall never be destroyed,
    and his dominion shall be to the end.
²⁷He delivers and rescues,
    he works signs and wonders
    in heaven and on earth,
he who has saved Daniel
    from the power of the lions."

²⁸So this Daniel prospered during the reign of Darius and the reign of Cyrus the Persian.

God delivered Daniel from all danger. Daniel teaches us that to witness to the faith, we need to trust not in our own strength but in God's power. Daniel could have chosen to stop praying to the Lord when he found out about the law. Instead, he continued to practice his faith and trusted in God. As a result, Daniel was able to witness to the Lord, the God of Israel. Darius could not help but admire the "God of Daniel" (6:26).

Daniel's success as the Lord's witness in a pagan land also proved that God was remaining faithful to his covenants. God had promised to make Abraham the father of a great nation, the Chosen People of Israel. But God also promised that his Chosen People would be the source of blessing for *all nations*. The Chosen People were to be God's witnesses to the rest of the world. The purpose of God's special relationship with Israel was to draw all people, including the Gentiles, into relationship with him.

Lion's head relief from ancient Babylon

The Prophecies of Daniel

"One like a Son of Man"

Daniel was more than a witness. He was also a great prophet who received visions from God. The purpose of these visions was to give the people of Judah hope as they suffered exile in a foreign land.

In one vision, Daniel saw four beasts. Each beast symbolized a different world power that persecuted God's people. In Daniel's vision, each of these beasts (world powers) was destroyed. After the destruction of the fourth and last beast, a mysterious figure would come. This figure would come to be called the Son of Man. After the coming of the Son of Man, the kingdom would be restored to the people of Israel. As Daniel wrote, "The saints of the Most High shall receive the kingdom, and possess the kingdom for ever, for ever and ever" (7:18). Daniel's vision of the Son of Man gave God's people hope as they suffered persecution under pagan rulers. Their suffering would not last forever. After the coming of the Son of Man, they would inherit God's kingdom.

Mosaic of the prophet Daniel at the Basilica of St. Paul Outside the Walls, Rome

Dan 7:13-14

7 ¹³And behold, with the clouds of heaven
there came one like a son of man,
and he came to the Ancient of Days
and was presented before him.
¹⁴And to him was given dominion
and glory and kingdom,
that all peoples, nations, and languages
should serve him;
his dominion is an everlasting dominion,
which shall not pass away,
and his kingdom one
that shall not be destroyed.

Recall that the Lord had promised King David a royal dynasty that would never be broken: "Your house and your kingdom shall be made sure for ever before me; your throne shall be established for ever" (2 Sam 7:16). This promise led God's people to look forward in hope to the coming of a new Davidic king, the Messiah, who would restore the kingdom. Now the Lord was revealing through the prophet Daniel that "one like a son of man" would be made king over the entire world (Dan 7:13). His kingdom would be everlasting. Many of God's people came to understand the Son of Man to be the future anointed king, the Messiah.

In Scripture, the phrase "son of man" is another way of saying "human being." According to Daniel's prophecy, the future king was *like* a human being, but also mysteriously different. Daniel did not say that this king was a son of man. He said he was "*like* a son of man" (7:13; emphasis added). After the coming of Jesus, it would be understood more clearly how passages such as this in the Old Testament pointed to the Messiah being both human and divine.

The prophecy also connected the "one like a son of man" with God's presence. Daniel described him as coming "with the clouds of heaven" (7:13). In Scripture, clouds symbolize God being present to his people. For example, when Moses went up Mount Sinai to meet with the Lord, a cloud hovered over the mountain (see Ex 24:16). To say that he comes "with the clouds of heaven" suggests the Son of Man would bring God's presence to his people.

The Resurrection of the Dead

Daniel's vision of the Son of Man gave his people hope for the earthly defeat of their enemies and the restoration of God's kingdom. In another vision, Daniel gave the people hope for the defeat of a more ancient enemy—death.

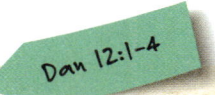
Dan 12:1-4

12 ¹"There shall be a time of trouble, such as never has been since there was a nation till that time; but at that time your people shall be delivered, every one whose name shall be found written in the book. ²And many of those who sleep in the dust of the earth shall awake, some to everlasting life, and some to shame and everlasting contempt. ³And those who are wise shall shine like the brightness of the firmament; and those who turn many to righteousness, like the stars for ever and ever. ⁴But you, Daniel, shut up the words, and seal the book, until the time of the end."

Death has entered human life because of Adam and Eve's sin. According to Daniel, however, death will not have the last word. At some point in the future, many of the dead will rise to new life. Those who are asleep "in the dust of the earth" will "awake" (12:2). In other words, the dead will rise and their souls will be reunited once again with their bodies for all eternity. Daniel described two different groups in the resurrection. Those who were wise and righteous during their lives would rise to "everlasting life," while the wicked would experience "shame and everlasting contempt" (12:2).

Chapter 19 Summary

1. While living in exile in Babylon, the prophet Daniel was a witness to the one true God.

2. Daniel predicted the coming of "one like a son of man," the Messiah, who would fulfill God's covenant with David.

3. Daniel spoke of a future resurrection of the dead. At the resurrection, the righteous and wicked will be separated.

Being a Faithful Witness

Read Matthew 10:16–23 on page 8.

In this passage from Matthew 10, Jesus was teaching his Apostles. What did Jesus say would happen to them?

_____

_____

Jesus reminded his Apostles that being a witness to the faith would not always be easy. Some people—even family members—would hate them for their faith. Jesus' words are also intended for us. *We* must be prepared. If we choose to follow Christ, we should expect to face opposition too. What do we need to help us bear witness to Jesus Christ in a hostile world?

Jesus told the Apostles they must be "wise as serpents and innocent as doves" (10:16). The prophet Daniel is a good example of someone who was both wise and innocent. He thought carefully about his actions and had a deep knowledge of his faith. Yet he was also humble and innocent. He sought to do what is right and obey God's law. He treated even those who disliked or hated him with respect. Even Daniel's enemies realized that he was "faithful, and no error or fault was found in him" (Dan 6:4). Through his wisdom and innocence, Daniel was able to be a strong witness to the faith, even as an exile in the hostile pagan environment of Babylon.

What are some specific ways you can grow in wisdom and knowledge of your faith?

_____

_____

Why do you think knowing your faith is so important to being an effective witness?

_____

_____

Why do you think living rightly is so important to being an effective witness?

_____

_____

Reread Matthew 10:16–23.

Jesus told the Apostles not to be anxious about what they would say when people attacked them for their faith. Why? What did Jesus promise to give them?

_____

_____

Jesus' words to the Apostles are important for us to hear too. We cannot be effective witnesses simply by our own efforts; we need God's help. Jesus promised to send the Holy Spirit to the Apostles to strengthen them as witnesses. Jesus sends us the same Spirit to guide us in our lives, especially when we suffer for our faith. In the Sacrament of Confirmation, we receive a special grace of the Spirit to strengthen us as witnesses to Jesus Christ and the Gospel. Even if we have not yet received this sacrament, we can pray for the strength we need each day, confident that God is with us.

Prayer is essential for the Holy Spirit to work in our lives. It is through a life of prayer that we can become witnesses to God. God can do amazing things in and through us if we remain close to him in prayer. Daniel prayed to the Lord at a set three times each day. Through his life of prayer, his faith in God was strengthened and he could trust God, even when he was sent to the lions' den.

What can you do to strengthen your prayer life and allow God to strengthen you to be a more effective witness to the Gospel?

_____

_____

Let Us Pray—Psalm 93

In Psalm 93, the psalmist reminds us that God is King of the Universe. He is the Creator of all things and governs the universe with justice and mercy. Let us entrust ourselves to him as we look with hope for the perfection of God's kingdom in Heaven.

Ps 93:1-5

93 ¹The Lord reigns; he is robed in majesty;
   the Lord is robed, he is girded with strength.
Yes, the world is established; it shall never be moved;
² your throne is established from of old;
   you are from everlasting.
³The floods have lifted up, O Lord,
   the floods have lifted up their voice,
   the floods lift up their roaring.
⁴Mightier than the thunders of many waters,
   mightier than the waves of the sea,
   the Lord on high is mighty!
⁵Your decrees are very sure;
   holiness befits your house,
   O Lord, for evermore.

Chapter 19 Review:
An Everlasting Kingdom

1. What is a witness? _____

   _____

   _____

2. Who was the Old Testament witness and prophet discussed in this chapter? _____

3. In what foreign land was this man a witness to the Lord God of Israel? _____

4. Who was the king who threw the prophet of the Lord into the lions' den? _____

5. What is the name of the mysterious figure that Daniel said would appear when Israel's enemies were defeated? _____

6. How would this figure fulfill God's covenant with David?

   _____

   _____

   _____

7. Why is it mysterious that the figure in Daniel's vision is described as "one *like* a son of man" (Dan 7:13; emphasis added)?

   _____

   _____

8. One of Daniel's visions gave the people hope that death was not the end. What did this vision describe?

   _____

   _____

Song of the Three Young Men

While Daniel was serving in the court of King Nebuchadnezzar, three of his friends and fellow exiles got into trouble. The king had created a golden idol for the Babylonians to worship. He required all people in his realm to worship it or face death in a fiery furnace.

One day, Daniel's friends—Shadrach, Meshach, and Abednego—were caught not bowing down to the idol. The king confronted them and warned them that if they did not worship the golden image, no one could rescue them from the fiery death that awaited them. The young men were defiant, telling the king, "Our God whom we serve is able to deliver us . . . out of your hand, O king" (Dan 3:17). Nebuchadnezzar ordered the three young men thrown into the fire. To the amazement of the Babylonians, the fire did not harm them even a bit. While in the furnace, Shadrach, Meshach, and Abednego sang praises to God:

The Three Young Men in the Fiery Furnace, Russian School, 16th century

Dan 3:29-34

3 ²⁹"Blessed are you, O Lord, God of our fathers,
and to be praised and highly exalted for ever;
³⁰And blessed is your glorious, holy name
and to be highly praised and highly exalted
for ever;
³¹Blessed are you in the temple of your holy glory
and to be extolled and highly glorified for ever.
³²Blessed are you, who sit upon cherubim and look
upon the deeps,
and to be praised and highly exalted for ever.
³³Blessed are you upon the throne of your kingdom
and to be extolled and highly exalted for ever.
³⁴Blessed are you in the firmament of heaven
and to be sung and glorified for ever.

When they exited the furnace, Nebuchadnezzar also praised the God of Israel: "Blessed be the God of Shadrach, Meshach, and Abednego, who . . . delivered his servants, who trusted in him, and set at nothing the king's command, and yielded up their bodies rather than serve and worship any god except their own God" (3:28).

The Church continues to sing the song of these three young men. It is included in the Liturgy of the Hours, which men and women around the world, both lay and religious, pray daily. The story of the three young men reminds us that to obey God, we must sometimes *disobey* the evil desires or commands of others.

Journal Reflection

Is there a relationship in your life that is causing you to disobey God? Is there something you are watching or listening to that is drawing you away from serving God as you should? What can you do to get your life back in proper order—with God at the top?

Living with Hope

Read

At some point, we all wonder, *What comes after this life on earth?* It is a fair question! After all, life on earth, according to Scripture, is seventy years, or eighty for those who are strong (see Ps 90:10). That is not very long, considering the age of the universe. As Catholics, we believe in the resurrection of the body and life everlasting, spoken of in Daniel 12. We have hope in the resurrection because Christ, the Son of Man, won it through his Paschal Mystery.

Imagine that after your death, there was nothing. You just stopped existing. Death would be the end. Nothing would come afterward. It would be like running a long race and, instead of winning a medal or a prize, you had everything taken away. Our lives would be extremely sad and unfulfilling.

Living with hope in eternal life in Heaven and the resurrection has the opposite effect. We run the race of life and work even harder to love God and others because we realize that there is a reward for our hard work. We do not lose everything but instead *win* everything. All our suffering and struggle is worth it! The best part is that the end of the race is only the beginning of sharing in eternity with God, where there is no suffering or pain. Living with such hope helps us live with purpose.

Reflect

Spend 5–10 minutes reflecting on the following:

- Do I live with hope for the resurrection? How is it expressed in my actions?
- How would a person's attitude toward challenges and suffering change if he went from not believing in the resurrection to believing in it?
- Who in my life needs to see the hope of resurrection in me?

Pray

Pray the Act of Hope on page 335.

Act

Find a crucifix and put it up in your room as a daily reminder of your hope in the resurrection to new life that Jesus won for us.

CHAPTER 20
I Will Bring Them Back

Words to Know

> Jew

> Samaritans

Proclaiming the Good News

"I will take you from the nations, and gather you from all the countries, and bring you into your own land. I will sprinkle clean water upon you, and you shall be clean from all your uncleannesses, and from all your idols I will cleanse you." —Ezekiel 36:24–25

Continuing the Story of Salvation

List a few key events that took place in the prophet Daniel's life. Then give a brief description of the prophecies from Daniel 7 and Daniel 12 discussed in Chapter 19.

_____
_____
_____
_____
_____
_____

Ezra Reads the Law, Jewish School, 2nd century

243

The Return from Exile

Bronze statue of Cyrus the Great

Rebuilding the Temple

The Southern Kingdom (Judah) was conquered by the Babylonians. For nearly seventy years, the people of Judah lived in exile. They had no Temple, no king, no land of their own. God had punished the Kingdom of Judah for their evil and murderous ways. But he did not *abandon* them. Moses had foretold that "he will gather you again from all the peoples where the LORD your God has scattered you" (Deut 30:3). A remnant of the people of Judah would be brought back from exile. Thus, the term "Jew" came to mean not only a person from the tribe of Judah but also one who resided in the land of Judea. After the Exile, the term "Jew" was also used to describe anyone who followed the religion of Judaism.

The Lord ended the Babylonian exile through an unlikely leader: Cyrus, the pagan king of Persia. He defeated the Babylonians. In 538 B.C., Cyrus issued a proclamation allowing the Jews to return to their land and begin rebuilding:

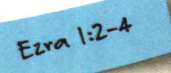

Ezra 1:2-4

1 ²"Thus says Cyrus king of Persia: The LORD, the God of heaven, has given me all the kingdoms of the earth, and he has charged me to build him a house at Jerusalem, which is in Judah. ³Whoever is among you of all his people, may his God be with him, and let him go up to Jerusalem, which is in Judah, and rebuild the house of the LORD, the God of Israel—he is the God who is in Jerusalem; ⁴and let each survivor, in whatever place he sojourns, be assisted by the men of his place with silver and gold, with goods and with beasts, besides freewill offerings for the house of God which is in Jerusalem."

Cyrus gave the Jews generous gifts of gold and silver to assist them in building a new Temple. He also returned costly items that the Babylonian king Nebuchadnezzar had stolen from the original Temple. The Jews began to return to the land of Judea under the leadership of the governor, Zerubbabel [zeh-RUB-uh-bull], who was a descendant of King David. When the Jews returned to Jerusalem, they laid the new Temple's foundation. But the rebuilt Temple was met with mixed emotions from the Jews who had returned.

Ezra 3:11–13

3 [11]All the people shouted with a great shout, when they praised the LORD, because the foundation of the house of the LORD was laid. [12]But many of the priests and Levites and heads of fathers' houses, old men who had seen the first house, wept with a loud voice when they saw the foundation of this house being laid, though many shouted aloud for joy; [13]so that the people could not distinguish the sound of the joyful shout from the sound of the people's weeping, for the people shouted with a great shout, and the sound was heard afar.

While many were rejoicing, the older people, who had been children when the Jews were taken into exile, wept because they remembered the glory of Solomon's Temple. Compared to the original Temple, this Second Temple was much less impressive. The Second Temple also fell short of the prophecies of a new Temple given by Ezekiel during the Babylonian exile. So, even as the Second Temple was being built, many Jews began to look forward to a new and even greater Temple.

From the Saints

"The Lord made Cyrus similar to his only-begotten Son, our God and Lord Jesus Christ. Just as Cyrus, after destroying the empire of the Chaldeans, freed the people of God, and sent them back to their homeland and ordered them to rebuild the temple . . . so the mediator between God and humanity, after destroying all over the world the kingdom of the devil, called back from that tyranny his elect, who had been scattered, and now gathers them in his church."[1]

—Saint Bede the Venerable

The Samaritans

When the Northern Kingdom (Israel) was conquered by the Assyrians, many from the ten northern tribes were exiled from the land. Moreover, the Assyrians forcibly relocated people from five other Gentile nations into the land of Israel. The people of these other nations all brought with them their worship of different false gods. Some of the Israelites who had been left in the land intermarried with members of these other nations, adopting many of their practices. The *Samaritans* were the descendants of these people.

When the Jews returned from exile, they were met by the Samaritans. The Samaritans asked Zerubbabel if they could help rebuild the Temple. Zerubbabel refused. The Samaritans were angry at being excluded and repeatedly tried to stop the Temple from being built. Their efforts failed. The Temple was eventually completed.

After they completed building the Second Temple, the Jews celebrated the Feast of Passover. The Passover ritual recalled the Lord's action during the Exodus, when he freed the Israelites from slavery in Egypt. This celebration of Passover had added meaning for the exiles who returned to the Promised Land. Once again, God had been faithful to his Word and freed his people from captivity in a foreign land.

Looking to the Future

The Walls That Had Fallen

Exiles from Judah continued to return to the Promised Land in the decades following Cyrus' proclamation. One of those who returned was a man named Ezra, who was a priest and a scribe with a great knowledge of the Law of Moses. Ezra oversaw the restoration of the priesthood and of worship in the new Temple. Ezra reminded the Jews that they were God's Chosen People. The Lord had called them so that all nations would come to know the true God. However, they could not be God's witnesses if they ignored his law. So, Ezra and the people renewed their covenant with God and vowed to live differently from the "peoples of the lands" (Neh 10:28). They swore an oath "to observe and do all the commandments of the LORD our Lord and his ordinances and his statutes" (10:29).

Rebuilding the Wall of Jerusalem under Nehemiah, William Brassey Hole

To separate themselves from other nations and secure their lives, the Jews rebuilt the walls and gates around Jerusalem. A man named Nehemiah [NEE-huh-MIGH-uh] led this massive construction project. Once again, the Samaritans attempted to stop them. They mocked the Jews, telling them they would never succeed. The Samaritans made violent threats against Jewish workers. Yet the Jews put their trust in the Lord and did not give up. Sanballat, a Samaritan leader, made one last effort to stop Nehemiah and the Jews:

Neh 6:5-7

6 ⁵Sanballat for the fifth time sent his servant to me with an open letter in his hand. ⁶In it was written, "It is reported among the nations, and Geshem also says it, that you and the Jews intend to rebel; that is why you are building the wall; and you wish to become their king, according to this report. ⁷And you have also set up prophets to proclaim concerning you in Jerusalem, 'There is a king in Judah.' And now it will be reported to the king according to these words. So now come, and let us take counsel together."

Sanballat knew his accusations were false. There was no rebellion. The Jews had no king. Jerusalem was under the political rule of the Persian king Artaxerxes [ar-tuh-ZURK-seez]. Sanballat tried to prevent the Jews from rebuilding the walls with the rumor of a Jewish king rebelling against Artaxerxes. Nehemiah resisted Sanballat's manipulation, trusting in the Lord's strength and protection. The Jews finished rebuilding the walls of Jerusalem in 445 B.C.

Awaiting Fulfillment

There was much to celebrate in Jerusalem: the return from exile, the construction of the new Temple, the rebuilding of the walls of Jerusalem, and the renewal of the covenant. Yet the conflict with Sanballat highlighted something missing—there was no son of David ruling as king. Ezra expressed the great sorrow of God's people as they continued under the burden of foreign rule, even after returning from exile:

Neh 9:32-33, 36-37,

9 ³²"Now therefore, our God, the great and mighty and awesome God, who keep covenant and mercy, let not all the hardship seem little to you that has come upon us . . . since the time of the kings of Assyria until this day. ³³Yet you have been just in all that has come upon us, for you have dealt faithfully and we have acted wickedly. . . . ³⁶Behold, we are slaves this day; in the land that you gave to our fathers to enjoy its fruit and its good gifts, behold, we are slaves. ³⁷And its rich yield goes to the kings whom you have set over us because of our sins; they have power also over our bodies and over our cattle at their pleasure, and we are in great distress."

Ezra trusted that the Lord would continue to be faithful to his people, as he had been in the past. God's people awaited the perfect fulfillment of God's promises to David. They looked for the coming of the Messiah, the anointed one who would restore the kingdom. The Lord continued to nurture his people's hope through the prophets.

The last prophet God sent was Malachi. He foretold the glorious return of the Lord to his people: "Behold, I send my messenger to prepare the way before me, and the Lord whom you seek will suddenly come to his temple" (3:1). God was preparing his people for the time of fulfillment, when he would accomplish all he had promised. The sign of this coming "day of the LORD" would be the arrival of a new Elijah, who would prepare the way for the Lord (4:5). As the Jews awaited the Messiah, they also looked for the return of Elijah.

The prophet Malachi

Chapter 20 Summary

1. Through King Cyrus of Persia, the Lord brought the Jews back from exile.

2. The Jews constructed a Second Temple, renewed their covenant with God, and rebuilt the walls of Jerusalem.

3. The Jews looked forward to a time when a king from the royal house of David would rule over them.

The Sin of Scandal

The *Catechism* defines the sin of scandal as "an attitude or behavior which leads another to do evil" (*CCC* 2284). A person is guilty of scandal when he leads others to sin by his bad example. The Old Testament prophets had harsh words for those who committed this sin. For example, the prophet Malachi had this to say to scandalous priests in his day:

An ancient millstone in Capernaum

Mal 2:1-3, 7-9

2 ¹"And now, O priests, this command is for you. ²If you will not listen, if you will not lay it to heart to give glory to my name, says the LORD of hosts, then I will send the curse upon you. . . . ³I will rebuke your offspring, and spread dung upon your faces, the dung of your offerings, and I will put you out of my presence. . . . ⁷For the lips of a priest should guard knowledge, and men should seek instruction from his mouth, for he is the messenger of the LORD of hosts. ⁸But you have turned aside from the way; you have caused many to stumble by your instruction; you have corrupted the covenant of Levi, says the LORD of hosts, ⁹and so I make you despised and abased before all the people."

Malachi called for the conversion of priests who "caused many to stumble" (2:8) by their bad example. When the people of Israel—especially their priests and leaders—set a bad example, they were betraying their very identity as God's Chosen People. As the Chosen People, Israel was called to be an example for the whole world. They were supposed to lead others to God, not draw them away from God by their sinful actions.

Read Matthew 18:1–7 on page 16.

 What did Jesus say is *worse* than drowning with a millstone around one's neck?

_____

Like the Old Testament prophets, Jesus had harsh words for those who commit scandal. As Christians, we are called to be Christlike and lead others to God. Leading another into sin endangers a person's soul.

Read Matthew 13:24–30 on page 12.

Why did the master in the parable not get rid of the weeds?

_____

_____

248 **Chapter 20**

When will the weeds finally be separated from the wheat?

_____

Jesus' parable reminds us that in the Church there will always be both "wheat" and "weeds" growing together. In the Church, we will always find good, holy men and women (wheat). Yet there will also be bad examples, even among priests (weeds). The two will not be separated until "harvest time," that is, until Christ comes again at the end of the world to judge the living and the dead.

We should not lose faith when we see Catholics, even priests, causing scandal. Christ said it would be so. He knew there would be evil in the Church. At the same time, Christ promised never to abandon the Church. As Jesus promised Saint Peter, "The gates of hell shall not prevail against [the Church]" (Mt 16:18). Evil will never overcome the Church. Christ promises to be with us, even amid scandals.

What are two specific things I can do to be a better example for those around me?

_____

_____

When I fail to live as I should, do I seek Christ's mercy in the Sacrament of Reconciliation? If not, what holds me back?

_____

_____

Let Us Pray—Psalm 19

It is easy to think of God's law as a restriction on our freedom. In these moments, we can forget that God's law frees us to love and flourish. Sin enslaves, but God's law liberates. As we pray Psalm 19, let us rejoice in the goodness of God's law.

Ps 19:7-10, 14

19 ⁷The law of the LORD is perfect,
     reviving the soul;
the testimony of the LORD is sure,
     making wise the simple;
⁸the precepts of the LORD are right,
     rejoicing the heart;
the commandment of the LORD is pure,
     enlightening the eyes;
⁹the fear of the LORD is clean,
     enduring for ever;
the ordinances of the LORD are true,
     and righteous altogether.
¹⁰More to be desired are they than gold,
     even much fine gold;
sweeter also than honey
     and drippings of the honeycomb. . . .
¹⁴Let the words of my mouth and the
          meditation of my heart
be acceptable in your sight,
     O LORD, my rock and my redeemer.

Chapter 20 Review:
I Will Bring Them Back

1. What does the term "Jew" refer to? _____

   _____

   _____

2. Who were the Samaritans? _____

   _____

   _____

3. Which foreign leader decreed that the Jews could return from exile?

   _____

4. Who was the descendant of David who, as governor, led the early return of Jews back to the land? _____

5. What are two things the Jews rebuilt after returning from exile? _____

   _____

6. Which priest and scribe of God's people led them in renewing their covenant with the Lord?

   _____

7. Which group of people tried to stop the rebuilding efforts of the Jews?

   _____

8. Even after the return from exile, the Jews were living under the rule of a foreign power. What was missing from Jewish life? _____

A New Temple

The original Temple of Solomon was destroyed by the Babylonians when they conquered Jerusalem in 586 B.C. Psalm 79 is a lament over this destruction:

Ps 79:1, 8-9

79 ¹O God, the heathen have come into your inheritance;
they have defiled your holy temple;
they have laid Jerusalem in ruins. . . .
⁸Do not remember against us the iniquities of our forefathers;
let your compassion come speedily to meet us,
for we are brought very low.
⁹Help us, O God of our salvation,
for the glory of thy name;
deliver us, and forgive our sins,
for your name's sake!

After the Jews returned from exile, the Temple was rebuilt. However, in A.D. 70, the Romans destroyed this Second Temple. To this day, only part of the western and southern retaining walls of the Temple remain. Every day, devout Jews gather in Jerusalem at the Western Wall. Many recite Psalm 79 as they mourn the loss of the Temple and pray for the restoration of God's Temple.

As Catholics, we believe that Jesus Christ, the Son of David, has raised up the true Temple—the Temple of his Body (see Jn 2:21). Through Baptism, Christians become members of Christ's Body, the Church. As Saint Paul said to the Church in Corinth, "Do you not know that you are God's temple and that God's Spirit dwells in you?" (1 Cor 3:16). As God's Spirit dwelt in the Temple in Jerusalem, now he dwells in a more wonderful way within the Church.

We experience God's presence in the Church in a special way through the sacraments. Since the Holy Spirit comes to dwell in us through Baptism, we must honor, care for, and respect ourselves and others.

In a particular way, we must respect our *bodies*. Our bodies are God's sacred dwelling places. We must follow Saint Paul's command to the Church: "Glorify God in your body" (1 Cor 6:20).

The Western Wall in Jerusalem

Journal Reflection

Do you treat yourself as though God's Holy Spirit dwells within you? Do you expect others to treat you as God's holy dwelling place? How can you better glorify God in your body?

Where We Worship

Read

In an age when we can watch the Mass from our computers, it may be hard to remember why we need church buildings at all. It may seem that the church building itself is not necessary anymore. Yet even with all our technological advancements, human beings remain creatures with both a soul *and a body*. We primarily interact with our world through our senses. Experiencing a physical place with all our senses has a real effect on what we imagine, think, desire, and do.

- **Imagination and thoughts:** When we see a beautiful church, full of beautiful images of the Lord, his angels, and the saints, our imagination and thoughts are drawn to focus on God's majesty, beauty, and power.
- **Desires:** The more we think of something good or beautiful, the more we desire it—for instance, the thought of a glass of ice-cold water on a hot summer day. Similarly, a beautiful church directs our thoughts to God so that we desire him more and more.
- **Actions:** When we desire something, we are pulled to be united with that thing. So, in a breathtaking church, the desire for God leads us to be with him in worship and prayer.

Reflect

Spend 5–10 minutes reflecting on the following:

- What within my parish church leads me to deeper prayer and worship by influencing my imagination, thoughts, desires, and actions?
- How can I incorporate certain aspects of the beauty of the church in my home to make it more fully a house of prayer?

Pray

Prayerfully meditate on these words from Psalm 27:4:

"One thing have I asked of the LORD,
    that will I seek after;
that I may dwell in the house of the LORD
    all the days of my life,
to behold the beauty of the LORD,
    and to inquire in his temple." Amen.

Act

Call your parish office and ask for ways that you could assist with keeping the church beautiful (for example, cleaning the sanctuary or assisting with gardening and lawn care).

CHAPTER 21
Zeal for the Law

Words to Know

> Gentile

> Hanukkah

> martyr

Proclaiming the Good News

"The souls of the righteous are in the hand of God, and no torment will ever touch them. . . . For though in the sight of men they were punished, their hope is full of immortality." —Wisdom 3:1, 4

Continuing the Story of Salvation

Summarize the key events that followed Cyrus' proclamation allowing the Jews to return to the Promised Land.

_____
_____
_____
_____
_____
_____
_____

The Triumph of Judas Maccabeus, Peter Paul Rubens

Persecution of the Jews

Judas Maccabeus

Following the return from exile, the Jews lived under the rule of various Gentile nations. The word "Gentile" refers to any member of a non-Jewish nation. The Jews were first ruled by various Persian kings. The Persians, however, were defeated by the Greek king Alexander the Great in 332 B.C. For several hundred years following, the Jews lived under Greek rule. Some Greek kings allowed the Jews to practice their faith, but others treated the Jews harshly.

Coin depicting Antiochus IV. The Greek text reads, "King Antiochus, God Manifest, Bearer of Victory."

Antiochus IV [an-TIE-uh-kuhs] was one of the harshest Greek rulers. He invaded Jerusalem, pillaged the Temple, murdered many Jews, and captured many Jewish women and children. To unite his realm, he forced all people to abandon their own religious practices and instead to adopt Gentile customs. This meant Jews would have to abandon observing the Sabbath and keeping the kosher food laws, among others. Many Jews went along with his commands. Yet some resisted.

Many Jews who resisted Antiochus were executed. But others escaped and formed an armed resistance. One of the most important leaders in this resistance was a man named Judas, whose nickname was Maccabeus, which meant "Hammer." Judas Maccabeus led a Jewish revolt against Antiochus. He succeeded in winning several battles. In a great rage, Antiochus sent all his forces to destroy the Jews completely.

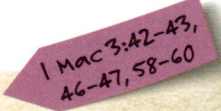

3 ⁴²Now Judas and his brothers saw that misfortunes had increased and that the forces were encamped in their territory. They also learned what the king had commanded to do to the people to cause their final destruction. ⁴³But they said to one another, "Let us repair the destruction of our people, and fight for our people and the sanctuary." . . .
⁴⁶So they assembled and went to Mizpah, opposite Jerusalem, because Israel formerly had a place of prayer in Mizpah. ⁴⁷They fasted that day, put on sackcloth and sprinkled ashes on their heads, and tore their clothes. . . .
⁵⁸And Judas said, "Gird yourselves and be valiant. Be ready early in the morning to fight with these Gentiles who have assembled against us to destroy us and our sanctuary. ⁵⁹It is better for us to die in battle than to see the misfortunes of our nation and of the sanctuary. ⁶⁰But as his will in heaven may be, so he will do."

Despite being vastly outnumbered, Judas and his men trusted in the Lord. In the end, they won the battle. Lysias, the commander of Antiochus IV's armies, was amazed at the courage and strength of the Jews.

The Feast of Dedication

After their victory, the first thing Judas and his men did was cleanse and repair the Temple in Jerusalem which the Gentiles had looted and desecrated.

1 Mac 4:36-43, 49-56

4 ³⁶Then said Judas and his brothers, "Behold, our enemies are crushed; let us go up to cleanse the sanctuary and dedicate it." ³⁷So all the army assembled and they went up to Mount Zion. ³⁸And they saw the sanctuary desolate, the altar profaned, and the gates burned. In the courts they saw bushes sprung up as in a thicket, or as on one of the mountains. They saw also the chambers of the priests in ruins. ³⁹Then they tore their clothes, and mourned with great lamentation, and sprinkled themselves with ashes. ⁴⁰They fell face down on the ground, and sounded the signal on the trumpets, and cried out to Heaven. ⁴¹Then Judas detailed men to fight against those in the citadel until he had cleansed the sanctuary.

⁴²He chose blameless priests devoted to the law, ⁴³and they cleansed the sanctuary and removed the defiled stones to an unclean place. . . . ⁴⁹They made new holy vessels, and brought the lampstand, the altar of incense, and the table into the temple. ⁵⁰Then they burned incense on the altar and lighted the lamps on the lampstand, and these gave light in the temple. ⁵¹They placed the bread on the table and hung up the curtains. Thus they finished all the work they had undertaken.

⁵²Early in the morning . . . ⁵³they rose and offered sacrifice, as the law directs, on the new altar of burnt offering which they had built. ⁵⁴At the very season and on the very day that the Gentiles had profaned it, it was dedicated with songs and harps and lutes and cymbals. ⁵⁵All the people fell on their faces and worshiped and blessed Heaven, who had prospered them. ⁵⁶So they celebrated the dedication of the altar for eight days, and offered burnt offerings with gladness; they offered a sacrifice of deliverance and praise.

Judas and his men cleansed and rededicated the Temple in 164 B.C. after the Gentiles had defiled it. The Jews would remember this rededication each year in what became known as the Feast of *Hanukkah*. The word "Hanukkah" comes from a Hebrew word meaning "to dedicate." To this day, Jews celebrate the Feast of Hanukkah. The celebration involves the lighting of a menorah, which is a nine-branched candelabra (a stand that can hold many candles). On each of the eight days of Hanukkah, a new candle is lit to recall the eight-day celebration after the rededication of the Temple.

The Hope of the Martyrs

The Mother and Her Seven Sons

Judas and his men violently resisted the persecution by Antiochus IV. However, others resisted nonviolently. Rather than take up arms, these Jews were willing to be martyred. A *martyr* is a person who is killed because of his faith. The Book of Second Maccabees records a famous story of seven brothers and their mother who were martyred by King Antiochus IV for refusing to violate the Law of Moses.

2 Mac 7:1-14, 20

7 ¹It happened also that seven brothers and their mother were arrested and were being compelled by the king, under torture with whips and cords, to partake of unlawful swine's flesh. ²One of them, acting as their spokesman, said, "What do you intend to ask and learn from us? For we are ready to die rather than transgress the laws of our fathers."

³The king fell into a rage, and gave orders that pans and caldrons be heated. ⁴These were heated immediately, and he commanded that the tongue of their spokesman be cut out and that they scalp him and cut off his hands and feet, while the rest of the brothers and the mother looked on. ⁵When he was utterly helpless, the king ordered them to take him to the fire, still breathing, and to fry him in a pan. The smoke from the pan spread widely, but the brothers and their mother encouraged one another to die nobly, saying, ⁶"The Lord God is watching over us and in truth has compassion on us. . . ."

⁷After the first brother had died in this way, they brought forward the second for their sport. They tore off the skin of his head with the hair, and asked him, "Will you eat rather than have your body punished limb by limb?" ⁸He replied in the language of his fathers, and said to them, "No." Therefore he in turn underwent tortures as the first brother had done. ⁹And when he was at his last breath, he said, "You accursed wretch, you dismiss us from this present life, but the King of the universe will raise us up to an everlasting renewal of life, because we have died for his laws."

¹⁰After him, the third was the victim of their sport. When it was demanded, he quickly put out his tongue and courageously stretched forth his hands, ¹¹and said nobly, "I got these from Heaven, and because of his laws I disdain them, and from him I hope to get them back again." ¹²As a result the king himself and those with him were astonished at the young man's spirit, for he regarded his sufferings as nothing.

¹³When he too had died, they maltreated and tortured the fourth in the same way. ¹⁴And when he was near death, he said, "One cannot but choose to die at the hands of men and to cherish the hope that God gives of being raised again by him. But for you there will be no resurrection to life!" . . .

²⁰The mother was especially admirable and worthy of honorable memory. Though she saw her seven sons perish within a single day, she bore it with good courage because of her hope in the Lord.

The mother and her seven sons were willing to face death because they loved the Lord God above all else. They would rather obey God's law than save their own lives. They also had a firm hope in the resurrection of the dead, as foretold by prophets like Daniel. They firmly believed that the righteous would rise to everlasting life. Death was not the end; a glorious resurrection awaited them. But for the wicked, like Antiochus IV, there would be only "the judgment of the almighty, all-seeing God" (2 Mac 7:35).

Prayers for the Dead

Many had hope during persecution because of their belief in the resurrection of the dead. The righteous would experience everlasting happiness after death. But what about those who were *mostly* righteous but found themselves still attached to their sins? What hope would they have if they were to die? Another event recorded in Second Maccabees sheds light on this question.

One day, Judas Maccabeus and his men were collecting the bodies of Jewish soldiers who had died in battle. They found idolatrous amulets hidden under the clothes of these men. The soldiers had clearly violated God's law. Yet these men were dead and could not offer sacrifices to God for their sins. So, Judas and his men prayed to God on their behalf, asking "that the sin which had been committed might be wholly blotted out" (2 Mac 12:42). Then they offered sacrifices to God for the sins of the dead men. Judas and his men believed that the prayers and sacrifices of the living could have a positive impact on the dead.

The Catholic Church embraces belief in the power of the prayers for the dead. Today Catholic Masses are frequently offered for those who have died. Catholics believe there are some who die in God's grace and friendship but need to enter a state of

final purification called Purgatory before entering Heaven. They are assured of their salvation but must still be purified of any venial sins, attachment to sin, or unhealthy attachment to created things. After this purification, the soul reaches the holiness necessary to enter the joy of Heaven. The prayers of the Church and of individual Catholics can assist those in Purgatory on their journey to Heaven.

Chapter 21 Summary

1. Judas Maccabeus led a violent resistance to the unjust persecution of Jews by King Antiochus IV.

2. The Temple in Jerusalem was rededicated to the Lord after being defiled by the Gentiles. The Feast of Hanukkah celebrates this rededication.

3. Some Jews freely chose to face persecution nonviolently by becoming martyrs. Many had hope in the resurrection of the dead.

The Virtue of Zeal

Imagine finding out the tragic news that your best friend has cancer. Your first reaction to the news would probably be some mixture of shock, sadness, anger, confusion, and fear. After the first wave of emotions had passed, you would probably feel something else—a strong pull to help your friend any way you can. If he was discouraged, you would want to encourage him. If sad, you would want to cheer him up. If confused, you would want to comfort him. If lonely, you would spend time with him. No matter what he needed, you would be compelled to do something about it.

This strong pull or impulse to help your friend describes the virtue of zeal. Zeal is an intense love that motivates a person to do good for someone and to fight off anything that is not good for the person. We can have zeal for God too. A person who is zealous for God has an intense love for him. Such a person seeks to honor God and avoid anything that offends or disrespects him.

Jesus Cleanses the Temple, Onofrio Bramante

Judas Maccabeus had zeal. Judas saw Antiochus IV persecuting and murdering his people and felt a strong desire to protect the innocent and fight off all attacks against them. His actions were motivated by an intense love for his people.

 Judas also had zeal for God. What was the first thing Judas and his men did after they defeated the large army seeking to wipe out the Jews?

___

Judas' actions in the Temple show his zeal for God. The Temple had been looted and treated with disrespect by Antiochus IV. Judas and his men mourned over the offense shown to God. Out of love for God, they sought to cleanse the Temple of evil and restore proper worship of God.

Read Matthew 21:12–13 on page 19.

How were Jesus' actions in the Temple similar to Judas Maccabeus' actions in the Temple?

___
___

Judas and his men were not the only ones to show zeal for God during the persecution of Antiochus. How did the martyred seven brothers and their mother show zeal for God?

_____

_____

Like Judas and the martyred mother and her seven sons, we, too, should seek to have zeal for God in our lives. We can grow in zeal by striving to pray each day, attend Mass at least every Sunday, go to Reconciliation regularly when we disobey God's commandments, and perform acts of service for others. Committing ourselves to daily prayer, regular reception of the sacraments of Reconciliation and the Eucharist, and acts of service can intensify our love for God and help us grow in our desire to respect God in our lives.

Think about the role that prayer, Mass, confession, and acts of service currently have in your life. Which of these areas are you doing well in? Which areas need improvement? What are two specific things you can do to make these more central?

_____

_____

_____

Let Us Pray—Psalm 17

In Psalm 17, the psalmist expresses trust that God will hear him in his difficulty. He has hope that he will see God face-to-face one day. Let us now entrust our own difficulties to the Lord and have hope that in the resurrection, we, too, will see God face-to-face in Heaven.

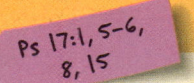
Ps 17:1, 5-6, 8, 15

17 ¹Hear a just cause, O LORD; attend to my cry!
  Give ear to my prayer from lips free of deceit! . . .
⁵My steps have held fast to your paths,
  my feet have not slipped.
⁶I call upon you, for you will answer me, O God;
  incline your ear to me, hear my words. . . .

⁸Keep me as the apple of the eye;
  hide me in the shadow of your wings. . . .
¹⁵As for me, I shall behold your face in righteousness;
  when I awake, I shall be satisfied with beholding your form.

Chapter 21 Review:
Zeal for the Law

1. What is a Gentile? _____

2. List some ways that Antiochus IV persecuted the Jews.

   _____
   _____
   _____
   _____

3. How did Judas Maccabeus respond to Antiochus IV's actions?

   _____

4. Which Jewish feast celebrates the rededication of the Temple after it had been defiled by the Greek armies? _____

5. What is a martyr? _____

6. What gave the Jewish mother and her seven sons hope in the face of torture and death at the hands of Antiochus IV? _____

7. Why did Judas and his men pray for and offer sacrifices on behalf of certain Jewish soldiers who had died in battle? _____

   _____

8. Catholic teaching affirms the value of praying for the dead. These prayers can benefit those who are in _____, those who have died in friendship with God but are still in need of final purification.

Freedom of Religion

Dignitatis Humanae, 2

"The human person has a right to religious freedom. This freedom means that all men are to be immune from coercion on the part of individuals or of social groups and of any human power, in such wise that no one is to be forced to act in a manner contrary to his own beliefs, whether privately or publicly, whether alone or in association with others, within due limits."

Under Antiochus IV, the Jews were unable to practice their faith freely. Antiochus forced the Jews to violate their religious beliefs and participate in Gentile religious practices. If they did not, they would be executed. Throughout history, people of faith have experienced persecution. Most of the Apostles were martyred for their faith. The first few generations of Christians lived under the constant threat of persecution from the Roman Empire. Today millions of Christians throughout the world live under the threat of violent persecution because of their faith in Jesus Christ.

But violent attacks are not the only way religious freedom can be attacked. Pope Francis has spoken about another form of attack, which he calls "polite persecution."[1] Polite persecution does not operate by means of violence. Rather, it uses the law or public pressure to force people of faith to violate their Christian values.

Even in the United States, Christians can become victims of polite persecution. Employees have been fired and business owners forced out of business because they refused to act in ways contrary to Christian beliefs about marriage and sexuality. The Little Sisters of the Poor, a community of Catholic nuns, spent years in a legal battle with the U.S. government. They were forced to participate in actions that went against their religious beliefs or face huge fines. Many Christians today face backlash on social media and in their workplaces for publicly expressing their faith. Not surprisingly, many choose to keep their faith and beliefs to themselves.

The Church teaches that each person has a right to religious freedom. People should be free to express their religious beliefs not just privately but also publicly without fear of persecution or backlash. At the same time, when facing persecution, the Church reminds us that we have an obligation to not deny our faith. As Jesus taught, "Everyone therefore who confesses me before men, I also will confess before my Father who is in heaven. But whoever denies me before men, I also will deny before my Father who is in heaven" (Mt 10:32–33).

Journal Reflection

What would you do if you felt pressured by your friends to go against your religious beliefs? How would you respond in word and deed to being asked to violate your faith in Christ?

Purgatory, God's Gift of Mercy

Read

We have every reason to hope in the resurrection and the joy of Heaven because of Jesus' saving actions. However, even with this hope, we might feel uneasy when we read verses in the Bible such as this: "Nothing unclean shall enter [Heaven], nor any one who practices abomination or falsehood" (Rev 21:27).

Can any of us claim to be completely clean or never to have sinned? We must remember that grave sin results in eternal punishment, being deprived of communion with God. But all sins, even venial sins, bring about temporal punishment. Temporal means related to the realm of time. The *Catechism* teaches that temporal punishment refers to the fact that sin creates within us an unhealthy attachment to created things that needs to be purified (see *CCC* 1472). The Sacrament of Reconciliation forgives all *eternal* punishment for sin, but some temporal punishment may remain. Temporal punishment can be purified on earth through prayer, penance, bearing our sufferings patiently, and performing works of mercy and charity. If we are not purified on earth, we will need to be purified in Purgatory before entering Heaven.

Purgatory is frequently described as a cleansing fire. As one heats precious metals like gold to remove impurities, so Purgatory is the merciful means that God has made available to purify us of any venial sins, attachment to sin, or unhealthy attachment to created things so we can enter fully into the joy of Heaven.

Reflect

Spend 5–10 minutes reflecting on the following:

- What sins do I need to begin to detach from now so that I can better love God?
- Which of my deceased friends and relatives can I pray for?

Pray

Pray this prayer from Saint Gertrude the Great:

> Eternal Father,
> I offer you the Most Precious Blood of your Divine Son, Jesus,
> in union with the Masses said throughout the world today,
> for all the holy souls in Purgatory,
> for sinners everywhere,
> for sinners in the universal Church,
> those in my own home, and within my family.
> Amen.

Act

Examine your conscience each night and identify those sins that require detachment. Ask the Lord daily to give you the grace and means to begin to overcome those sinful attachments.

CHAPTER 22

Jesus, the Son of Man

Words to Know

> *blasphemy*

> *Sanhedrin*

Proclaiming the Good News

"As Moses lifted up the serpent in the wilderness, so must the Son of man be lifted up, that whoever believes in him may have eternal life." —John 3:14–15

The Crucifixion with the Virgin and Saint John, Hendrick ter Brugghen

The Glorious Son of Man

Seated at the Right Hand of the Father

After Jesus was betrayed by Judas Iscariot, he was led before Caiaphas, the Jewish high priest, and the Sanhedrin. The *Sanhedrin* was a Jewish council of judges. If someone was accused of a crime, the Sanhedrin would listen to testimony and judge whether he was guilty or innocent.

Read Saint Matthew's account of Jesus' trial before the Sanhedrin (26:57–68) on page 25.

Jesus initially remained silent when questioned. But then Caiaphas placed Jesus under oath to reveal whether he is the Messiah, the Son of God. Jesus declared in reply, "You will see the Son of Man seated at the right hand of Power and coming on the clouds of heaven" (26:64). These words led to him being charged with blasphemy. *Blasphemy* is the sin of speaking hatefully or with contempt of God. But how was claiming to be the Messiah blasphemy? To understand why Jesus was accused of blaspheming, we must carefully examine his words.

Jesus answered Caiaphas by quoting from two Old Testament books—Daniel and Psalms—to reveal his identity more fully. He wove together language from Daniel's prophecy about the Son of Man (see page 236) with words from the opening of Psalm 110, a messianic psalm.

Ps 110:1–3

110 ¹The LORD says to my lord:
    "Sit at my right hand,
till I make your enemies your footstool."
²The LORD sends forth from Zion
    your mighty scepter.
    Rule in the midst of your foes!
³Yours is dominion
    on the day you lead your host
    in holy splendor.
From the womb of the morning
    I begot you.

When Jesus said that he would be "seated at the right hand of Power," he was claiming that he would be seated alongside God. As the Church teaches, "Being seated at the Father's right hand signifies the inauguration of the Messiah's kingdom, the fulfillment of the prophet Daniel's vision concerning the Son of man" (*CCC* 664). The high priest correctly understood that Jesus was making himself equal to God by identifying himself as the glorious Son of Man seated on God's throne. What Caiaphas failed to see, but we know by the light of faith, is that Jesus committed no blasphemy. Rather, he was truthfully revealing his divine identity—Jesus is the Divine Son of God made man.

Crucified under Pontius Pilate

The Sanhedrin found Jesus guilty of blasphemy and handed him over to the Roman authorities to be executed. Pontius Pilate, the Roman governor of Judea, did not think Jesus was guilty of anything. His own wife told him that Jesus was a "righteous man" (Mt 27:19). Yet Jesus again remained silent, even when the Jewish authorities condemned him before Pilate. Pilate was worried that if he did not condemn Jesus, the crowds would start a riot. So, Pilate treated Jesus like a criminal. Even though he knew Jesus to be innocent, he still had him whipped by Roman soldiers and handed over to be crucified.

Jesus knew in advance that all this would happen. Saint Matthew records three different occasions before Jesus' arrest when he foretold his Death and Resurrection.

Mt 16:21-22

16 ²¹Jesus began to show his disciples that he must go to Jerusalem and suffer many things from the elders and chief priests and scribes, and be killed, and on the third day be raised. ²²Then Peter took him aside and began to rebuke him, saying, "Far be it from you, Lord! Surely this shall never happen to you."

Mt 17:22-23

17 ²²While they were gathering in Galilee, Jesus said to them, "The Son of Man is about to be betrayed into the hands of men. ²³They will kill him, and on the third day he will be raised." And they were very sorrowful.

Mt 20:17-19

20 ¹⁷As Jesus was going up to Jerusalem, he took the twelve disciples aside by themselves, and he said to them on the way, ¹⁸"Behold, we are going up to Jerusalem, and the Son of Man will be handed over to the chief priests and scribes, and they will condemn him to death. ¹⁹And they will hand him over to the Gentiles to be mocked and scourged and crucified, and on the third day he will be raised."

Jesus' prophecies caused much distress and confusion for his disciples. His prediction that the Son of Man would *suffer* clearly came as a great shock. The way Jesus fulfilled Daniel's prediction of an everlasting kingship was also unexpected. Jesus perfectly fulfilled Daniel's prophecies through the Paschal Mystery. Many hoped Jesus would establish his kingdom through a glorious earthly victory. Instead, out of love, Jesus offered himself for our sins and was put to death on a Cross. His kingdom was established through his suffering, Death, and Resurrection. After his Resurrection from the dead, Jesus could appear to his Apostles and declare, "All authority in heaven and on earth has been given to me" (Mt 28:18).

Catechism of the Catholic Church, 440

"[Jesus] unveiled the authentic content of his messianic kingship both in the transcendent identity of the Son of Man 'who came down from heaven,' and in his redemptive mission as the suffering Servant: 'The Son of Man came not to be served but to serve, and to give his life as a ransom for many.'¹ Hence the true meaning of his kingship is revealed only when he is raised high on the cross.² Only after his Resurrection will Peter be able to proclaim Jesus' messianic kingship to the People of God: 'Let all the house of Israel therefore know assuredly that God has made him both Lord and Christ, this Jesus whom you crucified.'"³

According to the Scriptures

The Suffering Servant

When Jesus was in Gethsemane, he declared to the crowd who came to arrest him, "All this has taken place so that the writings of the prophets might be fulfilled" (Mt 26:56). Jesus knew that his suffering, Death, and Resurrection had been foretold in the Old Testament Scriptures. Through Jesus' Paschal Mystery, the hidden meaning of those Scriptures was unveiled.

Jesus perfectly fulfilled not only the words of the prophet Daniel but also the words of the prophet Isaiah. In the Book of Isaiah, we find four different prophecies about a figure known as the Suffering Servant of the Lord. In the last of these prophecies, Isaiah described in detail how the Servant would suffer and die for the sins of his people.

Is 52:13—53:12

52 ¹³Behold, my servant shall prosper,
he shall be exalted and lifted up,
and shall be very high.
¹⁴As many were astonished at him—
his appearance was so marred, beyond human semblance,
and his form beyond that of the sons of men—
¹⁵so shall he startle many nations;
kings shall shut their mouths because of him;
for that which has not been told them they shall see,
and that which they have not heard they shall understand.

53 ¹Who has believed what we have heard?
And to whom has the arm of the Lord been revealed?
²For he grew up before him like a young plant,
and like a root out of dry ground;
he had no form or comeliness that we should look at him,
and no beauty that we should desire him.
³He was despised and rejected by men;
a man of sorrows, and acquainted with grief;
and as one from whom men hide their faces
he was despised, and we esteemed him not.
⁴Surely he has borne our griefs
and carried our sorrows;
yet we esteemed him stricken,
struck down by God, and afflicted.
⁵But he was wounded for our transgressions,
he was bruised for our iniquities;
upon him was the chastisement that made us whole,
and with his stripes we are healed.
⁶All we like sheep have gone astray;
we have turned every one to his own way;
and the Lord has laid on him
the iniquity of us all.
⁷He was oppressed, and he was afflicted,
yet he opened not his mouth;
like a lamb that is led to the slaughter,
and like a sheep that before its shearers is silent,
so he opened not his mouth.
⁸By oppression and judgment he was taken away;
and as for his generation, who considered
that he was cut off out of the land of the living,
stricken for the transgression of my people?
⁹And they made his grave with the wicked
and with a rich man in his death,
although he had done no violence,
and there was no deceit in his mouth.
¹⁰Yet it was the will of the Lord to bruise him;
he has put him to grief;
when he makes himself an offering for sin,
he shall see his offspring, he shall prolong his days;
the will of the Lord shall prosper in his hand;
¹¹ he shall see the fruit of the travail of his soul
and be satisfied;
by his knowledge shall the righteous one, my servant,
make many to be accounted righteous;
and he shall bear their iniquities.
¹²Therefore I will divide him a portion with the great,
and he shall divide the spoil with the strong;
because he poured out his soul to death,
and was numbered with the transgressors;
yet he bore the sin of many,
and made intercession for the transgressors.

Jesus Fulfilled Isaiah's Prophecy

Jesus perfectly fulfilled the words of Isaiah the prophet. Consider some of the ways that Matthew's account of Jesus' Paschal Mystery unveils him to be the Suffering Servant spoken about by Isaiah hundreds of years earlier.

The Suffering Servant *Book of Isaiah*	Jesus Christ *Gospel of Matthew*
"He makes himself an offering for sin. . . . He bore the sin of many" (53:10, 12).	Jesus taught that his blood "is poured out for many for the forgiveness of sins" (26:28).
"He was oppressed, and he was afflicted, yet he opened not his mouth" (53:7).	Jesus remained silent when he was repeatedly accused of wrongdoing (see 26:63; 27 12, 14).
"He was wounded for our transgressions . . . and with his stripes we are healed" (53:5).	The Roman soldiers tortured Jesus by scourging him (see 27:26).
"He shall be exalted and lifted up, and shall be very high" (52:13).	Jesus was lifted high on the wood of the Cross (see 27:35–44).
"[He] was numbered with the transgressors" (53:12).	Jesus was crucified along with two robbers (see 27:38).
"He was despised and rejected by men" (53:3).	On the Cross, Jesus was mocked and reviled by both Jews and Romans (see 27:39–44).

No one expected the Son of Man figure in Daniel and the Suffering Servant in Isaiah to be the same person. Through his actions and words, Jesus proved that he was exactly who he claimed to be—the Son of Man, who "bore the sin of many" (Is 53:12).

Through his Death and Resurrection, Christ won for us the forgiveness of our sins. By his grace, made available to us through the sacraments, we are now able to be "accounted righteous" (Is 53:11) and are restored to friendship with God.

Chapter 22 Summary

1. When questioned by Caiaphas and the Sanhedrin, Jesus claimed to be the glorious Son of Man spoken of by the prophet Daniel.

2. Jesus was convicted of blasphemy and handed over to the Roman governor, Pontius Pilate, to be crucified.

3. Through his Paschal Mystery, Jesus perfectly fulfilled Isaiah's prophecy about the Suffering Servant.

Suffering for Others

In Daniel's prophecy, he foretold that the People of God would share in the everlasting kingdom of the Son of Man (see 7:18, 22, 27). As Christians, we believe that Daniel spoke the truth. We can truly share in the kingdom of Jesus, the Son of Man. Jesus entered the glory of his heavenly kingdom only *after* suffering on the Cross. In our earthly journey, we, too, will face suffering. We will have our own "crosses" to bear. Saint Paul reminds us that if we unite our own suffering with Christ's, we, too, can share in his glory (see Rom 8:17). Christ can bring good out of our suffering. He can draw us closer to himself and to his kingdom.

Saint Paul the Apostle

When you suffer, do you share your struggles with Christ in prayer? Or do you try to handle it on your own?

_____

_____

As the Suffering Servant, Jesus suffered on the Cross out of love for others. United with Christ, we, too, can offer our own suffering for the good of others. Writing to the Colossians, Saint Paul said this: "Now I rejoice in my sufferings for your sake, and in my flesh I complete what is lacking in Christ's afflictions for the sake of his body, that is, the Church" (1:24). Saint Paul suffered many things because of his devotion to Christ and his Church. He was persecuted, tortured, and imprisoned for his faith. Saint Paul could *rejoice* in his suffering because he suffered for the good of the Church. His mission to spread the faith helped so many people. He was willing to suffer because he loved others.

When has a person suffered out of love for you? List two specific examples.

_____

_____

_____

_____

What are two specific ways you might use the suffering and struggles you experience to help others?

_____
_____
_____
_____
_____
_____

Think of someone in your life who is going through a hard time. The next time you experience suffering, offer your suffering to Christ for that person. You can do this through a simple prayer: "Jesus, I offer you my suffering for the good of _____."

Let Us Pray—Psalm 8

As we pray Psalm 8, we recall how Jesus, the Son of Man, was crowned with glory and honor after suffering Death on the Cross. We, too, can share in Jesus' glory and honor by taking up our own crosses and uniting them with his Cross.

Ps 8:1-9

8 ¹O LORD, our Lord,
 how majestic is your name in all the earth!
You whose glory above the heavens is chanted
² by the mouth of babies and infants,
you have founded a bulwark because of your foes,
 to still the enemy and the avenger.
³When I look at your heavens, the work of your fingers,
 the moon and the stars which you have established;
⁴what is man that you are mindful of him,
 and the son of man that you care for him?
⁵Yet you have made him little less than the angels,
 and you have crowned him with glory and honor.
⁶You have given him dominion over the works of your hands;
 you have put all things under his feet,
⁷all sheep and oxen,
 and also the beasts of the field,
⁸the birds of the air, and the fish of the sea,
 whatever passes along the paths of the sea.
⁹O LORD, our Lord,
 how majestic is your name in all the earth!

Chapter 22 Review:
Jesus, the Son of Man

1. Who was Caiaphas? _____

2. The Jewish council of judges who would listen to testimony and judge whether a person was guilty or innocent of a crime was known as the _____.

3. To which psalm did Jesus refer when he declared to the Sanhedrin that they would "see the Son of Man seated at the right hand of Power" (Mt 26:64)? _____

4. What is the sin of blasphemy? _____
_____

5. Why did Caiaphas and the Sanhedrin think Jesus was guilty of blasphemy?
_____
_____

6. Saint Matthew records three separate times that Jesus foretold his Paschal Mystery. What specifically did he say would happen?
_____
_____

7. Which Old Testament prophet wrote at length about God's Suffering Servant?
_____

8. What are two specific ways that Matthew reveals Jesus to be the Suffering Servant from Isaiah's prophecy?
_____
_____

The Church and the Jews

Nostra Aetate, 4

"Even though the Jewish authorities and those who followed their lead pressed for the death of Christ (cf. John 19:6), neither all Jews indiscriminately at that time, nor Jews today, can be charged with the crimes committed during his passion. It is true that the Church is the new people of God, yet the Jews should not be spoken of as rejected or accursed as if this followed from holy Scripture."[4]

Jesus was falsely accused and unjustly condemned by the Jewish authorities. Crowds of Jews shouted for Jesus to be crucified. Unfortunately, some Christians throughout history have used the evil actions of some Jews toward Jesus as a justification for hatred and discrimination against the entire Jewish people.

The Church clearly teaches that hatred and unjust discrimination are always wrong. "Guilt by association"—blaming an entire group for the bad actions of a few within that group—is also never acceptable. While some Jews were guilty of evil against Jesus, most Jews at the time were innocent. Most of Jesus' own followers were Jewish. We must also remember that many pagans contributed to Jesus' murder. Pilate allowed Jesus to be crucified. Roman soldiers mercilessly mocked and beat Jesus and put him on the Cross.

Throughout history, the Church has repeatedly condemned anti-Jewish actions. When the Nazi Party began its rise to power in Germany, Pope Pius XI issued an encyclical, which is a letter written to the entire Church.[5] It was the first encyclical ever written in German, and the pope required it to be read in every Church in Germany on Palm Sunday in 1937. In that letter, Pius XI condemned those who idolize a particular race. This was a clear critique of the Nazis, who saw the Aryan race as superior to all other races and who hated the Jewish people. He reminded the people of Germany that God loves *all people* and does not value one race over others. He criticized those who are blinded by prejudice and cannot see God's love for the Chosen People. Not surprisingly, once the Nazi government found out about the encyclical, they tried to stop it from being printed and distributed. Some priests were imprisoned by the Nazis for reading it at Mass.

Pius XI's words remind us that one cannot be a Christian and hate the Jews. The Church sees the Jewish faith as special compared to all other non-Christian religions. God uniquely revealed himself to the Jewish people in salvation history. God continues to love the Jewish people and does not revoke the gifts he has given to them.

Pope Pius XI

Journal Reflection

What are some examples of "guilt by association" that you see in the world today?

Who Is Jesus Christ?

Read

In all four Gospels, Jesus is revealed as the Divine Son of God through his deeds and words. One of the most important ways we see this truth of our faith unfold is through the different titles and names that Jesus uses to refer to himself. Some of these, such as Son of Man, reveal Jesus' divinity in the Gospels. In response to this, someone might say, "Well, Jesus sounds like a good guy, but he wasn't God."

This objection seems reasonable, but it is ultimately not logical. Jesus could not have been a "good guy" while claiming to be a Divine Person, unless he was in fact divine. We have to think about who Jesus is. There are three possible identities for Christ:[6]

1. **Jesus could have been a liar.** This would have made him, in fact, the worst of blasphemers. He could not have been a "good guy" while deceiving countless people throughout history into believing that he is God.

2. **Jesus could have been out of his mind.** He could have truly believed he was God but been wrong. Only someone who is out of his mind would claim to be God.

3. **Jesus was (is) actually God.** He could have actually been who he said that he was. He actually is the Son of God, the Second Person of the Blessed Trinity.

Let's think about what the Gospels reveal. Liars tell lies for selfish gain like power or money. Jesus was poor and was even killed for his claims. Why would Jesus lie? People who are out of their minds are often confused and their messages are incoherent. Jesus' teachings never contradict. He was in complete control of himself. Truly we can say that Jesus is the Divine Son of God made man. The best way to verify this is to read, know, and live out the Gospel. When we live out the Gospel, we come to experience the divine power of God at work in and through us.

Reflect

Spend 5–10 minutes reflecting on the following:

- Based on how I live, do I act as though Jesus is truly the Son of God, who proclaimed the truth and who desires my heart? Or do I live as though he were a liar or a man out of his mind?

- Am I unfamiliar with some parts of the Gospel? If so, which parts do I need to read more?

Pray

Pray the Act of Faith on page 335.

Act

Spend 5–10 minutes reading Matthew's Gospel each day this week before school or before going to bed.

Unit 6

God with Us

All of salvation history finds its fulfillment in the Person of Jesus Christ. The Old Testament sheds light on Jesus' mission of salvation. In particular, the covenants with Abraham and David find their perfect fulfillment in Jesus' Paschal Mystery—his suffering, Death, Resurrection, and Ascension.

In the Great Commission, Jesus sent out his Church to evangelize by proclaiming the Good News of the Gospel and making disciples of all nations. The early Church began fulfilling this commission after receiving power from on high through the gift of the Holy Spirit on Pentecost.

Jesus Christ is Emmanuel, the Divine Son of God made man, who is present to his Church in all ages, especially through the liturgy and sacraments.

Chapters 23–24

Chapter 23: The Fullness of Time

Chapter 24: Jesus, Emmanuel

Grade 6 Road Map

Unit 1
The Good News
The Gospel of Matthew reveals who Jesus is through both his deeds and words. God speaks to us in Sacred Scripture through human authors inspired by the Holy Spirit.

Unit 2
In the Beginning
Genesis describes the beginning of the universe and humanity, the beginning of sin, and the beginning of God's plan to restore mankind's relationship with himself through the covenant with Abraham and his descendants. In Jesus, God's covenant with Abraham is fulfilled.

Unit 3
You Shall Be My People
Through Moses, God delivered his people from slavery in Egypt and made a covenant with them at Mount Sinai. Despite their unfaithfulness, God brought his people into the Promised Land after they wandered for forty years in the desert. Jesus is the New Moses, who gives the New Law.

Unit 4
The Kingdom of the Lord
The Lord made a covenant with King David and swore to give him an everlasting kingdom. The sins of God's people led to the division and downfall of the kingdom, eventually leading to the destruction of the Temple and the Babylonian exile. In Jesus, God's covenant with David is fulfilled.

Unit 5
The Coming of the Anointed One
God brought his people back from exile to the Promised Land, where they rebuilt the Temple in Jerusalem. The prophets foretold of the coming of the Messiah, who would rebuild the kingdom of David. Jesus, the Son of Man, brings the kingdom through his suffering and Death.

Unit 6
God with Us
The Gospel of Matthew provides reliable testimony that Jesus is the Divine Son of God made man, who delivered us from sin through his Paschal Mystery. Jesus continues to be present to his Church through Word and sacrament—above all, the Holy Eucharist.

Saint Teresa of Avila

Teresa Learns to Pray

The year was 1515. The sun rose over the yellowed stones of the medieval tower walls that surrounded the city of Avila, Spain. On that early spring morning, Don Alphonsus and his wife, Doña Beatriz, welcomed their third child, Teresa. It would be Teresa's work and witness that led to the nickname of Avila as the "city of saints and stones."

Teresa was born into a wealthy family that was well respected in Avila; however, her upbringing wasn't unusual for a girl of that time. She was raised by pious parents who read many good books, gave to the poor, and taught their children how to pray. Her parents' love for reading wasn't lost on her. She loved reading about the lives of the saints, which were considered the adventure stories of Teresa's time. When she was seven, she and her brother Rodrigo were so inspired by these stories that they attempted to run away to be martyred (only to be thwarted by their uncle).

Teresa's focus shifted away from saintliness when she turned thirteen years old. After the death of her mother, her selection of reading turned to romances that her father disapproved of. This influence, as well as the influence of a vain cousin, turned her to the things of this world. Teresa later recounted, "I began to imitate the fashions, to enjoy being well dressed, to take great care of my hands, to use perfumes, and wear all the vain ornaments which my position in the world allowed."[1] Her pious father became concerned that these obsessions were leading her away from God. He sent her off to the local Augustinian convent with other young girls of her societal class to take part in finishing school when she was fifteen.

About a year into school, Teresa fell seriously ill, and her father sent her to a cousin's country villa to recover. The witness of her cousin's holy marriage and the spiritual books the couple provided prompted her to discern religious life. With the help of the letters of Saint Jerome, Teresa heard God's call to

become a nun. When she told her father, he said she could do as she pleased after his death. In other words, he didn't approve. So, instead of returning to the Augustinian convent, and despite her father's wishes, she secretly left for the nearby Carmelite Convent of the Incarnation. But her time there was cut short.

A year later, when she was in her early twenties, Teresa fell ill once again after taking her solemn profession. Her father saw this as an opportunity to take her from the convent and bring her back home. There, her illness became progressively worse, and she was partially paralyzed for a time. At one point, she was in a coma for four days. When she awoke, she learned that they had dug a grave for her! But when she had the strength, she began reading a book called *The Third Spiritual Alphabet* that would change her life. It was a guide to mental and contemplative prayer. When she finished it, she said, "[I was] determined to follow that way of prayer with all my might."[2]

She finally recovered after three years and returned to the Carmelite convent (this time, with the blessing of her father). Upon her return, she became more aware of the worldliness of the 120 nuns who lived there. They arranged their habits in such a way to show off their jewelry, and it was common to entertain frequent visitors. Teresa found herself falling back into the snares of vanity. She described it like this: "On the one hand God was calling me, on the other I was following the world."[3] For more than ten years there, she struggled with having the relationship with God that she wanted. She later said, "Over a period of several years I was more occupied in wishing my hour of prayer over."[4] However, she persevered in prayer even though it didn't "feel" good. In the midst of this, God began to gift her with frequent visions of beautiful spiritual realities.

Her flip-flopping between worldliness and true devotion to God came to an end one day when she passed by an image of Jesus covered in the wounds of his Passion. Although she had seen it many times, this time something moved in her. She burst into tears and threw herself on the ground, begging the Lord to give her the strength never to hurt him again with her sins. She said, "I felt Mary Magdalen come to my assistance. . . . From that day I have gone on improving in my spiritual life."[5] She withdrew from the worldliness that surrounded her and committed wholly to mental prayer.

Teresa, the True Reformer

As her relationship with God deepened, she heard the call to begin her own convent, one that wouldn't repeat the mistakes of the one she was in. She proposed to start a small community that was poor and enclosed (meaning the sisters chose to stay inside the grounds in order to remain focused on God instead of getting distracted by the world). Her fellow nuns didn't like her proposal. They felt like their comfortable way of life would be threatened if she followed through with her desires. The opposition didn't change the fact that God was calling her to a radical life of prayer and poverty. "When I fell to prayer again and looked at Christ hanging poor and naked upon the Cross, I felt I could not bear to be rich. So, I besought him with tears to bring it to pass that I might be as poor as he."[6]

Teresa wasn't the only one seeking to reform her religious community. She was living in the immediate aftermath of the Protestant Reformation, when many people had left the Catholic Church. The Church was working to counter the Reformation, partly by identifying and fixing the problems that led to so many leaving the Church. One of these areas was reforming religious orders to be more faithful to their original way of life.

Teresa opened her new convent, the Carmelite Convent of Saint Joseph's, in 1562, when she was in her late forties. It was so small that, as it was being built, people thought it was going to be a house for a family rather than a convent. As she had envisioned, she kept the community small. Four sisters started the community (she wouldn't let it grow bigger than thirteen). Those around them found them strange. They didn't wear shoes and so became known as the "discalced," or "shoeless," Carmelites. Instead of relying on the money of any of the nuns' wealthy families, they relied on donations. Sometimes they skipped a meal because there was no food. In the face of these challenges, the convent remained open and drew both positive and negative attention.

In 1567, she was asked by authorities in the Carmelite order to found more convents. She would establish twelve convents during the next fifteen years! During this time, Pope Pius V himself appointed Teresa and others to check on various convents. Their job was to ensure that they were actually living out the rule of life of their religious order (living lives of prayer, poverty, and obedience). One convent she was sent to was the Carmelite Convent of the Incarnation—the very one she had left. To say it was humbling and difficult is an understatement. She was met with jealousy, and the sisters initially refused to listen to her or obey. Eventually, however, she won them over with her charm and reestablished discipline. Finances were set in order and frequent visitors were forbidden. After three years of hard work, worldliness was cleansed from the convent and God was back at the center of their lives.

Her original convent wasn't the only one to resist her attempts at reform. Many of the nonreformed Carmelites were afraid they themselves would have to reform. They worked hard to get a Church leader to call Teresa a "restless, disobedient . . . woman, who under the cloak of piety has invented false [teachings]."[7] There was a push to force her and other true reformers to stop their work. However, Teresa went to the king, King Philip II of Spain, and convinced him that these good reforms should continue. In the end, Teresa and her allies won and were able to continue their work.

By the grace of God, Teresa lived to the age of sixty-five. Even at that age she continued to travel and help convents live with true devotion. She did this on poor roads over dangerous terrain, sometimes in carts or drawn carriages with little food. During one such trip, her life of illness caught up with her. When she arrived at the convent, she collapsed in bed, exhausted. Three days later, she told her traveling companion (a nun), "At last, my daughter, I have reached the house of death."[8] Shortly after, she was given Last Rites and received the Eucharist. Upon receiving Jesus in the Blessed Sacrament, she said, "O my Lord, now is the time that we shall see each other!"[9]

Journal Reflection

1. Teresa strove to have a personal relationship with Jesus by engaging in contemplative prayer. **How can the Gospels help you grow closer to Jesus?**

2. **What distracted Teresa from God when she was your age? Are there any things in your life that keep you from focusing on God and the Good News of the Gospel?**

3. Teresa was met with resistance when she was sent to reform her old convent. **Have you ever been ridiculed or mocked by people you know when you tried to change or live better? What was that like?**

4. There were many who tried to keep Teresa from carrying out the mission God gave her. **What can you do to avoid discouragement as you try to live a truly Catholic life?**

CHAPTER 23

The Fullness of Time

Words to Know

> *Emmanuel*

> *redeemer*

> *Savior*

Proclaiming the Good News

"When the time had fully come, God sent forth his Son, born of woman, born under the law, to redeem those who were under the law, so that we might receive adoption as sons." —Galatians 4:4–5

The Annunciation, Fra Angelico

God's Plan of Salvation

Bad News and Good News

Although the Bible is a collection of 73 distinct books written by different authors over many centuries, these books tell a single story. This story tells us about salvation history, God's plan to save us from sin and unite all things in himself. Near the story's very beginning, we hear the terrible news of sin, when Adam and Eve disobeyed God and rejected his love and grace. Through their Original Sin, sin and death entered the world. But as soon as sin separated mankind from God, God announced his plan to fix it.

God loved us so much that he did not let sin have the last word. As soon as Adam and Eve sinned, God immediately announced his promise of the *Savior*, the person who would rescue mankind from the powers of sin and death and reconcile us to God. Jesus is the Savior of the World. Immediately after Adam and Eve's Fall, God told Satan, "I will put enmity between you and the woman, and between your seed and her seed; he shall bruise your head, and you shall bruise his heel" (Gen 3:15).

God promised that, in the future, the woman's seed, or descendant, would confront Satan and his evil ways. In this confrontation, the Savior and Satan would strike at each other, but the Savior would be victorious. This plan that God announced to conquer evil, sin, and death would unfold through the rest of salvation history.

The Lord Prepared His People

God announced his plan for the Savior in Genesis 3:15, and we read about the fulfillment of that plan in the Gospels. But throughout salvation history, the Lord prepared his people and revealed his plan, piece by piece. When God first called Abraham (named Abram at the time of his call) to follow him to a new land, he made three promises:

Gen 12:1-3

12 ¹Now the LORD said to Abram, "Go from your country and your kindred and your father's house to the land that I will show you. ²And I will make of you a great nation, and I will bless you, and make your name great, so that you will be a blessing. ³I will bless those who bless you, and him who curses you I will curse; and in you all the families of the earth shall be blessed."

Abraham and his wife, Sarah, had one son: Isaac. Isaac had only two sons: Esau and Jacob. Isaac and his sons were shepherds and nomads, as Abraham had been. Abraham never saw the fulfillment of the Lord's promise to make him a great nation, to make his family line into a royal dynasty, or to bless the whole world through his descendants. Those promises would ultimately be fulfilled by the Savior whom God planned to send.

Another way the Lord prepared his people for the Savior was by sending Moses to save the Israelites from slavery in Egypt and lead them to the Promised Land. After the Exodus, God taught his people how to live as part of his covenant family through the gift of his law. Through his law, God taught his Chosen People to know what was right and wrong. When the Savior came, he gave us God's grace to transform us in the depths of our hearts and enable us to keep God's law.

After God helped his Chosen People settle in the Promised Land, he made a covenant with King David. In this covenant, the Lord made three special promises to David:

> 2 Sam 7:11-14, 16
>
> 7 ¹¹"The LORD declares to you that the LORD will make you a house. ¹²When your days are fulfilled and you lie down with your fathers, I will raise up your offspring after you, who shall come forth from your body, and I will establish his kingdom. ¹³He shall build a house for my name, and I will establish the throne of his kingdom for ever. ¹⁴I will be his father, and he shall be my son. . . . ¹⁶And your house and your kingdom shall be made sure for ever before me; your throne shall be established for ever."

The Lord promised David he would establish his house, meaning he would make his descencants into a royal dynasty that would last forever. He also promised that David's son would build a house for God—a Temple where the people would always be able to worship God and offer sacrifices to him. Lastly, God promised to make the kings of David's line sons of God by divine adoption.

Although David's son Solomon did reign after him as king and built the Temple in Jerusalem for God, David's kingdom split into two after Solomon's reign. Some of David's descendants were righteous kings who ruled the people like God's sons, but many were wicked and did not keep God's covenant. By the time of the Babylonian Exile, there was no longer any descendant of David reigning as king and the Temple had been destroyed. The promises of a Davidic king reigning forever as a son of God would be fulfilled only when God sent the Savior—the Messiah, the king descended from David, who would be anointed with the Holy Spirit and would rule God's people forever.

Finally, the Lord announced his love and mercy in various ways through the prophets he sent to his people. Through all these people and events, God prepared the world for the coming of his Son, Jesus Christ. He is the Savior, who perfectly fulfilled all the promises God made throughout salvation history.

La Gloria, Titian

Both Lord and Christ

Announcing the Savior

Saint Matthew began his announcement of the Good News of the Savior with a list of the names of Jesus' ancestors, going back to Abraham. This genealogy reveals Jesus as the long-awaited Savior: "Jesus Christ, the son of David, the son of Abraham" (1:1). The long list of ancestors in Matthew 1 reveals how God prepared his people for the Savior. It further reveals that in Jesus, the promises the Lord made to Abraham and David have been fulfilled.

The opening chapter of Matthew's Gospel reveals another crucial detail about Jesus' identity: he is both the Son of Mary *and* the Divine Son of God. Matthew hinted at the mystery of Jesus' Divine Sonship when he described Saint Joseph as "the husband of Mary, of whom Jesus was born," rather than calling him the father of Jesus (1:16). And when the angel appeared to Saint Joseph in a dream, he both confirmed Jesus' Divine Sonship and announced his mission (see 1:20–25). Jesus' divine identity is found in his fulfilling the prophecy from Isaiah, which foretold a virgin giving birth to a son called Emmanuel. Jesus is truly *Emmanuel*, which means "God with us," as Matthew himself wrote (1:23).

But the angel revealed that this child's name would be Jesus, "for he will save his people from their sins" (1:21). The name Jesus (meaning "God saves") revealed his mission of salvation. The word "mission" comes from a Latin word meaning "sent." That Jesus had a mission of salvation means that he was sent to us by the Father to save us from our sins. God has not only sent *someone* to save us from sin—as he promised—but he *himself* has come to be our Savior!

Catechism of the Catholic Church, 517

"Christ's whole life is a mystery of redemption. Redemption comes to us above all through the blood of his cross,[1] but this mystery is at work throughout Christ's entire life:

- *already in his Incarnation through which by becoming poor he enriches us with his poverty;[2]*
- *in his hidden life which by his submission atones for our disobedience;[3]*
- *in his word which purifies its hearers;[4]*
- *in his healings and exorcisms by which 'he took our infirmities and bore our diseases';[5]*
- *and in his Resurrection by which he justifies us."[6]*

Jesus' Mission of Salvation

The Bible calls Jesus both our Savior and our Redeemer. A *redeemer* is someone who pays a debt and buys back another person's possessions or freedom. The Bible uses this title for Jesus because sin is a debt we cannot pay. God created us to belong to him in loving friendship. When we sin, we choose *not* to belong to God. Instead, we become slaves to sin and death. We cannot reverse that on our own—we cannot "buy" ourselves back from slavery. But Jesus can. Jesus redeemed us and paid our debt so we could belong to God again. This is why Jesus said he came "to give his life as a ransom for many" (Mt 20:28). His Death on the Cross was the ransom, or the price, for our debt of sin. As Saint Paul wrote, God took our debt of sin and "set [it] aside, nailing it to the cross" (Col 2:14).

The Church teaches that Jesus' "whole life is a mystery of *redemption*" (*CCC* 517). Every word and action during his life is about his mission to redeem us from the powers of sin and death and restore us to relationship with God. During his public ministry, Jesus performed great deeds of power (his miracles) that revealed more fully his mission. Jesus came to heal not just physical illness but also our spiritual illness of sin. The healing of the paralyzed man (see Mt 9:1–8) is one example of how Jesus revealed his mission of salvation through both his deeds and words.

Jesus forgave the paralytic's sins first because this was the heart of his mission. Physical healing is good, but spiritual healing is even more important and a greater miracle. The scribes were shocked by Jesus' words because only God can forgive sins. They realized that Jesus claimed to be God when he said he could forgive sins. When Jesus also healed the man physically, it was a sign of his divine authority to forgive sins.

Poured Out for Many

Jesus fulfilled his mission of redemption in his Paschal Mystery, which is his suffering, Death, Resurrection, and Ascension. Jesus is God's solution to the problem of sin. Through his Paschal Mystery, Jesus freed us from sin and death and made it possible for us to be reunited with God and share in his life. In the Old Testament, the blood of animal sacrifices symbolized the forgiveness of sins. But when Jesus poured out his blood on the Cross, he redeemed us. At the Last Supper, Jesus announced that he was this final and perfect sacrifice for the forgiveness of sins (see Mt 26:27–28).

Jesus' Paschal Mystery redeemed us from sin. But Jesus did not just save us from sin—he made it possible for us to enjoy eternal happiness with God in Heaven. Through his Paschal Mystery, we can become like him in love and holiness through grace. We can be totally united with the Blessed Trinity in a covenant relationship, just as God created us to be.

Chapter 23 Summary

1. Immediately after Adam and Eve committed the first sin, God announced his plan to send the Savior. God's plan unfolded throughout salvation history.

2. Jesus, the Divine Son of God, is the solution to the problem of sin. He perfectly fulfilled the promises of God's covenants with Abraham and David.

3. Jesus' whole life is focused on his mission of redemption. He frees us from the powers of sin and death through his Paschal Mystery.

Embodying the Gospel

From the Saints

"The Spirit is truly the dwelling of the saints and the saints are for the Spirit a place where he dwells as in his own home, since they offer themselves as a dwelling place for God and are called his temple." [7]

—Saint Basil the Great

We can understand the Bible better when we look at the lives of the saints. According to Pope Benedict XVI, the lives of the saints are crucial to our understanding of Scripture: "The interpretation of sacred Scripture would remain incomplete were it not to include listening to *those who have truly lived the word of God: namely, the saints*. . . . The most profound interpretation of Scripture comes precisely from those who let themselves be shaped by the word of God through listening, reading and . . . meditation." [8] Why do we understand the Bible better when we look to the saints, those holy men and women who knew, loved, and lived the Scriptures? It is because the Bible is the story of our salvation. The Bible teaches us that the key to salvation is imitating and living like Christ, our Savior. Those who best imitate Christ, in turn, best reflect the story of the Bible.

As Saint Paul wrote, "Those whom [God] foreknew he also predestined to be conformed to the image of his Son, in order that he might be first-born among many brethren" (Rom 8:29). We can use the family as an analogy. Family members bear a certain resemblance to one another. For example, children often look and act similarly to their parents. Likewise, in God's family, grace makes it possible for us to bear a certain resemblance to God. Through grace, we can live as Jesus did; we can become "conformed" to him. We can love others as God loves.

The saints show us what this "family resemblance" looks like in all sorts of different ways. They are holy men and women precisely because they are *like* Jesus. We learn how to be like Jesus from reading the Gospels, but we also learn how to be like him from considering the lives of the saints. Saint Paul encouraged the Corinthians, saying, "Be imitators of me, as I am of Christ" (1 Cor 11:1). This advice is true for all the saints. We see what being like Jesus looks like when people in different times and places imitate him.

Who is a saint you particularly admire? In what ways was this person like Jesus?

_____
_____
_____

How does the life of this saint inspire you and help you be more like Jesus?

_____
_____
_____
_____

Let Us Pray—Psalm 32

The Book of Psalms includes not only prayers of contrition, in which we express sorrow for our sins, but also prayers of rejoicing and thanksgiving, in which we celebrate God's great gift of mercy and salvation. Psalm 32 is one of these prayers. It reflects on the joy we find in God's mercy and forgiveness. As big and overwhelming as the problem of sin seems at times, God's mercy is always bigger and stronger.

Ps 32:1-2, 5-7, 11

32 ¹Blessed is he whose transgression is forgiven,
　　whose sin is covered.
²Blessed is the man to whom the LORD
　　imputes no iniquity,
　and in whose spirit there is no deceit. . . .
⁵I acknowledged my sin to you,
　　and I did not hide my iniquity;
　I said, "I will confess my transgressions to the LORD";
　　then you forgave the guilt of my sin.
⁶Therefore let every one who is godly
　　offer prayer to you;
　at a time of distress, in the rush of great waters,
　　they shall not reach him.
⁷You are a hiding place for me,
　　you preserve me from trouble;
　　you surround me with deliverance. . . .
¹¹Be glad in the LORD, and rejoice, O righteous,
　　and shout for joy, all you upright in heart!

Chapter 23 Review:
The Fullness of Time

1. What promise did God make in Genesis 3:15? _____

2. Why do we call Jesus our Savior? _____

3. What is a redeemer? _____

4. What three promises did God make to Abraham? _____

5. What three promises did God make to David? _____

6. Matthew identified Jesus as fulfilling the prophet Isaiah's prophecy about Emmanuel. What does "Emmanuel" mean? _____

7. What are three or more key details from Matthew's Gospel that reveal Jesus' mission of salvation? _____

The Rosary: A Summary of the Gospel

The Rosary has been one of the most familiar and beloved forms of prayer for many Catholics for centuries. Pope Saint John Paul II called the Rosary "a prayer of great significance, destined to bring forth a harvest of holiness."[9] Because we recite more Hail Marys than any other prayer in the Rosary, many people think of the Rosary as mainly asking for Mary's prayerful intercession. Asking for Mary's intercession is certainly an important aspect of the Rosary, but Pope Saint John Paul II highlighted another very important way that we pray when we recite the Rosary. He called the Rosary a compendium, or a summary, of the Gospel, and he said that when we pray the Rosary, we meditate on the Gospel.

In the Christian tradition, meditation means using our minds to try to understand the truths of our faith; it is a quest for understanding (see *CCC* 2705). More than saying particular words in prayer, meditation is a prayer where we think deeply about truth. In the mysteries of the Rosary, we have the opportunity to think deeply about the mysteries of Christ's life, particularly as seen through the eyes of his Blessed Mother.

When we pray the Rosary, Mary helps us listen to God. The Rosary is "directed to the contemplation of Christ's face,"[10] meaning that the whole purpose of the Rosary is to gaze on Christ in order to know and love him better. As we pray ten Hail Marys for each mystery, we reflect on the saving work of Jesus in the company of Mary, the Mother of our Lord. From her mother's heart, she helps us look upon her Son in love and see more deeply into each mystery. Pope Saint John Paul II also reminds us that "the recitation of the Rosary calls for a quiet rhythm and a lingering pace, helping the individual to meditate on the mysteries of the Lord's life as seen through the eyes of her who was closest to the Lord."[11] We should not rush through the Rosary just to get all the prayers said. Rather, the repetition in the Rosary is an opportunity for us to engage our minds and hearts fully in prayer as we contemplate our Lord Jesus Christ.

Journal Reflection

How can praying the Rosary help you know Jesus better? How can it help you love him more?

Needing a Savior

Read

The Bible's message of salvation is Good News, but that does not mean it is comfortable news. It requires us to acknowledge something about ourselves: we need a Savior. The Good News makes sense only if we acknowledge the problem of sin. And sin is not a popular idea. Often the world tells us we should not feel guilty about anything. Sin is too negative. After all, nobody is perfect, so why beat yourself up? Or we are even told that we are perfect just the way we are.

But if we're honest, we can recognize that we're not perfect yet, but we want to be better; we want to be happier. Something in our hearts recognizes the truth that we need help. We need not just someone to give us good advice but someone with the power to heal what is broken in us. We need a Savior.

Those feelings of guilt that we get when we sin are a gift from God. They call our attention to the fact that something is wrong. They point us toward the only real solution: Jesus Christ. Denying the reality of sin does not solve this problem. Only when we recognize the problem of sin do we start to realize how amazing the Good News of the Gospel is.

Reflect

Spend 5–10 minutes reflecting on the following:

- Do I acknowledge the problem of sin in my own life? Do I recognize my own need for a Savior?
- How do I handle feelings of guilt when I sin? Do they lead me to contrition and confession? Do I ignore them or make excuses?
- Do I relate to Jesus as my Savior? Or do I think of him primarily in some other way?

Pray

Make a simple act of contrition and entrust yourself to God's mercy with the Jesus Prayer:

> Lord Jesus Christ, Son of the living God,
> have mercy on me, a sinner.
> Amen.

Act

Take a few minutes each night this week to make an examination of conscience (see page 342). Think back over your day, asking God to forgive you for the sins you committed and thanking him for his grace and blessings.

CHAPTER 24

Jesus, Emmanuel

Words to Know

> *disciple*

> *evangelization*

> *liturgy*

Proclaiming the Good News

"Behold, the dwelling of God is with men. He will dwell with them, and they shall be his people, and God himself will be with them." —Revelation 21:3

The Last Supper, Joseph Edward Nuttgens

The Great Commission

Sharing in Jesus' Mission

What comes to mind when you think about missionaries? Most people think of missionaries as people who travel far from home to tell people about Jesus and the Christian faith. Their focus is *evangelization*—the proclamation of Jesus and the Good News through one's words and way of life. While there are people who dedicate their whole lives to this kind of missionary work around the world, *all Christians* are called to share the Gospel. The task of evangelization is not just for professional missionaries; it is for every single member of the Church.

From the very moment sin entered the world, God was preparing to send the Savior to restore our friendship with him. All God's plans and promises that are recorded in the Old Testament were fulfilled when he sent his own Divine Son. Jesus of Nazareth is truly God with us. Jesus freed us from the powers of sin and death through his Paschal Mystery. But that was not the end of his mission. Before he ascended into Heaven, Jesus instructed his Apostles to continue his mission by proclaiming the Good News to the whole world.

Read the account of the Great Commission in Matthew 28:16–20 on pages 27–28.

In the Great Commission, Jesus sent his Apostles out to continue his mission of salvation. The Church continues Jesus' mission by making disciples. A *disciple* is a student or follower of a teacher. A disciple imitates the teacher's way of life. To make disciples of Jesus means teaching people not only who Jesus was and what he taught and did but also how to follow him by obeying his teachings and trying to become like him with the help of God's grace.

There are two steps to Jesus' command to make disciples: baptize and teach. We become disciples of Jesus through faith and the Sacrament of Baptism. Baptism cleanses us from sin and brings us into a covenant relationship with God. It makes us a son or daughter of God and a member of Christ's Body, the Church. The grace of Baptism makes it possible for us to begin to follow Jesus as his disciples. We live as disciples by becoming like Jesus through obedience. We cannot be disciples of Jesus without obeying his teachings. Consider Jesus' own words about living as his disciples:

Jn 13:34-35; 15:7-10

13 ³⁴"A new commandment I give to you, that you love one another; even as I have loved you, that you also love one another. ³⁵By this all men will know that you are my disciples, if you have love for one another." . . .

15 ⁷"If you abide in me, and my words abide in you, ask whatever you will, and it shall be done for you. ⁸By this my Father is glorified, that you bear much fruit, and so prove to be my disciples. ⁹As the Father has loved me, so have I loved you; abide in my love. ¹⁰If you keep my commandments, you will abide in my love, just as I have kept my Father's commandments and abide in his love."

It is not enough just to believe what Jesus said; we also have to obey what he taught, especially his commandment to love others as he has loved us. Jesus gives us the grace to abide in his love. He empowers us with his own Holy Spirit to love as he loves.

Life in the Early Church

Jesus gave the Apostles the Great Commission before he ascended into Heaven. In the Acts of the Apostles, we read that he also told them to wait in Jerusalem until he sent them the Holy Spirit:

Acts 1:4-5, 8

1 ⁴"While staying with them he charged them not to depart from Jerusalem, but to wait for the promise of the Father, which, he said, "you heard from me, ⁵for John baptized with water, but before many days you shall be baptized with the Holy Spirit." . . .

⁸"You shall receive power when the Holy Spirit has come upon you; and you shall be my witnesses in Jerusalem and in all Judea and Samaria and to the end of the earth."

Nine days later, on the Feast of Pentecost, the Holy Spirit came upon the Apostles and the other disciples gathered together in prayer. Immediately, the Apostles started fulfilling what Jesus commanded in the Great Commission.

The Great Commission *Gospel of Matthew*	Pentecost *Acts of the Apostles*
"Go therefore and make disciples of all nations" (28:19).	"[The Apostles] were all filled with the Holy Spirit and began to speak in other tongues, as the Spirit gave them utterance. Now there were dwelling in Jerusalem Jews, devout men from every nation under heaven" (2:4–5).
"[Baptize] them in the name of the Father, and of the Son, and of the Holy Spirit" (28:19).	"[The people] said to Peter and the rest of the apostles, 'Brethren, what shall we do?' And Peter said to them, 'Repent, and be baptized every one of you in the name of Jesus Christ for the forgiveness of your sins'" (2:37–38).
"[Teach] them to observe everything I have commanded you" (28:20).	"Those who received his word were baptized, and there were added that day about three thousand souls. And they held steadfastly to the apostles' teaching and fellowship, to the breaking of the bread and to the prayers" (2:41–42).

When Peter first preached the Good News about Jesus to the crowds in Jerusalem, over three thousand people came to believe that Jesus was the Messiah and wanted to become his disciples! We find this same pattern throughout the rest of the Acts of the Apostles: the Good News about Jesus was proclaimed, those who believed were baptized, and they began to live their new lives as disciples of Christ by imitating him in love and seeking to obey everything he taught. This is how the Church continues to fulfill the Great Commission throughout all of history, continuing Jesus' mission of salvation until he comes again in glory at the end of time.

Pentecost, Navarro Perez Dolz

"I Am with You Always"

Jesus' Promise

Imagine how the Apostles felt when Jesus ascended into Heaven. They had suffered through the grief of his Death and then experienced the indescribable joy of his Resurrection. But after forty days of Jesus remaining with them, suddenly it looked like he was leaving them again. And yet, Jesus said he was not really leaving them. He promised to remain with his Church "even until the end of the age" (Mt 28:20). This was not the first time that Jesus promised to remain with his disciples forever. At the Last Supper, Jesus explained to the Apostles that he was going to return to the Father. But he also told them that he would continue to be with them.

> Jn 14:18-21, 23
>
> **14** ¹⁸"I will not leave you desolate; I will come to you. ¹⁹Yet a little while, and the world will see me no more, but you will see me; because I live, you will live also. ²⁰In that day you will know that I am in my Father, and you in me, and I in you. ²¹He who has my commandments and keeps them, he it is who loves me; and he who loves me will be loved by my Father, and I will love him and manifest myself to him. . . . ²³And we will come to him and make our home with him."

Present in His Church

God upholds and is present to his creation all the time. As the Book of Proverbs reminds us, "The eyes of the LORD are in every place, keeping watch on the evil and the good" (15:3). But Jesus, the Divine Son of God made man, is present in a special way in the liturgy and sacraments of his Church. *Liturgy* is our worship of God through which we participate in his work of salvation. In liturgy, we worship God through signs, words, and actions. Through the Church's liturgy, Jesus invites us to participate in his great work of salvation.

Sacrosanctum Concilium, 7

"To accomplish so great a work, Christ is always present in His Church, especially in her liturgical celebrations. He is present in the sacrifice of the Mass, not only in the person of His minister, 'the same now offering, through the ministry of priests, who formerly offered himself on the cross',¹ but especially under the Eucharistic species. By His power He is present in the sacraments, so that when a man baptizes it is really Christ Himself who baptizes. He is present in His word, since it is He Himself who speaks when the holy scriptures are read in the Church. He is present, lastly, when the Church prays and sings, for He promised: 'Where two or three are gathered together in my name, there am I in the midst of them'²."

The seven sacraments of the Church are efficacious signs, instituted by Christ and entrusted to the Church, by which grace, God's divine life, is given to us (see *CCC* 1131). The seven sacraments are Baptism, Confirmation, Eucharist, Reconciliation, Anointing of the Sick, Holy Orders, and Matrimony.

Jesus is present with us in each of these sacraments in two ways.

- He is present because he is the one performing the work of the sacrament through the words and actions of the minister.
- He is present because in the sacraments he gives us grace, which is "a participation in the life of God" (*CCC* 1997). By sanctifying grace, we are spiritually alive with a share in God's own life. God is not just present *to* us; he is present *in* us. As Saint Paul said about the gift of grace, "It is no longer I who live, but Christ who lives in me" (Gal 2:20).

Medieval painting of Jesus holding the Eucharist

We call the Eucharist the Most Blessed Sacrament because it is the "'source and summit of the Christian life'³" (*CCC* 1324). The other sacraments and all other aspects of our lives as disciples of Jesus point us toward the Eucharist and find their perfection and fulfillment in the Eucharist. Why? Because the Eucharist *is* Jesus himself.

In the Eucharist, Jesus is not only present in the work he does and the grace he offers; he is *substantially* present (see *CCC* 1374). "Substance" means the full reality or essence of something. All of who Jesus is, both as God and man—Body, Blood, Soul, and Divinity—is truly and completely present in the Eucharist. What we see and taste has the physical characteristics of bread and wine, but it is *actually* Jesus, present with us, just as he promised. Jesus made this clear at the Last Supper when he instituted the Eucharist, declaring the bread and wine to be his Body and Blood (see Mt 26:26–28).

At the beginning of Matthew's Gospel, the angel declared to Saint Joseph that Jesus would be born of the Virgin Mary and would fulfill Isaiah's prophecy about Emmanuel (see 1:20–23). Jesus certainly fulfilled that prophecy during his life here on earth. But he continues to be Emmanuel throughout all of history as he remains faithfully present to his Church, above all in the sacraments. The sacraments, especially the Eucharist, are how Jesus fulfills his promise to be with us always, "even until the end of the age" (28:20).

Chapter 24 Summary

1. The Church continues Jesus' mission of salvation by making disciples of all nations in obedience to Christ's command in the Great Commission.

2. Jesus is with us always in the liturgy and sacraments of the Catholic Church.

3. The Eucharist is the source and summit of the Christian life.

Be Prepared

When Saint Peter received the outpouring of the Holy Spirit on Pentecost, he immediately began to share the Good News about Jesus with the crowds in Jerusalem, and three thousand people believed in Jesus and were baptized. Later in his life, Peter wrote a letter in which he reminded the Church that all Christians are called to evangelize, no matter what.

1 Pet 3:15

> **3** ¹⁵"Always be prepared to make a defense to any one who calls you to account for the hope that is in you, yet do it with gentleness and reverence."

Icon of Saint Peter

This call to evangelization has two parts. As Peter said, we need to be ready to "make a defense," or to explain what we believe. We need to do this bravely and strongly but also with "gentleness and reverence," meaning we need to remember that we are trying to win souls, not arguments. But being ready to explain our faith when we are asked assumes the second part of the call: our hope and joy in the Good News of salvation should make a difference in how we live. When people see this difference, they will want to know why we are different. Evangelization involves both how we live our lives and how we explain our faith.

Peter was writing to the whole Church in his letter. The call to evangelization is for all the baptized, not just for certain Christians. Each one of us has a necessary role to play in the Church's continuation of Christ's mission of salvation. We have a share in this mission by virtue of our Baptism. And one of the graces of the Sacrament of Confirmation is to give us the strength and courage to carry out this mission. Confirmation "gives us a special strength of the Holy Spirit to spread and defend the faith by word and action as true witnesses of Christ, to confess the name of Christ boldly, and never to be ashamed of the Cross" (*CCC* 1303).

We are called, and we are equipped for the mission. But this is not some extra duty that the Church adds on to all the other things we are supposed to do as Christians. Rather, it is simply the natural result of our own experience of God's love and mercy. Pope Saint Paul VI put it this way:

> The person who has been evangelized goes on to evangelize others. Here lies the test of truth, the touchstone of evangelization: it is unthinkable that a person should accept the Word and give himself to the kingdom without becoming a person who bears witness to it and proclaims it in his turn.⁴

We share the Good News about Jesus simply because the truth is too good *not* to share!

Select two verses from Matthew's Gospel that you want to memorize for the purpose of sharing the Gospel with others. Copy the references and the verses below.

Mt _____ : _____
    (Chapter)   (Verse)

_____
_____
_____

Mt _____ : _____
    (Chapter)   (Verse)

_____
_____
_____

Let Us Pray—Psalm 84

In the Old Testament, God dwelt with his people in the tabernacle in the wilderness and the Temple in Jerusalem. In the New Covenant, God is present to us in an even more powerful way through the sacraments of his Church. Psalm 84 reflects on encountering God's presence in his Temple. Praying this psalm can help us better understand what it means that God dwells with us by making our hearts his Temple now.

Ps 84:1-4, 10-12

84 ¹"How lovely is your dwelling place,
    O LORD of hosts!
²My soul longs, yes, faints
    for the courts of the LORD;
my heart and flesh sing for joy
    to the living God.
³Even the sparrow finds a home,
    and the swallow a nest for herself,
    where she may lay her young
at your altars, O LORD of hosts,
    my King and my God.
⁴Blessed are those who dwell in your house,
    ever singing your praise! . . .

¹⁰For a day in your courts is better
    than a thousand elsewhere.
I would rather be a doorkeeper in the house
    of my God
    than dwell in the tents of wickedness.
¹¹For the LORD God is a sun and shield;
    he bestows favor and honor.
No good thing does the LORD withhold
    from those who walk uprightly.
¹²O LORD of hosts,
    blessed is the man who trusts in you!

Chapter 24 Review:
Jesus, Emmanuel

1. What does the word "commission" mean? _____
   _____

2. What did Jesus command his Apostles, and the Church, to do at the Great Commission?
   _____
   _____

3. To make disciples, what are the two steps Jesus commanded the Apostles, and the Church, to do? *Hint: See chart on page 291.*
   _____
   _____

4. What is a disciple? _____
   _____

5. What does it mean to be a disciple of Jesus? _____
   _____
   _____

6. What does the word "evangelization" mean? _____
   _____

7. Through what two aspects of the Church's life is Jesus present to us in a special way?
   _____

8. The Eucharist is the _____ and _____ of the Christian life.

Eucharistic Adoration

God is present to us in many ways. But Jesus' presence in the Eucharist is totally unique. Jesus is fully present to us—Body, Blood, Soul, and Divinity. The Church refers to Jesus' presence in the Eucharist as his *Real* Presence. The *Catechism* tells us this is not because other ways of God being present are not real but because the Eucharist is "'presence in the fullest sense . . . by which Christ, God and man, makes himself wholly and entirely present'"[5] (*CCC* 1374).

Because Jesus is really and entirely present in the Eucharist, we not only show respect for the sacrament but also worship Jesus in this sacrament. One of the ways we express our belief in Christ's presence and offer him worship is through eucharistic adoration: spending time in prayer before Jesus in the Eucharist. We can do this in any Catholic church, where Jesus is present in the tabernacle, but it is especially powerful when the Blessed Sacrament is exposed for adoration in a monstrance (a special case for displaying a consecrated Host so it is visible while we pray).

Eucharistic adoration is a very special way of showing our love for God. While we can of course talk to God in prayer anytime and anywhere, it shows a greater commitment and devotion to set aside a particular time in a particular place. We are not just fitting God into our busy schedules—we are making him a priority.

Eucharistic adoration can also help us grow in the virtues of faith, hope, and love. We wouldn't adore the sacrament if we did not believe Jesus was truly present. And acts we perform because of our faith also strengthen our faith. Eucharistic adoration also helps us grow in hope because as we spend this special time in the presence of Jesus, we are reminded of his promise to remain with us always and we see how he is keeping that promise. This strengthens our hope in Jesus' ultimate promise that we will be with him in Heaven.

Finally, Eucharist adoration helps us grow in love. The best way to strengthen a friendship is to spend time together. And because Jesus is present in a unique way in this sacrament, it is a very special way to spend time with him. Many spiritual writers have connected spending time in eucharistic adoration with the Apostles keeping watch with Jesus in the Garden of Gethsemane. We show our love for Jesus during this time, and we receive his love as we sit in his presence.

Journal Reflection

How important do you think presence is to a good relationship? How can being in Jesus' Real Presence in eucharistic adoration strengthen your friendship with him?

Radical Presence, Radical Change

Read

The Eucharist is not only the sacrament of Jesus' continual presence with us but also the true food and true drink that will give us eternal life (see Jn 6:54–55). We need this spiritual nourishment even more than our bodies need physical food! The *Catechism* lists the many ways in which this awe-inspiring sacrament bears fruit in our lives. The Eucharist does the following:

- Unites us ever more closely to Christ, the principal fruit of the sacrament and the reason we call it Holy Communion (see *CCC* 1391)
- Provides essential nourishment so that we can grow in our spiritual life as it "preserves, increases, and renews the life of grace" that we received at our Baptism (*CCC* 1392)
- Washes away past venial sins and strengthens us against committing sins in the future when received worthily (see *CCC* 1393–95)
- Unites us more closely to all other members of the Church and to all those who are poor and in need (see *CCC* 1396–97)

The Eucharist is really Jesus, no matter how much we believe in it or understand it. But a greater awareness of the reality of the sacrament can prepare us for a more fruitful reception of it. The more open we are to the graces of the Eucharist, the more Jesus will transform our hearts to be like his when we receive him in this sacrament.

Reflect

Spend 5–10 minutes reflecting on the following:

- How can I approach the Eucharist with greater faith and reverence?
- Which grace or effect of the Eucharist do I feel I need the most?
- How can I be more open to this grace the next time I receive the Eucharist?

Pray

Spend a few minutes before the Most Blessed Sacrament and repeat these words from Saint Thomas Aquinas in prayer:

> O Sacrament Most Holy,
> O Sacrament Divine,
> all praise and all thanksgiving
> be every moment thine.

Act

Each day this week, ask Jesus to help you see all the ways he is present in your life. Ask him especially for a greater awareness of and love for his eucharistic presence.

LITURGICAL YEAR
Advent

Words to Know
> *Advent*
> *liturgical calendar*

Proclaiming the Good News
"Establish your hearts, for the coming of the Lord is at hand." —James 5:8

Isaiah the Prophet, Anonymous

Advent: Preparation and Expectation

The First Vocation of the Apostle Andrew, Domenichino

Celebrating Advent

Good things in life are worth waiting for. Whether waiting in line for our favorite amusement park ride, waiting for a new game to download, or waiting for Christmas, we must learn to wait patiently.

God's Chosen People of Israel had to wait patiently for centuries as God prepared them for the coming of the Messiah. God then sent his Son to take on flesh and become man. This event, known as the Incarnation, is one of our faith's greatest mysteries. The Church celebrates the mystery of the Incarnation every Christmas.

God prepared for the Incarnation through the people, events, and symbols that we read about in the Old Testament. During this time, God's people longed for the coming of the Messiah. The Church invites us to share in this longing for Jesus' coming each year during Advent. *Advent* is the liturgical season of preparation and expectation during the four weeks leading up to Christmas.

Beginning the Liturgical Year

Most societies use a calendar to mark months and seasons. Likewise, the Church has a *liturgical calendar* that marks various events in the life of Jesus and invites us to participate in and celebrate those events (i.e. Advent, Christmas, Lent, Easter, Holy Week, and Pentecost).

As we journey through the liturgical calendar, we celebrate the whole mystery of Christ's life, Death, Resurrection, and Ascension. Advent marks the Church's "new year." During Advent, we prepare to celebrate Jesus' Incarnation and Nativity at Christmas. From there, we move through Jesus' life during Ordinary Time and Lent, to his Resurrection at Easter, his Ascension, and the coming of the Holy Spirit at Pentecost. We anticipate Jesus' Second Coming with blessed hope throughout the year.

Every liturgical season invites us to enter the story of salvation history and see it as our own. Through our participation in these mysteries, we are transformed to be like Christ. For example, during the forty days of Lent, we fast and pray just as Jesus fasted and prayed for forty days in the wilderness.

During Advent, which means "to come," we identify with the people in the Old Testament who longed for the Messiah's coming. We prepare ourselves with expectation and hope for Jesus' coming.

Advent in the Liturgy

Advent is a season of "devout and expectant delight."[1] The Church's liturgical worship during Advent makes present the ancient longing of God's people for the Messiah (see *CCC* 524). The Church invites us to share in this preparation for the Savior today by (1) preparing ourselves for the Christmas celebration and (2) looking forward with joyful hope to Jesus' Second Coming.

We participate fully in Advent through the Church's liturgy and prayer:

- **Purple vestments and decorations** signify penance and preparation. On the third Sunday of Advent, known as "Gaudete" Sunday, which means "to rejoice," the priest usually wears **rose-colored vestments** at Mass. This color is a sign of joy at the nearness of Christmas.
- When we have to do without something joyful and delightful, we start to long for it. For this reason, **the Gloria**, the hymn of joy we normally sing during Mass, is not recited or sung during Advent. This inspires within us a sense of expectation and longing.
- We light one of the four candles on the **Advent wreath** each Sunday during Advent. The Advent wreath reminds us that we are waiting for Jesus, the Light of the World.
- From December 17 to 23, the Church prays the **O Antiphons**. Each antiphon is a short verse inspired by Old Testament prophecies of the Messiah and expresses longing for his coming.

The readings at Mass during Advent prepare us to live with patience and expectation:

- The **Old Testament readings** contain prophecies of the Messiah and his kingdom, often from the prophet Isaiah.
- The **New Testament readings outside the Gospel** instruct us to live with patience, hope, and expectation while preparing for Jesus' Second Coming.
- The **first week's Gospel** passage reminds us of Jesus' promise to come again to judge the living and the dead at the end of time.
- The **second and third weeks' Gospel** readings tell of John the Baptist's ministry to prepare the way of the Messiah by calling people to repentance.
- The **fourth week's Gospel** tells of the events immediately leading up to Jesus' Incarnation and Nativity.

The Lord Will Come

The readings during Advent help us understand how the season can strengthen our faith. In the reading from the Old Testament, Isaiah prophesies the miracles that the Messiah would perform.

Is 35:1-6

35 ¹The wilderness and the dry land shall be glad,
 the desert shall rejoice and blossom;
like the lily ²it shall blossom abundantly,
 and rejoice with joy and singing.
The glory of Lebanon shall be given to it,
 the majesty of Carmel and Sharon.
They shall see the glory of the LORD,
 the majesty of our God.
³Strengthen the weak hands,
 and make firm the feeble knees.
⁴Say to those who are of a fearful heart,
 "Be strong, fear not!
Behold, your God
 will come with vengeance,
with the recompense of God.
 He will come and save you."
⁵Then the eyes of the blind shall be opened,
 and the ears of the deaf unstopped;
⁶then shall the lame man leap like a deer,
 and the tongue of the mute sing for joy.

God spoke through the Old Testament prophets to prepare his people for the Messiah's coming. God's words inspired hope and expectation in the people.

Now read Matthew 11:2–11 on page 9.

At every Mass, the Gospel reading fulfills what was said or done in the First Reading from the Old Testament. In this passage from Matthew's Gospel, Jesus revealed that John the Baptist was like the prophets of old. He prepared the way for Christ. John's mission was to usher in the Messiah's kingdom by calling people to repent and turn away from their sins.

Jesus also revealed that he fulfilled the prophecy in the reading from Isaiah 35. These readings show that our Savior, Jesus Christ, fulfilled God's promise in the Old Testament to save us from sin.

Waiting Patiently for the Lord

The New Testament reading comes from the Letter of Saint James, which encourages us to practice patience as we wait for Jesus' Second Coming at the end of time.

Saint James the Less, Pompeo Girolamo Batoni

Jas 5:7-10

5 ⁷Be patient, therefore, brethren, until the coming of the Lord. Behold, the farmer waits for the precious fruit of the earth, being patient over it until it receives the early and the late rain. ⁸You also be patient. Establish your hearts, for the coming of the Lord is at hand. ⁹Do not grumble, brethren, against one another, that you may not be judged; behold, the Judge is standing at the doors. ¹⁰As an example of suffering and patience, brethren, take the prophets who spoke in the name of the Lord.

As Christians, we believe if we persevere in charity and obedience, we have nothing to fear at Christ's Second Coming. The Church gives us the liturgical season of Advent as a time to prepare ourselves for this moment with joyful hope, patience, and expectation.

The Last Judgment, Michelangelo

Patience and Perseverance

In the passage from James 5:7–10, God encourages us to live with patience and perseverance in faith. There are several ways we can put this advice into practice in our lives.

For example, if we want to practice more patience, we can adopt the tradition of using an Advent calendar. During Advent, some families purchase an inexpensive calendar that counts down the days of Advent till Christmas. Each day on the calendar usually contains a short Scripture passage for prayer and reflection.

How can the Advent calendar help you practice patience?

_____
_____
_____

Other examples of practicing patience can come before and during Christmas. While we wait with joyful expectation for the opportunity to open our Christmas presents, we can grow in patience. We can focus more on making and giving gifts than receiving them during this time. By focusing on others, we tend not to allow so much time to think of ourselves and what we may receive at Christmas.

Which person in your life can you give a gift to this year, even if you normally don't?

_____

Saint James also tells us to stop grumbling, or complaining, about other people (see 5:9). This Advent, we should avoid situations where we gossip about others. We may be tempted to grow angry at our siblings or family members during Christmas for whatever reason, but God calls us to exercise patience with others instead.

Who is one person with whom you struggle to be patient? What can you do to avoid grumbling or being angry toward this person?

_____
_____
_____

Liturgical Year: Advent

Saint James also calls all Christians to look to the prophets as examples of perseverance in suffering. The prophets were often persecuted for speaking the truth and obeying God's will. But they suffered with perseverance, always trusting God's will and plan for them.

We all must prepare ourselves for persecution, even if we are not greatly persecuted like the prophets. One way we can learn to suffer with perseverance is by practicing fasting.

Fasting is a way in which we can show our repentance to God. We may consider fasting for a few days during Advent. Perhaps we abstain from eating meat on Fridays during Advent. Or maybe we fast from sweets or watching videos online one of the weeks of the season.

When we fast, we long for and joyfully anticipate enjoying what we have sacrificed. For example, if you give up your favorite app for a few days, you will long to use it again. Fasting also helps us become less attached to earthly joys so we can find lasting joy in eternal, heavenly things.

Fasting helps us get in the right frame of mind for Advent. It can remind us that we long for the upcoming Christmas celebration as we do the eternal joy of everlasting life with God in Heaven.

How can fasting help us learn to suffer with perseverance?

_____

_____

_____

Let Us Pray—"O Come, O Come, Emmanuel"

"O Come, O Come, Emmanuel" is an ancient hymn inspired by the O Antiphons and recalls Old Testament prophecies about the Messiah's great deeds of power. As we pray by singing this hymn, we ask the Holy Spirit to direct our minds and hearts to the true meaning of Advent, preparing with joyful hope for Jesus' coming in glory.

1. O come, O come, Emmanuel,
   And ransom captive Israel,
   That mourns in lonely exile here,
   Until the Son of God appear.

Refrain: Rejoice! Rejoice! Emmanuel
   Shall come to thee, O Israel.

2. O come, thou Wisdom from on high,
   Who ord'rest all things mightily;
   To us the path of knowledge show,
   And teach us in her ways to go. (Refrain)

3. O come, O come, thou Lord of might,
   Who to thy tribes on Sinai's height
   In ancient times didst give the Law
   In cloud and majesty and awe. (Refrain)

4. O come, thou Rod of Jesse's tree,
   Free them from Satan's tyranny
   That trust thy mighty pow'r to save,
   And give them vict'ry o'er the grave. (Refrain)

A Time of Giving

Read

"It is well with the man who deals generously and lends, who conducts his affairs with justice" (Ps 112:5).

Advent is an exciting time of year as we prepare for the Birth of Christ on Christmas. Jesus' coming into the world is a truly wonderful and awesome gift! We celebrate the gift of his Birth by giving gifts to others. We are most often excited to receive presents from others, but sadly, many young people and families cannot afford gifts and presents.

For this reason, many churches have a Giving Tree somewhere in the church. This tree often is decorated with paper ornaments listing items that can be purchased for families who have less money. Members of the church are encouraged to take an ornament and purchase the items for the families.

Churches and other charitable organizations also have toy drives and collection boxes where you can donate toys and gifts for families in need. You can support these drives by donating unused or gently used items you no longer need or want.

Reflect

Spend 5–10 minutes reflecting on the following:

- What items do I have that I no longer use or need?
- Is there someone I know who could use these items?
- What other ways can I help those in need in my community this Advent and Christmas?

Pray

Turn to the Lord in faith and pray:

> Jesus, the Light of the World, as we celebrate your Birth, may we begin to see the world in the light of the understanding you give us. As you chose the lowly, the outcasts, and the poor to receive the greatest news the world has ever known, so may we worship you in meekness of heart. May we also remember our brothers and sisters less fortunate than ourselves in this season of giving. Amen.

Act

This Advent, contribute to a Giving Tree or charitable organization by offering some of your own money to put toward requested items. Or, on your Christmas list, ask for a gift to be given to someone in need on your behalf.

LITURGICAL YEAR

Epiphany

Words to Know

> *epiphany*

> *Magi*

> *Solemnity of the Epiphany*

Proclaiming the Good News

"Arise, shine; for your light has come, and the glory of the LORD has risen upon you." —Isaiah 60:1

Adoration of the Magi, Federico Zuccari

307

Jesus, Light of the World

A Light Shining in Darkness

Imagine sitting in a dark room. There is no light, so you cannot see around you or find the way out. You reach out for a light switch, your phone, or any source of light that will help you see, but you cannot find anything. You need help out of the darkness.

Sacred Scripture uses the image of darkness to represent the world and mankind before the Incarnation. Before the Messiah, humanity lived in the shadow of sin and ignorance. Many people chose to sin and wounded their relationship with God. They were unaware that God wanted them to love and forgive others as he loves and forgives. Humanity also had not received the grace of the Holy Spirit to obey God's commandments perfectly.

The prophet Isaiah foretold of the Messiah's coming, saying, "The people who walked in darkness have seen a great light; those who dwelt in a land of deep darkness, on them has light shined" (9:2).

The Church proclaims Isaiah 9:2 as part of the Old Testament reading at Mass during the night on Christmas. Even Jesus referred to himself as light: "I am the light of the world; he who follows me will not walk in darkness, but will have the light of life" (Jn 8:12).

At the Incarnation, the Eternal Word of God, the Second Divine Person of the Blessed Trinity, became man while remaining fully God. Jesus is the long-awaited Messiah and Savior. The Church acknowledges that Jesus is the Light of the World. We use this title for Jesus because he came to cast out the darkness of sin and ignorance by revealing the truth of God's plan so that we may know the path to Heaven.

The Solemnity of the Epiphany

Christmas is the liturgical season when the Church remembers and celebrates the Incarnation and Jesus' Nativity. The liturgical season of Christmas lasts longer than just one day. It extends for multiple weeks after Christmas Day. The Christmas season ends with the Feast of the Baptism of the Lord. Near the end of the Christmas season, the Church celebrates the Solemnity of the Epiphany.

The *Solemnity of the Epiphany* is the liturgical feast that celebrates the mystery of Jesus' manifestation as the Messiah and Savior of all peoples. On this day, we offer thanksgiving to God for sending his Beloved Son to bring us healing and forgiveness for our sins through grace. He opened the way to salvation for us through his life, Death, Resurrection, and Ascension.

A solemnity is the highest rank of a liturgical feast on the Church's liturgical calendar. There are fourteen solemnities in the Church's calendar. Epiphany is one of these days. The word "*epiphany*" means "a manifestation or revealing of God."

On the Solemnity of the Epiphany, we commemorate events in Jesus' life that revealed him as the Messiah. The Church remembers Jesus' baptism in the Jordan and his miracle of turning water into wine at the Wedding Feast at Cana in her liturgical prayer on this day. But the primary event the Church commemorates on the Epiphany is the wise men from the East coming to adore Jesus after his Birth. Each of these events manifests Jesus as the Messiah of Israel, Son of God, and Savior of all people (see *CCC* 528).

A Light to the Nations

The Scripture readings at Mass on the Solemnity of the Epiphany teach us to see and believe that Jesus is the Messiah and Savior of all people. The Old Testament reading comes from the prophet Isaiah. God spoke through Isaiah to prepare for the Messiah's coming:

Is 60:1-6

60 ¹Arise, shine; for your light has come,
and the glory of the LORD has risen upon you.
²For behold, darkness shall cover the earth,
and thick darkness the peoples;
but the LORD will arise upon you,
and his glory will be seen upon you.
³And nations shall walk by your light,
and kings in the brightness of your rising.
⁴Lift up your eyes round about, and see;
they all gather together, they come to you;
your sons shall come from far,
and your daughters shall be carried in the arms.
⁵Then you shall see and be radiant,
your heart shall thrill and rejoice;
because the abundance of the sea shall be turned to you,
the wealth of the nations shall come to you.
⁶A multitude of camels shall cover you,
the young camels of Midian and Ephah;
all those from Sheba shall come.
They shall bring gold and frankincense,
and shall proclaim the praise of the LORD.

This prophecy speaks of the Messiah as a "light" (60:1). This "light" would drive out the darkness covering the earth and lead all nations and kings to God's eternal dwelling place with mankind. Jesus Christ, the Light of the World, casts out the darkness of sin. Through Jesus' Death and Resurrection, we receive new life in the Holy Spirit. In the sacraments, the Holy Spirit gives us grace that cleanses us from sin and makes us holy and worthy of the gift of eternal life.

Jesus also casts out the darkness of ignorance. In him, the truth of God's loving plan to unite all people to himself in the Church has been fully revealed and accomplished. If we obey Jesus and live according to the truth he has revealed, he will bless us with abundant life and joy.

Detail from *Adoration of the Shepherds*, Philippe de Champaigne

This prophecy of Isaiah also foretold that when the Messiah would come, Gentiles—people who are not Israelites—would join God's Chosen People in offering him gifts and also in worshipping him. These Gentile nations would bring gifts of gold and frankincense, a type of incense that creates sweet-smelling smoke when burned.

Our King and Lawgiver,
Apse Mosaic of Saint Pudenziana

The King of All Nations

Read Matthew 2:1–12 on page 1.

At Mass on the Solemnity of the Epiphany, we hear from the passage of the Gospel of Matthew that tells of the fulfillment of Isaiah's prophecy. Matthew records that wise men, led by the light of a star, journeyed from a distant Gentile nation to offer gifts of gold, frankincense, and myrrh to Jesus, the Messiah.

These wise men, also known as the *Magi*, sought truth by studying the stars and writings of other religions, including God's Word in the Old Testament.

The Magi sought the one prophesied about in the Old Testament who would be the king of all nations. These wise men, who looked for truth in the stars and various religions, discovered by God's grace the fullness of truth in Jesus, who drives away the darkness of sin and ignorance. With faith and humility, the Magi recognized and worshipped Jesus as the Son of God and Savior of the world.

In Matthew's Gospel, the Magi are the first Gentiles to recognize the kingship of Jesus. The Magi represent all people and nations outside of Israel who accept Jesus and his teachings with faith. This event revealed that all nations who believe in Jesus as the Messiah, as the Magi did, can join the family God began with the patriarchs Abraham, Isaac, and Jacob.

Offering Our Gifts

The Magi offered gifts of gold, frankincense, and myrrh as sacrifices of worship to Jesus. The Church sees that each of these gifts reveals certain aspects of the mystery of Jesus' Incarnation and mission as the Savior of the world.

- *Gold* is a gift usually given to royalty. It symbolizes that Jesus is the *King* of the Universe.

- *Frankincense* is used in the worship of God. When we light incense, it releases a sweet-smelling smoke that floats up to God. It symbolizes that Jesus is *fully God*.

- *Myrrh* is an ointment used to anoint bodies at burial. It signifies that, while remaining fully God, Jesus became *fully human* and offered himself as the sacrifice for our sins on the Cross.

Which of these three gifts reveals who Jesus is to you personally and why?

_____

_____

According to Pope Saint Gregory the Great, the Magi's gifts represent spiritual gifts we can offer to Christ in our daily lives.[1]

- *Gold* symbolizes *Christ's wisdom*, which shines in us through grace. In Baptism, the Holy Spirit enables us to live with wisdom, meaning we can see the truth of God's purpose and plan in the world.

  We can offer this wisdom back to Christ as a gift to him by using wisdom as he wants us to use it. For example, we can help others see the truth of God's plan by assisting them in understanding Scripture. We can also offer our wisdom as a gift to Christ by advising those doubting their faith.

  Describe one situation in your life in which you can offer Christ's wisdom as a gift to him.

  _____

  _____

- *Frankincense* is symbolic of our *prayer and adoration* to Christ. When we see this sweet-smelling smoke rising to Heaven, we imagine our prayers, in which we raise our hearts and minds to God, rising to God's throne.

Liturgical Year: Epiphany

Write a prayer of adoration showing you are raising your heart and mind to God.

_____

_____

- *Myrrh* is symbolic of our *daily self-sacrifices*. Jesus offered himself as the perfect sacrifice to take away the sins of the world. In Baptism, we are united with Jesus in his Death and Resurrection. Because of this unity with Christ, we can unite our sacrifices with Jesus' perfect sacrifice.

  No matter how small our sacrifice—for example, giving up chocolate, helping a family member instead of playing video games, or donating to a charity—we can unite it with Jesus' sacrifice. God looks with favor on the sacrifices we unite with his Son's perfect sacrifice. In response, he pours out grace in our lives or in the life of someone else for whom we pray.

  List three sacrifices you will offer to Christ to show your love for him and others.

  1. _____

  2. _____

  3. _____

Let Us Pray—Psalm 72

Jesus is the Messiah, the Light of the World, and the King of All Nations. The Church prays Psalm 72 at Mass on the Solemnity of the Epiphany. As we pray the following verses from Psalm 72, let us approach our King with humility, reverence, and love, trusting that he will light our way on the path to salvation:

Ps 72:1-2, 7-8, 10-13

72 ¹Give the king your justice, O God,
 and your righteousness to the royal son!
²May he judge your people with righteousness,
 and your poor with justice! . . .
⁷In his days may righteousness flourish,
 and peace abound, till the moon be no more!
⁸May he have dominion from sea to sea,
 and from the River to the ends of the earth! . . .
¹⁰May the kings of Tarshish and of the isles
 render him tribute,
 may the kings of Sheba and Seba bring gifts!
¹¹May all kings fall down before him,
 all nations serve him!
¹²For he delivers the needy when he calls,
 the poor and him who has no helper.
¹³He has pity on the weak and the needy,
 and saves the lives of the needy.

Arranging Our Schedules

Read

The Church's liturgical calendar unfolds the Paschal Mystery. What do you think is the greatest and most central celebration in the liturgical calendar?

Easter is the greatest celebration of the liturgical calendar. It is known as the "Feast of feasts" and the "Solemnity of solemnities" (*CCC* 1169). But every year, the date of Easter is different. The dates of many of our liturgical feasts also change from year to year. The dates for feasts such as Ash Wednesday, Ascension, and Pentecost, and seasons such as Lent and Advent, all depend on the date of Easter Sunday.

One ancient tradition in the Church connects these dates to the Solemnity of the Epiphany. In ancient times, Catholics learned the dates of Easter and all these other feasts and seasons at Mass on Epiphany Sunday. Traditionally, the priest or someone else at Mass proclaimed an announcement called the Epiphany proclamation after the Gospel reading.

Some parishes still keep this tradition. In this announcement, the dates for Ash Wednesday, Lent, Easter Sunday, Ascension, Pentecost, the Solemnity of the Most Holy Body and Blood of Christ (Corpus Christi Sunday), and the First Sunday of Advent are announced to the congregation.[2]

Reflect

Spend 5–10 minutes reflecting on the following:

- Why is knowing liturgical dates important?
- How can knowing these dates ahead of time influence how I arrange my schedule?
- What can I do to make sure my family and I know the dates of these feasts and seasons?

Pray

Pray this prayer from the Roman Missal:

> May the splendor of your majesty, O Lord, we pray, shed its light upon our hearts, that we may pass through the shadows of this world and reach the brightness of our eternal home. Through our Lord Jesus Christ, your Son, who lives and reigns with you in the unity of the Holy Spirit, one God, for ever and ever.[3]

Act

Find out the dates of the feasts announced in the Epiphany proclamation. Add these dates to your personal calendar and your family's paper or digital calendar. Add any other dates important to you, such as other solemnities, saint feast days, or other liturgical seasons. Plan ways to join the Church in celebrating these feasts and seasons as a family.

Liturgical Year: Epiphany

LITURGICAL YEAR

Lent

Words to Know

> *almsgiving*

> *fasting*

> *prayer*

Proclaiming the Good News

"Take your share of suffering for the gospel in the power of God, who saved us and called us with a holy calling, not in virtue of our works but in virtue of his own purpose and the grace which he gave us in Christ Jesus ages ago."
—2 Timothy 1:8–9

The First Adam and the Last Adam

Detail from *Adam, Eve, and the Forbidden Fruit*, Notre Dame de Paris Cathedral

Three Disordered Desires

God created Adam and Eve in his image and likeness. He created them to share in his own divine life. God commanded them not to eat from the Tree of the Knowledge of Good and Evil. Soon, however, Adam and Eve were tempted by Satan, who approached them as a serpent. He persuaded them to disobey God's command and reject his love and friendship. Satan successfully tempted Eve to eat from the Tree of the Knowledge of Good and Evil.

Gen 3:6-7

3 ⁶When the woman saw that the tree was good for food, and that it was a delight to the eyes, and that the tree was to be desired to make one wise, she took of its fruit and ate; and she also gave some to her husband, and he ate. ⁷Then the eyes of both were opened, and they knew that they were naked; and they sewed fig leaves together and made themselves aprons.

Adam and Eve disobeyed God and committed the Original Sin. This sin wounded our human nature. One effect of this wounded human nature is concupiscence, the inclination to sin. Because of concupiscence, every human person experiences disordered desires for pleasure called lust. Genesis says that the Tree of the Knowledge of Good and Evil was "good for food," "a delight to the eyes," and "desired to make one wise." According to Saint John, these three temptations relate to three common disordered desires.

1 Jn 2:15-17

2 ¹⁵Do not love the world or the things in the world. If any one loves the world, love for the Father is not in him. ¹⁶For all that is in the world, the lust of the flesh and the lust of the eyes and the pride of life, is not of the Father but is of the world. ¹⁷And the world passes away, and the lust of it; but he who does the will of God abides for ever.

In other words, we may be tempted by disordered desires for *bodily pleasures* ("lust of the flesh"), for *possessing created things* ("lust of the eyes"), and for *loving ourselves* above God and others ("pride of life"). Every human person must combat these three temptations with the help of God's grace.

Three Temptations in Eden *Genesis 3:6*	Threefold Lust *1 John 2:16*	Three Temptations
"Good for food"	"Lust of the flesh"	Bodily pleasures
"A delight to the eyes"	"Lust of the eyes"	Possessions, wealth
"Desired to make one wise"	"Pride of life"	Pride

Jesus, the New Adam

At his Incarnation, the Divine Son of God took to himself our human nature while remaining fully divine. Jesus is the New Adam, whose mission was to redeem us from sin and bring mankind healing from the wounds of Original Sin. Jesus came to save man from all sin and from the three disordered desires that lead to sin. Saint Paul described Jesus' mission as the New Adam in his Letter to the Romans:

Rom 5:12-14, 17-18

> **5** ¹²Therefore as sin came into the world through one man and death through sin, and so death spread to all men because all men sinned—¹³sin indeed was in the world before the law was given, but sin is not counted where there is no law. ¹⁴Yet death reigned from Adam to Moses, even over those whose sins were not like the transgression of Adam, who was a type of the one who was to come. . . .
>
> ¹⁷If, because of one man's trespass, death reigned through that one man, much more will those who receive the abundance of grace and the free gift of righteousness reign in life through the one man Jesus Christ.
>
> ¹⁸Then as one man's trespass led to condemnation for all men, so one man's act of righteousness leads to acquittal and life for all men.

Adam's disobedience brought sin and death into the world. Saint Paul noted that this Original Sin led to "condemnation for all men" (5:18). In contrast to Adam's disobedience, Jesus was perfectly obedient to God the Father, above all in his Paschal Mystery. Jesus' "act of righteousness" (5:18) led to grace, life, and acquittal for all his faithful.

Overcoming Temptation

Victory over Satan

Just as Adam and Eve were tempted by Satan in the Garden of Eden, the New Adam was also tempted. Satan came to Jesus in the wilderness and tempted him. Jesus had to combat the same three temptations as Adam and Eve: lust of the flesh, lust of the eyes, and pride of life. Where they failed, he succeeded.

Read Matthew 4:1–11 on page 2.

Satan offered Jesus what was "good for food," "a delight to the eyes," and "desired to make one wise." The demand that he turn stones into bread tempted Jesus with the disordered desire for bodily pleasures ("lust of the flesh"). The action of falling from the Temple tempted Jesus to prove his Divine Sonship by a miraculous display of power ("pride of life"). The promise of all the kingdoms of the world tempted Jesus to give in to a disordered desire for possessions ("lust of the eyes").

Jesus did not give in to these temptations. His responses counteracted the three disordered desires of our wounded human nature. Man lives by God's Word, not by bread alone (see Mt 4:4). God is never to be tempted, especially not for the purposes of pride. God alone is worthy of worship—not the self, not possessions, and certainly not Satan. In these replies, Jesus undid the sin of Adam, who gave in to these temptations. Jesus showed that we overcome these three disordered desires by remaining obedient to God in the face of temptation.

The Temptation of Christ by the Devil, fresco, 12th century

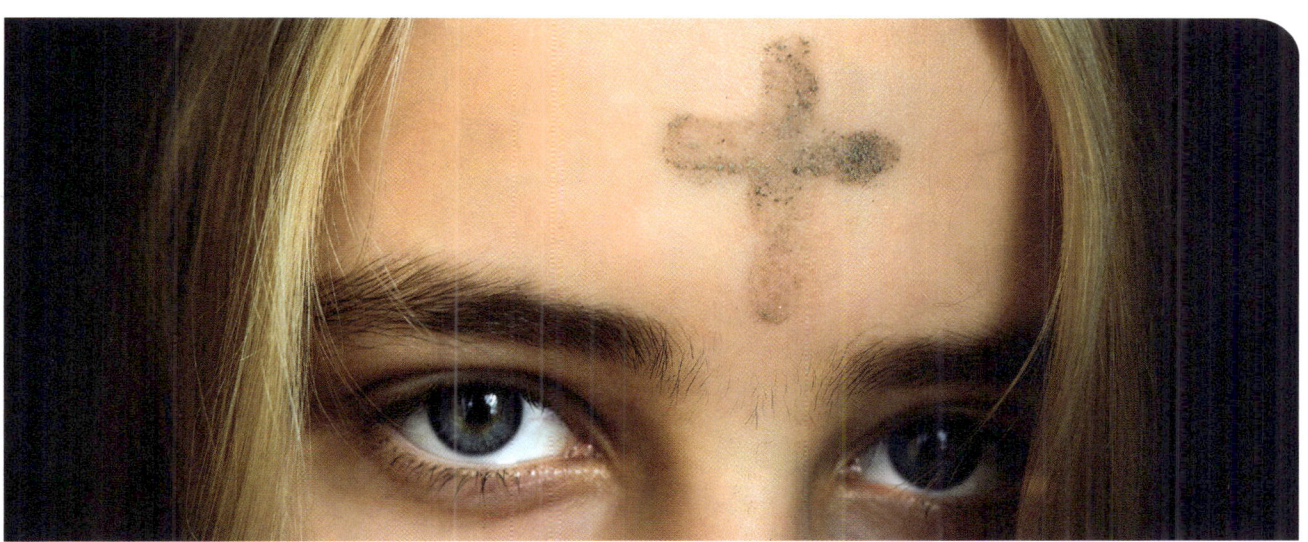

Fasting, Almsgiving, and Prayer

In his Sermon on the Mount, Jesus taught his disciples three spiritual acts to help overcome the three disordered desires that belong to our wounded human nature.

Read Matthew 6:1–18 on pages 4–5.

Jesus teaches us to practice fasting, almsgiving, and prayer.

- *Fasting* is when we intentially limit or keep from eating and drinking as a way to grow closer to God. We also may fast from other things we enjoy to show our love for God and to grow closer to him.

- *Almsgiving* is the practice of performing charitable acts for others, particularly giving money or other possessions to the poor.

- *Prayer* is the lifting up of our minds and hearts to God by listening and talking to him. The goal of all prayer is union with God.

Fasting, almsgiving, and prayer combat our disordered desires. By fasting, we counter the lust of the flesh. Through almsgiving, we become detached from our worldly possessions and oppose the lust of the eyes. Through prayer, we humble ourselves and counter the pride of life.

Lent is the liturgical season of forty days of fasting, almsgiving, and prayer. By performing these three virtuous actions, we enter into the wilderness with Christ to combat the same temptations that both he and our first parents did. Through grace, God uses our acts of fasting, almsgiving, and prayer to sanctify us. These actions prepare us to celebrate the Easter season, in which we celebrate Christ's Resurrection and our share in his victory over temptation, sin, and death.

Lent: Participation in Redemption

In his Sermon on the Mount, Jesus taught about how those who want to be a part of his new kingdom should live. To live as members of the Kingdom of God, we must continue to repent from sin and live according to the New Law with the help of God's grace. If we live according to Jesus' law of love, we allow the seed of God's grace given to us in Baptism to grow. God's grace sanctifies us and orders our desires to virtue and holiness rather than to sin and evil. We live according to Jesus' New Law and cooperate with God's grace by performing actions of fasting, almsgiving, and prayer.

Jesus used the word "when" to direct his disciples on how often to perform these virtuous actions. How often do you fast, give alms, and pray?

_____
_____
_____

Jesus mentioned that the virtuous actions he described should be done "in secret." How can you do these spiritual acts without drawing attention to yourself?

_____
_____
_____
_____

In the past, what obstacles have you encountered when fasting, giving alms, and praying during Lent?

_____
_____
_____
_____

What areas of your life related to fasting, almsgiving, and prayer need attention?

_____

_____

_____

_____

This week in prayer, make at least one resolution for each virtuous action of Lent. Plan when, where, how, and how often to carry them out.

Let Us Pray—Psalm 51

The Church prays Psalm 51 at Mass during Lent. In this psalm, we express sorrow and repentance for our sins. By praying these words, we also express hope in God's merciful love and his abundant grace that delivers us from temptation and sin.

Ps 51:1, 3–6, 12–13, 17

51 ¹Have mercy on me, O God,
according to your merciful love;
according to your abundant mercy blot out
my transgressions. . . .
³For I know my transgressions,
and my sin is ever before me.
⁴Against you, you only, have I sinned
and done that which is evil in your sight,
so that you are justified in your sentence
and blameless in your judgment.
⁵Behold, I was brought forth in iniquity,
and in sin did my mother conceive me.

⁶Behold, you desire truth in the inward being;
therefore teach me wisdom in my secret
heart. . . .
¹²Restore to me the joy of your salvation,
and uphold me with a willing spirit.
¹³Then I will teach transgressors your ways,
and sinners will return to you. . . .
¹⁷The sacrifice acceptable to God is a broken
spirit;
a broken and contrite heart, O God, you
will not despise.

Intentional Fasting

Read

Fasting is one of the primary exercises of the Lenten season, and it is a powerful way of redirecting our hearts and minds to God through disciplining our bodies. Often, we can eat or drink too much and feel bloated or lethargic. We might also consume something that puts us in an unstable mental state. Other times, we can become obsessed with looking a certain way, to the point of stressing about eating anything at all.

When we become more concerned about the goods of the body than the goods of the soul, we experience disorder and disharmony. An unhealthy focus on the goods of the body draws us away from spiritual goods, like performing works of charity and growing in our relationship with God. As we fast, we can repair this disorder and grow closer to God by refocusing our desires. Even small acts like giving up desserts can start this process. Fasting requires self-restraint and attentiveness that in turn support a vibrant and disciplined prayer life.

Reflect

Spend 5–10 minutes reflecting on the following:

- How is my relationship with food and drink? Do I eat or drink too much? Do I eat or drink too eagerly? Am I too particular? Do I avoid eating for the sake of appearance?
- What other good am I overfocused on? Is it appearance, possessions, reputation, social life, etc.?
- What are two good things that I value more than I should? How can I change my relationship with these to allow for more time for prayer?

Pray

Spend time in prayer before the Blessed Sacrament and reflect on how you see Jesus, your dependence on him, and his love for you. Ask for the grace to focus on both spiritual and physical matters in the proper balance.

Act

This week, fast from one food or drink and one other physical good (such as hot showers, extra time on appearance, social media posts/scrolling) and use the time to say a quick prayer asking for the grace to prioritize God and his will.

LITURGICAL YEAR

Easter

Words to Know

> *spiritual body*

Proclaiming the Good News

"Do you not know that all of us who have been baptized into Christ Jesus were baptized into his death? We were buried therefore with him by baptism into death, so that as Christ was raised from the dead by the glory of the Father, we too might walk in newness of life." —Romans 6:3–4

The Supper at Emmaus, Caravaggio

Jesus' Resurrection

The Prophet Ezekiel, Pietro Gagliardi

The Promise of God's Spirit

At the time of the Babylonian Exile, the Lord promised his people that they would be delivered from their exile and given a fresh start. He delivered this message of hope through the prophet Ezekiel:

> Ezek 36:24-28
>
> **36** ²⁴For I will take you from the nations, and gather you from all the countries, and bring you into your own land. ²⁵I will sprinkle clean water upon you, and you shall be clean from all your uncleannesses, and from all your idols I will cleanse you. ²⁶A new heart I will give you, and a new spirit I will put within you; and I will take out of your flesh the heart of stone and give you a heart of flesh. ²⁷And I will put my spirit within you, and cause you to walk in my statutes and be careful to observe my ordinances. ²⁸You shall dwell in the land which I gave to your fathers; and you shall be my people, and I will be your God.

The Church proclaims this reading each year during the Easter Vigil. The Easter Vigil is the most solemn celebration of the liturgical year. It is celebrated on the evening of Holy Saturday, the day before Easter Sunday. During this liturgy, the Church celebrates Christ's Resurrection and receives new members into the Church through the sacraments of initiation—Baptism, Confirmation, and the Holy Eucharist. This reading from the prophet Ezekiel helps prepare us to hear again the Good News of Jesus' Resurrection, which makes possible the gift of the Holy Spirit to all the baptized.

The Man of Heaven

Jesus' Resurrection was an actual event that took place in history. The disciples' discouragement at Jesus' Death and their initial doubts about his rising help attest to the truth of their insistence that Jesus died and rose. These men were willing to die rather than deny Jesus' Resurrection from the dead. The New Testament contains a variety of evidence that attests to Jesus' Resurrection, including the discovery of the empty tomb as well as the Risen Lord's appearances to Mary Magdalene, the other disciples, and even five hundred witnesses at one time (see 1 Cor 15:6). As the *Catechism* summarizes, "The mystery of Christ's resurrection is a real event, with manifestations that were historically verified" (*CCC* 639).

After his Resurrection, Jesus appeared glorified. His body was still the same body born of the Virgin Mary, which hung on the Cross and was laid in the tomb. But Jesus' resurrected body was changed; it was a spiritual body. A *spiritual body* is a human body that is incorruptible because it is enlivened by God's own Holy Spirit. Consider what is unusual and remarkable about Jesus' resurrected body in John's account of one of the Risen Lord's appearances.

The Resurrection, Jan Boeckhorst

Jn 20:19–20

20 ¹⁹On the evening of that day, the first day of the week, the doors being shut where the disciples were, for fear of the Jews, Jesus came and stood among them and said to them, "Peace be with you." ²⁰When he had said this, he showed them his hands and his side. Then the disciples were glad when they saw the Lord.

Jesus still had the wounds of the Crucifixion, revealing that this body was not a totally new body. It was the same body he had on earth but was now glorified. Jesus could appear in a room with locked doors. He no longer was bound by the rules of space or time in the same way.

Our Resurrection

Saint Paul the Apostle

Our Glorified Bodies

Faced with this magnificent reality, Saint Paul wondered about our own resurrection. He described how our bodies will be transformed to become like Christ's when we, too, are raised from the dead at the Last Judgment.

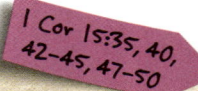

1 Cor 15:35, 40, 42-45, 47-50

15 ³⁵But some one will ask, "How are the dead raised? With what kind of body do they come?" . . . ⁴⁰There are celestial bodies and there are terrestrial bodies; but the glory of the celestial is one, and the glory of the terrestrial is another. . . .
⁴²So it is with the resurrection of the dead. What is sown is perishable, what is raised is imperishable. ⁴³It is sown in dishonor, it is raised in glory. It is sown in weakness, it is raised in power. ⁴⁴It is sown a physical body, it is raised a spiritual body. If there is a physical body, there is also a spiritual body. ⁴⁵Thus it is written, "The first man Adam became a living soul"; the last Adam became a life-giving spirit. . . .
⁴⁷The first man was from the earth, a man of dust; the second man is from heaven. ⁴⁸As was the man of dust, so are those who are of the dust; and as is the man of heaven, so are those who are of heaven. ⁴⁹Just as we have borne the image of the man of dust, we shall also bear the image of the man of heaven. ⁵⁰I tell you this, brethren: flesh and blood cannot inherit the kingdom of God, nor does the perishable inherit the imperishable.

As with Christ, our weak, dishonorable bodies will be made strong and glorious. Had Christ not come to raise us from the dead, our bodies would return to dust, as our first father Adam's did. This would be the end of our bodies. But because of Jesus' Resurrection, our bodies will rise again. They will resemble the "man of heaven," Jesus, whose image and likeness we bear. By his Resurrection, Christ gives us a share in his eternal life. In some mysterious way, as with Christ, we will still have our bodies, but these same bodies will be glorified to become spiritual bodies.

After we die and are raised with Christ, the image and likeness of God will shine through with greater clarity. We will pass beyond "flesh and blood," which "cannot inherit the kingdom of God," and will be renewed into that which is "imperishable," or unending.

A Foretaste of the Resurrection

This mystery of Christ's Resurrection from the dead is the source of the Church's joy during Easter. Easter is the most important of all Christian feasts. On Easter Sunday, the Church celebrates the day Jesus rose from the dead (the Sunday after Good Friday), knowing that the powers of sin and death have been defeated. The fifty days following are the Easter season. Throughout this season, all Christians are to give thanks to Jesus for his Death and Resurrection and rejoice with the sure hope that one day we will share in the eternal glories of Heaven with our Savior.

We already experience a foretaste of the joy of the resurrection of the dead every time we go to Mass. As the *Catechism* teaches, drawing upon the great wisdom of Saint Irenaeus, "Our participation in the Eucharist already gives us a foretaste of Christ's transfiguration of our bodies: 'Just as bread that comes from the earth, after God's blessing has been invoked upon it, is no longer ordinary bread, but Eucharist, formed of two things, the one earthly and the other heavenly: so too our bodies, which partake of the Eucharist, are no longer corruptible, but possess the hope of resurrection'" (*CCC* 1000).

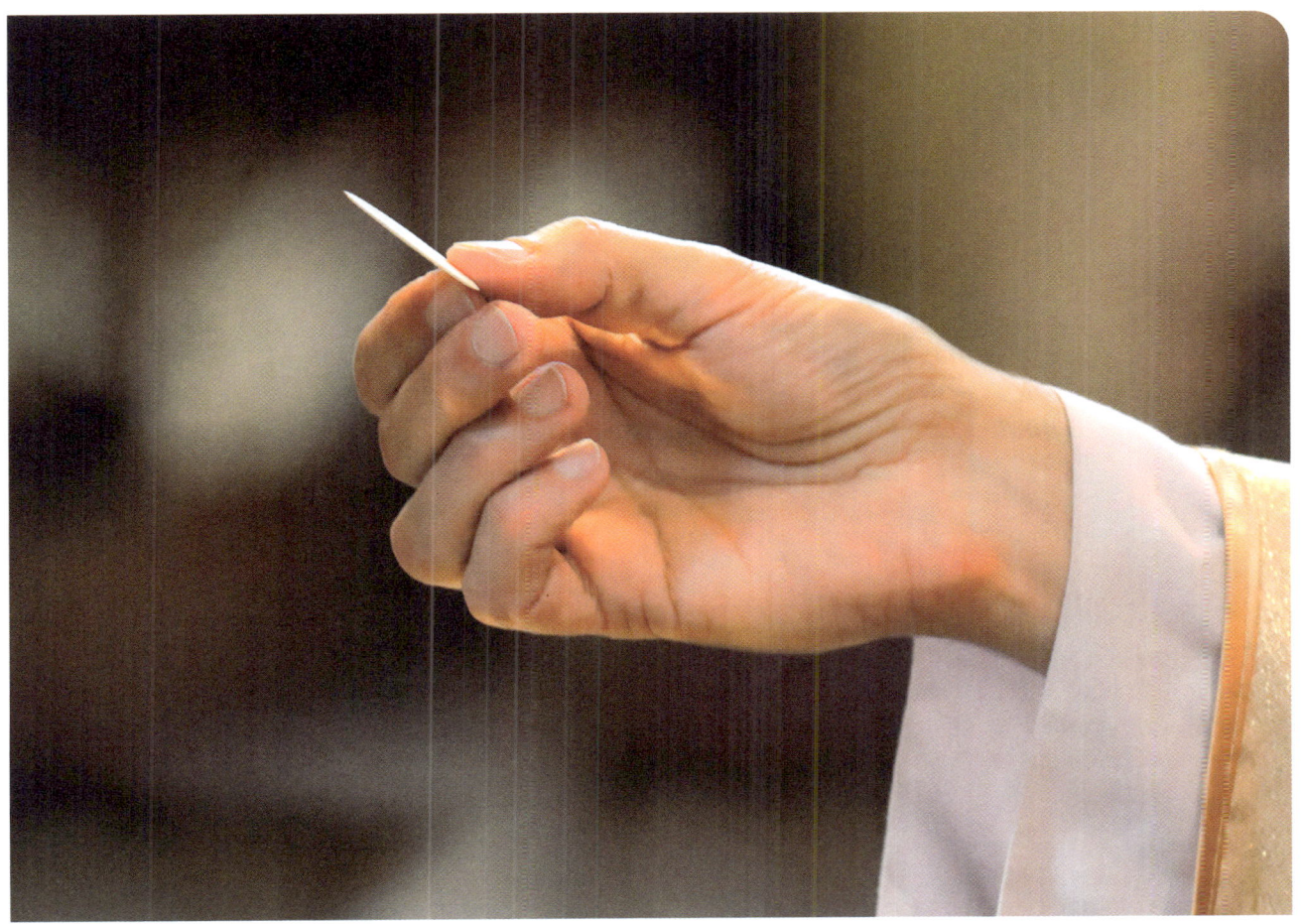

Baptized into Christ's Death

We know that we are to be conformed to the "man of heaven," Jesus Christ. But how are we incorporated into this relationship? Saint Paul went into detail in his Letter to the Romans:

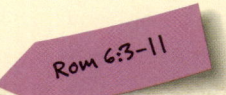

Rom 6:3-11

6 ³Do you not know that all of us who have been baptized into Christ Jesus were baptized into his death? ⁴We were buried therefore with him by baptism into death, so that as Christ was raised from the dead by the glory of the Father, we too might walk in newness of life.

⁵For if we have been united with him in a death like his, we shall certainly be united with him in a resurrection like his. ⁶We know that our former man was crucified with him so that the sinful body might be destroyed, and we might no longer be enslaved to sin. ⁷For he who has died is freed from sin. ⁸But if we have died with Christ, we believe that we shall also live with him. ⁹For we know that Christ being raised from the dead will never die again; death no longer has dominion over him. ¹⁰The death he died he died to sin, once for all, but the life he lives he lives to God. ¹¹So you also must consider yourselves dead to sin and alive to God in Christ Jesus.

Saint Paul said we are "crucified" with Jesus, and should be "dead to sin." What do you think he meant by someone being "dead to sin"? Are you "dead to sin"?

_____

_____

Saint Paul tells us that we must be "alive to God in Christ Jesus." How would you make it clear to others that you live a life "alive to God"?

_____

_____

_____

328 Liturgical Year: Easter

Through Baptism, we are incorporated into the Death and Resurrection of Christ. We enter into water, which symbolizes both death and new life. Water symbolizes death due to its dangerous potential to suffocate and drown. Through the waters of Baptism, we are "baptized into his death." At the same time, Baptism gives us the grace to "walk in newness of life." Water is also critical for life. It cleanses and sustains life.

Our Baptism conforms us with Christ's baptism in the Jordan and with his Death and Resurrection. By rising from the dead, Jesus gives us the power to rise from the dead if we remain united to him, sharing in the life of the Trinity.

In what ways are you walking in "newness of life" according to your baptismal call?

_____

_____

_____

This week in prayer, specify one major vice that you are struggling with and plan a way to draw on the support of God and others to counteract that fault.

Catechism of the Catholic Church, 1003

"United with Christ by Baptism, believers already truly participate in the heavenly life of the risen Christ, but this life remains 'hidden with Christ in God.'² The Father has already 'raised us up with him, and made us sit with him in the heavenly places in Christ Jesus.'³ Nourished with his body in the Eucharist, we already belong to the Body of Christ. When we rise on the last day we 'also will appear with him in glory.'⁴"

Let Us Pray—Psalm 118

The Church prays Psalm 118 during Easter. In this psalm, we offer God our praise and thanksgiving for his loving mercy. Jesus' Resurrection shows us God's mercy because it tells of God's plan to call all mankind into everlasting life with his Beloved Son.

Ps 118:1-2, 16-17, 22-24

118 ¹O give thanks to the LORD, for he is good;
  his mercy endures for ever!
²Let Israel say,
  "His mercy endures for ever." . . .
¹⁶ "The right hand of the LORD is exalted,
  the right hand of the LORD does valiantly!"
¹⁷I shall not die, but I shall live,
  and recount the deeds of the LORD. . . .

²²The stone which the builders rejected
  has become the cornerstone.
²³This is the LORD's doing;
  it is marvelous in our eyes.
²⁴This is the day which the LORD has made;
  let us rejoice and be glad in it.

The Faithful Departed

Read

The Christian belief in the resurrection of the body at the end of time follows from Christ's Resurrection. This is why, for millennia, Catholics have taken pains to show respect not just for the memory of the dead but also for the bodies of the dead. The Church addresses this with respect to cremation and burial: "The bodies of the dead must be treated with respect and charity, in faith and hope of the Resurrection. The burial of the dead is a corporal work of mercy; it honors the children of God, who are temples of the Holy Spirit. . . . The Church permits cremation, provided that it does not demonstrate a denial of faith in the resurrection of the body" (*CCC* 2300–1).

The *Order of Christian Funerals* states that "although cremation is now permitted by the Church, it does not enjoy the same value as burial of the body. The Church clearly prefers and urges that the body of the deceased be present for the funeral rites, since the presence of the human body better expresses the values which the Church affirms in those rites."[5] Regardless of the method of preservation used for the body after death, respect for the dead is an essential element of Christian piety.

Reflect

Spend 5–10 minutes reflecting on the following:

- What do I believe about the resurrection of the body? Do I find it hard to fathom how we will be reunited with our bodies?
- When was the last time I visited a cemetery or attended a visitation or funeral?
- Who are the deceased friends and relatives in my life? Do I pray for them to help ease their suffering if they are in Purgatory?

Pray

Spend a few minutes in prayer, calling to mind any friends and family who have died and gone to their rest.

> Eternal rest grant unto them, O Lord,
> and let perpetual light shine upon them.
> May the souls of all the faithful departed,
> through the mercy of God, rest in peace.
> Amen.

Act

This week, visit the grave of a friend or relative who has passed over to the Heavenly Father. Clear away any dirt or leaves from the headstone. Make an act of respect for the deceased person by bringing flowers or saying a prayer for the repose of the person's soul.

The Canon of Sacred Scripture

Old Testament (46 Books)

Genesis (Gen)
Exodus (Ex)
Leviticus (Lev)
Numbers (Num)
Deuteronomy (Deut)
Joshua (Josh)
Judges (Judg)
Ruth (Ruth)
1 Samuel (1 Sam)
2 Samuel (2 Sam)
1 Kings (1 Kings)
2 Kings (2 Kings)
1 Chronicles (1 Chron)
2 Chronicles (2 Chron)
Ezra (Ezra)
Nehemiah (Neh)
Tobit (Tob)
Judith (Jud)
Esther (Esther)
1 Maccabees (1 Mac)
2 Maccabees (2 Mac)
Job (Job)
Psalms (Ps)
Proverbs (Prov)
Ecclesiastes (Eccles)
Song of Solomon (Song)
Wisdom (Wis)
Sirach (Sir)
Isaiah (Is)
Jeremiah (Jer)
Lamentations (Lam)
Baruch (Bar)
Ezekiel (Ezek)
Daniel (Dan)
Hosea (Hos)
Joel (Joel)
Amos (Amos)
Obadiah (Obad)
Jonah (Jon)
Micah (Mic)
Nahum (Nahum)
Habakkuk (Hab)
Zephaniah (Zeph)
Haggai (Hag)
Zechariah (Zech)
Malachi (Mal)

New Testament (27 Books)

Matthew (Mt)
Mark (Mk)
Luke (Lk)
John (Jn)
Acts of the Apostles (Acts)
Romans (Rom)
1 Corinthians (1 Cor)
2 Corinthians (2 Cor)
Galatians (Gal)
Ephesians (Eph)
Philippians (Phil)
Colossians (Col)
1 Thessalonians (1 Thess)
2 Thessalonians (2 Thess)
1 Timothy (1 Tim)
2 Timothy (2 Tim)
Titus (Tit)
Philemon (Philem)
Hebrews (Heb)
James (Jas)
1 Peter (1 Pet)
2 Peter (2 Pet)
1 John (1 Jn)
2 John (2 Jn)
3 John (3 Jn)
Jude (Jude)
Revelation (Rev)

Looking Up Bible Passages: Luke 15:2

Book **Chapter** **Verse**

Book — LUKE 14,15

Page Number — 66

¹²He said also to the man who had invited him, "When you give a dinner or a banquet, do not invite your friends or your brothers or your kinsmen or rich neighbors, lest they also invite you in return, and you be repaid. ¹³But when you give a feast, invite the poor, the maimed, the lame, the blind, ¹⁴and you will be blessed, because they cannot repay you. You will be repaid at the resurrection of the just."

The Parable of the Great Banquet

¹⁵When one of those who sat at table with him heard this, he said to him, "Blessed is he who shall eat bread in the kingdom of God!" ¹⁶But he said to him, "A man once gave a great banquet, and invited many; ¹⁷and at the time for the banquet he sent his servant to say to those who had been invited, 'Come; for all is now ready.' ¹⁸But they all alike began to make excuses. The first said to him, 'I have bought a field, and I must go out and see it; please, have me excused.' ¹⁹And another said, 'I have bought five yoke of oxen, and I go to examine them;

was not able to finish.' ³¹Or what king, going to encounter another king in war, will not sit down first and take counsel whether he is able with ten thousand to meet him who comes against him with twenty thousand? ³²And if not, while the other is yet a great way off, he sends an embassy and asks terms of peace. ³³So therefore, whoever of you does not renounce all that he has cannot be my disciple.

About Salt

³⁴"Salt is good; but if salt has lost its taste, how shall its saltiness be restored? ³⁵It is fit neither for the land nor for the dunghill; men throw it away. He who has ears to hear, let him hear."

The Parable of the Lost Sheep

15 Now the tax collectors and sinners were all drawing near to hear him. ²And the Pharisees and the scribes murmured, saying, "This man receives sinners and eats with them." ³So he told them this parable: ⁴"What man of you, having a hundred sheep, if he has lost

Passage Title | **Chapter** | **Verse** | **Passage**

Follow these steps to look up this Bible verse: Luke 15:1–7.

1. Identify the book, chapter, and verse:
Luke; chapter 15; verses 1–7.

2. Go to the table of contents.
Find the name of the book. Sometimes the name of the book is shortened to two to three letters. This is called an abbreviation. Look for the abbreviation in the table of contents in your Bible.

3. Go to the book. Turn to the page number of the book that is listed in the table of contents.

4. Go to the chapter. Look for chapter numbers at the top of the page. Turn the pages to the chapter number. Then go to the paragraph that begins with the chapter number.

5. Go to the verses. In each chapter, there are small numbers before each sentence. These are the verse numbers. Find the verses you need, and read the passage.

THE NEW TESTAMENT
Matthew 1
Mark 30
Luke 48
John 78
Acts 100
Romans 126
1 Corinthians 133

The Parable of the Lost Sheep

15 Now the tax collectors and sin were all drawing near to him. ²And the Pharisees and the scr murmured, saying, "This man rece sinners and eats with them."
³So he told them this parable: ⁴"V

The Parable of the Lost Sheep

15 Now the tax collectors and sinners were all drawing near to hear him. ²And the Pharisees and the scribes murmured, saying, "This man receives sinners and eats with them."
³So he told them this parable: ⁴"What man of you, having a hundred sheep, if he has lost one of them, does not leave the ninety-nine in the wilderness, and go after the one which is lost, until he finds it? ⁵And when he has found it, he lays it on his shoulders, rejoicing. ⁶And when he comes home, he calls together his friends and his neighbors, saying to them, 'Rejoice with me, for I have found my sheep which was lost.' ⁷Just so, I tell you, there will be more joy in heaven over one sinner who repents than over ninety-nine righteous persons who need no repentance."

Salvation History Overview

Following the Six Ages Outlined by Saint Augustine

1. Adam to Noah	Out of love, God created Adam and Eve in his image and likeness. Adam and Eve disobeyed God. After their sin, God promised to send a Savior, who would conquer the powers of sin and death. Sin and evil spread throughout the world because of Adam and Eve's Original Sin. God washed away sin and evil from the world in the Flood. He protected Noah and his family in the ark, and after the Flood, he made an everlasting covenant with Noah and his family.
2. Noah to Abraham	God chose Abram and called him to leave his homeland and journey to the Promised Land. God changed Abram's name to Abraham, made a covenant with him, and promised to bless the entire world through Abraham's descendants. Through this covenant, God formed Abraham's descendants into his Chosen People.
3. Abraham to David	Abraham's beloved son Isaac had two sons: Jacob and Esau. Jacob's twelve sons and their families became the twelve tribes of Israel. Jacob brought his sons to live in Egypt to protect them from famine. Eventually, the Egyptians enslaved the Israelites, but God heard his people's cries. God called Moses and sent him to deliver his people from slavery. God made a covenant with the Israelites through Moses. After Moses' death, God led his people into the Promised Land under the leadership of Joshua. God grew his Chosen People into a kingdom with David as their king. God made a covenant with David and promised that one day a son of David's would rule God's everlasting kingdom.
4. David to the Exile in Babylon	Sadly, the Israelites were unfaithful to their covenants with God. God allowed the kingdom to be divided: the Kingdom of Israel in the north and the Kingdom of Judah in the south. God sent prophets to call his people to repentance and prepare them for the Messiah. But they continued to disobey God. He allowed both kingdoms to be conquered by neighboring nations. The kingdom of Assyria conquered the Northern Kingdom (Israel). The people were taken captive and became part of other nations. The kingdom of Babylon conquered the Southern Kingdom (Judah). The people were taken captive and exiled from the Promised Land.
5. Exile to the Coming of Christ	Eventually, the people of the southern Kingdom of Judah, known as Jews, were allowed to return to the Promised Land to rebuild Jerusalem and the Temple. For centuries, the faithful Jews longed for the coming of the Messiah. In the fullness of time, the Eternal Word of God became man in the Incarnation. Jesus Christ, the promised Savior, fulfilled the promise God had made after Adam and Eve's Original Sin. Jesus perfectly and fully revealed God and his loving plan, fulfilling the Old Testament Law and the Prophets. He established the Kingdom of God on earth through his teaching and miracles. He offered himself as the perfect sacrifice to take away the sins of the world and open for us the way to eternal life.
6. Current Age	Jesus' coming began the current age we are living in today. Through Jesus, we enter into the new and everlasting covenant with God in this age. God shares his grace with mankind and offers salvation to all people through Jesus Christ and his Church.

Catholic Prayers

Sign of the Cross
In the name of the Father
and of the Son
and of the Holy Spirit. Amen.

Our Father
Our Father, who art in Heaven,
hallowed be Thy name;
Thy kingdom come,
Thy will be done on earth as it is in Heaven.
Give us this day our daily bread,
and forgive us our trespasses as we forgive those
who trespass against us;
and lead us not into temptation,
but deliver us from evil. Amen.

Hail Mary
Hail, Mary, full of grace,
the Lord is with thee.
Blessed art thou among women
and blessed is the fruit of
thy womb, Jesus.
Holy Mary, Mother of God,
pray for us sinners,
now and at the hour of our death. Amen.

Glory Be
Glory be to the Father
and to the Son
and to the Holy Spirit,
as it was in the beginning
is now, and ever shall be
world without end. Amen.

Grace before Meals
Bless us, O Lord, and these Thy gifts, which we are
about to receive, from Thy bounty, through Christ
our Lord. Amen.

Grace after Meals
We give Thee thanks for all Thy gifts, Almighty God,
who lives and reigns forever. Amen.

Jesus Prayer
Lord Jesus Christ, Son of the living God, have mercy
on me, a sinner. Amen.

Fatima Prayer
O my Jesus, forgive us our sins,
save us from the fires of Hell,
and lead all souls into Heaven,
especially those in most need of Thy mercy. Amen.

Prayer to Saint Michael the Archangel
Saint Michael the Archangel, defend us in battle.
Be our protection against the wickedness and
snares of the Devil.
May God rebuke him, we humbly pray,
and do thou, O prince of the heavenly hosts,
by the power of God,
thrust into Hell Satan and all the evil spirits
who prowl about the world
seeking the ruin of souls. Amen.

Prayer to the Holy Spirit (by Saint Augustine)
Breathe into me, Holy Spirit,
that my thoughts may all be holy.
Move in me, Holy Spirit,
that my work, too, may be holy.
Attract my heart, Holy Spirit,
that I may love only what is holy.
Strengthen me, Holy Spirit,
that I may defend all that is holy.
Protect me, Holy Spirit,
that I may always be holy. Amen.

Eternal Rest
V. Eternal rest grant unto them, O Lord.
R. And let the perpetual light shine upon them.
All. May the souls of all the faithful departed,
    through the mercy of God, rest in peace. Amen.

Act of Faith
O my God, I firmly believe that You are one God in
three Divine Persons: Father, Son, and Holy Spirit.
I believe that Your Divine Son became man and died
for our sins and that He will come to judge the living
and the dead. I believe these and all the truths which
the Holy Catholic Church teaches because You have
revealed them, who are eternal truth and wisdom,
who can neither deceive nor be deceived. In this
faith, I intend to live and die. Amen.

Act of Hope
O Lord God, I hope by Your grace for the pardon
of all my sins and after life here to gain eternal
happiness because You have promised it, who are
infinitely powerful, faithful, kind, and merciful. In this
hope, I intend to live and die. Amen.

Act of Love
O Lord God, I love You above all things, and I love
my neighbor for Your sake because You are the
highest, infinite, and perfect good, worthy of all my
love. In this love, I intend to live and die. Amen.

Act of Contrition (Traditional)
O my God, I am heartily sorry for having offended Thee, and I detest all my sins because of Thy just punishments, but most of all because they offend Thee, my God, who art all-good and deserving of all my love. I firmly resolve with the help of Thy grace to sin no more and to avoid the near occasion of sin. Amen.

Act of Contrition (Modern)
My God, I am sorry for my sins with all my heart. In choosing to do wrong and failing to do good, I have sinned against You, whom I should love above all things. I firmly intend, with Your help, to do penance, to sin no more, and to avoid whatever leads me to sin. Our Savior, Jesus Christ, suffered and died for us. In His name, my God, have mercy. Amen.

Divine Praises
Blessed be God.
Blessed be His holy name.
Blessed be Jesus Christ, true God and true man.
Blessed be the name of Jesus.
Blessed be His Most Sacred Heart.
Blessed be His Most Precious Blood.
Blessed be Jesus in the Most Holy Sacrament of the Altar.
Blessed be the Holy Spirit, the Paraclete.
Blessed be the great Mother of God, Mary most holy.
Blessed be her holy and Immaculate Conception.
Blessed be her glorious Assumption.
Blessed be the name of Mary, Virgin and Mother.
Blessed be Saint Joseph, her most chaste spouse.
Blessed be God in His angels and in His saints.
Amen.

Act of Spiritual Communion
My Jesus, I believe that You are present in the Most Holy Sacrament. I love You above all things, and I desire to receive You into my soul. Since I cannot at this moment receive You sacramentally, come at least spiritually into my heart. I embrace You as if You were already there and unite myself wholly to You. Never permit me to be separated from You. Amen.

Anima Christi
Soul of Christ, sanctify me. Body of Christ, save me.
Blood of Christ, inebriate me.
Water from the side of Christ, wash me.
Passion of Christ, strengthen me.
O good Jesus, hear me.
Within Your wounds conceal me.
Do not permit me to be parted from You.
From the evil foe protect me.
At the hour of my death call me.
And bid me come to You, to praise You with all Your saints for ever and ever. Amen.

Prayer before a Crucifix
Look down upon me, good and gentle Jesus, while before Your face I humbly kneel and, with burning soul, pray and beseech You to fix deep in my heart lively sentiments of faith, hope, and charity; true contrition for my sins; and a firm purpose of amendment. While I contemplate, with great love and tender pity, Your five most precious wounds, pondering over them within me and calling to mind the words which David, Your prophet, said to You, my Jesus: "They have pierced My hands and My feet; they have numbered all My bones." Amen.

Prayer before Mass by Saint Thomas Aquinas
Almighty and ever-living God, I approach the sacrament
of Your only begotten Son, our Lord Jesus Christ;
I come sick to the Doctor of life, unclean to the fountain of mercy,
blind to the radiance of eternal light, and poor and needy to the Lord of Heaven and earth.

Lord, in Your great generosity, heal my sickness,
wash away my defilement, enlighten my blindness, enrich my poverty,
and clothe my nakedness.
May I receive the Bread of angels,
the King of Kings and Lord of Lords,
with humble reverence, with the purity and faith,
the repentance and love, and the determined purpose
that will help to bring me to salvation.
May I receive the sacrament of the Lord's Body and Blood,
and its reality and power.

Kind God, may I receive the Body
of Your only begotten Son, our Lord Jesus Christ,
born from the womb of the Virgin Mary,
and so be received into His Mystical Body
and numbered among His members.

Loving Father, as on my earthly pilgrimage
I now receive Your beloved Son
under the veil of a sacrament,
may I one day see Him face-to-face in glory,
who lives and reigns with You for ever. Amen.

Some Prayers of the Mass

Confiteor (I Confess)
I confess to almighty God
and to you, my brothers and sisters,
that I have greatly sinned,
in my thoughts and in my words,
in what I have done and in what I have failed to do,
(strike your breast)
through my fault, through my fault,
through my most grievous fault;
therefore I ask blessed Mary ever-Virgin,
all the Angels and Saints,
and you, my brothers and sisters,
to pray for me to the Lord our God.

Gloria (Glory to God)
Glory to God in the highest,
and on earth peace to people of good will.
We praise you, we bless you, we adore you, we
 glorify you,
we give you thanks for your great glory,
Lord God, heavenly King, O God, almighty Father.
Lord Jesus Christ, Only Begotten Son,
Lord God, Lamb of God, Son of the Father,
you take away the sins of the world, have mercy
 on us;
you take away the sins of the world, receive
 our prayer;
you are seated at the right hand of the Father, have
 mercy on us.
For you alone are the Holy One,
you alone are the Lord,
you alone are the Most High, Jesus Christ,
with the Holy Spirit, in the glory of God the Father.
Amen.

Sanctus (Holy, Holy, Holy)
Holy, Holy, Holy Lord God of hosts.
Heaven and earth are full of your glory.
Hosanna in the highest.
Blessed is he who comes in the name of the Lord.
Hosanna in the highest.

Agnus Dei (Lamb of God)
Lamb of God, you take away the sins of the world,
have mercy on us.
Lamb of God, you take away the sins of the world,
have mercy on us.
Lamb of God, you take away the sins of the world,
grant us peace.

The Rosary

1. The Rosary begins by holding the cross of the rosary and making the Sign of the Cross. While still holding the cross, we then profess our beliefs as we pray the Apostles' Creed.

2. On the first bead, we pray the Our Father. This is traditionally offered for the intention of the pope.

3. Three Hail Marys are then prayed on the next three beads for the virtues of faith, hope, and charity.

4. We then pray the Glory Be. On the fifth bead, we say the first mystery (see list of mysteries), and while meditating on the mystery, we say one Our Father and ten Hail Marys (one on each of the next ten beads) and a Glory Be. Then, as requested by Our Lady of the Rosary at Fatima, we pray the Fatima Prayer.

5. The fourth step is then repeated for the next four mysteries.

6. At the end of the five decades, the Hail, Holy Queen is prayed.

7. We end with the Sign of the Cross.

Joyful Mysteries
The Annunciation
The Visitation
The Nativity
The Presentation in the Temple
The Finding in the Temple

Luminous Mysteries
The Baptism of Christ in the Jordan
The Wedding Feast at Cana
Jesus' Proclamation of the Coming of the Kingdom of God
The Transfiguration
The Institution of the Eucharist

Sorrowful Mysteries
The Agony in the Garden
The Scourging at the Pillar
The Crowning with Thorns
The Carrying of the Cross
The Crucifixion and Death

Glorious Mysteries
The Resurrection
The Ascension
The Descent of the Holy Spirit
The Assumption
The Coronation of Mary

Our Catholic Faith

The Apostles' Creed
I believe in God, the Father Almighty, Creator of Heaven and earth, and in Jesus Christ, His only Son, our Lord, who was conceived by the Holy Spirit, born of the Virgin Mary, suffered under Pontius Pilate, was crucified, died, and was buried; He descended into Hell; on the third day He rose again from the dead; He ascended into Heaven and is seated at the right hand of God the Father Almighty; from there He will come to judge the living and the dead. I believe in the Holy Spirit, the holy catholic Church, the Communion of Saints, the forgiveness of sins, the resurrection of the body, and life everlasting. Amen.

The Nicene Creed
I believe in one God, the Father Almighty, maker of Heaven and earth, of all things visible and invisible. I believe in one Lord Jesus Christ, the Only Begotten Son of God, born of the Father before all ages. God from God, Light from Light, true God from true God, begotten, not made, consubstantial with the Father; through Him all things were made. For us men and for our salvation He came down from Heaven, and by the Holy Spirit was incarnate of the Virgin Mary, and became man. For our sake He was crucified under Pontius Pilate, He suffered death and was buried, and rose again on the third day in accordance with the Scriptures. He ascended into Heaven and is seated at the right hand of the Father. He will come again in glory to judge the living and the dead and His kingdom will have no end. I believe in the Holy Spirit, the Lord, the giver of life, who proceeds from the Father and the Son, who with the Father and the Son is adored and glorified, who has spoken through the prophets. I believe in one, holy, catholic, and apostolic Church. I confess one Baptism for the forgiveness of sins and I look forward to the resurrection of the dead and the life of the world to come. Amen.

The Ten Commandments
1. I am the LORD your God: you shall have no other gods before me.
2. You shall not take the name of the LORD your God in vain.
3. Remember to keep holy the LORD'S Day.
4. Honor your father and your mother.
5. You shall not kill.
6. You shall not commit adultery.
7. You shall not steal.
8. You shall not bear false witness.
9. You shall not covet your neighbor's wife.
10. You shall not covet your neighbor's goods.

The Beatitudes
"Blessed are the poor in spirit, for theirs is the kingdom of heaven.
"Blessed are those who mourn, for they shall be comforted.
"Blessed are the meek, for they shall inherit the earth.
"Blessed are those who hunger and thirst for righteousness, for they shall be filled.
"Blessed are the merciful, for they shall receive mercy.
"Blessed are the pure in heart, for they shall see God.
"Blessed are the peacemakers, for they shall be called sons of God.
"Blessed are those who are persecuted for the sake of righteousness, for theirs is the kingdom of heaven.
"Blessed are you whenever they insult you and persecute you and say all kinds of evil things against you falsely because of me. Rejoice and be glad, for your reward is great in heaven. For in the same way they persecuted the prophets who came before you" (Mt 5:3–12).

Three Conditions of a Mortal Sin
1. **Grave Matter:** The sin must be of grave matter, meaning it is very serious.
2. **Full Knowledge:** We must know that the serious sin is wrong.
3. **Deliberate Consent:** We must deliberately and freely choose to commit the serious sin anyway.

Corporal Works of Mercy
- Feed the hungry
- Give drink to the thirsty
- Shelter the homeless
- Visit the sick
- Visit the prisoners
- Bury the dead
- Give alms to the poor

Spiritual Works of Mercy
- Counseling the doubtful
- Instructing the ignorant
- Admonishing the sinner
- Comforting the sorrowful
- Forgiving injuries
- Bearing wrongs patiently
- Praying for the living and the dead

The Seven Sacraments

The Sacraments of Initiation

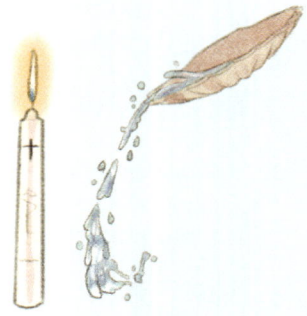

Baptism

Matter: Water.

Form: "N. [Name], I baptize you in the name of the Father, and of the Son, and of the Holy Spirit."

Minister: Ordinarily a bishop, priest, or, in the Latin Rite, a deacon. However, anyone can baptize another person in case of an emergency as long as he shares the same intention as the Church and uses the proper form.

Confirmation

Matter: Anointing of the forehead with sacred chrism and the laying on of the minister's hand.

Form: "Be sealed with the gift of the Holy Spirit."

Minister: In the Latin Rite, the ordinary minister is the bishop. In the Eastern Catholic churches, a priest ordinarily confirms immediately after Baptism.

Holy Eucharist

Matter: Wheat bread and grape wine.

Form: "This is my body. . . . This is the chalice of my blood . . ."

Minister: A validly ordained bishop or priest.

The Sacraments of Healing

Matter: A person's sins, his contrition, intention to make reparation, the confession of his sins to the priest, and doing penance.

Form: The prayer of absolution.

Minister: A validly ordained bishop or priest.

Reconciliation

Matter: The anointing with holy oil of the forehead and hands of the sick person or of other parts of the body (in the Eastern Catholic churches).

Form: "Through this holy anointing may the Lord in his love and mercy help you with the grace of the Holy Spirit" (while anointing the forehead). "May the Lord who frees you from sin save you and raise you up" (while anointing the hands).

Minister: A validly ordained bishop or priest.

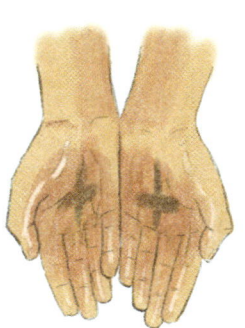

Anointing of the Sick

The Sacraments at the Service of Communion

Matter: The bride's and groom's desire and consent to be united in the Sacrament of Matrimony.

Form: The consent of the bride and groom given publicly in front of the church.

Minister: The bride and the groom confer the sacrament upon each other; however, a priest or deacon must be present to receive their public consent on behalf of the Church.

Matrimony

Matter: The laying on of hands by the bishop.

Form: The specific prayer of consecration said at the ordination of either a bishop, priest, or deacon.

Minister: A validly ordained bishop.

Holy Orders

Examination of Conscience

1. **I am the LORD your God: you shall have no other gods before me.**

    Have I failed to pray to God every day? Have my relationship with God and being with him in Heaven been important to me? Or have things like TV, games, or popularity been more important to me?

2. **You shall not take the name of the LORD your God in vain.**

    Have I said "God" or "Jesus" in a disrespectful or thoughtless way? Have I been respectful toward God and his Church? Or have I been disrespectful and uncaring toward him?

3. **Remember to keep holy the LORD's Day.**

    Have I missed Sunday Mass on purpose or complained about going? Have I played around or not paid attention at Mass?

4. **Honor your father and your mother.**

    Have I failed to obey or respect my parents, priests, or teachers? Have I been disrespectful or unkind to my family members?

5. **You shall not kill.**

    Have I hurt anyone on purpose or because I was not careful? Have I been mean to anyone because of how he looks, acts, or talks? Have I said bad words?

6. **You shall not commit adultery.**

    Have I used others for what they can give me instead of treating them with love and respect? Have I been faithful to my friends?

7. **You shall not steal.**

    Have I stolen, broken, or not returned anything that was not mine? Have I been selfish and not given to those in need?

8. **You shall not bear false witness.**

    Have I spread rumors about someone or said hurtful things about someone behind his back? Have I lied to, tricked, or exaggerated to others? Have I cheated in games or on schoolwork?

9. **You shall not covet your neighbor's wife.**

    Have I failed to keep my heart pure by turning away from sinful images, shows, songs, and other temptations?

10. **You shall not covet your neighbor's goods.**

    Have I been jealous of others' things or abilities? Have I been greedy and ungrateful? Have I failed to thank God or share with others when I should have?

Have I lived the theological virtue of *faith*? Have I chosen to turn away from God when I am angry or any other time? Have I chosen not to believe or to ignore what I have learned about God?

Have I lived the theological virtue of *hope*? Have I trusted that God has a plan for my life and will help me accomplish it? Have I trusted that God will forgive my sins so I can be with him in Heaven one day?

Have I lived the theological virtue of *charity*? Have I failed to love God with all my heart, mind, and soul? Have I skipped prayer for my hobbies or games instead?

Have I lived the virtue of *prudence*? Have I ignored what God wants for my life? Have I chosen only what I want? Have I acted against the guidance of my parents and chosen to sin?

Have I lived the virtue of *fortitude*? Have I been pressured by my friends into doing something that I knew was wrong? Have I failed to stand up for my faith and talk courageously about God or my faith?

Have I lived the virtue of *temperance*? Have I thought or complained about wanting more instead of being grateful? Was I grateful or thankful for the many blessings I have?

Have I lived the virtue of *justice*? Have I failed to treat others fairly? Have I failed to give God the time and honor he deserves? Have I failed to honor my parents the way they deserve?

The Sacrament of Reconciliation

Making a Good Confession

1. **Know your sins:** Do an examination of conscience (see page 342). Pray to the Holy Spirit to help you know your sins. Think of times when you may have broken God's laws and not lived with virtue. You can remember or write your sins down. Do not share your sins with other people.

2. **Be sorry:** To make a good confession, you need to be truly sorry. If you are not sorry for sinning, ask the Holy Spirit to help you be sorry.

3. **Repent:** To repent means to choose not to sin again. Before confessing your sins, make up your mind not to sin again.

4. **Go to the Sacrament of Reconciliation:** You will confess your sins to the priest, who will give you a penance and absolve you of your sins. Your sins will be forgiven.

5. **Do your penance:** The priest will give you penance. Penance can be a prayer or action. We show God we are turning away from sin. You should always do the penance the priest gives you.

How to Celebrate the Sacrament of Reconciliation

1. **The priest will welcome you.**

2. **Begin with the Sign of the Cross:** Say, "In the name of the Father, and of the Son, and of the Holy Spirit. Amen."

3. **Start your confession:** Say, "Bless me, Father, for I have sinned. It has been _____ since my last confession." Tell the priest how long it has been since your last confession. If it is your first confession, say, "This is my first confession."

4. **Confess your sins:** Tell the priest your sins. Be sure to confess all mortal sins. Try to say how often you committed the mortal sins. For example, "I hit my friend two times."

5. **Receive your penance:** The priest may give you some advice to avoid sin. Listen to the priest's words.

6. **Pray the Act of Contrition:** When you pray the Act of Contrition, you tell God you are sorry. Pray the Act of Contrition (see page 336).

7. **Through the priest, Jesus absolves you of your sins:** The priest says, "God, the Father of mercies, through the Death and Resurrection of His Son, has reconciled the world to Himself and poured out the Holy Spirit for the forgiveness of sins; through the ministry of the Church may God grant you pardon and peace. And I absolve you from your sins, in the name of the Father, and of the Son, and of the Holy Spirit. Amen."

8. **The priest will end your confession:** The priest says, "Give thanks to the Lord, for He is good." You respond, "His mercy endures forever." The priest will end your confession by saying, "The Lord has freed you from your sins. Go in peace." You respond, "Thanks be to God."

9. **Do your penance right away.**

The Liturgical Year

The liturgical year is made up of six seasons. Each season is symbolized by a color.

White or Gold: light, life, triumph, glory, purity, celebration

Green: life eternal, growth, hope, new life

Violet: penance, preparation

Black: death, mourning

Rose: joy, anticipation

Red: the Passion, Christ's blood, sacrifice, zeal, martyrdom, God's love, the Holy Spirit

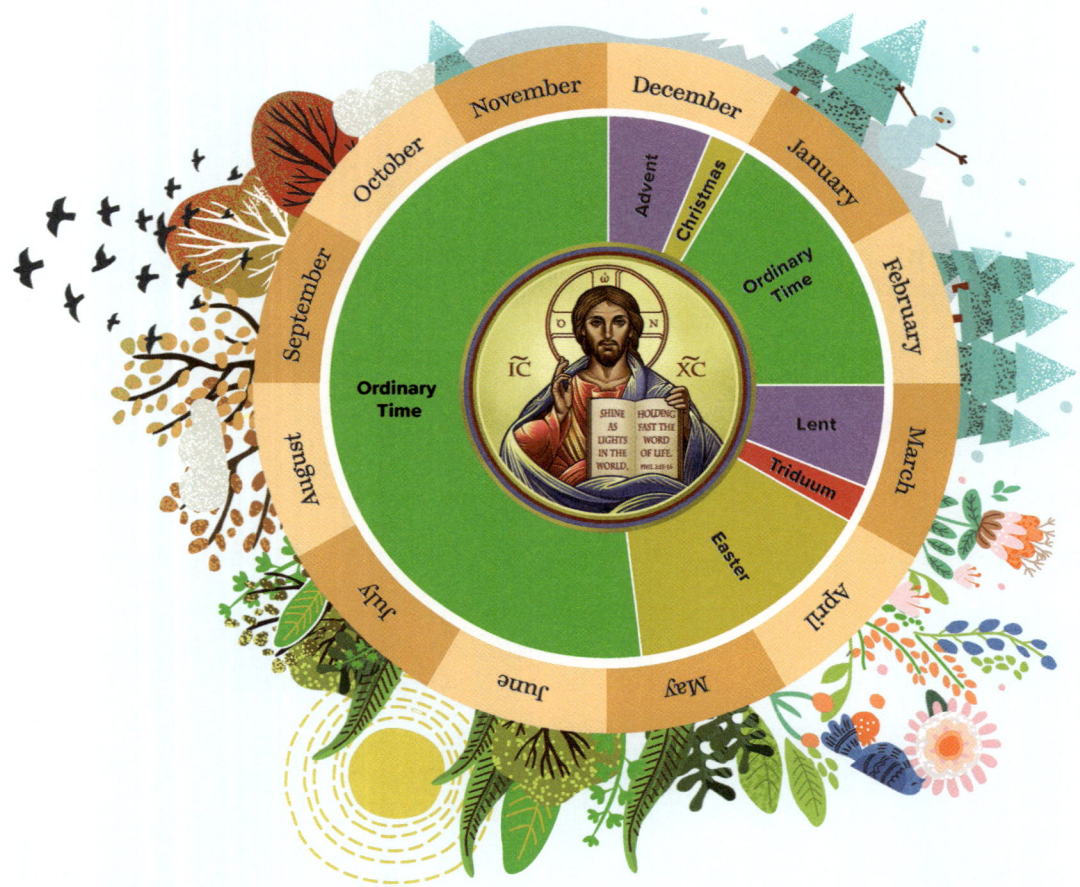

Holy Days of Obligation

The following are Holy Days of Obligation in the United States of America:

- January 1, the Solemnity of Mary, Mother of God*
- Thursday of the Sixth Week of Easter, the Solemnity of the Ascension
- August 15, the Solemnity of the Assumption of the Blessed Virgin Mary*
- November 1, the Solemnity of All Saints*
- December 8, the Solemnity of the Immaculate Conception
- December 25, the Solemnity of the Nativity of Our Lord Jesus Christ

*Whenever these Holy Days fall on a Saturday or a Monday, the obligation to attend Mass may be lifted in some dioceses.

Growing in Virtue

Virtue Tree

Since medieval times, the analogy of a tree has been used to show how the virtues are related to one another. It demonstrates how an integrated life of virtue forms a cohesive whole and is necessary for human flourishing. This Virtue Tree is based on the distinctions made by Saint Thomas Aquinas.

The **theological virtues** are the roots because they are the foundation of the Christian moral life. The centrality of charity shows that it is the most important root and the perfection of all the virtues.

The **cardinal virtues** form the trunk and main branches to show their unique importance; the moral life hinges on them. Prudence is the trunk because it connects all the virtues; a person must have prudence to act virtuously.

Virtue Shields

The virtues are like a shield because they strengthen and protect us against temptations and sin. The truly virtuous and holy person of character is a soldier and servant for Christ.

FAITH

Faith is depicted as the Cross of Christ and the keys of Peter. Christ reveals the fullness of the faith, which is protected by the Church.

HOPE

Hope is represented as a dove and olive branch because this was the sign of hope that God sent to Noah.

CHARITY

Charity is depicted with the Sacred Heart of Christ because through charity we can love like God loves.

PRUDENCE

Prudence is depicted as a compass because it enables us to know what is right in a situation.

JUSTICE

Justice is represented as scales because we must give what is due to others and to God.

TEMPERANCE

Temperance is represented as the reins of a horse because it helps us guide and control our desires.

FORTITUDE

Fortitude is depicted as armor because it fortifies us against fear.

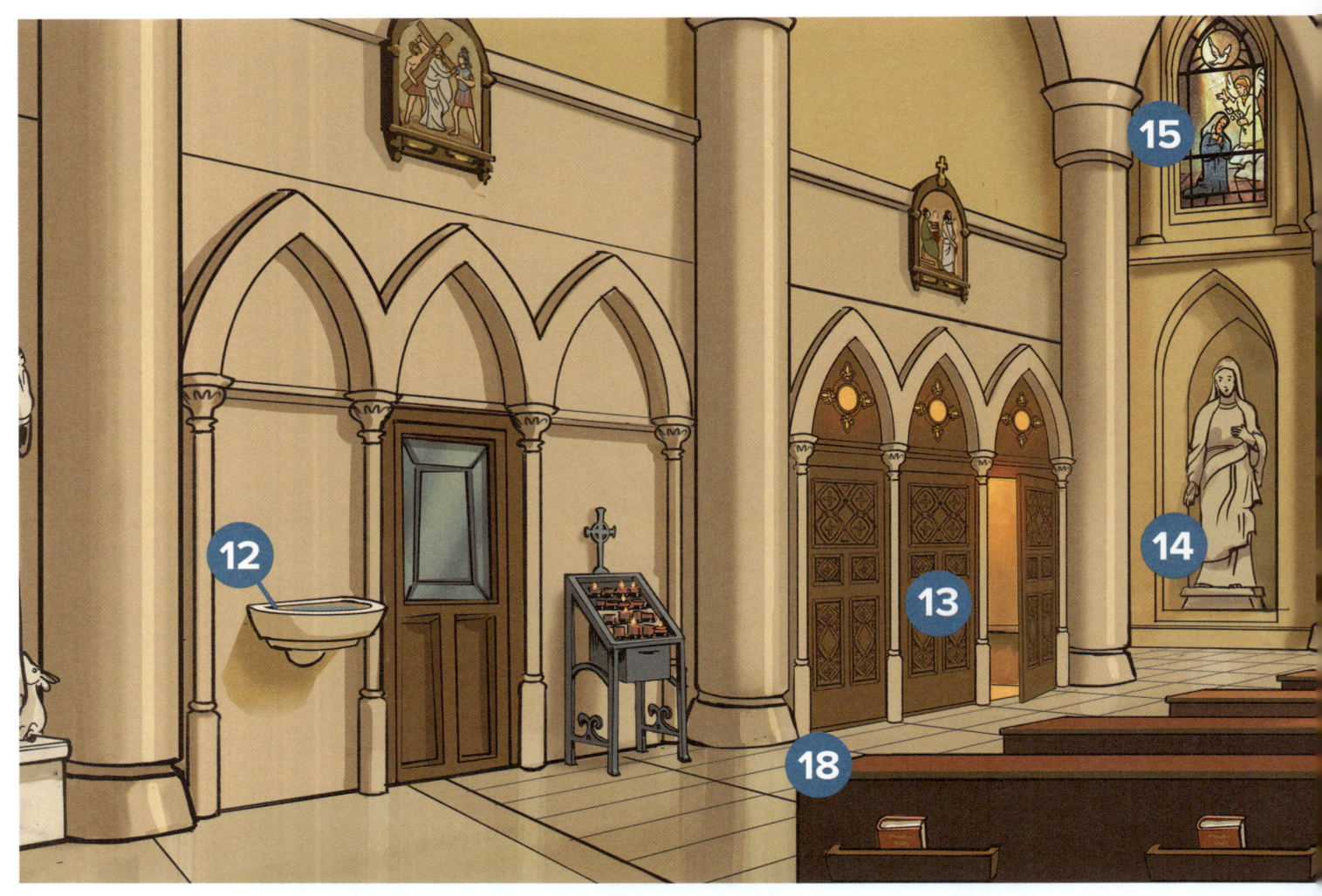

Tour of a Catholic Church

1. **sanctuary**: The holiest area of the church. This is where Mass is celebrated. The space that is directly around the altar, usually at the top of some steps.

2. **tabernacle**: A sacred metal or wood box in the church. It holds the Holy Eucharist.

3. **sanctuary lamp**: A special candle that is near the tabernacle. When the candle is lit, Jesus is present in the tabernacle.

4. **altar**: The sacred table in the front of the church. The priest celebrates the sacrifice of the Mass on the altar.

5. **candles**: Candles lit during Mass remind us that Jesus is the Light of the World.

6. **ambo**: The stand or platform where readings from the Bible are read during Mass.

7. **Lectionary**: The large book with the readings from the Bible that are read at Mass.

8. **crucifix**: A sacred cross with an image of the body of Jesus on it. It shows us Jesus' sacrifice and great love for us.

9. **hymnal**: A book of songs and prayers that helps us participate at Mass.

10. **paschal candle**: The tall candle lit at Easter. It reminds us that Jesus is the Light of the World.

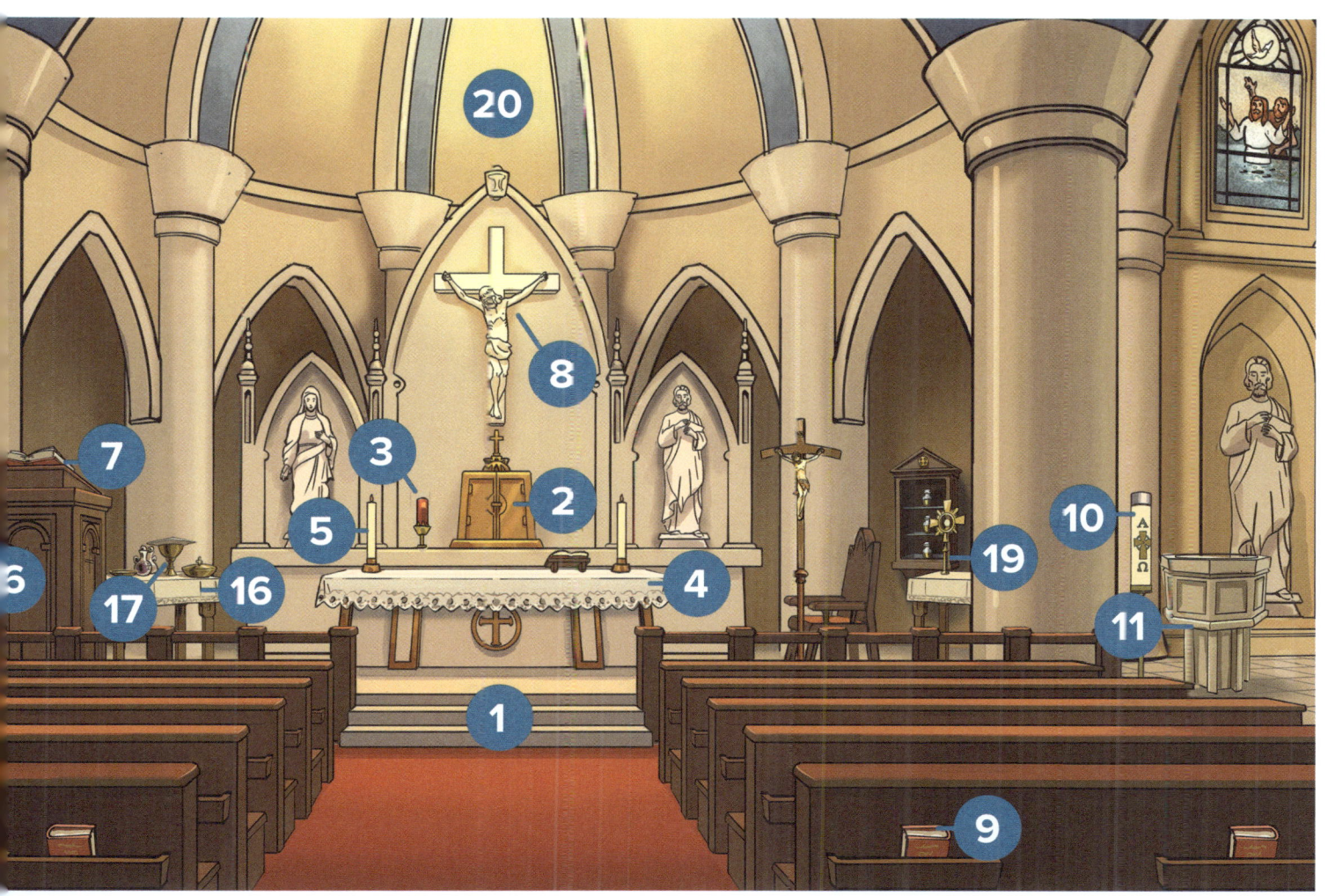

11	**baptismal font:** The font or other sacred container for the consecrated water. It is used for Baptisms.	16	**credence table:** A table in the sanctuary. Items like water, wine, a host, patens, a towel, and a bowl are kept on this table.
12	**holy water:** Water that has been blessed by a bishop, priest, or deacon. It reminds us of our Baptism.	17	**chalice:** A sacred cup made of precious metal. It holds the wine that becomes the Blood of Christ at Mass.
13	**confessional:** The private space set aside for the Sacrament of Reconciliation.	18	**pew:** A long bench that people sit in during Mass.
14	**statues:** Carved images of saints. Statues remind us to live holy lives like the saints.	19	**monstrance:** A sacred container made of precious metals. It displays the Holy Eucharist. It is used so we can adore Jesus in eucharistic adoration.
15	**stained glass windows:** Colorful windows that reflect the light of the sun. They tell stories of our Catholic faith.	20	**apse:** A semicircular area above the altar that lifts our eyes upward.

347

Words to Know

Note: Sentences in italics provide helpful context but are not required for memorization.

Advent: The liturgical season of preparation and expectation during the four weeks leading up to Christmas. *It means "to come."*

almsgiving: The practice of performing charitable acts for others, particularly giving money or other possessions to the poor.

Ark of the Covenant: A wooden chest plated with gold where God made himself present to his people.

Baal: One of the false gods worshipped by the Canaanites. *God's Chosen People were tempted by the Canaanites to worship the false god Baal.*

Beatitudes: Jesus' teachings about how to achieve eternal happiness with God in Heaven. *The word "beatitude" means "happiness." We find the Beatitudes at the beginning of Jesus' Sermon on the Mount.*

blasphemy: The sin of speaking hatefully or with contempt of God.

Canaanites: The people already dwelling in the Promised Land, which is also called Canaan.

canon: The Church's official list of books in the Bible. *The canon contains a total of 73 books: 46 in the Old Testament and 27 in the New Testament.*

charity: Love of God above all else, and the love of our neighbor as ourselves for the love of God. Charity is one of the three theological virtues (faith, hope, and charity). *Charity is the greatest virtue.*

Chosen People: Abraham and his descendants. *They were chosen by God as a sign to prepare the world for the day when God would gather all faithful people into the unity of his family, the Church.*

Christ: Another name for Messiah, or "anointed one." *This title reveals that Jesus is the long-awaited Savior and King, who is filled with the power of the Holy Spirit.*

covenant: An agreement between God and humans that forms a sacred bond. *Like an adoption or marriage, a covenant is an agreement where humans become part of God's family.*

Decalogue: The Ten Commandments. It is from the Greek for "ten words." *These "ten words" of God lead his people to freedom in living as God designed.*

disciple: A person who is a student or follower of his teacher and who imitates his way of life. *Being a disciple of Jesus means following him by obeying his teachings and trying to become like him.*

divine providence: God's guidance of salvation history according to his wisdom and love. *God guides his people to cooperate with his help so that they reach fulfillment and perfection.*

Emmanuel: A title for Jesus, the Messiah, which means "God with us."

epiphany: A manifestation or revealing of God.

evangelist: Someone who proclaims the Good News of Jesus Christ.

evangelization: The proclamation of Jesus and the Good News through one's words and way of life. *The mission of evangelization is not just for professional missionaries—it is for every single member of the Church.*

exile: When people are taken from their homeland and sent to live in a foreign land.

ex nihilo: A Latin expression meaning "out of nothing." The term is used to refer to God bringing the universe from not existing into existence.

fasting: When we limit or keep from eating and drinking as a way to grow closer to God. *We also may fast from other things we enjoy to show our love for God and to grow closer to him.*

Gentile: Any member of a non-Jewish nation. *Following the return from exile, the Jews lived under the rule of various Gentile nations.*

Great Commission: The act of Jesus appearing to his eleven Apostles after his Resurrection and giving them their mission to go and make disciples of all nations (see Mt 28:16–20).

Hanukkah: The Jewish feast that celebrates the rededication of the Temple after it had been defiled by the Greek armies. *The word "Hanukkah" comes from a Hebrew word meaning "to dedicate."*

hesed: The Hebrew word for God's merciful, steadfast love.

Hosanna: A word that means "Save!" or "Give salvation!" *The people called Jesus Hosanna and celebrated him as the long-awaited Son of David, who would save them when he entered Jerusalem riding a donkey.*

idolatry: Worshipping any created thing in place of the Creator. *The First Commandment forbids idolatry.*

image of God: The way that God made us to be like him. Human persons are created to share in God's divine life. Because we are made in God's image, we can reason, act freely, love, and imitate God's loving care of creation.

inspiration: The belief that while God is the single Divine Author of the Bible, through the grace of the Holy Spirit the human authors of the Bible freely and creatively wrote what God wanted to reveal for our salvation.

Jesus: The name of the Son of God made man, the Savior of the World. It means "God saves." *Jesus is God himself, who saves us from the powers of sin and death.*

Jew: A person who had returned from exile and dwelt in the land of Judea and anyone after the Exile who followed the religion of Judaism.

judges: Leaders who delivered God's people during times of great distress. *Through God's power, these judges brought restoration to God's people by saving them from their enemies and restoring their loving covenant relationship with the Lord.*

judgment: An act of justice in which God punishes or rewards people according to their actions. *God is perfectly just and merciful in his judgments.*

liturgical calendar: The Church's calendar that marks various events in the life of Jesus and invites us to participate in and celebrate those events (i.e., Advent, Christmas, Lent, Easter, Holy Week, and Pentecost).

liturgy: Our worship of God through which we participate in his work of salvation. *In liturgy, we worship God through signs, words, and actions.*

Lord: The title commonly used in the Gospels to show respect to an authority figure. *When Christians confess Jesus as Lord, we express our greatest respect and adoration for Jesus, who has been given "all authority in heaven and on earth"* (Mt 28:18).

Magi: The wise men who, led by the light of a star, journeyed from a distant Gentile nation to offer gifts of gold, frankincense, and myrrh to Jesus, the Messiah. *With faith and humility, the Magi recognized and worshipped Jesus, the Son of God and Savior of the World.*

magnanimity: The virtue that allows us to do great and noble things confidently for God and others. *A magnanimous person does not trust only in his own abilities. The magnanimous person has faith that God will give the strength that is needed to accomplish great things.*

martyr: A person who is killed because of his faith. *The Book of Second Maccabees records a famous story of seven brothers and their mother who were martyred by King Antiochus IV for refusing to violate the Law of Moses.*

New Law: The grace of the Holy Spirit given to us through faith in Christ and the sacraments, beginning with Baptism. *It is expressed above all in Jesus' Sermon on the Mount (see Mt 5–7).*

Original Sin: The first sin of Adam and Eve and the effects their sin has on us. *By committing Original Sin, Adam and Eve fell from grace and lost the gifts of original holiness and original justice. We all inherit their wounded human nature.*

Paschal Mystery: The events of Jesus' Passion, Death, Resurrection, and Ascension. By these events, Jesus brings salvation from the power of sin and death.

patriarch: A father and ruler of God's Chosen People. The patriarchs of God's people were Abraham, Isaac, and Jacob (Israel).

prayer: The lifting up of our minds and hearts to God by listening and talking to him. *The goal of all prayer is union with God.*

presumption: The sin we commit when we believe that God will forgive us even if we do not repent.

prophet: Someone chosen by God to speak God's words and remind people of his promises. *Prophets called the Israelites to repent of their sins and be faithful to the Lord.*

pure in heart: Seeking to love God above all else and avoiding sin. *A person who is pure in heart puts his trust in God.*

ransom: A payment required for the release of a captive. *Jesus ransomed us from captivity to the powers of sin and death by freely giving his life on the Cross.*

redeemer: Someone who pays a debt and buys back another person's possessions or freedom. *Jesus is our Savior and Redeemer.*

repent: To change our mind or heart. We repent by turning away from sin. *To enter the Kingdom of Heaven, we must repent from sin and do the will of God the Father in all things.*

Resurrection: The historical event when Jesus, having died on the Cross and been buried in the tomb, truly rose from the dead on the third day and appeared to his disciples.

salvation history: God's plan throughout history, as told in the Bible, to save us from sin and unite the Church to himself in love.

Samaritans: The descendants of the northern ten tribes who intermarried with Gentile nations after Assyria invaded the Northern Kingdom.

Sanhedrin: A Jewish council of judges who would determine the innocence or guilt of a person accused of breaking the law.

Savior: Jesus, who rescued mankind from the power of sin and death and reconciled us to God.

Sermon on the Mount: The extended teaching Jesus gave about how those who want to be part of his new kingdom should live. It is found in chapters 5–7 of Matthew's Gospel. *In this teaching, Jesus teaches us the New Law of love.*

shalom: The Hebrew word for "peace." *The name Solomon comes from the word "shalom."*

sin: A free choice to disobey God's law and reject his love.

Solemnity of the Epiphany: The liturgical feast that celebrates the mystery of Jesus' manifestation as the Messiah and Savior of all peoples. *The Church remembers Jesus' baptism in the Jordan and the miracle at the Wedding Feast at Cana in her liturgical prayer on this day. But the primary event the Church commemorates on Epiphany is the wise men from the East coming to adore Jesus after his Birth.*

Son of Man: The mysterious figure that Daniel said would appear when Israel's enemies were defeated.

spiritual body: A human body that is incorruptible because it is enlivened by God's own Holy Spirit. *At the end of time, our souls will be reunited with our glorified bodies for eternity.*

Temple: The place where God's people could offer sacrifice in worship to the Lord. *The Temple in Jerusalem was meant to reflect God's beauty, and it foreshadowed the glory of Heaven.*

theophany: A visible appearance of God in the world. *For example, the Lord spoke to Moses in the theophany of the burning bush on Mount Sinai.*

twelve tribes of Israel: Israel's (Jacob's) sons and their families. *Reuben, Simeon, Levi, Judah, Dan, Naphtali, Gad, Asher, Issachar, Zebulun, Joseph, and Benjamin. Through covenants with God, they grew into the nation of Israel and eventually the Kingdom of Israel.*

type: A person or event that foreshadows a future fulfillment. *The sacrifice of Isaac is a type of Jesus' sacrifice on the Cross.*

typology: The way we discern how deeds and words in the Bible foreshadow the fulfillment of God's plan in Jesus Christ. *Typology helps us see how "the New Testament lies hidden in the Old, and the Old Testament is unveiled in the New,"[1] as Saint Augustine once wrote.*

wisdom: A spiritual gift that allows a person to know God's purpose and plan and to see the world from God's perspective.

witness: Someone who proclaims God's truth to others through words and actions based on his experience and knowledge.

Endnotes

Unit 1 Saint Story: Saint Jerome
1. Saint Jerome, *Letter* 22, trans. W. H. Fremantle, G. Lewis, and W. G. Martley, in *Nicene and Post-Nicene Fathers*, 2nd series, vol. 6, ed. Philip Schaff and Henry Wace (Buffalo, N.Y.: Christian Literature Publishing, 1893). Revised and edited for New Advent by Kevin Knight, 2021, www.newadvent.org/fathers/3001022.htm.
2. Origen of Alexandria, *On First Principles* IV, 1, 7 (New York: Harper and Row, 1966), 267.
3. Saint Jerome, *Ep.* 22, 25, quoted in Pope Benedict XVI, General Audience (November 14, 2007).
4. Saint Jerome, *Commentary on Isaiah*, foreword (PL 24:17).

Chapter 1
1. Tertullian, *De orat.* 1: PL 1, 1251–55.
2. Saint Thomas Aquinas, *Summa Theologiae* II-II, q. 83, art. 9.

Chapter 2
1. Guigo the Carthusian, *Scala Paradisi*: PL 40, 998; emphasis added.

Chapter 3
1. Saint Jerome, *Commentary on Matthew*, trans. Thomas P. Scheck, ed. Thomas P. Halton, vol. 117 of *The Fathers of the Church* (Washington, D.C.: The Catholic University of America Press, 2008), 327.

Chapter 4
1. Pope Saint Gregory the Great, *Morals on Job* (Preface, iv; PL 75, 515).
2. Saint Jerome, *In Psalmum* 147: CCL 78, 337–38, quoted in Pope Benedict XVI, post-synodal apostolic exhortation *Verbum Domini* (September 30, 2010), no. 56.

Chapter 5
1. Saint Jerome, *Praefatio in Librum Paralipomenon LXX*, 1.10–15: *Sources Chrétiennes* 592, 340, quoted in Pope Francis, apostolic letter *Scripturae Sacrae Affectus*, under "From Rome to Bethlehem" (September 30, 2020).
2. Saint Jerome, *Ep.* 52, 7, quoted in Pope Benedict XVI, General Audience (November 14, 2007).
3. Ibid.
4. Saint Jerome, *In Tit.*, 3:9, quoted in Pope Benedict XV, *Spiritus Paraclitus* (September 15, 1920), no. 40.

Unit 2 Saint Story: Saint Teresa Benedicta of the Cross (Edith Stein)
1. "Teresa Benedicta of the Cross: Edith Stein," Vatican.va, accessed March 10, 2023, www.vatican.va/news_services/liturgy/saints/ns_lit_doc_19981011_edith_stein_en.html.
2. *Catholic News Agency*, "St. Teresa Benedicta of the Cross (Edith Stein)," accessed March 10, 2023, www.catholicnewsagency.com/saint/st-teresa-benedicta-of-the-cross-edith-stein-557.
3. "Edith Stein," Vatican.va, accessed March 10, 2023.
4. Robert Royal, *The Catholic Martyrs of the Twentieth Century: A Comprehensive World History* (New York: Crossroad Publishing, 2015), 183.
5. Ibid.
6. Ibid., 191.

Chapter 8
1. Verse 3, here and throughout, is the alternate text in the RSV-2CE footnote.

Chapter 9
1. Saint Augustine, *Quaest. in Hept.* 2, 73, quoted in *CCC* 129; cf. *Dei Verbum*, 16.
2. Saint Augustine, *The City of God*, ed. Boniface Ramsey, trans. William Babcock, vol. 7 of *The Works of Saint Augustine: A Translation for the 21st Century* (Hyde Park, N.Y.: New City Press, 2012–2013), 223.

Unit 3 Saint Story: Saint Josephine Bakhita
1. Roberto Italo Zanini, "Childhood in Africa," in *Bakhita: From Slave to Saint*, trans. and ed. Andrew Matt (San Francisco: Ignatius Press, 2013), 638, Kindle.
2. Zanini, "A Saint among Saints," in *Bakhita*, 1585.
3. Zanini, "Childhood in Africa," in *Bakhita*, 186.
4. Ibid., 259.

Chapter 12
1. Saint Augustine, *Quaest. in Hept.* 2, 73, quoted in *CCC* 129; cf. *Dei Verbum*, 16.
2. Saint Peter Chrysologus, *Sermo* 67: PL 52, 392, quoted in *CCC* 2837; cf. Jn 6:1.

Unit 4 Saint Story: Saint Gregory the Great
3. Quoted in Warren H. Carroll, *The Building of Christendom* (Front Royal, Va.: Christendom Press, 1987), 197.
4. Quoted in Father John Laux, M.A., *Church History* (Rockford, Ill.: Tan Books, 1989), 192.
5. Quoted in ibid., 193.
6. Quoted in ibid., 197–98.

Chapter 14
1. Cf. 1 Jn 4:20.

Chapter 16
1. Cf., e.g., Hos 2:15, 21–25; Is 54:6–8.
2. Cf. Jer 31:20; Ezra 39:25–29.
3. Pope John Paul II, encyclical letter *Dives in Misericordia* (November 30, 1980), 4.
4. Martin Luther King, Jr., "I Have a Dream" (speech, Lincoln Memorial, Washington, D.C., August 28, 1963), History.com, www.history.com/topics/black-history/i-have-a-dream-speech.
5. Saint Augustine, *Serm.* 186, 1: PL 38, 999.
6. Lk 1:38.

Chapter 18
1. Mt 26:28.
2. C. S. Lewis, *Mere Christianity* (New York: HarperCollins, 2001), 46.

Unit 5 Saint Story: Blessed Franz Jägerstätter
1. Quoted in Robert Royal, *The Catholic Martyrs of the Twentieth Century: A Comprehensive World History* (New York: Crossroad Publishing, 2015), 161.
2. Ibid.
3. *Franz Jägerstätter: Letters and Writings from Prison*, ed. Erna Putz (Maryknoll, N.Y.: Orbis Books, 2009), 6.
4. Quoted in "Saint of the Day: Blessed Franz Jägerstätter's Story," Franciscan Media, June 7, 2023, www.franciscanmedia.org/saint-of-the-day/blessed-franz-jagerstatter.
5. Quoted in Royal, *Catholic Martyrs of Twentieth Century*, 163.
6. *Jägerstätter: Letters and Writings from Prison*, 243.
7. Ibid., 129–30.
8. Quoted in Royal, *Catholic Martyrs of Twentieth Century*, 165.

Chapter 20
1. Bede, *On Ezra and Nehemiah*, PL 91:811, quoted in Marco Conti and Gianluca Pilara, eds., *1–2 Kings, 1–2 Chronicles, Ezra, Nehemiah, Esther*, Ancient Christian Commentary on Scripture (Downers Grove, Il.: InterVarsity Press, 2008), 304.

Chapter 21
1. Pope Francis, "Morning Meditation in the Chapel of the *Domus Sanctae Marthae*: Two Kinds of Persecution (April 12, 2016)," *L'Osservatore Romano*, Weekly ed. in English, April 22, 2016.

Chapter 22
1. Jn 3:13; Mt 20:28; cf. Jn 6:62; Dan 7:13; Is 53:10–12.
2. Cf. Jn 19:19–22; Lk 23:39–43.
3. Acts 2:36.
4. *Vatican Council II: The Conciliar and Post Conciliar Documents*, electronic ed. of the new revised ed., vol. 1 of Vatican Collection, ed. Austin Flannery (Northport, N.Y.: Costello Publishing, 1992), 741.
5. Pope Pius XI, Encyclical on the Church and the German Reich *Mit Brennender Sorge* (With Deep Anxiety) (March 14, 1937).
6. See C. S. Lewis, *Mere Christianity* (New York: HarperCollins, 2001), 52.

Unit 6 Saint Story: Saint Teresa of Avila
1. "Saint Teresa of Avila, Virgin, Foundress," EWTN, www.ewtn.com/catholicism/library/saint-teresa-of-avila-virgin-foundress-5209.
2. *Butler's Lives of the Saints, New Full Edition: October*, ed. Alban Butler, revised by Peter Doyle (Collegeville, Minn.: Liturgical Press, 1998), 95.
3. Ibid.
4. Ibid., 96.
5. "Saint Teresa of Avila, Virgin, Foundress."
6. *Butler's Lives of the Saints*, 97.
7. Ibid., 98.
8. "Saint Teresa of Avila, Virgin, Foundress."
9. Ibid.

Chapter 23
1. Cf. Eph 1:7; Col 1:13–14; 1 Pet 1:18–19.
2. Cf. 2 Cor 8:9.
3. Cf. Lk 2:51.
4. Cf. Jn 15:3.
5. Mt 8:17; cf. Is 53:4.
6. Cf. Rom 4:25.
7. Saint Basil, *De Spiritu Sancto* 26, 62: PG 32, 184, quoted in *CCC* 2684.
8. Pope Benedict XVI, post-synodal apostolic exhortation *Verbum Domini* (September 30, 2010), 48.
9. Pope John Paul II, apostolic letter *Rosarium Virginis Mariae* (October 16, 2002), 1.
10. Ibid., 18.
11. Ibid., 12.

Chapter 24
1. Council of Trent, Session XXII, Doctrine on the Holy Sacrifice of the Mass, c. 2.
2. Mt 18:20.
3. Vatican Council II, Dogmatic Constitution on the Church *Lumen Gentium* (November 21, 1964), 11.
4. Pope Paul VI, apostolic exhortation *Evangelii Nuntiandi* (December 8, 1975), 24.
5. Pope Paul VI, encyclical *Mysterium Fidei* (September 3, 1965), 39.

Advent
1. On the Liturgical Year, Roman Missal, no. 39.

Epiphany
1. See Saint Gregory the Great, *Hom. in Evan.* 10.
2. See the Announcement of Easter and the Moveable Feasts, Various Chants for the Order of Mass, Roman Missal.
3. Collect, At the Vigil Mass, Epiphany of the Lord, Roman Missal.

Easter
1. St. Irenaeus, *Adv. haeres*. 4, 18, 4–5: PG 7/1, 1028–29.
2. Col 3:3; cf. Phil 3:20.
3. Eph 2:6.
4. Col 3:4.
5. International Commission on English in the Liturgy, *Order of Christian Funerals* (Totowa, N.J.: Catholic Book Publishing Corp., 2019), 413.

Appendix: Words to Know
1. Saint Augustine, *Quaest. in Hept.* 2, 73, quoted in *CCC* 129; cf. *Dei Verbum*, 16.

Art Credits

All images not credited below are drawn from Shutterstock.com and Lightstock.com.

Chapter	Title	Artist	Credit
Road Map / Unit 1	*Christ Pantocrator*	Viktor Mikhaylovich Vasnetsov	State Tretyakov Gallery, Moscow / Photo © Fine Art Images / Bridgeman Images
Road Map / Unit 2	Detail from *Baptism of Christ*	Pietro Perugino	© NPL-DeA Picture Library / G. Nimatallah / Bridgeman Images
Road Map / Unit 3	*The Sermon on the Mount*	Fra Angelico	Museo di San Marco, Florence, Italy / Photo © Nicolò Orsi Battaglini / Bridgeman Images
Road Map / Unit 4	*Entry into Jerusalem*	Giotto	Cappella degli Scrovegni, Padova, Italia / Cameraphoto Arte Venezia / Bridgeman Images
Road Map / Unit 5	*Christ on the Cross*	Bartolomé Esteban Murillo	Courtesy of Restored Traditions
Road Map / Unit 6	*The Supper at Emmaus, 1601*	Michelangelo Caravaggio	National Gallery, London, UK / Bridgeman Images
Unit 1	Portrait of Saint Jerome	Alessandro Valdrighi	
Unit 1	Vision of Saint Jerome	Alessandro Valdrighi	
1	*Isaiah with Saint Matthew on His Shoulders*	French School, 13th century	Chartres Cathedral, Chartres, France / Bridgeman Images
1	*The Baptism of Christ*	Byzantine School, 13th century	San Marco, Venice, Italy / Mondadori Portfolio / Electa / Paolo e Federico Manusardi / Bridgeman Images
1	*Friar's Badge with the Nativity*	José de Páez	Courtesy of Los Angeles County Museum of Art, US
2	*Sermon on the Mount*	Carl Bloch	Courtesy of Restored Traditions
2	*The Sower*	James Tissot	The Brooklyn Museum, purchased by public subscription
2	*The Handing Over of the Keys*	Pietro Perugino	Courtesy of Restored Traditions
2	Detail from *The Ladder of Divine Ascent*	Sucevita Monastery, Moldavia	Dannilovski / Shutterstock
3	*Christ on the Cross*	Diego Velázquez	Courtesy of Restored Traditions
3	*Christ Glorified in the Court of Heaven*	Fra Angelico	Courtesy of Restored Traditions
3	*The Appearance of Christ on Mountain in Galilee*	Duccio di Buoninsegna	©NPL-DeA Picture Library / G. Nimatallah / Bridgeman Images
3	*Light of the World*	William Holman Hunt	Keble College, Oxford, UK, by Kind Permission of the Warden, Fellows, and Scholars of Keble College, Oxford / Bridgeman Images
4	*The Sermon on the Mount*	Fra Angelico	Museo di San Marco, Florence, Italy / Photo © Nicolò Orsi Battaglini / Bridgeman Images
4	*Saint Matthew and the Angel*, formerly in Kaiser Friedrich Museum, Berlin	Caravaggio	Department of Image Collections, National Gallery of Art Library, Washington, DC

Chapter	Title	Artist	Credit
4	*The Inspiration of Saint Matthew*	Caravaggio	Courtesy of Restored Traditions
4	*Site of Jesus' Baptism at the Jordan River*	Anonymous	Evanessa / Shutterstock
4	*Saint Jerome Writing*	Caravaggio	Courtesy of Restored Traditions
4	*Pope Francis elevating the Book of the Gospels*	Anonymous	Shutterstock image 10437332k
5	*Jesus Appearing to Two Disciples on the Road to Emmaus*	William Brassey Hole	Private Collection / ©Look and Learn / Bridgeman Images
5	*Road to Emmaus, Resurrection Appearances of Jesus*	Giovanni and Francesco Cagnola	https://commons.wikimedia.org/wiki/File:Momo_Chiesa_SS_Trinit%C3%A0_Discepoli_Emmaus.jpg
5	Detail from *Adoration of the Trinity*	Albrecht Dürer	Courtesy of Restored Traditions
5	*Supper at Emmaus, Resurrection Appearances of Jesus*	Giovanni and Francesco Cagnola	https://commons.wikimedia.org/wiki/File:Momo_Chiesa_SS_Trinit%C3%A0_Cena_in_Emmaus.jpg
5	*Moses Striking the Rock*	Corrado Giaquinto	Courtesy of Restored Traditions
Unit 2	*Portrait of Saint Teresa Benedicta of the Cross*	Alessandro Valdrighi	
Unit 2	*Saint Teresa Benedicta at the deportation train*	Alessandro Valdrighi	
Unit 2	*The German philosopher and theologian Edith Stein*		Bridgeman Images
6	*Creation of Adam*	Michelangelo	Courtesy of Restored Traditions
7	*The Expulsion of Adam and Eve from Paradise*	Benjamin West	Courtesy National Gallery of Art, Washington, DC
7	*Vanitas Still Life with a Tulip, Skull and Hour-Glass*	Philippe de Champaigne	Musee de Tesse, Le Mans, France / G. Dagli Orti / © NPL-DeA Picture Library / Bridgeman Images
7	*Tower of Babel*	Pieter Brueghel the Elder	Jorisvo / Shutterstock
7	*Divine Mercy*	Anonymous	Renata Sedmakova / Shutterstock
8	*Abraham's Journey from Ur to Canaan*	József Molnár	Courtesy of Restored Traditions
8	*Joseph Cast into the Well by His Brothers*	Anonymous	Jorisvo / Shutterstock
8	Detail from *Abraham*	Joseph Schonman	Renata Sedmakova / Shutterstock
9	*Arrest of Christ*	Fra Angelico	Courtesy of Restored Traditions
9	*The Sacrifice of Isaac*	Giovanni Domenico Tiepolo	Metropolitan Museum of Art, NY
9	*Crucifixion*	Benozzo Gozzoli	Courtesy of Restored Traditions
9	*Agony in the Garden*	El Greco	Courtesy of Restored Traditions

Chapter	Title	Artist	Credit
9	Details from *Abraham and Isaac Climbing Mount Moriah; Christ Bearing the Cross with Veronica Receiving the Veil Imprinted with the Face of Christ*	Biblia Pauperum	British Library, London, UK / © British Library Board. All Rights Reserved / Bridgeman Images
9	*Christ Crowned with Thorns*	Filipino School, 20th century	Private Collection / Photo © Boltin Picture Library / Bridgeman Images
Unit 3	Portrait of Saint Josephine Bakhita	Alessandro Valdrighi	
Unit 3	Saint Josephine Bakhita welcoming guests	Alessandro Valdrighi	
Unit 3	Saint Josephine Bakhita in prayer		With permission from the Canossian Sisters
10	*Moses and the Burning Bush*	Sébastien Bourdon	Pictures from History / Bridgeman Images
10	Fresco in the cupola with the name of God in Saint Clement's Church, Eastcheap	Anonymous	Renata Sedmakova / Shutterstock
10	*The First Passover Feast*	Peinture d' Huybrecht Beuckelaer	Private Collection / Photo © Fine Art Images / Bridgeman Images
10	*Moses and the Tablets of the Law*	Laurent de La Hyre	Private Collection / Photo © Bonhams, London, UK / Bridgeman Images
10	*The Golden Calf and the First Commandment*	Anonymous	Stig Alenas / Shutterstock
10	*The Tabernacle in the Wilderness*	English School, 19th century	Private Collection / © Look and Learn / Bridgeman Images
11	*Moses and the Messengers from Canaan*	Giovanni Lanfranco	Digital image courtesy of Getty's Open Content Program
11	*The Fall of Jericho*	Jean Fouquet	Photo © Tamsin Lewis / Bridgeman Images
11	*Crucifixion*, from a missal	French School, 13th century	Metropolitan Museum of Art, NY
12	*Scene of the Massacre of the Innocents*	Leon Cogniet	Musee des Beaux-Arts, Rennes, France / Bridgeman Images
12	*Moses with the New Tablets of the Law on Mount Sinai*	Anonymous	Photo © The Holbarn Archive / Bridgeman Images
12	*Sermon on the Mount*	Henrik Olrik	Courtesy of Restored Traditions
12	*The Communion of the Apostles*	James Tissot	Courtesy of Restored Traditions
Unit 4	Portrait of Saint Gregory the Great	Alessandro Valdrighi	
Unit 4	Vision of Saint Gregory the Great	Alessandro Valdrighi	
Unit 4	*Protectress of the Roman People* icon	Basilica Santa Maria Maggiore, Rome	Bill Perry / Shutterstock
13	*Othniel*	James Tissot	Lebrecht History / Bridgeman Images
13	The storm god Baal with a thunderbolt, from Ugarit (Ras Shamra), c. 1350–1250 B.C.		https://commons.wikimedia.org/wiki/File:Baal_Louvre_Thunder.jpg

Chapter	Title	Artist	Credit
13	*The Angel and Gideon*	Gerbrand van den Eeckhout	Courtesy of the National Museum, Stockholm, Sweden
13	*Ruth and Naomi*	Ary Scheffer	© National Museums Liverpool / Bridgeman Images
14	*King David Playing the Lyre*	Ethiopian School, 15th century	Photo © AISA / Bridgeman Images
14	*Hannah's Prayer*	Julius Schnorr von Carolsfeld	Lebrecht Authors / Bridgeman Images
14	*Anointing of David by Samuel, 1842*	Felix-Joseph Barrias	Musee de la Ville de Paris, Musee du Petit-Palais, France / Bridgeman
14	*David*	Lorenzo Monaco	Metropolitan Museum of Art, NY
15	*King Solomon*	Simeon Solomon	Courtesy National Gallery of Art, Washington, DC
15	*Solomon before the Ark of the Covenant*	Blaise Nicolas Le Sueur	Bridgeman Images
15	*The Idolatry of King Solomon*	Jacob Hogers	Rijks Museum
15	*The Baldacchino, the high altar and the chair of Saint Peter*	Gian Lorenzo Bernini	Bridgeman Images
16	*The Prophet Elias Prays on Mount Carmel*	Visigothic-Mozarabic Bible of St. Isidore's, A.D. 960	Archivo Capitular de la Real Colegiata de San Isidoro. Leon, Spain / Bridgeman Images
16	*The Rival Sacrifices of Elijah and the Priests of Baal*	Lucas Cranach the Younger	© Staatliche Kunstsammlungen Dresden / Bridgeman Images
16	*Elijah in the Desert of Horeb*	William Brassey Hole	Eyre & Spottiswoode, London / Lebrecht History / Bridgeman Library
16	*Dr. Martin Luther King, Jr., addresses an audience in Washington, DC*		Everett Collection / Bridgeman Images
16	*The Nativity with the Prophets Isaiah and Ezekiel*	Duccio di Buoninsegna	Courtesy National Gallery of Art, Washington, DC
17	*The Destruction of Jerusalem by Nebuchadnezzar*	William Brassey Hole	© Look and Learn / Bridgeman Images
17	*King Hezekiah Spreads His Case before the Lord*	English School, 19th century	© Look and Learn / Bridgeman Images
17	*The Prophet Jeremiah*	Byzantine School	San Marco, Venice, Italy / Cameraphoto Arte Venezia / Bridgeman Images
17	*The Good Shepherd*	Philippe de Champaigne	Palais des Beaux-Arts de Lille, France / Bridgeman Images
17	*Jonah Preaching to the Ninevites*	Gustave Doré	Nicku / Shutterstock
18	*The Good Shepherd*	Paleo-Christian, 5th century	Oratorio di Galla Placidia, Ravenna, Italy / Bridgeman Images
18	*The Entry of Christ into Jerusalem*	Louis Felix Leullier	Musee des Beaux-Arts, Arras, France / Bridgeman Images
18	*The Crucifixion*	Follower of Peter Paul Rubens	Philadelphia Museum of Art

Chapter	Title	Artist	Credit
18	Consecration	Augustine Institute Studios	
Unit 5	Portrait of Blessed Franz Jägerstätter	Alessandro Valdrighi	
Unit 5	Wedding photograph of Franz and Franziska, spring 1936	Erna Putz	Courtesy of Communications Department of the Diocese of Linz
Unit 5	Blessed Franz Jägerstätter writing to Franziska	Alessandro Valdrighi	
19	*Daniel the Prophet*	Duomo di Santa Maria, Milan, Italy	Zvonimir Atletic / Shutterstock
19	*Daniel in the Lion's Den*	Briton Rivière	Walker Art Gallery, National Museums Liverpool / Bridgeman
19	Lion's head relief from ancient Babylon		Yury Zap / Shutterstock
19	Mosaic of the prophet Daniel at the Basilica of St. Paul Outside the Walls, Rome		Zvonimir Atletic / Shutterstock
19	*The Three Young Men in the Fiery Furnace*	Russian School, 16th century	State Russian Museum, St. Petersburg, Russia / Bridgeman
19	Orthodox icon of the Resurrection of Jesus Christ	Ljubljana, Slovenia	Godongphoto / Shutterstock
20	*Ezra Reads the Law*	Jewish School, 2nd century	Dura-Europos Synagogue, National Museum of Damascus, Syria / Bridgeman Images
20	Bronze statue of Cyrus the Great		KatMoys / Shutterstock
20	*Rebuilding the Wall of Jerusalem under Nehemiah*	Willian Brassey Hole	Private Collection / Bridgeman Images
20	The prophet Malachi		Renata Sedmakova / Shutterstock
20	An ancient millstone in Capernaum		alefbet / Shutterstock
20	The Western Wall in Jerusalem		Stavchansky Yakov / Shutterstock
21	*The Triumph of Julius Maccabeus*	Peter Paul Rubens	Musee des Beaux-Arts, Nantes, France / Bridgeman Images
21	Coin depicting Antiochus IV		https://commons.wikimedia.org/wiki/File:Antiochos_IV_Epiphanes.jpg
21	Votive candles	Augustine Institute Studios	
21	*Jesus Cleanses the Temple*	Onofrio Bramante	Renata Sedmakova / Shutterstock
22	*The Crucifixion with the Virgin and Saint John*	Hendrick ter Brugghen	Metropolitan Museum of Art, NY
22	*Ecce Homo*	Spanish School, 16th century	Renata Sedmakova / Shutterstock
22	Saint Paul the Apostle		Nancy Bauer / Shutterstock
22	Pope Pius XI		Library of Congress

Chapter	Title	Artist	Credit
Unit 6	Saint Teresa of Avila with the Holy Spirit	Alessandro Valdrighi	
Unit 6	Saint Teresa of Avila	Alessandro Valdrighi	
23	*The Annunciation*	Fra Angelico	Courtesy of Restored Traditions
23	*La Gloria*	Titian	Prado / Bridgeman Images
23	*Peter Opening Gates of Heaven*	Rila Monastery, Bulgaria	A_Lesik / Shutterstock
24	*The Last Supper*	Joseph Edward Nuttgens	Renata Sedmakova / Shutterstock
24	*Pentecost*	Navarro Perez Dolz	Renata Sedmakova / Shutterstock
24	Medieval painting of Jesus holding the Eucharist		jorisvo / Shutterstock
24	Icon of Saint Peter		Sebastian Photography / Shutterstock
Advent	*Isaiah the Prophet*	Anonymous	Godongphoto / Shutterstock
Advent	*The First Vocation of the Apostle Andrew*	Domenichino	Sant' Andrea della Valle, Rome, Italy / Ghigo Roli / Bridgeman Images
Advent	*Saint James the Less*	Pompeo Girolamo Batoni	Basildon Park, Berksire, UK (National Trust) / The Iliffe Collection / National Trust Photographic Library / John Hammond / Bridgeman Images
Advent	*The Last Judgment*	Michelangelo	Courtesy of Restored Traditions
Epiphany	*Adoration of the Magi*	Federico Zuccari	Zvonimir Atletic / Shutterstock
Epiphany	*Three Kings*	Anonymous	Godongphoto / Shutterstock
Epiphany	Detail from *Adoration of the Shepherds*	Philippe de Champaigne	© Wallace Collection, London, UK / Bridgeman Images
Epiphany	*Our King and Lawgiver*	Apse Mosaic of Saint Pudenziana	Photo by Father Lawrence Lew, O.P
Lent	*The Temptation of Christ by the Devil*	Spanish School, 12th century	Metropolitan Museum of Art, NY
Easter	*The Supper at Emmaus*	Caravaggio	Courtesy of Restored Traditions
Easter	*The Prophet Ezekiel*	Pietro Gagliardi	Renata Sedmakova / Shutterstock
Easter	*The Resurrection*	Jan Boeckhorst	Courtesy of the Los Angeles County Museum of Art
	Maps	David LeMerrer	

Notes

Notes

Notes